DEVELOPMENT OF INDIA'S RESOURCE BASE

DEVELOPMENT OF INDIA'S RESOURCE BASE

PATTERNS, PROBLEMS AND PROSPECTS

Prof. V. Vidyanath
Dr. R. Ram Mohan Rao

GYAN

ISBN : 978-81-212-0210-7

Published, 2018

Published by

Gyan Publishing House
5, Ansari Road
Daryaganj, New Delhi-110002
Phone: 011-47034999, 9811692060
www.gyanbooks.com
E-mail: books@gyanbooks.com

Printed at: G. Print Process, Delhi.

FOREWORD

The need for maximum and efficient utilisation of resources indigenously available in the countryside needs no emphasis. A major constraint in this respect relates to quantification of the resource potential under microlevel situations. No doubt, some attempts have been made in this direction but the information available is still insufficient for implementation of programmes on a massive scale. Moreover, the work of different research groups, including scientists, engineers, geographers and economists, needs to be expanded and pooled together.

It is noteworthy therefore that Prof. V. Vidyanath and R. Ram Mohan Rao of Osmania University have consolidated and brought out the proceedings of the National Seminar on Resource base and pattern of development in India held at Hyderabad during 1986. A perusal of the contents reveals that it covers the following sectors: Resource base in relation to developmental problem, prospects and regional imbalances; Human resources, energy resources, water resources, land and agricultural resource and biotic resources. The 33 papers included in this volume present a broad spectrum of the work relating to the resource base of the country. This publication should serve as a useful reference source for all those interested in the assessment of resources and their utilisation for meeting the growing needs of the country.

Department of Non-Conventional
Energy Resource, Ministry of Energy
New Delhi

MAHESHWAR DAYAL
SECRETARY

PREFACE

There exists much material on the resources of India and on the problems of economic development, but there are not worthwhile studies linking resource base of the country with its economic development. So far, most of the geographers tend to confine themselves to the studies on resource base while economists limited the scope of their analysis mostly to the analysis of development patterns and processes. This volume contains articles by eminent scientists, social scientists, administrators and others who adopt largely an inter-disciplinary approach in analysing the problem in its totality. The papers included in this book were presented at the National Seminar on 'Resource Base: Pattern of Economic Development in India' held at Osmania University in March, 1986.

The following pages must be regarded as personal analysis of the contributing authors of the problems connected with the development of India's resource base. Much opposition to many of the views expressed in the volume can perhaps be expected. The present study does not necessarily provide definite answer to many questions. It simply starts the process and presents the material in the best and most scientific way. The book is only a preliminary attempt to survey the necessary range of material and, the editors hope, it should be soon superceded. The editors would consider their work worth-while if the ideas expressed by the contributing authors cause discussions, growing interest and enlightenment. If such be the case our efforts have not been in vain.

We are very thankful to the contributing author's for readily consenting to include their esteemed articles in the book. This book would not have been published but for their full co-operation.

Our Vice-Chancellor, Prof. T. Navaneeth Rao offered encouragement and thoughtful counsel for organising the seminar. He has always been a great source of inspiration for all of us in all our academic ventures. We are extremely grateful to him.

Many of our colleagues in the University have provided valued assistance in both the organisation of seminar and in bringing out this book. We record our sincere thanks to all of them. We would like to place on record our sincere thanks to University Grants Commission, New Delhi, for sanctioning funds for organising the seminar. Our thanks are also due to the Co-ordinating Officer, and Deputy Registrar, U.G.C. Unit. We would like to acknowledge the excellent secretarial assistance provided by Mr. B. Damodar and Mr. A.K. Basava Roa. We appreciate the assistance of Mr. Rajanikanth in proof reading, Finally, we must recognise the superb production assistance provided by Gian Publishing House, Delhi.

V. VIDYANATH
R. RAM MOHAN RAO

LIST OF FIGURES

SECTION I

SECTION II

SECTION III

SECTION V

SECTION VI

SECTION VII

CONTENTS

SECTION II

Resource Base and Regional Imbalances

SECTION III

Human Resources

SECTION VI

Land and Agricultural Resources

SECTION VII

Biotic Resources

SECTION-I

RESOURCE BASE: DEVELOPMENT PROBLEMS AND PROSPECTS

Resource endowments may shape the form of economic development in a country, or may impose constraints on it. Adequate or excess endowment of resources itself may not necessarily lead to development, unless the country has achieved sufficient level of technological development in utilising such resources. It also requires adequate and trained man power. On the other hand, deficiencies in particular resources may require particular strategies to overcome them. Shortage or surplus of trained man power requires emphasis on right education and proper planning of human resources.

The present section is devoted to the discussion of developmental problems and prospects of India's resource base. M.G. Bhasin in the first article of this section and the book, thought-provokingly analyses some of the aspects of the conflict between resource use and environmental degradation. While stressing that resource use and environmental degradation have cause and effect relationships, Bhasin argues that the techniques of mechanics of urban, regional and environmental management need new dimensions towards socially relevant spatial organisation that makes the decision makers more rational and consistent.

The need for an integrated and perspective approach for assessing the resource potential is brilliantly discussed by D.N. Singh in the second article. He underlines that the problem of resource assessment should not be construed as a mere calculation of its existing and potential amount. It is rather a complex problem necessitating conceptualization of the role of resource creating factor and processes involved therein. He adds that it will be more rational to assess, putting them under identifiable—techno—economic, social—ecological and political perspectives whereby all inter-related issues could be brought to focus and a viable approach could be evolved. Singh advocates a simultaneous and coherent view after a careful perusal of the problem.

In the next paper entitled 'A Study in Planning Strategy for Resource Utilization in Sikkim Himalays' S.C. Mukhopadhyay lucidly works out the planning strategies and cultural developmental sequence against a backdrop of applied geomorphological frame and considerations of environmental hazards. He is of the view that the large scale geomorphological maps and soil maps relating to the development of Pedo-geomorphological problems would be helpful to locate areas with high erosional potential, especially, the unstable sectors like geologically or tectonically unstable sectors in the area. He suggests that a detailed drainage status map, including ground-water resources and vegetational map of the area should be prepared and judicious irrigation practices should be adopted giving attention to land development.

In the next article of the present section K. Adinarayana Reddy and C.R. Pathak emphasise the need of data base management system of resources for planning and development. They opine that planning for resource development is a complex process, intimately connected with socio-economic, cultural and political factors, the control on the progress of which is exercised by many departments and agencies. This results in the creation of parallel data systems in various agencies, each limited to the requirement of the function it serves. 'Therefore it is essential to develop an integrated information system of resources which give insight into the totality of interaction that come into play in taking a particular decision and provide a timely feed back to various agencies involved to help them perform their individual function affectively'.

Chobi Nag and R.N. Chattopadhyay examine the techniques of resource base analysis for industrialising backward areas. They attempt an analytical study of developing industries based on local resources in resource rich backward areas with or without a local resource base. A transaction matrix reveals the very weak inter-linkages between resource and industry, resource to resource, industry to resource and industry to industry. The authors establish the necessity of a resource based approach for industrial planning of backward areas.

In the penultimate article of this section, K. Sita highlights the changing patterns of resource base due to metropolitan growth of Bombay through two case studies. The first deals with Ratnagiri and Sindhurg and the second area comprises urban sprawl around Bombay. The author establishes that there is a quantitative and qualitative change in the resource base ushered in due to metropolitan growth.

1

RESOURCE USE AND ENVIRONMENTAL DEGRADATION: A CONFLICT

BHASIN M.G.*

Both resource use and environmental degradation are unique not only in having a meaning and a history, but also a fundamental conflict between individual and group interests, as well as, private and public interests. This conflict in them is basic and eternal. It emerges when we study who gets what, where, why and how. Logically considered, this question forms the core of Human Geography. According to Vidal de la Blache, 'Human Geography is a recent sprout from venerable trunk of geographical science——.' In the words of Miss Ellen Semple 'Human Geography is the study of the changing relationship between the unresting man and the unstable earth.' In other words, this is what the discipline means in the spatial context.

Both the terms 'resource use' and 'environmental degradation' are functional *i.e.*, operational. In other words they are reflections or expressions of human appraisal; always presupposing a person. One of the best ways of understanding is to

---

*Head, Department of Geography and Meteorology, D.B.F. Dayanand College of Arts and Science, SOLAPUR (Maharashtra State).

seek or build relationship between its three most mysterious and thrilling elements:

(i) *MAN*—his numbers, distribution, perception, attitude and behaviour etc.

(ii) *CULTURE*—generated and developed by interaction between real and felt needs with his ego value—system influencing and affected variously by man's thought and action, and

(iii) *NATURE*—whose mysteries—visible and hidden remain unexplained; All these are in ugly and dangerous condition.

Historical Linkages

Curiously enough there arrived a time, 50,000 or more years ago, when the genus 'Homo' was singled out of all organic creatures to travel a road closed to all others—the role of active man-willed adaptation or adjustments. Man having learnt to stand erect, used his hands largely to degrade resources which were available in plenty. This he could achieve through his superior brain power. Today, skills and abilities—good and bad, make him run a mad race whose two termini are resource wastage, and environmental degradation. In addition, it will be interesting and profitable to list a few of its linkages viz:

(i) The Resource patterns, processes and stages' from a specific discipline. Their nature and extent is, today, much more complex and involving;

(ii) The harms and abuses exaggerated by careless, irrational behaviour and action of man is ongoing *i.e.*, increasing. One is, therefore, almost ready to join the prophets of doom and gloom. What they say is:

(a) The world we live in is finite and has set in mysterious limits within which we evolve, develop and achieve our real and felt needs;

(b) Culture has emerged as a dynamic force. It perceives change induces change; making one conscious also of merits and demerits of the change. In the historic words of the American Geographer—Miss Ellen Semple 'Man is a geographical agent and not the least. He everywhere contributes his share towards investing the physiogonomy of the earth with those changing expressions' which is the special charge of Geography to study.

(c) As the future is purchased by the present, we must tackle the real world problems and bring about a just and fair world.

Realities

Many ecologists point out that the role of man in designing or shaping the world has reached a critical stage. This point of view is well-expressed by Dr. D.B. Collier: 'Man is forced with an ecological crisis. This crisis has developed as a consequence of increasing mismanagement of the world environment and unrestrained growth of human populations. It not only threatens the chances of achieving adequate standard of living for the population, but also threatens his chances of continued existence as a species.' He presented such like evidences in support of his thesis:

1. Deserts have expanded, pollution has increased, water shortages have developed, famine and malnutrition have persisted, and poverty has not been conquered, and
2. Human populations are getting overloaded by social strife, tensions and violence, with ward, terrorism or civil riot-man threatens his own destiny.

H.G. Wells, on the other hand, wisely observed that human history is becoming more and more a race between education and catastrophe:

In spite of such conditions or situations, let us have a search or an enquiry into 'Patterns of development in India' that have generated or developed in the post-independence era. For this one must recall some images and elitism connected with the perception of the need for change and advantages or otherwise of the change. These are as below:

1. The images of change, at least in the early years were derived from foreign sources. In all this, the Delhi-centred bureaucrat in particular played a very significant role in providing advice, guiding development and formulating plans. Secondly change in India has had two basic attitudes: modernisers and traditionalists. A difference perhaps best epitomised by the contrast between Pandit Nehru and Gandhiji and their very distinct views as to what India represented as a system;
2. Our democratic structure is now showing dangerous signs of stress and strain. While one thinks of the recent times and future with a great deal of concern, he is to chew the following:

   (a) The politico-administrative map of India has been in flux; boundaries and territories always changing. Hence the number and sizes of States could never acquired a stability;

   (b) Politics has become a cesspool of degradation. This is because the noble processes of our Constitution have been trivialized by the power holders, the power-seekers and the power-brokers, more especially, in the urban India, 'One Indian is an intelligent human being, two Indians are a political group, three Indians are two political groups,' observe the Indian diplomat Jurist N.A. Palkhiwala.

   (c) An eminent scientist of our day said, 'We do not run the place; it runs itself. We are a part of the running.' Albert Einstein refused to believe that

TABLE—I

Inter-State Disparities

S. No.	State	Per Capita income at current prices (Index 1960-61) 1961			(Index 1970-71) 1971			1981		
		Aggre-gate	*Rural*	*Urban*	*Aggre-gate*	*Rural*	*Urban*	*Aggre-gate*	*Rural*	*Urban*
1.	Punjab	119	121	113	168	195	140	202	245	171
2.	Delhi	217	29	423	188	26	350	201	18	333
3.	Haryana	106	128	182	137	177	97	150	182	127
4.	Maharashtra	133	106	162	123	70	175	141	96	173
5.	Gujrat	118	94	131	129	126	133	132	123	139
6.	Himachal Pradesh	N.A	N.A.	N.A.	106	121	90	102	132	80
7.	West Bengal	127	103	152	113	101	123	101	99	101
	All India	100	100	100	100	100	100	100	100	100

Yojana, Mar 1-15, 1986. Vol. No. 30, No. 4.

'God plays dice with the universe. It is equally difficult to believe that he will permit the human race to play dice even with an insignificant planet in a small galaxy, located in an unimportant part of the universe.'

(d) The highlights in the economic scenario are undoubtedly as follows:

(i) We have failed to catch up fast with the nations in the developed world;

(ii) Our insular outlook and spatial neglect has widened the regional imbalance or spatial disparities. Table I shows inter-state disparities of States exceeding All-India according to per capita income.

Table II presents annual growth rate of States exceeding All-India.

(iii) The problem in India is not only of relative poverty but of absolute proverty as well—More than 40 per cent of the Indian people are in such misery which no indicators of well-being can measure. Their condition of life is in itself a degradation or degeneration of the three "i"s—integrity, intellect, and industry.

(e) Despite our commitment to the goal of NRR (net reproduction rate) of one by the year 2000 A.D.; one becomes pessimistic in glancing through following demographic facts:

(i) India's growth of population was slow in the past, but it increased by 24.5 per cent between 1961-71 and 25 per cent between 1971-81. Moreover it has been estimated that the population of India will be as in Table III.

TABLE—II

Annual Growth Rates of States Exceeding All-India Average

S. No.	*State*	*1981-82/1970-71*	
1.	Andhra Pradesh	4.0--VII	7
2.	Haryana	4.5—VI	6
3.	Jammu and Kashmir	4.6—V	5
4.	Maharashtra	4.6—V	5
5.	Manipur	4.8—IV	4
6.	Punjab	4.9—III	3
7.	Tripura	5.0--II	2
8.	Delhi	5.9—I	1
9.	Orissa	3.4—IX	9
10.	Gujarat	3.7—VIII	8
	All India	3.4	

*This is a pointer for the need of reappraisal.

TABLE—III

Census Year	*Population*	*Decennial Growth Rate in per cent*
1981	685.2	
1991	837.2	2.0
2001	996.0	1.6

(ii) Both life expectancy and child survival are increasing and its burden falls on public as well as on private resources. They need new aims, new approach, and new action plans for bettering the socio-economic well-being.

(iii) Like that of all other countries of the world, the resources of India are different at war, than the resources of India at peace. Of these ultimate resource of the nation is the human resource. Thus investment in human development is more productive than investment in physical assets. Moreover it leads to a faster rate of national growth. This task is achievable by improving capacity, optimising abilities and developing skills. In case done, it will open a new epoch or a new era!

(iv) The ecosystem are being largely degraded mainly through unwise use, and this too under the two unprofitable monsters demonstrating that human beings do not exist. These are: (a) Urbanisation and (b) Industrialisation. Infact these have reduced man to a tool of tools! He has become plaything of scientists, engineers and planners. This is visible in hills and mountains wherein live the tribal people, as well as in the river valleys which cradled our culture and civilisations.

Outlook

In the last two to three decades our perception and awareness toward resource use and environmental degradation is towards the increase. Secondly it is also experienced that 'The Resource Development Process' is functioning under various aims and forces; the dominant one being limited, emotional or irrational. Strangely enough these have come in sharp conflict with invariably defeated and brought into contempt!

It is true that our view of the future is myopic and/or blurred. Furthermore it is being overstimulated by new sight, sound and bombardment from world-wide mass media, that breaks us up at first psychologically and then physiologically. At this time, more especially, we must realise that the real issue at stake is the nature of man himself, and the problems that arise therefrom. The preamble of UNESCO states, 'War starts not in the battlefield but in the minds of men. And it is in the minds of men that bastions of peace must be erected——.' If one were to denote in a word, it is the Sanskrit word, *buddhi*—the capacity to perceive the Truth. This is capacity which few individuals have, and they can develop it by self-realization. In turn, it leads to other mystic Sanskrit words—*Karma* and *Moksha*. This implies that the time has come to proceed to a higher and larger consciousness which would offer the solution, for the problems which are perplexing and vexing him since the first began to think of a just, fair and perfect world.

The question that, therefore, needs to be answered by the galaxy of 'The Welfare Geographers' is what ought to be done, where, why, when, and how? In case this question is answered with conviction, courage, and ethical neutrality the grossly immoral, world will become a heaven on the earth. Shift of emphasize, I believe, is the greatest challenge that awaits year acceptance. It will stop the rot, and we will achieve the greatest good of the greatest number for a longer time. And no one to blame.

SELECTED BIBLIOGRAPHY

1. Blundin John, Haggett Peter, Hammett Christopher and Sarre Phillip (Eds.) (1978) '*Fundamentals of Human Geographer*: *A Reader*, Harper and Row Publishers, New York.

2. Knox Paul L. (1978) '*Spatial Well-Being—A Spatial Perspective*,' Oxford University Press London.

3. Palkhiwala N.A. (1984) '*We, The People*' Strand Book Stall, Bombay.

4. Prakasa Rao V.L.S. and others (Eds.) (1976) '*Readings in Planning and Development*' Indian Geographical Society, Madras.

5. Smith David M. (1977) '*Human Geography: A Welfare Approach,*' Arnold Heinemann, London.

6. Southwish Charles H. (1976) '*Ecology and the Quality of our Environment*' D. Van Nastrand Company, New York.

7. Zimmerman E.W. (1951), '*World Resources and Industries*', *Harper and Row* Publishers, New York.

2

ASSESSING THE RESOURCE POTENTIAL: NEED FOR A PERSPECTIVE AND INTEGRATED APPROACH

D.N. SINGH*

The present paper attempts to discuss precisely some methods of perspective assessment of natural resource potential with an emphasis on integrated approach. It, however, does not claim to be exhaustive; it is rather illustrative in nature and brings together some relevant facts from diverse sources in an order by manner so as to clinch the major issues. Since conceptualization of resource itself is not an unambiguous problem, its assessment necessitates adoption of a wider framework involving identifiable but inter related perspectives, viz., techno-economic socio-ecological and political, etc.

It is, indeed, remarkable that inspite of full realisation of the pivotal role of natural resources in all kinds of development and consequent vigorous human efforts to tap them, there are still many areas where no significant achievement could be made so far. Notable among them are vast polar regions, much of the tropical lands, gigantic ocean floors and some planets already within reach of the man. Interestingly, what man has to

*Reader in Geography, Banaras Hindu University, Varanasi

his knowledge, that is by and large distributed sporadically and in lopsided manner both with respect to quantity and quality. This is more so in case of minerals associated with geological structure of the earth which is widely dissimilar and uneven in character. It holds true for biotic resources, land types and general agricultural patterns associated with them. To this situation much is added by the ironical production/consumption patterns at different levels. The owners (many of the developing countries) have not yet been able to make exhaustive survey of their resources and whatever is on their record, the lion's share of that goes to developed countries. Such problems are considered in this paper *under political* perspective.

There are certain resources which are supposed to be abundant but subject to exploitation only under much more developed technological and economic conditions, as has been exemplified through increase in the use efficiency of many resources by application of modern technology. This aspect has been discussed in techno-economic perspective. Many achievements on this front have, to a large extent, been nullified by side effects such as their devastative exploitation, wastages, misutilization and environmental pollution, all threatening the prospect of future generation. No wonder, from this stand point, the modern man of 20th century has brought to his credit more in the form of destruction of resources as compared to its creation and regeneration. So this aspect needs very careful analysis, not taking for granted all favourable benefits that are likely to accrue from introduction of growing new production technologies. Parson's warning that human technology often exceeds his wisdom, which well reflects in ever continuing hostility between nature and man, is to be reckoned with. Thus, socio-ecological perspective has enormous significance in the context of resource assessment, as has been emphasized in the last section of the paper.

Here, it can be observed that the problem of resource assessment has largely been related to the description of a particular resource or group of resources with emphasis on their distributional pattern. Although Zimmerman, a doyen of the subject, gave enough indications about philosophical aspect, its implications were realised in right spirit only in recent years. But still complexity of the problem associated with conceptual or methodological framework for resource assessment remained an unsolved problem rather an ignored aspect.

In this connection, the problem of suitable data even for illustrative purposes emerge as a major constraint. Obviously, geographers on their own have little to do with technical aspect of the resource surveys and as such they have to rely largely on figures procured from diverse secondly sources. The data are by and large available on the world scale and that too mostly for U.S. or some other developed countries which maintain better recording system. In case of the developing countries which require rather more rigorous analysis, the problem is more serious, as they have limited resource surveys and the information available therein are baffled by inadequacy, less specifications, inconsistency and more so lack of authenticity and desirability. Since most of the countries at present are pursuing planned development in regional framework, the collection and maintenance of data under a definite outline has now assumed greater significance.

The next question of consequence in this context is the structure of spatial framework, *i.e.*, the size and level of spatial unit to be used for survey or assessment of various resources. For some resources like soil or cultivable land, village level surveys are of better use, whereas for water, mineral and forests, assessment is by and large made in regional or national contexts. Recently, in planning perspective, it is found to be more convenient, first, to define region and then take stock of its various resources. Such regions may be groups of administrative areas or geographical units. The south-east resource region, as carved out by planning commission of India, serves as example of the former kind. But so far such attempts, although part of a grand plan of the central government, are limited to sample areas. So identification and adoption of geographical units/regions, *viz.*, river basins may prove to be of greater utility for the purpose, as thereby all kinds of resources can be developed within an integrated framework. Including multipurpose projects and being vested with special authorities, such regions, *e.g.*, T.V.C. (U.S.A.) and D.V.C. (India), exercise stronger influence. The main idea behind adoption of this kind of spatial units for resource assessment purpose is that they have zonal as well as local character. Their physiographic, climatic and geological structures determine their natural resource potentiality. Moreover, with hierarchical arrangement, natural units at different levels necessitate special methods for exploiting the same. The rivers therein serve as sources of hydel power as well as that of irrigation accounting for saving of limited oil and coal resources. Thus they are of special significance for countries where resources are developed essentially under agricultural setting (Sengupta 1965).

Regarding the temporal frame work, data for trend analysis purpose may be procured for short intervals, but the projections for a period beyond twenty to thirty years should ordinarily not be acceptable. It will otherwise have greater probability of changes in techno-economic, political and sociological circumstances with their obvious impact on the degree of accuracy, feasibility and practical value of evaluation and prediction. For limited purposes, the questionnaires prepared by certain research organization like NIRD and AVARD (India) for data collection at grass-root level, are quite useful being designed for gathering comprehensive information, particularly with reference to consumption and availability patterns of certain resources. These can be of special significance in suggesting measures for regulated and or alternative use of fund resources like energy and water. While identifying the areas for resource exploitation and development, the role of perception becomes very important, because viewing of elements of physical environment as constraints or opportunities depends, to a large extent, on the perception which is an outcome of personality and cultural background of decision maker. Gerasimov (1976) underlined this aspect and ascribed the massive developments in desert and steppe central Asia to the continuing significance in Soviet policy making of attitudes originally formalized in Stalin's programme for 'Transformation of nature.' In fact, the personality and ambitions, largely linked to psychological elements, affect the perception of the leader and his government which are ventilated in the policy decisions as to resource utilization. The two totally opposite views about earth's resourcefulness to support the growing population are in essence reflection of the perception of the two schools about the future of the world.

Notably, the resource assessment techniques are, more often than not, subject to question and hence they ought to be chosen keeping in view their limitations. The selection of resources for analysis is based on their relative significance and data availability for illustration purpose.

Techno-Economic Perspective

For assessing resources in techno-economic perspective it is a prerequisite to have a proper understanding of resource process that may be defined as the means by which certain substances or elements of physical environment acquire potential utility to man and are thus recognized as 'natural resources.' The said process is a function of a complex of interrelated variables which undergo changes in spatial as well as temporal context. To illustrate, the technology in the form of knowledge and tools appears as the first requirement of man to enable him both to perceive the utility of an element and to overcome the problem of its utilization/exploitation at a particular time. But when the question of final decision to undertake the operation, *e.g.*, mining of an iron ore deposit comes, its economic evaluation as to feasibility becomes rather imminent. Such feasibility is dependent on market mechanism[1] as well as some other considerations, *e.g.*, the then government policy etc. Thus, there is needed simultaneous consideration of several favourable conditions.

The type and level of technology through time exercises notable influence upon man's evolving relationship with the components of physical environment. Accordingly, there emerge various resource utilization patterns. In this process, many elements associated with appropriate technology acquire value while others loose it.[2] Although it may not be fully logical to talk of a simple relationship between technological level and the degree of resource development, there are identified certain general stages in the utilizatian of natural resources which parallel man's level of technical achievement, in general, and his control and application of energy in particular (Zobler 1962). A review of economy from hunting/gathering society through the age of sedentary agriculture to date thr(ws much light on this issue. In fact, the sophisticated technology is said to have brought the notion of limitless natural resources and the concept of phantom resource, as advanced by Zimmerman (1951), well elucidates the point. According to the said concept, although because of use and misuse, the weight and volume of resources shrinks considerably, with progress in technological knowledge their per unit and total use efficiency expands many more times. To elaborate, assume that in Nineteen hundred India had a coal reserve of Sixty thousand million tonnes. Then according to American technology seven pound of coal was necessary to generate one kilowatt-hour. By now, the technique of coal utilization has advanced to the point where one pound of coal generates one kilowatt-hour. Thus, its value has been enhanced seven folds and taking general increase in efficiency of coal utilization also in other fields, we may envisage the original Sixty thousand tonnes pile expanding to a phantom pile of Four Hundred and Twenty million tonnes. The way of reasoning may well be applicable to metals or other resources also.

For practical purpose, it is inevitable to distinguish between potentially present and actually available resources. Such a distinction is largely based on techno-economic conditions which witness variations both through space and time. The vicissitudes in the economic history of Brazilian rubber resource, a very popular example, bears testimony to the fact. The techno-economic circumstances enabled it to reach its zenith on world scale but subsequently through time they accounted for its relegated position.[3] Similarly, the attainment of higher level of economic development by countries like Switzerland, and Netherland, which have meagre resources but more sophisticated technology, is too glaring an example stressing the role of technology.

As a matter of fact, while analysing what is physically available and what could be really availed, there emerge two types of situations making the role of technology quite obvious. Under one situation, there is noticed correspondence between the unfavourable conditions and poor socio economic achievements, whereas the other, the outcome of the interaction between the physical environment and man results in a strikingly different shape. A comparative explanation of the maps depicting environmental constrains (in terms of annual growing season under ninty days and annual rainfall below ten inches) and agricultural production (as shown by nutritional output of cereals and livestock)[4] conforms to the former situation wherein large areas characterized with hazardous (unconducive) conditions have low productivity. Most of the desert lands fall in this category. On the other hand, the biological productivity map, if compared with actual production map, reveals that some of the most important food production areas like wheat lands of North America and European Russia are found in zone of low biological productivity pointing to the dominance of techno-economic factors. Zimmeraman (1951,87) also pleaded for considering, in case of wheat, not only availability of land, but its being equipped with other factors of production. He observed that land available for the varied from forty one million sq. miles (suitable only from view-point of temperature) through eleven million sq. miles (suitable from view-point of temperature and moisture) to 5.5 million sq. miles (suitable from view-point of temperature, moisture and soil conditions). This principle may be applied to assess potential oil supposed to have been embedded in continental shelves of the world oceans. As surveys in a few countries have revealed, it varies greatly in quality, the size of occurrence (deposits) and the distance from the coast, and its actual obtainability soley depends on the availability of technology, indigenous or imported. Unfortunately, because of ocean oil survey being quite expensive involving sophisticated technology, very few countries could so far fully or partially afford it. Surprisingly, it could not yet be known if the oil belt of gulf countries extends up to

India through continental shelf of Pakistan, although such possibilities have been indicated.

In view of the foregoing, it should, not be generalised that resource possession without indigenous technology is meaningless, as in such cases many countries have procured capital and knowledge on resource credit that could gear the process of their economic development. In this regard, Zelinsky (1966) very nicely protrayed the relationship between technology and physical resources[5] leading to the conclusion that some areas like U.S.A. and parts of U.S.S.R. have both and other like India and China lack both, especially in view of their huge requirement.

While enlisting obvious contributions of technology, *viz.*, possibility of use of lower grade of resources, raising of output per unit of time, in other words, increasing the quantity of a resource available at a point, extension in life of a product through application of improved techniques and enabling of recycling of junk heap for reuse etc., it should be underlined that the economic aspects of the technological propositions have to be carefully studies, because the complex technology required for the purpose needs enormous amount of energy for processing and transformation of resources. Now the question remains: if the energy which is rather a dearer resource can be made available for all such kinds of processing and transformation? Thus, the promises of technology and the resource assessment associated with that cannot be accepted unscrutinised.

Political Perspective

The occurrence of natural resources across the political boundaries of states and countries poses a serious problem in assessment of resources with reference to respective territories. Such problems are more acute in case of minerals and water resources as manifesting in many State, national and international level disputes. For example, the war of pacific (1879-83) between Peru, Bolivia and Chile was nothing other than a dispute over the ownership of Nitrate deposits of the Atakama. Similar reasons could be assigned to division of phosphate containing former

Spanish Sahara between Mauritania and Morocco in 1976. The issue of allocating ocean resources has added a further new dimension to the problem. Apart from general issues raised regarding renewable biotic resources like fisheries, special significance is now being attached to mineral deposits, particularly oil and gas under the continental shelves. In fact, its importance has accounted for formal international agreements on the division of seas.[6] It is noticeable that despite demarcation of economic jurisdiction of the concerned areas, there lies much discrepancy in the sense that the island States and those with long coast lines have gained larger share meaning denial of the due to land locked States. The problem is further aggravated by highly differential technological level of coastal developed and developing countries; the former being sole custodian of offshore exploration technology are in bargaining position while dealing with other nations.

It is, indeed, interesting to note that rivers, often treated as regional bonds, have accounted for many State level conflicts in India. All calculations of water resource potential related to respective rivers prove futile, as benefits associated with them cannot be reaped on equitable basis among the States and countries which they traverse through.[7] As a matter of fact, under several situations, the boundary lines demarcating territories have far reaching consequences on the allocation of resources, particularly when the question of opening manufacturing units to use them arises. Furthermore, the regional resource endowment not conforming the levels of economic development expected by the people therein have been found to raise issues of great implications.

A peculiar situation emerges where political factor prevails upon all other considerations even ignoring geographical location. The case of petroleum on world scale where its availability is more linked to the policies of OPEC as compared to any other element, is an example in point. In international context, some developed countries like U.S.A. have been pursuing the policy of 'blocking out' considerable amount of some of precious and scarce resources which they manage to import from other countries. Doubtless, continuation of such practice depends much on the friendly relations, but even friends may be diffident in making supplies available in view of their global political and strategic considerations. In fact, there is no guaranteed free flow of resources either on world or on national scale. In extreme cases, the exporting country may ban export to all or selected destinations and may prevent imports via devious routes. Within the nation, too, there are restrictions on movements of commodities from one state to another. So, in this connection it becomes important to identify regional affinities among countries which have resource deficiencies and potential complimentary resource relations. Thus, the international political stability emerges as an important strategic element.

However, still the fact remains that those countries, which can, are gradually stock piling a number of minerals whose supply is running out. The poor and backward countries are only too happy with whatever they can dig out of the earth crust. Unfortunately, to pay for their much needed imports for their developments and also for food, these countries have to dig deeper owing to rising costs of such imports (Ali, 1979, 62). Also, there are some other aspects of the problem which could be appreciated only in the context of political objectives. For example, the contribution of oil producing wells in U.S.A., which are rather uneconomical in world terms but fulfil political motive of minimizing the country's dependence upon imports, needs evaluation in such a perspective. Similarly, consistent encouragement to mineral production as a notable feature of Soviet economic policy since 1920 under communists political motivation is explained in the fact that the U.S.S.R.'s present position as leading producer of most of the major minerals has only been achieved by allowing political objectives to override economic consideration (Warren, 1973). America's view that it has to conserve natural resources not only to fulfil its own needs (Smith 1958) but also that of its allies does point out the complexity of the issue implying political sting.

Within a nation, the significance of Government policy in determining the value of a particular resource can be well exemplified by the petroleum industries in the two Latin

American countries, *viz.*, Mexico and Venezuela. It was nothing but the government policy of taking over properties of big oil companies that was responsible for reducing on time (about 1920) world's very important oil exporter Mexico to nothingness. The favour of these companies naturally went to Venezuela which consequently witnessed oil boom. As Zimmerman (1951, 16) could conclude, laws, political attitudes and government policies, along with basic geographical and geological facts, become the strategic factors in determining which oil field will be converted by foreign capital from useless 'neutral stuff' into the most coveted resource of modern times.

Socio-Ecological Perspective

Recently, several pertinent issue have been raised which show greater concern with welfare of society in terms other than economic considerations. The declaration of some areas as 'reserve' in the form of natural parks and sancturies are a kind of development in response to changed requirements in this direction. It has been noticed that aesthetic viewpoints and ecological aspects have received greater attention in such cases. An opposition to opening of Bauxite mines in Gandh Mardan Hills (Orissa) by local tribes and environmentalists has nothing but the same spirit. The main idea implied herein is that the price cannot necessarily be equated with value. This sort of controversy has often been raised while choosing between socially desirable and economically viable propositions. The case of Carnish tin minesin England and that of Silent Valley in India mav serve as examples wherein one can visualise an obvious conflict between business and amenity interests. As to the above mentioned mines, many of them are located on or near the coast which is one of the most attractive sites in England. Even if it were possible to estimate correctly the financial gain to be made by opening a mine, how could this be set against the aesthetic loss of an unspoilt coastline? The same is true with Silent Valley in Kerala (India). A similar situation exists in the case of Highland coast lines of England. These were regarded by the oil industry as excellent sites for construction of concrete production platform to be used in North Sea oil exploration but the amenity and conservation group adopted an entirely different perspective and view about them (Chapman 1979, 78, 79).

In the modern planning context, the land allocation plans provide for considerable areas under recreational uses like parks, playgrounds, beaches, golf courses, resorts and hunting reserve etc. For such a purpose, different norms have been prescribed on the basis of population attribute but these could rarely be observed either in case of urban or rural areas. It has, therefore, been found to be more advisable to provide for and acquire socially as well as economically viable proportion (5-10 per cent) of the total land under this category.

There can be visualized another type of impact caused by social and institutional prejudices where they have emerged stronger even against the objective evidence of the potential benefits to be gained by utilizing a particular material. For example, despite all convincing arguments regarding nutritional values, a significant proportion of world population comprising Muslims, Jews and Hindus refused to consume porks or beef. Also, someother sort of complex relationships between economic activities and social structures have been found to prevent the best use of resources, as is exemplified by the agricultural developments in parts of east Africa. There, Masai and other cattle rearing people are not prepared to reduce their herds despite the serious problem of overgrazing in the region. Being much conscious of the status symbol that is linked to size of herds these people fail of identify the danger of depletion of grassland resources. It does highlight the fact that resource problems under certain circumstances can be overcome merely by reforming the cultural whims with which most of the decisions are intimately associated.

Under certain constraints, ecological approach provides necessary guidelines for allocation of natural resources for different purposes and it also determines the extent of exploitation of resources in different areas. Obviously, herein the environmental control remains the key consideration. The forest resource illustrates the problem in unambiguous terms. Recently, some environmentalists have drawn attention towards importance of tropical forests in preservation of the global environment apprehending that conversion of these forests to other forms of land use might have global repercussions affecting the carbondioxide budget, the thermal balance and the climate. Although these forests are generally assumed to be of low economic value, they do provide general benefits available from forests and, as could be easily argues, the low value of many of the trees in these forests under present market condition may not remain the same for all times to come. Moreover, their elimination is also a deep worry of geneticists who are concerned much more with loss or extinction of the gene.

Environmental problems associated with mining and mineral processing[8] are growing fast but their control does not seem to be easy and feasible because of constantly growing demand for minerals. However, atleast the reduction of damage to environment in this field, though a costly proposition, is rather essential. Needless to mention that with application of new sophisticated technologies, there will be faster depletion of minerals apart from excess strain on dearer and limited energy sources and it can partly helped through the process of environmental conservation.

Summing up: The foregoing presents a sufficient account of some broad aspects of resource assessment under different perspectives. However, it has to be stressed upon here that the perspectives under reference are interrelated and, while formulating any plan and policy regarding assessment and development of resources, decisions must be guided by their simultaneous considerations. For example, in viewing the problems merely from techno-economic angle, there is probability of jeopardising ecological and social interests, whereas in ignoring the political aspect there may arise controversy as to allocation and also some programmes. Besides, propriety of assessment can also be obscured. Thus, for lack of integration in approach there can hardly be struck a compromise between aspects of desirability and the feasibility.

NOTES AND REFERENCES

1. The market mechanism is related to demand and supply situation wherein scarcity accounts for price rise on which depends economic viability of deposits or its substitution by other minerals.

2. For example, with advent of giant steel plant using huge amount of iron ore, many small iron ore deposits loose their significance and are rendered as neutral stuff.

3. There were developed alternative areas for much organised and better quality (through research) rubber production at much cheaper cost at Malaya and Sumatra with British and Dutch efforts. With this Brazil was by no means able to compete.

4. Originally prepared by the Times Concise Atlas of the World, 1972, and Simmons 1974, these maps have been reproduced by K. Chapman in his book *People, Pattern and Process, 1979, pp. 48-49.*

5. The map is presented in a modifed form in Abler *et.al.*, (Ed). *Spatiul Organisation,* 1971, p. 344.

6. In the case of world oceans, 200 mile zones were defined as areas within which coastal states could have exclusive economic rights to any resources contained in the sea itself and on or below the sea bed. In the case of North sea, most of the national sectors were defined by the application of a formula whereby a median line is drawn equidistant from a set of base lines parallelling the respective coast lines. It may be underlined that unlike land resources, the division of offshore areas normally takes place 'before (the precise distribution of resources is known. Thus, gain herein is not necessarily a function of the allocation mechanism but it may be described as a 'resource lottery' (Chapman 1979, 297).

7. For theoretical considerations, there may be evaluation on national levels, but for the practical purposes the States have invariably used their autonomy creating host of problems. However, with central government's intervention temporary solutions could be obtained through tribunals, but these have always been subject to defiance by the changing State Governments and/ or their chief ministers.

8. What happens to the minerals extracted from the earth's crust after they have been used and thrown away? In one sense they are lost. Their constituent atoms are rearranged and eventually dispersed in a diluted and unusable form into the air, soil and water of our Plannet (Meadows 1972, 68).

REFERENCES

Abler R. *et.al.*, (1971) *Spatial Organization*, Englewood Cliffs N.J.

Ali S.A. (1979), *Resources For Future Economic Growth*, V kas Publishing House, New Delhi.

Chapman, K. (1979), *People, Pattern and Process*, Edward Arnold, London.

Gerasimov, I.P. (1976), 'Problems of Natural Environment Transformation Soviet Constructive Geography', *Progress in Geography*, Vol. 9, pp. 73-100.

Meadows, D.H. *et al.* (1972), *The Limits to Growth*, Earth Island Press, London.

Sengupta, P. (1965), Methodology of Delineating Economic Planning Regions of Different Orders' (Memo) *Summer School in Applied Geography*, Geography Department, Banaras Hindu University, pp. 1-10.

Smith, E.W. (1958), *Conservation of American Resources* John Wiley and Sons, London.

Warren, K. (1973), *Mineral Resources*, Newton Abbot.

Zelinsky, W. (1966), *A Prologue to Population Geography*, Prentice Hall, New York.

Zimmerman, E.W. (1951) *World Resources and Industries*, Harper and Brothers, New York.

Zobler, (1962), An Economic Historical View of Natural Resource use and conservation; *Economic Geography*, Vol. 38, pp. 189-94.

3

A STUDY IN PLANNING STRATEGIES FOR RESOURCE UTILISATION IN THE SIKKIM HIMALAYAS, SIKKIM

S.C. MUKHOPADHYAY *

The need for studying the planning strategies for resource utilization in the backward Sikkim Himalayas, Sikkim with various treasure of flora, fauna and unsurpassed beauty in the context of evaluation of the resource base and pattern of development in this part of India, has gained recognition in recent times. It is of particular socio-economic significance relating to the increasing interest in planning for regions in India from an applied geographical point of view as there is marked inter-regional differences in the area of about 7,300 sq. km. (The 22nd State). The Sikkim Himalaya within the Eastern Himalayan environment (upto 7500 m., a.s.l.) is typified by the development of a series of ridge and vales with terraces, glaciers, snowfields and lakes and undulating plains, and complex drainage status on the one hand, and forest clad hills and valley slopes, pastures-grazing land, terraced-farmlands, irregular and discontinuous distribution of population and

* Professor in Geography, Calcutta University, Calcutta.

settlements at different regions of geomorphic contrasts ranging between 270 m, to 4000 m and more, on the other. The variegated landscape elements of the Sikkim Himalayas have been produced by the interactions of geological, climatic, edapthic complexes being expressed through a varied morphogenetic condition and environmental hazards relating to the frigid (above 4000 m), cold, coll-temperate, warm temperate and subtropical environments (below 1000 m). The polycyclic Sikkim Himalayan landscape presents a complex mixture of glacial-periglacial-fluvio-glacial-fluvial processes and lithotechnics. Again, it is a region of ecological pursuits where pastoralism, hill-terracing, fishing, hunting and lumbering as well as tourism dominated the scene of cultural landscapes incorporating various land use patterns (Fig. 1). This author has also considered some relevant points on the geo-ecological aspects including socio-economic aspects of the Sikkim Himalaya mentioning the different approaches made by the previous as well as contemporary earth scientists or agencies for a better comprehension (Mukhopadhyay, 1979a, 1979b, 1982).

The planning strategies for re ource utilization mainly in terms of cultural developmental sequence worked out in this stu ly is presented against a backdrop of geomorphological frame and considerations of environmental hazards especially the seismic shocks, landslides, local severe storms and floods, heavy rainfall, soil erosion in central and southern parts dominated by sehistose rocks compared to the northern and eastern parts made of greissie rocks along with the related phenomena occurring in this part of tectonically unstable—Eastern Himalayan terrain. Earlier, this author has endeavoured to reveal the varied factors and interactions to the present layout of the variegated landscape including the problems of cultural landscape in proper perspective over space and time. Previous attempts of understanding the Himalayan landscape—"to thrust the Himalayan kingdoms into world prominence"—by some geographers as well as earth scientists from our country and outside its geographic limits. (Bagchi 1944, Karan and Jenkins 1963, Chatterjee 1986, Mukhopadhyay 1979a, 1985b,

Karan 1984), suggest how this field of applied geography has become attractive and significant both in academic and economic spheres of research particularly since the mid-sixties. A variety of landscape, geoecological, and behavioural approaches have already been discerned mainly with macro and meso levels of geomorphic content. Moreover, it has been possible to have involvement of some effective national approaches (Geological Survey of India, Department of Environment, Survey of India, National Atlas & Thematic Mapping Organization etc.) towards the study of mountainous terrain, as applied geographic rather geomorphic problems are liable to be greatly influenced by their physical, cultural, social and even political environments as well as by their methods of enquiry (Vink 1983, Piesietal 1985, Vidyanath 1985). This author has made an attempt to focus upon the planning strategies for resource utilization especially involving the development of present cultural landscape in terms of an analysis and assessment of land use patterns and the related constraints that have affected the mutual ecological relations between landforms and land use at different agro-climatic regions in Sikkim Himalayan terrain, Sikkim, where about 91 per cent of population live in the rural sectors, and the land available for cultivation is only 10.83 per cent.

Natural Resource

The Sikkim Himalaya in Sikkim is endowed with various natural resources like forest, water, mineral, arable lands in the valleyside and hillside-slopes and variegated Himalayan landscapes—natural and cultural, lying between 270m to about 800 m, a.s.l. Apart from timber, the forest resource contains bamboos, fuelwood, fodder, minor forest produce (economic forest products), medicinal plants and other resource like orchids and wild life. Though any survey has not yet been conducted to estimate the fossil fuel or coal reserves, the area has a great potential for hydel power from the swift flowing mountain torrents of the Tista drainage system. It has been estimated that more than 500 M.W. power can be generated from the Tista and its major tributary—the Rangit river. The important minerals are copper, lead, zinc, graphite, dolomite and coal which are found at Rangpo, Dikchu and parts of the Western Sikkim Himalayas as well as Rangit valley areas. Here, the only effective means of communication is road negotiating the steeper hillside and valley side slopes of the rugged mountainous terrain being devoid of railways (Mukhopadhyay 1985a).

The great altitudinal variation with a variety of relief and agro-climatic situations has favoured the production of all kind of crops. The antecedent perennial Tista river is of particular geomorphic-economic importance which in many ways has decided the economic activity of the people of Sikkim and northern part of West Bengal in India. The economic value of the mountainous landscape with the sublime beauty of the Sikkim and its aesthetic and recreational values (tourism) is being more and more widely recognised in recent years. On the contrary, the series of ridge and valleys set in a greatly undulating terrain within Sikkim, is also noted for the high potentiality for several environmental hazards like landslide and landslips, floods, seismic shocks, soil erosion including accelerated soil erosion, fog etc. The Tista, the main channel for drainage has divided the Sikkim Himalayas into four distinct Regions synonimous with the four (4) districts of Sikkim (1982, 1985a).

Economic Activity and Landuse with special reference to Agriculture:

The economic structure of this Himalayan terrain is extremely primitive, and is deroid of any notable industries. The different economic activities associated with forestry, hill-agriculture including plantations, horticulture and animal husbandry, small scale industries, transportation, tourism, etc., have led to the development of a varied land use patterns in the area (Table 1). Actually, agriculture is mainly practised in the hillside and valleyside slopes in terms of wet terrace in the valleys and dry terrace in the upper hillsides raising maize, paddy, wheat, potato, cardamom, oranges (Mandarin) and miscellaneous vegetables occupying proportion of land in per cent as 55, 15, 5, 5, 9, 1 and 10 per cent respectively. However, orange (mandarin) is the major fruit crop and maize is the staple food for a large number of farmers.

TABLE 1

Broad land use patterns in the Sikkim Himalayas, Sikkim

Land Use patterns	%	*'000 hac.*
Barren and uncultivated	28.64	209.01
Land put to non-agricultural uses	9.58	69.96
Permanent pastures & grazing land including cultivable waste	14.04	102.49
Land under miscellaneous tree crops	0.57	4.17
Forest land	35.34	265.21
Land under operational holdings	10.83	79.06
Total	100.00	729.90

The tables (Table 1, 2 & 3) reveal that the land available for cultivation is only 10.83 per cent and substantial areas are barren, mountainous or under forests. Out of the total land under operational holdings 82.12 per cent is under crops, 9.52 per cent is fallow and 8.36 per cent is not available for cultivation. At present, about 80 per cent of the total workers (or 45 % per cent people) are engaged in agricultural pursuits mainly based on traditional farming on steep to moderate slopes in Sikkim. The per capita income of the Sikkim Himalaya is very low, nearly Rs. 30,000 per capita per annum (as estimated in 1971).

The present author has stressed much on the soil and water conservation measures in the land area including agricultural land, forest land, waste land etc. to develop agriculture, forestry and the related forest and agro-based industry with an integrated and more rational approach. The Table 2 indicates general land types at different altitudinal ranges in the Sikkim Himalayas, Sikkim, and Table 3 shows the agricultural land use parameter with operated area in the Sikkim Himalayas, Sikkim.

Measures for Agricultural Development in Sikkim

As mentioned above, in this extremely primitive economic structure more than 80 per cent of the population are associated with agricultural activities. The essential measures should immediately be taken for the economic development particularly of agricultural development of Sikkim areas are given below:

(a) Prevention of soil erosion;

(b) preservation and improvement of soil by levelling, terracing and embankment of fields;

(c) planning for sowing of trees, shrubs and grasses for the purpose of afforesting uncultivable land or providing shelter-bed (against wind of sand or for any other purposes);

(d) controls or maintenance of tree-growth;

(e) improvement of water supply by utilisation of water in rivers, springs, tube-wells, bordering or constructions of wells, conservation of rain water by constructing dams;

(f) Development of horticulture and planting of fruits trees;

(g) Reclamation of land lying waste through water logging, accumulation of sand, growth and jungle, soil erosion, or any other cause;

(h) Regulation or prohibition of grazing and browsing;

(i) Cultivation of land lying uncultivated owing to the negligence or absence of the owner;

(j) Improvement in the methods of cultivation;

(k) Introduction of dry farming methods;

(l) Supply of seed, improved implements of agriculture, manures and fertiiizers;

(m) Regulation or prohibition of firing of vegetation;

(n) Protection from disease and pests; and

(o) Making, improvement and maintenance of village paths and roads.

Soil Conservation on Agricultural land in Sikkim

As mentioned earlier, the topography of Sikkim is, in general, steep to very steep slopes with practically no flat land (Mukhopadhyay 1982). The rainfall pattern is monsoon based but with longer duration and heavy intensity. The annual rainfall of Sikkim varies from 2000mm to 500mm spread over more than six months (April-September). All these have made the lands of this State very prone to soil erosion which at present has become acute problems. Soil erosions have been not only removing the top fertile soils but also leaching the applied manures and fertilizers thereby making the lands not productive. The problem of accelerated soil erosion has been further intensified by the rapid deforestation.

Of the total area under cultivation only about 50 per cent of the lands farming about 1.00 lakh acres area have been well terraced but without the drainage. All the paddy acreage and 25 per cent of non-paddy lands are terraced leaving about one lakh acres without any land development. Realising the above indicated problem top priority has been given for controlling soil erosions by proper terracing and levelling, water ways protection, safe disposal of runoffs, gully plugging etc., including growing of crops having soil binding capacity. The

Department of Agriculture since 1976-77 has started a programme of taking up soil conservation work on compact area basis in farmer's fields for which this Agriculture Department extends assistance to the farmers in the form of subsidy at the rate of 50 per cent of the cost of soil conservation per acre with maximum amount of Rs. 1,000/. During the fifth plan, 1600 acres covering 650 households were brought under the programme of soil conservation on Agriculture lands.

Therefore, the soil conservation will be given importance and it is targetted to bring more than 15,400 acres under this programme within five years time. The subsidy proposed to be provided to the beneficiaries if 50 per cent of the cost of soil conservation per acre based on actual measurement which in terms of money on the average amounts to Rs. 1,000/ per acre. The soil conservation work will be taken up on project. This programme has the advantage of preventing further soil erosion to take place and also provide part time employment to the farming families and agriculture labourers.

TABLE 2

General land types and land covers at different altitudinal ranges in the Sikkim Himalayas, Sikkim

Land types and land cover	*Proportion of total land (Percentage)*	*Altitudinal range (m)*
Snowfields and Glacierised Surfaces with lakes (there are 180 perennial lakes)	28.29	5000-8500
Reserved Forest	26.66	400-3000
Alpine Pastures	14.14	3000-3600
Agriculture and Cultivation	11.14	300-3000
Settlements with Roads etc.	10.23	350-4000
Khasmahal and Garucharan Forest	5.30	1000-2500
Private Forest	4.24	700-3000

TABLE 3

Important Agricultural Land use Parameters with operated area in the Sikkim Himalayas, Sikkim

Land use parameters	*Area (hac.)*	*Proportion of total operated area (per cent)*
Total operated area	79062.13	
Net area sown	64926.80	82.12
Current fallows	500.90	0.63
Net cultivated area (net area sown and current fallows)	65427.70	82.75
Other uncultivated land excluding fallow	4924.63	6.23
Fallow land other than current fallow	944.33	1.19
Culturable waste land	1153.46	1.46
Total uncultivated land (other uncultivated land excluding fallow+fallow land other than current fallow+culturable waste land)	7022.42	8.88
Land not available for cultivation within the operated area	6612.01	8.37

Population Distribution and Occupational Structure

There are four districts in Sikkim—Mangan (North), Gangtok (East), Gyalshing (West) and Namchi (South), the division of the districts being based on the dividing lines of the two river systems—Tista and Rangit. The districts vary in size, density of population and other economic characteristics. The Mangan (North) district is the largest (1736 sq. miles) followed by the Western district Gyalshing (445 sq. miles), than Gangtok in the east (367 sq. miles) and Namchi in the south (270 sq.

miles). This means that the North district covers more than 60 per cent of land area. But the population and its density are very meagre in this district (fig. 2a).

Nearly 41 per cent of people of Sikkim live in Gangtok district or in the eastern part of the State; northern part of Sikkim is very thinly populated. Consequently, density of population in Sikkim is different in different areas. Average density of population of Sikkim is very small only -4 per sq. km. in 1981. When the total number is 3,15,682 of which males and females are 1,71,595 and 1,43,723 respectively. One of the reasons of the varying density in the different areas may be explained by the distribution of forests in Sikkim. The forest area covers 40 per cent of the south (Namchi), 64 per cent of the west (Gyalshing) and 54 per cent of the east (Gangtok). As the district of Mangan situated in the north is mainly under forest and glaciers, the density of population per square mile is very small.

Nor only the density of population is the highest in Gangtok district the rate of growth of population is also the highest in this area. The percentage change of population in between 1961 and 1971 census is about +50 per cent in Gangtok, +32 per cent in Mangan, +24 per cent in Namchi and +12 per cent in Gyalshing.

The rate of growth of urban population in Sikkim seems to be very high in comparison to the rural population. The rate of growth of population in rural and urban areas of different hill areas are given for comparison. It appears that the growth of population in Sikkim in between 1961 and 1971, and 1971 and 1981 has mainly been absorbed by the urban area (fig. 2b). About 70 per cent of the urban population in Sikkim live in Gangtok town—the capital town of Sikkim. The 'Urban population' in many other centres is very small. These urban areas are very small and are practically 'administrative outpost' of Sikkim. The decennial population growth during (1971-81) is 1,05,839 (absolute) *i.e.*, 50.44 per cent.

The sex ratio in Sikkim is very different from other hill areas, especially Darjeeling hill areas of West Bengal to the south. There are about 680 females per thousand males in the urban areas and 883 females per thousand males in the rural areas of Sikkim. In the same 1971 census, there were about 736 and 910 females in the urban and rural areas of Darjeeling hill areas. In some areas the sex ratio is very disproportionate; for example, in the 'urban centres' of Mangan there are only 497 females per thousand males. In the rural areas of Mangan the proportion is however higher—about 865 females per thousand males (1971). The provisional 1981 census also shows significant disparity in the sex ratio in Sikkim where female population is about 84 per cent of the male population thus causing a significant problem of socio-environmental concern to the Public Health Department.

The percentage of literacy is also very small in Sikkim. There are only 17 per cent literates in Sikkim. The proportion of literates among the males is 22 and 53 per cent in the rural and urban areas respectively. The proportion literates among the females is only 7 and 35 per cent in the rural and urban areas respectively; 56 per cent of the total literates are found in Gangtok area. There are about 8631 persons who are literate among the Sikkimese women and out of this 63 per cent live in Gangtok district. According to provisional 1981 census the percentage of literacy is 33.83 (total) where males and females have registered as 43.65 per cent 22.07 per cent respectively.

Sikkim's economy is agricultural. More than 80 per cent of domestic products are available from agriculture. But Skkim's agriculture and tenancy system, method of farming and nature of products are different from the plains. The land available for cultivation is only a small fraction of the total land namely less than 12 per cent. In the north 'jhum' cultivation was largely prevalent even a few decades ago. Now the farmers practise 'terrace farming.' In the Namchi area, however, where some 'plain lands' are found, the farmers practise ordinary cultivation. The land use patterns very widely in different areas at various attitudes. The cropping patterns are also different. More than 50 per cent of land is under maize cultivation. The maize is mainly cultivated in the north, west and in large part of the east, paddy is being cultivated mainly in the south. The southern part of the country is more fertile than the rest. An analysis of major occupational structure (1971 census) of Sikkim's total workers (in per cent) reveal the dominance of cultivation (80.98 per cent) followed by agricultural labourers (3.77 per cent), construction (3.40 per cent), trade and commerce (2.14 per cent), other than household industries (.93 per cent), livestock etc. (.55 per cent), mining and quarrying (0.1 per cent), and other services (6.22 per cent); and the primitive character of the economy becomes more apparent.

In regard to other agriculture characteristics, the farmers of Sikkim practise Mixed farming consisting of agriculture and animal husbandry. There are five types of general land use in the rural sectors:

(i) dry terraces at upper parts are prone to severe erosion in the hill slope;

(ii) wet terrace—(fertile) at lower elevations (effected by floods),

(iii) untilled land;

(iv) forest; and

(v) home-site.

Each household in the State (barring a few villages in North Sikkim) maintains *Sukha bari* (unirrigated land), *Dhankheti* (Rice land), fruit trees (mostly mandarines or Sikkim oranges), vegetable plots, a small patch of *Elaichi bari* (large cardamum plantation), cattle, goats and poulatry. Evidently, difficult terrain and remoteness within a mountain ecosystems necessitate the people to produce all requirements in their own farms. The agro-climatic situations vary greatly due to variations in elevation, topography and climate. The agricultural lands are situated at altitudes ranging from 270 m to as high as about 3000 metres, the majority of the cultivated land being located below 2000 m altitude. Attempts are being made to develop particularly horticulture and soil reclamation with a target of adding 2000 acres additionally each year. As mentioned earlier the prevailing climatic condition ranges from sub-tropical to alpine with major agricultural areas under crops falling within the sub-tropical and temperate climate (Mukhopadhyay 1982, 1985b).

Planning Strategies for Resource Utilization

1. Preparation of an illustrated book on (a) landscape patterns—natural and cultural, and (b) natural resources should be taken up jointly with appropriate agencies like Geological Survey of India (G.S.I.), Zoological Survey of India (Z.S.I.), National Atlas and Thematic Mapping Organisation (N.A.T.M.O.), and Forest Departments in particular.

2. Detailed geoecological data, information and evidences emphasising on the changing landscape patterns in the context of dynamic landscape ecology and land use *i.e.*, forestry, agriculture, plantations, grazing, settlements, roads, mining, canals, etc., should be collected in collaboration with G.S.I., Soil Survey and Land Use Department, Forest Department and Environment Department, Geohydrology Department etc., and interaction of landsat imageries. (Remote Sensing Techniques) should be availed of in addition to the intensive field investigation in some selected sector of geoecological importance.

3. The large scale geomorphological maps and soil maps relating to the development of pedo-geomorphological problems including landslide hazards would be helpful to locate areas with high erosional potential especially the unstable sectors like geologically or tectonically unstable sectors in the area.

4. A detailed drainage status map, including ground water resources, vegetational map and large scale land use map of the area should be prepared. These detailed maps would be useful aids in formulating the strategies

for resource utilization. In regard to the drainage problem an effective drainage of water from the roadside must be given top attention and necessary systems of drains constructed to lead the runoff to the natural water courses, *e.g.* Melli Bazar, Manjhitar, Gezing, Rargpo, Singtam, Khamdong, Sirwani, Mangkha, Ranipool, Gangtok, Chhanggu, Phodong, Phensang, Singhik, Dikchu, Mangan, etc.

5. Judicious irrigation practices should be adopted with due attention to land development, and over irrigation should be avoided. Irrigation should also be avoided on areas prone to landslides and accelerated soil erosion.

6. Here, intensive agriculture should be adopted in the gently undulating terrain (having slopes below 20°) while horticulture, agrohorticulture and agroforestry should be practised on slopes from 20° to 30°. Slopes beyond 30° should be put entirely under forestry and silvipasture. Mixed cropping of leagumes with cereals should be encouraged. Research in mixed farming, agro-forestry and other silvipastural systems should be strengthened combined with shaping the land use patterns. Suitable soil and water management practices be evolved for different soil and terrain conditions. Developments should also be monitored by remote sensing techniques. Proper guidelines should be worked out for allocation and felling of forests particularly for construction.

7. The present geoecological conditions especially the landforms and drainage status as well as the climate and vegetations at different altitudes, make this mountainous are in Sikkim largely suited to the development and expansion of non pollutive, small scale natural resource-based (*e.g.*, forest based, agro-based etc.) industries only. Attempt should be made to build up interrelation between population and economic change by utilizing the human resources of Sikkim, and a large

number of Sikkimese should be sent out to respective industries for work and technical education (training) to develop a local work-force thus reducing unemployment and migration. The mineral including power resources of the area should be properly assessed and tapped. Here, even the basic industries should be oriented on small units involving production, processing and marketing and all these should be made with an integrated approach.

8. A Master plan for establising a road net work and road maintenance should be evolved to meet the growing demands of tourism and communication linkages.

Concluding Remarks

Obviously, there are considerable inter regional differences and intra-regional disparities within the Sikkim Himalayas where the land system for a long time has been feudalistic. As mentioned earlier, economic structure of Sikkim is extremely primitive (subsisting on out moded traditional practices) though some modifications have been possible in the Eightees. Some progress is also made in the industries which were actually non existent even in the early Eightees in the area. Here, more than 80 per cent of the population are engaged in agriculture, but agriculture covers only a small fraction of the total land available in the rugged mountainous terrain of the Sikkim Himalayas. On the other hand, more than 80 per cent of its land portion are under forest or permanent waste. Normally, being influenced by the 'feudalistic structure' surplus from land is poor and this area is deficit in food grains, and consequently supplies are obtained every month through the F.C.I. Again, trade and commerce is mainly controlled by some groups of 'banias' and their 'roaming agents' who share much profits taking the advantage of the backward people's ignorance of the knowledge of the market especially in the northern and western districts which have also led to the development of such notable regional differences in the area. In sequel, most of the people in the higher altitude of North and West with prevalent barter trade, live in a poor condition with much lower per capita income (below Rs. 30 per capita per annum as estimated in 1971) than the East and South (nearly Rs. 30 per capita per annum, as estimated in 1971, now it has increased considerably) with subdued relief where most of the literates among male and females are found to be distributed mainly over the urban sectors particularly in and around Gangtok and Namchi towns. It is important to note that the problems and requirements of the people living at higher altitude under cool temperate environment in North and Western parts are different than the East and Southern parts with relatively subdued relief and warm temperate as well as sub tropical environments. Due weightage should be given on balanced regional development and integrated rural development as well as micro-level planning with a view to developing those small order centres even at the lower level *e.g.*, Nayabazar, Rangpo, Jorethang, Dikchu, Tadong, Duga, etc.

The planners and land policy makers should keep in mind the possibility of occurrences of ensuing notable changes in the variegated landscapes in sequel of the growing human interferences as well as improvement in the primitive economic structure over this critical (border-land) mountainous terrain. Although this rugged terrain is accompanied by several environmental hazards *viz.*, seismic shocks, heavy rainfall (2000 mm to 5000 mm), inundation and floods, frequent landaslides and accelerated soil erosion, dense fog and severe local storms, yet this area is going to provide increasingly important competition and markets in the Hill-States of Eastern India by the beginning of Ninetees. The remote terrain of the Sikkim Himalaya with a very little proportion of gently undulating plains being devoid of wide riverine flats, and backward economy has to husband every bit of its resource for an optimal growth in view of the increasing pressure on the comparatively level landmass set in a changing physical and socio-economic as well as political or cultural environments. Every care should be taken to protect those fertile hill-side and valley side slopes at Sorakh, Chawang, Karekkabby, Womchong, Sirwani, Maniram, Phungdanra, Samtok, Lingthem, Ratepani,

Rinchenpung Tadong, Wok, Mangkha, Rangpo, Namchi, etc. subject to heavy rainfall and prone to erosion and landslides in particular.

At present, part of the Sikkim Himalayan terrain have blossomed into a busy tourist centre for which its resource utilization have to be enhanced for catering to huge numbers of more or less affluent clientele. The people of the soil are also anxious to elevate their standard of living especially through the best utilization of land resources available in the area and preservation of rich flora and fauna with emphasis to organising forest-based industries. Such elaboration leads us to evolving some strategies for planning including the preparation of the series of technical maps *e.g.*, geomorphic maps, land use maps, cadastral maps based on a detailed survey particularly of the existing settlements to discern their potential for expansion to accommodate future migrants to notify their growth limits etc., (which are discussed in the foregoing paragraphs as above) so essential for the overall development of these backward regions within the Sikkim Himalayas, Sikkim. Emphasis should be laid upon the rapid growth of forestry, agriculture, horticulture, small scale industries, tourism as well as organized modern education including health education with special reference to the identification of 'population parameters' considering their problems and requirements at different altitudes (ecological sites) within the Sikkim Himalayan ecosystem, Sikkim.

Acknowledgements

The present author is grateful to Professor K. Bagchi, Department of Geography, Calcutta University (Retired) and Professor A.T. Sanyal, Adviser, Govt. of Sikkim, Gangtok, for their valuable suggestions in the preparation of this paper. This research work has been supported in part by University Grants Commission, UGC—Financial Assistance to Teachers in the Universities and College for undertaking minor research project in Science, 26-1 (1089).

REFERENCES

Bagchi, K. (1944), Kalimpong—Its land and people, Calcutta Geographical Review, No. 13, No. 1, pp. 37-43.

Chatterjee, S.P. (1986). Economic Geography of Asia, Allied Book Agency, Calcutta, pp. 156-158.

Karan, P.P. (1984). Response to environmental hazards on Sikkim Himalayas, Himalayan Research and Development, Himalayan Research Group, Nainital, vol. 2, pp. 45-46.

Karan, P.P. and Jenkins, W.W. (1963). The Himalayan Kingdom, Bhutan, Sikkim and Nepal. D. Van Nostrand Co. London, pp. 6, 56-74.

Mukhopadhyay, S.C. (1979 a). Some Techniques and Recent Trend of Geomorphological Studies, Recent Trends and Concepts in Geography. Vol. 1, Spond. by Geog. Research Centre, Patna, Concept Publishing Company, Delhi, pp. 274-282.

Mukhopadhyay, S.C. (1979 b). The Morphological Analysis of Landforms of the Tista Basin in the Eastern India. *Geographical Review of India*, Vol. 41, No. 4, pp. 247-256.

Mukhopadhyay, S.C. (1982). The Tista Basin. A Study in Fluvial Geomorphology, K.P. Bagchi and Company, Calcutta and New Delhi, pp. 101-134, 182-222.

Mukhopadhyay, S.C. (1985 a). Landscape Sphere, Environment and Applied Geomorphology of the Tista Basin, in Geography and Environment, Issues and Challenges (Professor S.L. Kayastha Felicitation Volume) (ed). H.H. Singh, P. Nag etc., Concept Publishing Company, New Delhi, pp. 231-243.

Mukhopadhyay, S.C. (1985 b). Morpho-based Land Use of the Upper Tista Basin, Indian Journal of Landscape Systems and Ecological Studies, Institute of Landscape, Ecology and Ekistics (ILEE), Calcutta, Vol. 8, No. 2, pp. 102-109.

Pecsi, M. and Retvari, L. (1985). Concept of the Geographical Environment in Geographical Mosaic (Professor K. Bagchi Felicitation Volume) (ed.) S.C. Mukhopadhyay, Modern Book Agency Pvt. Ltd., Calcutta, pp. 1-8,

Vidyanath, V. (1985). A New Method to Determine Arable Land Use Efficiency in Andhra Pradesh in Geographical Mosaic (Professor K. Bagchi Felicitation Volume) (ed.,) S.C. Mukhopadhyay, Modern Book Agency Pvt. Ltd., Calcutta, pp. 77-87.

Vink, A.P.A. (1983). Landscape Ecology and Land Use, Longmans, London and New York, pp. 1-18, 35-76.

4

DATA BASE MANAGEMENT SYSTEM OF RESOURCES FOR PLANNING AND DEVELOPMENT

K. ADINARAYANA REDDY*
C.R. PATHAK*

In a developing country like India, with its vast resource base and big size, planning and development on a decentralised area basis is almost axiomatic or inescapable. Since the Fourth Five Year Plan, a number of programmes focussed on small areas were specially introduced, to solve specific area problems and to bring about more balanced development in the country. A sound data base and efficient information system on resources is a prerequisite to rational planning and also for proper management of resources. An extensive and comprehensive information system can help in planning, policy framing, evaluation and making optimum investment and management decisions for various regional projects, and thus would improve the planning process substantially.

Planning for resources development is a complex process, intimately connected with physical, socio-economic, cultural

*Department of Architecture and Regional Planning, Indian Institute of Technology, Kharagpur-721 302, West Bengal, India.

and political factors. At present the control on the progress of these is collectively exercised by many departments and agencies. Each of them has typically developed its own information system, to fit it's particular needs. This practice leads to creation of parallel data systems in various agencies, each limited to the requirement of the function it serves. Data on a given subject is thus haphazardly scattered in the files of individual departments, institutions and agencies without proper co-ordination among the department/agencies. A great deal of time and effort is to be spent in extracting the information and presenting it in suitable formats for the use of planners and decision makers. Quite often, it may be impossible to locate it even though the information required is available somewhere in the files of some department/agency.

Due to jurisdictional and procedural problems, or perhaps due to to lack of interaction among institutions and agencies, they do not share the information items already available. Therefore it needs hardly any emphasis to say that, we need an integrated National Resource Information System (NRIS) which gives insight into the totality of interactions that come to play in taking a particular decision and provide a timely feedback to various agencies involved to help them perform their individual functions effectively. It will also help to evaluate and control the performance against pre-determined targets.

In the light of the above discussion, the importance and characteristics of National Resource Information System should be as follows:

1. Timeliness—The data needed should be acquired, processed and analysed for information extraction in the shortest possible time.
2. Accuracy —The information should meet the accuracy requirements of the user at the highest confidence level.
3. Reliability —The information made available to any agency/department should be reliable in terms of correctness, frequency and continuity.

4. Format —The information could be in the form of tables, graphs, or maps. The scales and details given in the map should meet requirements of the user for a given application. The format should be so designed so as to make efficient retrieval from a computerised data base.

5. Retrieval —Either the original data or the information derived should be made available in common place so that multi-user retrieval is possible.

6. Levels —The data should be arranged such that it can be used by all levels of study.

7. Costs —This should be economic (Although for the development of the NRIS, we have to spend considerably in the initial stages, thereafter we can minimise the cost a lot).

Existing Information System

The existing information system has three tiers with its own characteristics. The first tier is composed of agencies who collects primary data and analyse it to provide information. This tier consists of various State level agencies dealing with the State subject. The present data collection system in the State is principally operated through the State Bureau of Economics and Statistics, which has an extensive network from village to State level through blocks, taluks and districts which is very exhaustlve in nature. The second tier consists of sectoral agencies responsible for regional level programmes. These are the central agencies such as Forest Survey of India as well as specialised agencies such as the Narmada Valley Authority/ Damodar River Valley Authority etc. These agencies collect and analyse primary data and also have access to the State data base wherever necessary. The third tier is the C.S.O., Planning Commission and NSS who did not normally handle primary data but compile the State and regional data sources. The mode of communication is primarily in the form of statistical reports, tables, charts and maps.

A study of the existing system of information system reveals that there exists a fairly elaborate infrastructure and network for collecting, aggregating and reporting large volume of data. A notable characteristics of the system is that the data flows continuously from bottom to top *i.e.*, from villages to States and centre through numerous functional departments in a well defined hierarchy. Some times, the time available at different levels in this long chain to collect, compile and process the data is limited. Moreover, in the existing system there is so much duplication *i.e.*, the same information may be collected by so many departments at the same time period. Some time it will so happen that, if we compare the same data collected by two departments, there is variation. Therefore it is difficult to assess the reliability of such information in the final form. Moreover, the existing system of data collection seems to be very costly affair.

Need for New Approach to Integrated National Resource Information System

The National Resource Information System (NRIS) would deal with the collection of data on resources (Natural and man made resources) and the conversion of the data to user defined information. The overall structure of the National Resource Information System is represented in the fig. No. 1. The resource information collected would be modelled by the Management Information System (MIS) to provide information suitable for decision making. The decision making and implementation system would then generate/modify the necessary policies, plans, programmes and projects and implement the same.

The management decisions can be subdivided into three broad categories:

1. Strategic decisions: which results in the policy formulation.

2. Tactical decisions: which result in the formulation of plans and programmes for the implementation of the policy.

3. Technical decision: which identify actions required to implement the plans and programmes.

For example—a policy to increase land area for agriculture would lead to the formulation of a plan for land reclamation which would be implemented through specific actions such as reclamation of saline areas, deforestation, providing irrigation to barren land etc.

The point to be noted here is that the information needed at each level of decision making is different. Thus the NRIS should be able to provide the required information to each decision making level. In terms of levels of decision making the State and regional agencies operate at both the technical and tactical level, while the central agencies operate at the strategic level. This demarcation is not, however, very clearcut and there could be specific cases where strategic decisions are taken at the central level. Further since technical information is obtained and used at the district and block levels, for the purpose of this discussion State level will encompass the organisation down to district level also. The need of the decision makers thus determines the system.

In keeping with the existing model a configuration proposed for the NRIS is shown in figure 2. The existing information system is not disturbed but some changes are incorporated:

(a) The first and most obvious change is the use of satellite and aircraft derived remotely sensed data. This data would be used in conjunction with conventional data. Remote sensing is one of the techniques of scientific data collection. The department of space has considerable experience in the technology of remote sensing and its applications and currently a project is under way, to develop a semi-operational Indian Remote Sensing Satellite System (IRSS). It is expected that

IRS System would play a major role in providing data for the NRIS.

(b) With the help of soft ware/hard ware system we can store the data at apex level. For storing the spatial data see the the methodology developed by Rama Rao. Indian Space Research Organisation has already launched a programme to set up six regional remote sensing centres to collect and store the data in a scientific way.

(c) The State level user departments and the regional level sectoral agencies would be responsible for the field data collection and for the overall data analysis.

(d) The establishment of data bases at the State and regional levels. This would require certain amount of co-ordination between the agencies to standardise the data base.

(e) Exchange of information between States and between States and regions.

(f) The use of Regional Resources Information System as a starting point for the information flow from the States to the centre. This would be required to reduce information deplication wherever necessary between states and sectoral agencies.

The data base at the States, regions and centre would be interlinked State to State, States to region, region to regions andregions to centre. This interlinking would provide the flow of information envisaged in fig. No. 2.

Elements of NRIS

The important elements of NRIS are:

1. Data collection
2. Data processing and analysis

3. Data storage and retrieval system
4. Data presentation

1. Data collection

Data are the raw materials which are converted into the finished products of information and intelligence. Any information system will be good, if the data used, and the sources of information have been carefully selected. Regarding the data collection system we have to use mixed type of both scientific and conventional means of data collection.

2. Data processing and analysis

There is no use in collecting large amount of data without proper processing and analysis. Data collection is not an end in itself. Consequently it is necessary to pay attention to methods of data processing which fit minimal standards of analysis. The raw data would have to be re-organised and converted into a standard format and desired by the user agencies. The remotely sensed data should be analysed using machine processing techniques. Computer System is required for processing of such data. This should be merged with the conventional data for the user departments.

3. Data storage and retrieval system

Here the inputs from various agencies would be organised and stored for future retrieval. Now-a-days there are many methods of hardware and software computer systems are available for the storage of data. The input information should be in the form of statistics. There would have to be classified and indexed on the basis of their contents and organised into "files." The storage function would involve the physical filling of the information for easy retrieval.

The retrieval function is the selective abstraction of the data based on user needs. The retrieved data would have to be transformed to meet the specific user requirement. This would involve, for example preparing composite maps or rearranging the data to highlight the specific information. The transformation would also involve the reproduction of the information in the required format.

4. Data presentation

The total material collected, processed and meaningfully interrelated analytically must be presented clearly enough for decision makers to use as their main means of evaluation for future decisions.

From the foregoing discussion it is evident that, one of the urgent tasks before the Government of India is the evolution of a National Resource Information System (NRIS) through which, information about natural, and man made resources is scientifically gathered, and speedily disseminated to planners and decision makers.

A planning process can be rationalised by the utilisation of NRIS, which has a capacity to present statistics, projections themes as an integrated whole. A planner needs to arrive at the interactive systems desired for the boundary conditions of each attribute.

The planners have to give the levels of planning area, operational area and the implementation areas, given these conditions the NRIS programme has the capability to process the data that is stored in various files and present an area specific planning decisions.

REFERENCES

1. A.R. Dasgupta *et. al.*, A Remote Sensing Based Natural Resources Informations Systems—National Seminar on Natural Resource Management System' held at Bangalore during May 10-12, 1983.

2. A.R. Nagabhushana and V.R. Rao, A Remote Sensing Based National Resources Information System—System Specialised mainly for Agriculture.

3. A.K.S. Gopalan, D.S. Kamat and K.L. Majumdar. Some Experiences of Joint Experiments conducted at SAC/LSRO and their relevance to Information System needs.

4. R.V. Rama Rao, Natural Resources Data Management System concept and design.

5. P. Misra, T. Natarajan, O.P. Rao and G. Behera, National Natural Resources Management System—Some policy—issues and suggestions.

6. Leeman Virgina, *et al*, The NRSA earth Resources spectral Information System—A data completion NRSA contract Report—115757.

7. J.C. Camillus and Mohan, Kaul Information systems for economic development. M. Joseph and F.C. Kohli (ed.) North Hall and Publishing Company—1976.

5

METHODOLGY OF RESOURCE BASE ANALYSIS FOR THE INDUSTRIAL DEVELOPMENT OF BACKWARD AREAS CASE STUDY JHARGRAM SUBDIVISION

CHOBI NAG*
R.N. CHATTOPADHYAY**

The availability of natural resources of all types provides the basic support to man's existence. All production and consumption activities have been a process of utilising the natural resources which are limited in availability. Those resources which are physical in nature, exist as stock at a particular point of time, *e.g.*, fossil fuels, metal ores, land, water etc. Whereas those of a biological nature, *e.g.*, forests, animal and human resources etc., have their 'stocks' changing at a 'natural' (biological or biochemical) rate. This is the temporal limitation of natural resources. The areal limitation of natural resources is, that they are not distributed uniformly over a region. This

*Research Scholar, Department of Architecture and Regional Planning, I.I.T., Kharagpur.
**Professor, Department of Architecture and Regional Planning, IIT, Kharagpur,

limited supply of natural resources over time and space calls for their efficient utilisation such that there is maximum benefit and minimum misuse.

The abundance of resources in an area has not always led to the economic development of that area. Failure of man to assess the available resources and use them effectively did not allow these resource-endowed areas to forge ahead. Utilisation of the natural resources to their best extent is associated with their careful assessment. This will provide a better information base for the preparation of any economic development plan. This is particularly vital for backward areas where information programming ahead of time is made more difficult because of their scarce resource base. The present paper is based on this concept of resource assessment for the purpose of setting up industries in backward area. The paper emphasizes that any attempt to prepare an industrial development plan for a backward area must be preceeded by the thorough inventory of the resource potential, based on a sound information base. The resource assessment must provide information on the present use of available resources, their estimated future availability and the potential unutilised resources. This analysis of resource-use will fetch a technical guidance to the planner. He will be aware of how much of the available resources are being used, how much can best be used over the planning period to attain the desired goals and how much must be left over as stock. For this purpose, the present paper suggests a methodology of resource base analysis which provides a systematic and organised approach of identification and selection of right type of industry at the right moment of time.

The objective of the paper is to indicate the necessity of a methodology for resource base analysis, to illustrate the use of the methodology for selecting the industries in a backward area to point out the deficiencies in the information sources, which are vital to the methodology.

The procedure follows a classification of the resources and industries of the area, preparation of the transaction matrix showing the current 'flows' of commodities, preparation of the second transaction matrix incorporating the unutilised resources and identifying their possible 'flows' and preparation of the final transaction matrix depicting the prescribed flows for the planning period.

The Study Area

The above methodology has been demonstrated with the information on Jhargram Subdivision forming a part of the industrially backward district of Midnapore, West Bengal. The study area is endowed with resources like forests, minerals, livestock etc., though handicapped by less fertile soil, frequent droughts, concentration of tribal population and poor infrastructural builds. Extensive cultivation of land is restricted by the physical conditions and agriculture is rewarding only with the help of more scientific and intensive farming techniques. Hence any approach to develop the secondary sector as a source of income generation is a welcome proposal.[2] In fact, the current policy of industrial development is lacking in its objective of development of the backward area with appropriate appraisal and use of resources.[3] Inspite of many promotional policies, industrial development is yet to set in here. The certificate of backwardness conferred on the district because of Jhargram's disadvantageous situation, is being exploited by the rest of the district. The subsidies and incentives associated with backwardness are availed by educated entrepreneurs from Haldia, Kharagpur, Tamluk and other urban centres which serve as better locations for industrial investments. The few units which are set up in the study area have had little impact on its economy because neither input nor output is related to the local sectors. Besides, the low skill-formation of the local populaion also restricts their absorption as technical labour.

Development of the secondary sector in Jhargram needs to be approached from the view point of resource use. Small scale resource based processing activities located at a few centres will provide the stimulus for industrial growth. These activities will be directly linked with the surrounding area through the process of resource utilisation. Employment, income and other multiplier effects will 'trickle down' into the entire area subsequently. Therefore, effective resource use and industrialisation, it is essential to estimate the potential 'stocks' and 'flows' of resources through a systematic analytical approach.

The information source for resource 'flow' and 'stock' is based on primary and secondary surveys, undertaken with reference to: (a) existing resource availability as compiled from different government reports and annual plans and (b) a twenty per cent sample survey of operating industries. The resource flows and stocks have been recorded as per the annual reports of 1983-84 for the former and the corresponding financial year for the latter. The only exception is mineral resources whose 'stocks' have been estimated as available over a limited areal extent and depth. Data in the transaction tables correspond to 1983-84 for the first intersectoral matrix and to 1994-95 for the second and third matrices assuming a plan period of ten years from 1984-85.

The Methodology

The first step in the process of analysis is the preparation of the transaction matrix. The format of the transaction matrix corresponds to that of a basic input-output table. The elements of the table have been utilised, without going into the refinements for presenting a systematic and at the same time descriptive account of resource 'flows' within an economy. Just like the conventional input-output tables, such transaction matrices may also be constructed for a whole economy or a part thereof or for showing inter regional inter-sectoral flows. Only the dimensions of the tables vary according to the number of resources identified.

The procedure begins with the construction of the matrix recording the relevent transactions. The transaction items in this case may be grouped under agriculture, forest, livestock and mineral resources as well as industrial products. The matrix is divided along the rows to distinguish between intermediate use, final use (domestic, government and reports), total output, imports and reserves, for any supplying sector. The divisions along the column show the consumptions of a sector from the different resources and industries. In the inter-industy segment the upper left hand quadrant (II) will record the resource-transactions, the upper right hand qudrant (I) for resource-industry, lower lefthand quadrant (III) for industry, resource and lower righthand quadrant (IV) for industry-industry transactions. The flows are recorded for a particular time period and the unit of entry is quantity (mostly in metric tonnes). This is because the quantitative measures give a clear picture of the amount of availability, whereas monetary values fluctuate with spatial, temporal and qualitative differentiation of any commodity and thus reduces their long term utility for prediction purposes.

Matrix A: The entry of thirty six resources highlights the presence of a resource base which may be exploited for industrial purposes.[5] However the non-existent resource-industry and poor inter industry flow reveal the scope of better utilisation of resources. For example, paddy is used by sector 1 (for seeds) and by sector twenty four (for machine processing). This is the existing intermediate use of paddy as depicted in Matrix A. Similarly, pulpwood a forest product has no intermediate use. The total output is exported soap stone, manganese ore and china clay have sufficient 'stock' for establishing mineral based industries and call for techno-economic feasibility studies. The blank elements in the matrix is noteworthy.

Matrix B: These blank elements help in the construction of the second matrix. This matrix enters (a) those resources which are unutilised and (b) those resources which will be made available over the planning period through different sectoral policies. As illustrated in Matrix B, rice husk, clean rice and straw are the by-products of paddy. Rice husk can be consumed by secor five (as fodder), sector eighteen (for producing sodium silicate , sector nineteen (for detergent) and sector twenty (cattle-feed plants). Similarly clean rice can be utilised by sector thirty three (for household processing of flattened and puffed rice). Straw, which is another important by-product of paddy cultivation can be utilised by sector thirty three (for producing mats, bags, hats and thatch material). This transaction table illustrates the varsatile uses of paddy and its by-products for sustaining small scale industrial activities·

Similarly in Matrix B, pulpwood has been shown as being utilisable in sector twenty nine (for paper manufacturing).

Matrix C: From the above matrics it is now possible to compile the resource flows, which are feasible, for product identification and drawing up an industrial plan. This is the final matrix which will provide the base for the industrial development plan. It selects the resource 'flows' from matrix A and B, which can sustain industries successfully.

Cereals (paddy and wheat) and pulses as sector 1, can be utilised in sector 4 (for fodder), sector 10 (for machine processing of paddy) and sector 19 (for hand processing of paddy). Simultaneously, the machine processed grain yields clean rice, and a host of by-products. The latter are consequently used in sector 4 (as fodder), sector 11 (flattened and puffed rice, wheat flour for bakery products), sector 12 (wheat bran for cattlefeed) sector 13 (rice bran for non-edible oil), sector 17 (straw and husk for briquette), sector 18 (rice husk for household cleaning powder), sector 19 (hard processing of paddy) and sector 25 rice husk to sodium silicate).

Pulpwood is consumed by sector 16 (for paper making) sector 20 (for hand made paper) and sector 30 (for safety matches).

The flow-sheet presents a clear picture of the above mentioned transactions.

Limitations

The transaction matrix is an organised approach to small scale industrial development in backward areas. With further improvements made possible by a sound data base, they can become important analytical tools in industrial planning. However the method has its limitations. Firstly, the matrices cannot be constructed without a solid data base, which is sadly lacking.

Flow-sheet of Cereals and Pulpwood (based mainly on forward linkages)

1. Cereals
   - →Machine & Head processing of grains
     - →Clean rice
       - →Flattend rice
       - →Puffed rice
     - →Rice husk
       - →Sodium silicate
       - →Household clearing power
       - →Briquette
     - →Wheat flour →Bakery products
     - →Wheat brand
       - →Non-edible oil
       - →Cattle feed
   - →Straw
     - →Household industry products *e.g.*, mats hand made paper etc.
     - →Fodder
     - →Briquettee
   - →Seeds →Cereals

2. Pulp-wood →Paper and pulp.
   - →Craft paper, and other varieties of paper
   - →Safety matches

Because of this the uses of the matrices have been restricted. Secondly, the assumption that the percentage of consumption in different sectors will remain same over the planning period is subject to criticism.

Conclusions

The matrices provide a helpful guidance to the planner for resource based industrial development. It is a technique of sequential matrix construction, keeping in mind products in the forward linkage. It beings with the identification of resources presently used in industrial activity, thereby simultaneously focussing on those unutilised resources and their potential uses. Finally it selects the resource inventory which is best suited to further industrial activity generation.

As illustrated, the four quadrants of the inter-industry segment of the transaction tables have gradually altered their sizes, with the sequential progress from A to C. The resource—resource quadrant of Matrix A has been reduced considerably in size in Matrix C. The practically non-existent, industry—industry quadrant of Matrix A has been enlarged considerably in Matrix C, which indicates a better utilisation of the by-products. The zero or blank elements of Matrix A are characteristic of a backward economy. Though these elements are present in Matrix C, their number has been reduced. Blank elements occur where inter-linkage between industries are few. The inter-linkages established in Matrix C are few and mainly forward in nature. Only a well developed heavy industrial base can integrate industrial activities with maximum forward and backward linkages, and thereby reduce the number of blank elements. However, a heavy indusrtial base may not necessarily be local resource based. But the objective of the present work is essentially resource based small industrial development of backward areas. The process of bringing in industries into a stagnating backward economy must be gradual and essentially related with the local area. The technique employed stresses the need of maximum resource utilisation, and is therefore very much appropriate for backward area industrial planning.

RESOURCE INDUSTRY & INTERINDUSTRY LINKAGES

TABLE NO: MATRIX A

SECTORS	1	2	3	4	5	6	7	8	9	10	11	12	13	14	15	16	17	18	19	20	21	22	23	24	25	26	27	28	29	30	31	32	33	34	35	36	*
PADDY	810																																				
WHEAT																								[illegible]													
PULSES																								1,000													
OILSEEDS																														57							
SUGARCANE																														58							
OTHER AGRI PRODS																																					
BABUL GRASS																														[illegible]							
FRUITS																																			12,460		
STRAW																														17							
TIMBER (M^3)																																					
PULPWOOD																										4,000											
FUELWOOD (M^3)																																					
SEEDS																								20	72						986			92			
BAMBOO (NOS)																													9065								
LEAVES																											1,950										
FLOWERS																																				[illegible]	
MOORA GRASS																																					
CASHEWNUT																																					
RAW HIDE (NOS)																															50						
BONES																																					
CHINA CLAY																																					
MANGANESE ORE																																					
SOAPSTONE																																					
GRAINMILL PRODS																																			[illegible]		
NON-METALLIC MINL PRODS																	100													16	[illegible]						
WOOD PRODS																																					
PAPER PRODS																										100											
ENGG PRODS																																					
OIL & BD PRODS																									30												
FOOD PROCESSING																															500	1,760					
CATTLE FEED																																					
CHEMICAL PRODS																																					
TEXTILES (M^2)																										20		20									
STONEWARE (NOS)																																					
ARTISAN SECTOR PRODS																																					
OTHERS																																					

SECTORS	Inter-mediate Consumption	Domestic Consumption	Govt. Consumption	Exports	Final Use	Total Output	Imports	Reserves
PADDY								
WHEAT	38,616	82,947	0	95,565	208,512	218,830		218,530
PULSES	1,000	1,350	0	90	2,130	1,350		1,350
OILSEEDS	57	1,994	0	0	1,994	1,995		[illegible]
SUGARCANE	58	0	0	1,538	1,576	1,560		1,560
OTHER AGRI PRODS								
BABUL GRASS	[illegible]	43,960	0	0	43,960	43,960		43,960
FRUITS	12,460	0	0	0	0	12,460		12,460
STRAW	17	0	0	0	0	17		95
TIMBER (M^3)	0	395,276	0	171,300	566,575	566,575		566,575
PULPWOOD	4,000	0	7,300	7,300	14,600	18,600		18,600
FUELWOOD (M^3)	0	0	6,000	0	6,000	6,000		1,959,616
SEEDS	5,150	67,598	0	29,615	97,463	93,500		98,500
BAMBOO (NOS)	9065	0	0	0	0	400	7,947.56	
LEAVES	1,950	0	1,350	1,300	2,650	4,000		4,000
FLOWERS	175,500 67,560	18,000 0	0 0	0 100,000	18,000 100,000	193,500		193,567 67,500
MOORA GRASS	0	10	0	0	10	10		
CASHEWNUT	0	45	0	0	45	45		100
RAW HIDE (NOS)	50	0	0	0	0	50	150	96
BONES	0	0	0	171,630	171,630	171,630		171,630
CHINA CLAY	0	0	0	504	504	504		504
MANGANESE ORE	0	0	0	0	0	0		10,030
SOAPSTONE	0	0	0	0	0	0		700,000
GRAINMILL PRODS	1,500	0	0	0	0	1,500		[illegible]
NON-METALLIC MINL PRODS	1,500	479,996	1,200	50,000	480,396	482,836		28,400
WOOD PRODS	0	165,162	299,000	0	465,162	465,162		
PAPER PRODS	100	200	0	0	200	300		
ENGG PRODS	0	0	0	10,000	10,000	10,000		10,000
OIL & BD PRODS	30	0	0	0	0	30		
FOOD PROCESSING	1,998	0	0	6,351	6,351	8,249		
CATTLE FEED	0	5,568	0	88	5,567	5,567		
CHEMICAL PRODS	0	20	0	2,500	2,520	2,520		316
TEXTILES (M^2)	40	5,095	0	4,380	5,475	5,515		
STONEWARE (NOS)	0	384,000	0	0	0	384,000		480,000
ARTISAN SECTOR PRODS	0	16,986	0	1,360	18,350	18,350		
OTHERS	0	10,175 1,500	0 0	10,575 5,000	281,500 3,500	281,500 6,500		500,000
	200	5,500	0	0	5,500	6,000		

* Unless specified units are in metric tonnes

RESOURCE INDUSTRY & INTER-INDUSTRY LINKAGES

TABLE NO : MATRIX B

SECTORS	1	2	3	4	5	6	7	8	9	10	11	12	13	14	15	16	17	18	19	20	21	22	23	24	25	26	27	28	29	30	31	32	33	34	Total Interm Use	Dom Consmp	Govt. Consmp	Export	Final Use	Total Output
1 RICE HUSK					100													2,500	60	2,940															5,600	0	0	0	0	5,600
2 CLEAN RICE																																	5,040		5,040	0	6,720	5,040	11,760	16,800
3 STRAW																																	6,000		6,000	0	0	1,85,300	1,85,300	1,91,300
4 WHEAT BRAN																				1,980															1,980	0	0	0	0	1,980
5 FODDER							(II)													100					(I)										100	0	0	-0	0	100
6 WHEAT FLOUR																							2												2	4,018	0	0	4,018	4,020
7 CASHEWNUT																					175		356												531	0	0	0	0	531
8 LEAVES (NO'S)																	184,972			3,60,348					487,600										9,19,280	10,000	0	2,00,000	2,10,000	11,29,280
9 POTATOES																																	8,718		8,718	20,342	0	0	20,342	29,060
10 PULSES																																	1,800		180	3,000	0	1,200	4,200	6,000
11 BAMBOO																														5,150			2,510		7,650	0	1,350	0	1,350	9,000
12 SEEDS																	2,150																		2,150	0	0	0	0	2,150
13 TIMBER																											4,000								4,000	0	2,300	7,300	1,46,000	31,900
14 SUGARCANE																																								
15 SABAI																																	16,384		16,384	0	0	0	0	16,384
16 PULPWOOD																														18,000					18,000	0	6,000	50,318	56,318	74,318
17 NON-EDIBLE OIL																			1,598	700													85		1,900	0	0	6,363	6,363	8,263
18 SODIUM SILICATE							50												720			60								100		36			600	0	0	0	0	600
19 SOAP BY-PRDTS.																																			0	65	0	65	130	130
20 CATTLE FEEDS																																			0	0	10,000	0	10,000	10,000
21 C.N.S.L.																												8		22				5	35	0	0	0	0	35
22 ENGG. PRDTS.								(III)														5					(IV)					30		5	40	0	0	80	80	120
23 FOOD PROCESSING.																							535												535	4,832	0	356	5,188	5,723
24 FERTILISERS							00		10	150				180																					730	0	1,500	770	2,270	3,000
25 SAL LEAF PRDTS.																																			0	4,800	0	1,200	6,000	6,000
26 TIN CONTAINER (NO'S)																	6,00,000																		6,00,000	0	0	0	0	6,00,000
27 WOOD PRDTS.																																								
28 L.D.P.E.																																36			36	0	0	0	0	36
29 PAPER PRDTS.																														5,000					5,000	13	0	25,000	25,013	30,013
30 SEMI-FINISHED LEATHER																																								
31 NON-METALLIC MINL. PRDTS.																																			0	4,000	4,000	4,000	8,000	16,000
32 L.D.P.E. WRAPPERS																							11												11	0	25	0	25	36
33 HNLD. INDUSTRY PRDTS.																																								
34 CHEMICALS.																																								

Unless specified units are in metric tonnes

RESOURCE INDUSTRY & INTER-INDUSTRY LINKAGES

TABLE NO: MATRIX C

SECTORS	1	2	3	4	5	6	7	8	9	10	11	12	13	14	15	16	17	18	19	20	21	22	23	24	25	26	27	28	29	30	31	Total Inter. Use	Dom. Consump	Govt Consump	Exports	Total Final Use	Total Output
1 CEREALS / PULSES	1500									2840									6910													44368	90111	0	96075	186186	236654
2 MILLETS / OILSEEDS													13																			84	0	0	1376	1376	1460
3 OTHER AGRL. PRODUCE																			13720													6720	66182	0	0	66182	73002
4 STRAW / BABUL / FODDER																				21384												21384	355275	0	191300	546575	568959
5 HORTICULTURAL PRODUCE											373										175											548	0	0	0	0	548
6 MAJOR FOREST PRODUCE									749						6000	18000				4913		72								1.96		90567 m³ 18000 mt					
7 MINOR FOREST PRODUCE													8957			5836				25920			300							2.75,000		99475 m³ 74265 mt	10000	0	200000	210000	299475 m³ 282650 mt
8 LIVESTOCK PRODUCE														120000																		120000	0	0	0	0	120000
9 MINERAL PRODUCE																														6,500		6500	0				
10 GRAINMILL PRDTS				100								2,040	5980				6000	60	3040						2540							13611	5018	4720	5040	15778	29400
11 FOOD PROCESSING																																0	509	0	38	517	547
12 CATTLE FEED								10000																								10000	0	0	0	0	10,000
13 EDIBLE & NON-EDBL OIL												300						1888	535	0.5												24135	4832	0	6364	11196	35431
14 LEATHER PROC. PRDTS																				600000												600,000 ft²	0	0	60,000	60,000	120,00,000
15 WOOD BASED IND.															600																	100 m³	200	0	0	200	300 m³
16 PAPER & ITS PRDTS.																7500																5000 m³	13	0	25,000	25,013	30,013
17 BRIQUETTE																																0					
18 SOAP & BY-PRDTS											0.5																					0.5	60	0	69.5	129.5	130
19 HHLD. IND. (FOOD)																																0	38.5	0	154	0	192.5
20 HHLD. IND. (OTHERS)																																0					
21 C.N.S.L. ADHESIVE																8											10	17				35	0	0	0	0	35
22 NON-METALLIC MINL.																																0	4000	6000	8000	18,000	16,000
23 DISTILLATION PRDTS.																																0					
24 MIXED GRANULATED FERT.	150		380		200																											730	0	1500	770	2,270	3000
25 SODIUM SILICATE																	120	30	120		150					120	60					600	0	0	0	0	600
26 TEXTILES																																0	38,400 m²	0	0	0	38,400 m²
27 ENGG / FOUNDRY / ETC.																							30					5				40	0	0	90	120	120
28 RESIN, LDPE, CHEM. ETC.																20												20	36			76	0	0	14	0	90
29 L.D.P.E WRAPPERS, CONT'RS												9		600000						2												60,00,000 Nos	0	15	5	20	6,000,000 Nos
30 OTHERS.																																0					

Unless specified units are in metric tonnes

REFERENCES

1. John Mclnerney, 'Natural resources economics: the basic analytical principles, Journal of Agricultural Economics, 27, Jan. 1976.

2. W.E.B.C.O.N., 'Industrial persepective study on Jhargram Region,' study report sponsored by J.B.D. and I.D.B.I., 1984-85.

3. Planning Commission, 'Development of Backward Areas—Report on Industrial Despersal,' National Committee Report, 1980, Annexure IV 2.

4. A.P. Thirlwall, 'Growth and Development', Mcmillan Press, London, 1982, pp. 220-234.

5. Chhabi Nag, 'Planning for Industrial Development of backward Areas—Case study Jhargram Subdivision', Unpublished MRP Thesis, Dept. of Arch. & Regional Planning, I.I.T., Kharagpur, 1985.

6

METROPOLITAN GROWTH AND SHIFTS IN RESOURCE BASE

K. SITA*

A striking characteristic of the pattern of economic development in India is the spatial imbalances and the sharp changes that one finds within a short distance. This aspect is very evident in Maharashtra, particularly near the metropolitan cities. Brahme (1977) has clearly brought out through her study of Bombay the contrast between metropolitan cities and their hinterlands; this has not substantially changed during the last decade. The dominance of the metropolitan centres is reflected in the spatial pattern of urbanization in Maharashtra. Urban growth in 1971-81 was concentrated in the metropolitan centres themselves and in their immediate vicinity with a sharp fall at a distance of 25 to 50 kms. Beyond this distance, there is a marked metropolitan shadow-zone where urban growth appears to be inhibited due to the towering metropolitan centres. (Desai, 1985, p. 29) Friedmann's core-periphery paradigm is thus very appropriate in this context as metropolitan centres not only dominate their hinterlands but have also resulted in the spatial organization of activities in the hinterlands. It is against this

*Department of Geogrpahy, University of Bombay, Bombay.

background that it was felt desirable to focus on the changing patterns of the resource base, which are the result of Bombay's growth in two areas, one located in the metropolitan shadow-zone of Bombay and the other in the zone where the centrifugal forces due to Bombay's growth are operative.

South Konkan—A Weak Urban Sub-System

Ratnagiri district[1] or South Konkan lies in the metropolitan shadow of Bombay. In spite of its location in the western coastal plain between the highly developed pockets of Bombay and Goa, it is one of the most backward regions of Maharashtra. The urban sub-system which is operating in South Konkan is very weak as is evident from the low degree of urbanisation in the region and the stagnant or declining growth rates of the towns (Sita, 1980). In fact, the system is so weak as to raise the question as to whether there is a system functioning at all.

There is historical evidence to show that some of the towns of South Konkan are of great antiquity. Prior to the rise of Bombay they carried on a large amount of coastal and overseas trade and served as outlets for the products of the Deccan Plateau (Nairne, 1896). The complementary nature of South Konkan and the Deccan Plateau led to trade between the two areas which was facilitated by the east-west routes across the Sahyadri. The Konkan towns with their ghat linkages functioned as part of the plateau urban sub-system.

With the expansion of the British and Portuguese colonial rule in this part of India the ports of South Konkan lost their trade. The Portuguese developed their base at Goa while the British concentrated on Bombay. They strengthened the transport links of only these two bases with the plateau hinterland. South Konkan parts got more or less squeezed out of coastal and overseas trade as a result of the colonial economy centred mainly at Bombay. Nature also conspired in the decline of South Konkan ports as silting reduced their value for navigation while the larger size of sailing ships was an equally important factor. The links of the Konkan ports with the plateau were snapped and no substitute emerged. Since about 1930, the West

Coast road provided accessibility, but did not contributed to urban development; on the contrary it further eroded regional urbanisation. Hence the weak urban sub-system of South Konkan appears to be primarily due to the growth and influence of Bombay.

South Konkan—Depletion of Human Resources

South Konkan has been a traditional area of out-migration to Bombay and is the major source of migrants to the metropolis. In the initial stages, this was due to the growing labour demands of Bombay's docks and industries which resulted in South Konkan becoming a recruiting ground for labour. (Savur, 1979) Migration was particularly from the southern parts of Ratnagiri, and due to its selective nature, it left its mark on settlements in the form of stagnant and declining growth rates, high sex ratios and high dependency ratios (Sita, 1979).

However, during the last two decades, there have been changes. Ratnagiri continues to be an area of out-migration (Table 1) but the tendency appears to be towards family migration as is reflected in a decrease in sex ratios in many parts of the district.

Since, however, migration continues to be age selective, its impact is evident in the dependency ratios which are very high and are increasing in most parts of the district.[2] (Table 2).

The increase is particularly marked in some of the South Ratnagiri talukas such as Lanja, Rajapur, Kudal and Vengurla. Its effect is also evident in male and female participation in work which are on the decline. For example, in Vengurla, the female participation in work decreased from 17.53 per cent in 1971 to 12.14 per cent in 1981, which is a very steep fall.

This depletion of the productive sector of the work force has naturally affected the economy of the region. Ratnagiri has traditionally earned a reputation of noving a 'money-order economic.' Data collected in the field regarding money order remittances at selected places shows a trend to increase in remittances, but also indicates that the amounts received are on an average small per household; this raises a doubt as to the

TBALE 1

Migration from Ratnagiri District 1971-1981

S. No.	*Talukas*	*Actual Increase of Population 1971-81*	*Natural Increase of Population 71-81*	*Net migration 71-81*	*Net out migration as a percent of actual increase*
1.	Ratnagiri	22713	21907	806	×
2.	Guhagar	8580	8743	—163	—1.86
3.	Dapoli	12516	13563	—1047	—7.72
4.	Mandangad	4986	4218	—768	×
5.	Khed	10853	14469	—3616	24.99
6.	Chiplum	11423	21437	—10014	—46.71
7.	Sangameshwar	11948	15979	—4031	—25.22
8.	Lanja	6809	8528	—1719	—20.16
9.	Rajapur	7624	16864	—9240	—54.79
10.	Kankavli	3919	12363	—8444	—68 30
11.	Kudal	4820	13929	—9100	—65.37
12.	Sawantwadi	13518	22758	—9240	--40.60
13.	Vengurla	1405	8703	—7298	—83.86
14.	Malwan	5976	9520	—15496	—162.77
15.	Deogad	3467	9543	—6076	—63.67

TABLE 2

Ratnagiri District Dependency Ratios 1971 & 1981

S. No.	*Taluka*	*1971*	*1981*
1.	Ratnagiri	227.54	217.49
2.	Guhagar	173.27	176.99
3.	Dapoli	179.68	186.10
4.	Mandangad	162.18	151.50
5.	Khed	166.20	165.33
6.	Chiplum	178.77	177.39
7.	Sangameshwar	160.49	175.29
8.	Lanja	155.01	176.06
9.	Rajapur	191.00	209.81
10.	Kankavli	168.88	178.39
11.	Kudal	176.62	200.05
12.	Sawntwadi	195.56	213.98
13.	Vengurla	234.83	285.79
14.	Malwan	223.99	229.42
15.	Deogad	208.98	207.40

validity of the term 'money-order economy' under present economic conditions.

The negative impact of out-migration is evident in the stagnation of agriculture in the region. There is hardly no trend to double cropping and workers in the agricultural sector have decreased, particularly in South Ratnagiri (Table 3). Though the literacy rate has improved suggesting that the labour is better qualified, levels of unemployment are high (Table 4). It is clear that the number of candidates on the live register of the Employment Exchange has been swelling in the last two decades. This, along with the low level of placement to registration which decreased from thirteen per cent in 1971 to three per cent in 1981, suggests that a large pool of qualified labour is unemployed and hence sustains the stream of out-migration.

TABLE 3

Ratnagiri District: Workers in Agricultural Activities

Sl. No.	*Talukas*	*1971*	*1981*	*% Change 1971-81*
1.	Ratnagiri	37891	39400	3.98
2.	Guhagar	33241	30263	—8.95
3.	Dapoli	40613	38249	—5.82
4.	Mandangad	18554	20028	7.94
5.	Khed	49812	51104	2.59
6.	Chiplum	55531	58121	4.64
7.	Sangameshwar	59190	54838	—7.35
8.	Lanja	29898	29423	—1.59
9.	Rajapur	42111	47255	—10.88
10.	Kankavli	38364	*34612	—9.78
11.	Kudal	39154	34569	—11.71
12.	Sawantwadi	39440	35943	—68.87
13.	Vengurla	15305	9840	—35.71
14.	Malwan	28516	23608	—17.21
15.	Deogad	29195	28025	—4.00

TABLE 4

Candidates enrolled and Vacancies Notified in the Employment Exchange Office—Ratnagiri

	YEARS		
	1960-61	*1970-71*	*1979-80*
1. Candidates enrolled	3738	9046	9024
2. Vacancies notified	598	1740	933
3. Placement in vacancies	357	1193	279
4. Per cent of placement to registration	9	13	3
5. Candidates on live register at the end of the year	2840	7306	16260

These characteristics are due to the low level of capital accumulation in the district. The provision of services by the government has not stimulated private capital formation in the area; in fact it has led to a decelerated rate of capital accumulation in the district (Prabhu, 1985).

Developmental efforts in South Konkan have hence to take into account the strong economic pull of metropolitan Bombay. The proposed Konkan railway, if accompanied by a number of feeder east-west roads might improve accessibility in the region. But transport alone would probably not generate development it might only serve to funnel more migration to Bombay (Phadke *et.al.*, 1972-73). A degree of stabilisation of the economy of South Konkan can be achieved by strengthening of the agricultural base through development of small irrigation projects on the rivers. In addition South Konkan's physical setting and its historical background invest it with a potentiality for developing tourism. Its undulating topography gives it a great scenic beauty and this is enchanced along the coast by the beaches and headlands. The wild life and bird sanctuaries and the numerous historic points together with the proximity to Bombay should prove assets for promoting the tourist industry.

Immediate Vicinity of Bombay—Urban Sprawl

The second area is a zone around Greater Bombay where the spill-over effects of metropolitian growth are very evident. The area chosen for study is the Bombay Metropolitan Region and the analysis is based on village level secondary data on land-use. The "land not available for cultivation" has been considered as a good surrogate of "built-up" area changes in village boundaries between 1971 and 1981 enable only a qualitative picture of urban sprawl to be obtained (D'Souza, 1986).

In 1971, the extension of the built-up area was mainly along the railway corridors. Hence urban sprawl was noticeable only in two areas; one extended from Greater Bombay northwards into coastal Thane and Vasai talukas along the Western Railway. The second was associated with the Central Railway route and extended from the metropolis through Thane, Kalyan, Ulhasnagar to Badlapur. In the rest of the Metropolitan Region a rural land-use pattern was dominant. The continuity and expansiveness of this had completely been destroyed by 1981 due to the tremendous degree of urban sprawl. Though urban sprawl continued along the two railways routes, it is clear that considerable diffusion had taken place along the roads in their neighbourhood. However, the remarkable feature in 1981 was the urban sprawl in the trans-Thane Creek belt and along the Bombay-Pune road. These are associated with the opening of the Thane Creek bridge in 1972, the diversion of the Bombay-Pune traffic to it, and the development of New Bombay as a counter-magnet to Bombay. Urban sprawl in this area has developed to such an extent that the isolated patches in 1971 around centres like Khopli, Neral have now been engulfed in it.

An analysis of changes in the percentage of land under cultivation indicates that there has been a considerable reduction in the area under cultivation. There were vast expanses with over 50 per cent of the land under cultivation in 1971 while in 1981 large areas had less than twenty five per cent. Hence, it is evident that built-up area has encroached on cultivated land, and there has been a large scale coversion from agricultural to non-agricultural land-use in the fringe of the metropolis particularly along routeways. The routes to Bombay initially developed along the lines of least resistance provided by river valleys, and low-lying areas. It is unfortunate therefore that urban sprawl is at the expense of these fertile agricultural areas while vast tracts of infertile land remain under agriculture.

It is clear that unless strict zoning regulations are enforced the problems due to unplanned urban sprawl will be accentuated in the near future. On the one hand, Bombay's daily requirements of vegetables and other perishables will have to be obtained from areas further away and on the other, the magnitude of population concentration would pose severe infrastructural and other problems.

The metropolitan growth of Bombay has thus had varied effects on its hinterland. In the distant hinterland, the centripetal effects due to Bombay have led to an exodus of population, which in turn has affected the development of the region. The result has been the creation of the problem area of South Konkan, a region depleted of its valuable human resources. In the immediate vicinity of the metropolis, the growth of Bombay has ushered in changes in the resource base due to diversion of fertile agricultural areas to non-agricultural land-uses. As this shift is taking place in an unplanned and unorganized manner, it is likely to pose serious problems in the future. Since the metropolitan region has been delineated, strict zoning regulations along with well demarcated green belts would help to mitigate the problems.

NOTES

1. It now forms the 2 districts of Ratnagiri and Sindhudurg.

2. The increase in dependency ratio which is the ratio of non-workers to workers may be partly due to the stricter defination of 'worker' in 1981.

REFERENCES

Brahme, S. (1978) "The Role of Bombay in the Economic Development of Maharashtra" in A.G. Noble and A.K Dutt (ed.) *Indian Urbanisation and Planning, Vehicles of Modernization.* (Tata McGraw Hill, New Delhi), pp. 313-325.

Desai, R.J. (1985) "*Metropolitan Dominance in India—A Case Study of Maharashtra, 1971-81.*" Unpublished M. Phil. Dissertation, Department of Geography, University of Bombay.

D'Souza, H, (1986) "Urban Sprawl around Greater Bombay," Unpublished M.A. dissertation, Department of Geography, University of Bombay.

Nairne, A.K. (1986) "History of the Konkan" in *Gazetter of the Bombay* Presidency" (Bombay, Vol. I, Pt. II).

Phadke, V.S., Arunachalam, B, and Deshpande, C.D. (1972-73). "South Kolaba: A Study in Demographic characteristics as an as pect of rural-urban relations," *Bombay Geographical* Magazine, XX, XXI, pp. 49-67.

Prabhu, K.S. (1985) "Resource Base of Ratnagiri District" (University of Bombay) Mimeo.

Savur, M. (1979) "Ratnagiri Underdevelopment or an area of reserve labour', in R. Baxamusa *et.al.*, "*Underdevelopment of Ratnagiri—A Case of Rural metropolitan relations.*" (Department of Sociology University of Bombay), pp. 1-16.

Sita, K. (1979), "Migration and its effect on urbanisation in South Konkan," *Indian Geog. journal*, 54 (1), pp. 14-21.

Sita, K. (1980) "Some Aspects of Urbanisation in South Konkan," *Geog. Review of India*, 42 (3), pp. 238-244.

SECTION II

RESOURCE BASE AND REGIONAL IMBALANCES

It is apparent to any one who is well conversed with the developmental scenario in India that there are considerable imbalances in levels of development, between countryside and town, and between regions within the country. Can we attribute this to different patterns of resources endowment and utilisation? or, is it the result of defective planning? It may be difficult to find an answer to these questions without conducing detailed investigations. However, it is generally agreed that regional imbalances are manifestations of a spatial planning without taking into account of the location of projected development. The benefits of development in such a case tend to concentrate rather than spread.

In the first article of this section K.P.C. Rao and C.K. Ramanatha Chetty take a cursory look at the problem of imbalances in economic development of major states of India with/reference to their resource endowments. They are of the opinion that the co-efficient of variation of the per-capita incomes of the major states of India show an increasing trend over time, suggesting that regional imbalances are growing. The authors examine the distribution of natural resources with special refrence to agriculture, their exploitation and the resulting levels of development in the fifteen major states. The impact of financial and human resources in accelerating the process of development and the constraints of the poorer states are also investigated in some detail.

Regional imbalances and social well-being in two eastern states of India is the topic of a scholarly analysis by Swapna Banerjee, Nandini Das Gupta and Bharati Banerjee. They view the spatial dimension of socio-economic well-being as an expression of the movement of capital and functioning of control hierarchy. The pattern as studied by the authors, not only indicates extreme polarisation in a single core surrounded by a vast impoverished periphery, but also helps to expose gaps in planning of resources utilisation for improvement of the regional economies.

The third article in this section pertains to the study of regional resource base and pattern of economic development in Madhya Pradesh. The author, S.K. Sharma, portrays the broad pattern of the distribution of natural resources and correlates it with the present level of economic development in the State. Local/resources matter a great deal and economic activities related to the interaction of resources predominate. With the advancement in economic activities, supply of local resources appears to be inadequate to support them. and inadqeuacy of resources is met with the inter-regional transfer of resources. Thus the economy of the advanced society unties the bounds of local resource base. Contrary to these, there are certain regions which for some reason or the other, could not increase the efficiency of the resource use. and their resource bases appear much larger in relation to their level of economic development. These two types of regions present dependant-dominant relationship.

In the last article of this section 'Resource Regions of Telangana', P. Padmanabha Rao makes an attempt bring out the regions specificity based on significant variables. Three distinct sub-regions are delineated, *viz.*, urban-industrial, forest-mineral irrigation farming and dry farming regions.

7

RESOURCE ENDOWMENTS AND IMBALANCES IN ECONOMIC DEVELOPMENT OF MAJOR STATES IN INDIA

K.P.C. RAO**
C.K. RAMANATHA CHETTY**

India is often characterised as a rich country inhabited by poor people. It is implied in this statement that the country is rich in physical or natural resources, but the level of development attained by the people is not commensurate with the resource-base. To a large extent, this paradox is the legacy of the colonial rule for a period of nearly two centuries. Bairoch (1981) has estimated that in 1750 the per capita GNP in developed countries was only $ 182 against $ 188 in the third world, while in 1950 these were respectively $ 1054 and $ 202 all figures being in 1960 U.S. dollars and prices. Mehta (1980) observed that the income per person in the Indian sub-continent stagnated at the same level between 1600 and 1900 and possibly fell between 1900 and 1950.

**Scientist S-2 (Agricultural Economics) and Head, Division of Design and Analysis respectively at the CRIDA, Santoshnagar, Hyderabad—500 659.

In comparision to the dismal performance in the pre-independence era, India achieved a fairly rapid growth after Independence. At constant (1970-71) prices, the net national product grew at an average annual compound rate of 3.50 per cent between 1950-51 and 1981-82. But, in per capita terms, the growth rate was only 1.30 per cent per annum. It is a consequence of a fast growth in population at the rate of 2.2 per annum. The growth rate achieved in per capita income was very slow and at this rate, it would take nearly fifty four years to double the income or living standard of the people. Besides slow growth, another disturbing feature of economic development of the country has been the accentuation of the inequalities in income distribution. George (1980) analysed the per capita income of the urban and rural people between 1950-51 and 1974-75. The ratio of urban and rural per capita incomes increased from 2.02 in 1950-51 to 3.90 in 1974-75. Within the rural sector, the index of income inequality (Gini co-efficient) increased from 0.35 to 0.44 between 1963-64 and 1973-74 (Mehta 1980). These figures speak of the growing vertical imbalances in income distribution. Another important aspect of worsening income distribution could be found in the horizontal imbalances, which is the main theme of the present paper.

Growing Inequalities

Over the two decades period (1960-63 to 1980-83), there was a glaring accentuation of the income inequalities between the major states of the country Table 1). Bihar remained at the bottom rung of the ladder in all the three periods, while Punjab occupied the top spot displacing Maharashtra. Punjab and Haryana achieved the highest rate of growth during the two decades period, while West Bengal and Tamil Nadu registered the lowest growth rates. All the three measures of inequality employed in Table 1 suggested the same conclusion that the disparities in per capita income are growing over time. The ratio of highest to lowest per capita income steadily increased from 1.89 to 2.65 in the first decade and to 3.19 in the second decade. Similarly, the co-efficient of variation as well as the standard deviation of logarithmic values showed as a rising trend. These statistics testified to the fact that the imbalances in economic development of the major states increase alarmingly during the period under consideration.

In India, which is often referred as a sub-continent, the resource endowments of different states are not uniform. The country is known for its diversity not only in languages, religions and culture, but also in climate, soils, mineral wealth and people. There are no standard yardsticks with the help of which can pass judgments about the resource endowments, for quality aspects are as important as the quantities of resources. Yet a critical look into some of the indicators of resource endowments might help in understanding the process of economic development better. In spite of the rapid transformation of the economy in the recent past, agriculture continues to be the crucial sector of the country's economy.

Land Resource

Land and water are the key resources of the agricultural sector. Table 2 contains some key statistics pertaining to these resources. The geographical area per capita in different states is presented in the third column. There is a wide variation in it, with Rajasthan and Madhya Pradesh lying at one end of the spectrum and Kerala and West Bengal at the other. But this measure is not a proper indication of the endowment of land resource because there are wide differences in the types and varieties of the land masses in different states. In fact, the carrying capacity of the land might very inversely with it. A better index might be the net sown area per rural person presented in the fourth coloumn. There is a considerable reduction in the variation of this statistic when compared with that of the previous one. But what ultimately matters is the gross cropped area per rural person which is given in the fifth column. It exceeded 0.50 hectare in the states of Rajasthan, Punjab, Haryana, Madhya Pradesh and Maharashtra, while it was less than 0.25 hectare in the states of Kerala, Bihar, West

Bengal, Assam and Tamil Nadu. The remaining five states fall in the medium range of 0.25 to 0.49 hectares with respect to this statistic.

Water Resource

The average rainfall received in different states serves as a rough guide to the availability of moisture for the crops. The data on average rainfall are presented in column six of the Table 2. Kerala, Assam and West Bengal are better placed with respect to the rainfall, while the contiguous states of Rajasthan, Punjab and Haryana receive lowest quantities of rainfall. But the development or irrigation facilities has greatly reduced the dependence on rainfall in some of the states like Punjab, Haryana, Tamil Nadu and Uttar Pradesh. Column seven has the data on the percentage gross cropped area having irrigation facilities. There seems to be an inverse relationship between the rainfall and percentage irrigated area. But Rajasthan and parts of other states like Maharashtra, Andhra Pradesh, Karnataka and Gujarat are at a disadvantage due to scanty rainfall and underdevelopment of irrigation facilities. The last column of Table 2 gives information on the percentage irrigation potential achieved by different states. The exploitation of opportunities to develop irrigation facilities has been very much uneven across the states. While Punjab, Tamil Nadu, Haryana, Rajasthan and Uttar Pradesh achieved more than sevently per cent of the ultimate potential, Assam, Orissa, Kerala, Madhya Pradesh. Bihar and Mahrashtra achieved less than fifty per cent of the possible potential. There is a pressing need to invest more resources in the exploitation of water resources and to harness irrigation potential in the states where such an effort was going slow.

Modern Agricultural Inputs

Besides the endowments of the land and water resources, modern agricultural inputs are also assuming a greater role in influencing the productivity and income from the agricultural sector. Data on the use of modern inputs in different states are presented in Table 3. To achieve higher levels of productivity, fertiliser use has become crucial to replenish the nutrients removed by crops. Punjab is very much ahead of all other states in the use of fertilisers, distantly followed by Tamil Nadu, Andhra Pradesh, Uttar Pradesh and Haryana. At the lower end of the spectrum are Assam, Rajasthan, Orissa and Madhya Pradesh, using less than 20 kg. fertiliser per hectare of gross cropped area. Another index of progressiveness of agriculture is provided by the percentage area under high yielding varieties. The percentage area under high yielding varieties of the five major cereals, rice, wheat, jowar, maize and bajra, is worked out for each state and is presented in column 4 of Table 3. Six out of the fifteen states have more than fifty per cent coverage with the high yielding varieties. Tamil Nadu and Punjab lead them, while Haryana, Andhra Pradesh, Gujarat and Karnataka follow those two states distantly. Rajasthan, Orissa, Assam, Uttar Pradesh and Madhya Pradesh have less than one-third of the area under the high yielding varieties.

Although mechanisation has not made much dent in Indian Agriculture, tractorisation has been accepted as a means of increasing cropping intensity by hastening land preparation, threshing and transport operations. Punjab and Haryana states have achieved a high degree of tractorisation. The eastern states of Orissa, West Bengal and Assam are lagging behind other states in case of tractorisation. The eastern states are also backward in the use of power for minor irrigation. Tamil Nadu, Maharashtra and Gujarat lead others in the use of power for the agricultural sector. For the rapid use of modern inputs in agriculture, agricultural credit has a catalytic role to play. We find a lot of variation in the supply of institutional credit per hectare of gross cropped area across the states. It is less than Rs. 100 in the states of Madhya Pradesh and Rajasthan and is ranging between Rs. 100 and Rs. 200 in Orissa, Bihar and Uttar Pradesh. The amount of credit per hectare exceeded Rs. 500 in case of Kerala, Punjab and Tamil Nadu. All other states fall in the range of Rs. 200 to Rs. 500

per hectare. Thus, it can be observed that the states of Punjab, Tamil Nadu and Haryana displayed an intensive use of modern inputs in the agricultural sector. On the other hand, the use of modern inputs was very less in Assam, Orissa, Madhya Pradesh, Rajasthan, and Bihar. The other seven states fall in the intermediate category with respect to the use of the new inputs in agriculture.

Performance of the Agricultural Sector

Having surveyed the endowments of basic resources and the use of modern inputs, we shall now turn our attention to some indicators of the performance of agricultural sector in different states. The values of agricultural output per hecatare and per rural person are presented in columns three and four respectively in Table 4. The value of agricultural output per hectare of gross cropped area is highest in Kerala, followed by West Bengal, Assam and Punjab. It is lower than Rs. 2000 in the states of Madhya Pradesh, Rajasthan, Orissa, Maharashtra and Gujarat. But in terms of the value of agricultural output per rural person, the position is totally different. It is because of the differences in the availability of gross cropped area per rural person among the states. Punjab and Haryana have the highest levels of agricultural income per rural person, while Bihar and Tamil Nadu are at the lowest rungs of rural prosperity. The value of agricultural output per hectare seems to be correlated with the fertilizer consumption in kg per hecatre ($r=0.51$), percentage area under high yielding varieties ($r=0.45$) and percentage irrigated area ($r=0.31$).

The data on foodgrain production in kg per person is presented in column five of Table 4. An interesting feature is that the states of Kerala, Assam and West Bengal, which had very high values of agricultural output per hectare, produced very low quantities of foodgrains per person, along with Bihar and Tamil Nadu. This paradox is due to the specialisation of these states in the production of non-foodgrain crops. The foodgrain production per person in Punjab is more than four times the national average. Haryana stands distant second with four hundred seventy eight kg. per person. The growth rates of food production presented in the last two columns of the table reveal some interesting facts. The annual rates of increase in food production achieved by different states during the period 1952-55 to 1959-62 and 1959-62 to 1981-84 are given in the sixth and seventh columns of Table 4 respectively. The combined Punjab state, which already recorded a high rate of growth in the first period, has shown further acceleration in the growth of foodgrain production, after it was trifurcated into Punjab, Haryana and Himachal Pradesh states. Gujarat, Uttar Pradesh, West Bengal and Assam also improved their growth rates remarkably during the second period. Andhra Pradesh, Karnataka, Rajasthan, Maharashtra and Orissa suffered marginal reduction in their growth rates. The growth rates of foodgrain production declined steeply in case of Tamil Nadu, Kerala, Bihar and Madhya Pradesh.

Industrial Sector

Industrial sector is gaining importance with the passage of time. A large variety of commodities are being produced by this sector to meet the growing demand of the people. It is a source of employment to the skilled and educated labour force. Traditionally, the industries were concentrated in a few metropolitan cities, but the policy of the Government after Independence has been to encourage their dispersal throughout the length and breadth of the country. Table 5 contains information of percentage shares of different states in the employment and output of factory sector in the country. In the column 3, the shares of different states in the country's population are presented for a ready comparison with their shares in different variables of the factory sector given in column 4 through 7 of the Table 5. In terms of the number of factories, Maharashtra, Andhra Pradesh, Gujarat and Tamil Nadu, dominate the scene, with each of them accounting for more than ten per cent of the total factories. Orissa, Assam and Rajasthan have very few factories, each having less than three per cent of the total. But in terms of factory employment, Maharashtra is followed by

West Bengal, Tamil Nadu and Gujarat. Orissa, Assam and Rajasthan are worse off with respect to employment also. With respect to value of output or value added by the sector, the four states of Maharashtra Gujarat, Tamil Nadu and West Bengal together account for 55.5 per cent of the value of output and 54.3 per cent of the value added by the factory sector. Considering the fact that these four states account for only 29.3 per cent of the country's population, the degree of concentration in the industrial sector can very well be imagined. The last column of Table 5 contains information on the value added per person in the factory sector of different states. Besides the above four states which have been the traditional centres of Industry, Punjab and Haryana states have also attained a high degree of industrialisation. The value added per capita in all these six states has been more than Rs. 200 per year. In the three southern states of Karnataka, Kerala and Andhra Pradesh, the value added per capita was in the range of Rs. 100 to Rs. 200. In the central and eastern states (with the exception of West Bengal), the value added in factory sector per person was lower than Rs. 100 per year.

Structural Changes

Besides the industrial sector, services sector is also growing at a rapid pace in the Indian Economy. In any economy, development is characterised by a reduction in the share of primary sector in the national income and a corresponding increase in the shares of secondary and tertiary sectors. A study of the structures of income in different states helps in understanding their levels of development. The percentage contributions of primary, secondary and tertiary sectors of the economy in different states at two points of time, 1970-71 and 1981-82 are furnished in Table 6.

There was a reduction in the percentage contribution of the primary sector in all the states over the period of eleven years under consideration. The reduction was quite marginal in case of Maharashtra, Andhra Pradesh, Assam and Orissa. Of these, the contribution of primary sector to the Maharashtra income was low in the base period itself. In case of the other three states, the transformation has been quite slow. The share of primary sector declined at a moderate pace in case of West Bengal, Bihar, Madhya Pradesh and Kerala. In case of the other seven states, the decline in the percentage contribution of the primary sector was quite sharp.

In Andhra Pradesh, Orissa, Assam and West Bengal, the fall in the percentage contribution of the primary sector was chiefly compenstated by the increase in the percentage share of the secondary sector. The share of secondary sector marginally decreased in case of Bihar and Maharashtra and only the tertiary sector increased its share. In all other states, the percentage shares of both secondary and tertiary sector increased. But the increase in the share of secondary sector was much larger than that of the tertiary sector in case of Tamil Nadu, Madhya Pradesh and Kerala, while the reverse was the case with the other six states.

Human Resource Characteristics

Having discussed the levels of development in different sectors of the economy, it will be useful to have a glance at the economic characteristics of the human resources in different states. Data on some of these characteristics are given in Table 7. Kerala is well ahead of all other states (70 per cent) with respect to the literacy level. The percentage of literate persons ranged from forty to fifty per cent in the states of Maharashtra, Tamil Nadu, Gujarat, Punjab and West Bengal. It was lower than thrity per cent in Rajasthan, Bihar, Uttar Pradesh, Madhya Pradesh and Andhra Pradesh. Another indicator of the human resource development is the degree of urbanisation. Assam, Orissa and Bihar states have less than fifteen per cent of the population in the urban areas, while at the other extreme the per cent of urban population exceeded thirty per cent in Gujarat, Tamil Nadu and Maharashtra. Inversely related with the urbanisation, the percentage of labour force employed in agriculture reflects the level of underdevelopment. Bihar, Madhya Pradesh, Orissa, Uttar Pradesh and Andhra Pradesh have more than seventy per cent of the labour force in agriculture. On the other hand, Kerala, West Bengal and Punjab have less than sixty per cent of their labour force in agriculture. The incidence of unemployment was highest in the four southern states and in West Bengal. The unemployment problem was less serious in Assam, Madhya Pradesh, Uttar Pradesh and Punjab. The percentage of population below the poverty line is an indicator of the low level of Income as well as the inequality in income distribution. Orissa, Madhya Pradesh and Bihar have the largest percentages of population below the poverty line, while the incidence of poverty was lower in Punjab, Haryana, Rajasthan and Gujarat. Considering several aspects of development, the centre for monitoring Indian Economy has computed indices of economic development in different states, which are reproduced in the last column of the Table 7. Bihar, Assam, Madhya Pradesh, Orissa, Rajasthan and Uttar Pradesh have attained lower levels of development when compared with the country as a whole. Punjab has achieved a very high level of development, distantly followed by Haryana and Maharashtra. All other states are at an above average level in over all economic development.

Infrastructure and Financial Resource

Development of infrastructural facilities influences economic development to a considerable extent. Public investments can be channelised consciously to achieve equitability in the infrastructure facilities and to stimulate development in the poorer regions. The indices of infrasturcture for different states are presented in the thrid and fourth columns of Table-8 for the years 1966-67 and 1983-84 respectively. Over the period of seventeen years, there was some reduction in the inequality of infrasturctural facilities, as suggested by the three inequality measures. Financial resources are very crucial to the development as they can command materials and services through the market. A very high correlation of 0.93 is observed between the per capita plan outlay of different states over the past thrity five years and the per capita incomes of the states during 1980-83. The data on per capita plan outlay spent during 1951-85 are given in column five of the table-8. Haryana and Punjab states spent much higher resources than others, while the investment was the lowest in Bihar. The Central Government is giving more weightage to poverty in allocating its assistance to states, as evidenced by the data for 1982-83 presented in column six. Leaving aside Assam, which falls in the special category, central assistance was higher to the under developed states of Orissa, Rajasthan and Bihar. Despite such preferential treatment, the poorer states are unable to increase their plan outlay due to the paucity of internal resources. The plan outlays of different states during the Seventh Five Year Plan are presented in the last column of the table in per capita terms. A comparison of the past outlays and the outlays of the Seventh Plan do not reveal any radical shifts and the degree of inequality is more or less at the same level as in the past.

Strategy to Correct Imbalances

The data presented so far on various facts of the resource endowments and the levels of development in the fifteen major states of the country indicated that the horizontal imbalances are growing over time. There exist considerable differences in the endowments of basic resources both in terms of quantity and quality. The use of modern inputs is found to be crucial to achieve a fast growth in agricultural production. A stable and buoyant growth in agricultural production is the *sin qua non* of a strong performance in other sectors of the economy as well (Kanneda 1981). For overall development and reduction in poverty, a two-prong strategy, which combines improvements in agricultural production with greater labour absorption of the rural work force outside agriculture, is necessary (Adelman 1985). Plan outlays and investments are crucial to exploit the resource endowments and to harness the potential for development (Singh 1980).

The Seventh Five Year Plan (SFYP 1985) lays great stress on the reduction of inter-regional disparities in levels of development. Special efforts are being mounted for rice production in the eastern region and for dryland and rainfed agriculture.

With its stress on human resource development, it hopes to reduce inter-regional disparities in access to health services, education and other minimum needs like water supply, rural roads and rural electrification. The transfer of resources from the Central Government to the State Governments for meeting Plan expenditure takes in to account the relative economic backwardness of each state. The formula for the allocation of marker borrowings is revised to ensure higher allocations for states whose per capita income is below the national average. Backward-states would receive preferential treatment while allocating resources under centrally-sponsored schemes, institutional credit and various subsidy programmes for promoting industrial units.

In spite of these policy measures, the per capita plan outlays are still lower for the poorer states. The natural law of the 'Survival of the fittest' operates in the economy and the richer states are likely to do well. If the poorer states have to perform better than the richer ones, the institutional and infrastructural constraints have to be removed and investments should be stepped up radically. To achieve this, the necessary political will has to be mobilised and the concurrence of the richer states has to be obtained. Only then, the imbalances in the levels of economic development of different states can be corrected in a meaningful way.

REFERENCES

Adelman, I., K. Subba Rao and Prem Vashishta: Some Dynamic aspects of Rural Poverty in India, Economic and Political Weekly, Vol. XX. No. 39, September 28, 1985, pp. A-103 to A-116.

Bairoch, P: 'The main trends in National Economic Disparities since the Industrial revolution' in 'Disparities in Economic Development since the Indutsrial revolution', Bairoch, P. and Levy-Leboyer (eds.), Metheren Co. Ltd., London, 1981.

George, P.T.: Status of Agricultural Labour-Kurukshetra, Vol. XXVIII, No. 13, April 1, 1980, pp. 21-26.

Kan'eda, H Growth and equity in India's Agriculture, Indian Journal of Agricultural Economics, Vol. XXXVI, No. 1, January-March, 1981, pp. 39-58.

Mehta, A. The changing pressures and the rural poor—Kurukshetra, Vol. XXVIII, No. 8, Janaury 16, 1980: pp. 4-16.

Singh, D. Imbalances in Agricultural Growth, Presidential Address to the 40th Annual Conference, Indian Society of Agricultural Economics, Poona, December, 1980.

Seventh Five Year Plan: 1985-1990, Vol. 1, Planning Commission, Government of India, New Delhi, October, 1985, pp. 44.

TABLE 1

Growth of per capita income of major states of India at current prices (Rs)

Sl. No.	*State/Statistic*	*Three-year average of* 1960-61 to 1962-63	*Three-year average of* 1970-71 to 1972-73	*Three-year average of* 1980-81 to 1982-83	*Annual rate of increase (%) between 1960-63 and 1980-83*
1.	Punjab	366	1145	3144	10.6
2.	Haryana	327	951	2597	10.6
3.	Maharashtra	421	810	2427	9.2
4.	Gujarat	383	806	2067	8.8
5.	West Bengal	401	761	1644	7.3
6.	Karala	270	596	1494	8.9
7.	Assam	315	553	1373	7.6
8.	Andhra Pradesh	291	623	1486	8.4
9.	Rajasthan	282	592	1418	8.4
10.	Karnataka	316	698	1466	8.0
11.	Uttar Pradesh	259	529	1337	8.5
12.	Tamil Nadu	334	633	1358	7.3
13.	Madhya Pradesh	264	531	1249	8.1
14.	Orissa	240	509	1249	8.6
15	Bihar	223	432	986	7.7
	Ratio of highest to lowest	1.89	2.65	3.19	
	Co-efficient of variartion %	19.07	27.92	35.61	
	Standard deviation of Logarithmic values	0.1898	0.2596	0.3165	

Source: CMIE—Basic statistics relating to the Indian Economy, Vol. 2: States-September, 1984.

TABLE 2

Land and water resources in major states of India

Sl. No.	*States*	*Geographical area per capita (ha)* 1981-82	*Net sown area per rural person (ha)* 1981-82	*Gross cropped area per rural person (ha)* 1979-82	*Rainfall in cms* 1900-50	*Irrigated area as per cent of gross cropped area* 1981-82	*Per cent of irrigation potential achieved* 1983-84
1	2	3	4	5	6	7	8
1.	Andhra Pradesh	0.51	0.28	0.30	88	35.9	59
2.	Assam	0.39	0.15	0.19	252	16.6	19
3.	Bihar	0.25	0.13	0.18	127	33.7	47
4.	Gujarat	0.55	0.41	0.46	83	23.1	58
5.	Haryana	0.34	0.36	0.54	63	59.2	72
6.	Kerala	0.15	0.11	0.14	300	13.1	43

(Contd.)

1	2	3	4	5	6	7	8
7.	Karnataka	0.51	0.39	0.40	136	15.8	52
8.	Madhya Pradesh	0.85	0.45	0.51	122	12.4	36
9.	Maharashtra	0.49	0.45	0.50	131	12.3	48
10.	Punjab	0.30	0.35	0.56	63	86.1	85
11.	Rajasthan	1.00	0.57	0.64	59	20.0	72
12.	Tamil Nadu	0.27	0.18	0.20	101	49.6	83
13.	Uttar Pradesh	0.27	0.19	0.27	99	46.9	71
14.	West Bengal	0.16	0.14	0.19	165	23.5	52
15.	Orissa	0.59	0.26	0.38	136	23.0	42

TABLE 3

Use of modern agricultural inputs in major states of India

Sl. No.	States	Fertiliser consumption per hectare of gross cropped area (kg) (1984-85)	Per cent area under high yielding varieties (1980-81)	Number of tractors per 1000 hectares of cultivated area (1981)	Power consumption per 100 hectares of minor irrigation (units) (1980-81)	Bank credit per hectare of cropped area (Rs) (June 1981)	
1	2	3	4	5	6	7	8
1.	Andhra Pradesh	79.0	56.49	1.63	48.0	318	
2.	Assam	4.1	28.75	0.76	1.3	202	
3.	Bihar	34.8	44.49	1.69	17.6	161	
4.	Gujarat	48.0	53.66	2.66	91.7	220	
5.	Haryana	63.9	71.24	13.97	73.8	352	
6.	Karnataka	54.3	51.10	1.29	37.6	287	

(Contd.)

1	2	3	4	5	6	7	8
7.	Kerala	48.6	45.75	1.10	24.7	682	
8.	Madhya Pradesh	18.3	32.49	1.15	21.3	38	
9.	Maharashtra	29.5	49.43	1.27	102.9	203	
10.	Orissa	15.3	28.16	0.43	8.3	126	
11.	Punjab	157.3	90.59	21.75	62.6	553	
12.	Rajasthan	12.4	24.56	2.19	54.6	98	
13.	Tamil Nadu	104.7	92.63	2.03	123.5	549	
14.	Uttar Pradesh	67.3	32.28*	4.58	29.1	194	
15.	West Bengal	53.5	43.54	0.48	4.8	272	

TABLE 4

Value of agricultural output per hectare and per rural person and growth of food production in major states of India

Sl. No.	*States*	*Value of agricultural output (1979-82)*		*Per capita food-grain produc-*	*Annual rate of increase in food production (%) between*	
		Per hectare	*Per rural person*	*tion (kg) 1981-84*	*1952-55 to 1959-62*	*1959-62 to 1981-84*
1	*2*	*3*	*4*	*5*	*6*	*7*
1.	Punjab	3135	1756	805	3.70	6.30
2.	Haryana	2710	1463	478	3.70	4.60
3.	Maharashtra	1844	922	156	2.50	2.00
4.	Gujarat	1866	858	142	—0.02	4.20
5.	Karnataka	2093	837	177	3.10	2.60
6.	Andhra Pradesh	2785	836	204	3.10	2.40
7.	Rajasthan	1205	771	234	2.80	2.50

(*Contd.*)

1	2	3	4	5	6	7
8.	West Bengal	3612	686	126	0.30	1.40
9.	Orissa	1799	684	205	1.60	1.50
10.	Assam	3455	656	125	0.60	2.20
11.	Uttar Pradesh	2401	648	230	1.30	3.00
12.	Kerala	4510	631	50	4.40	1.00
13.	Madhya Pradesh	1186	605	248	3.20	1.60
14.	Tamil Nadu	2609	522	123	4.70	0.60
15.	Bihar	2500	450	113	2.70	0.70
	All India	2153	710	193	2.70	2.70

TABLE 5

Percentage shares of major states in employment and output of factory sector in India (1979-80)

Sl. No.	States	Percentage shares in country's					
		Population	Factory numbers	Factory employment	Value of output	Value added	Value added per capita (Rs)
1	2	3	4	5	6	7	8
1.	Maharashtra	9.2	15.6	17.5	23.8	24.9	440
2.	Gujarat	5.0	11.5	9.3	11.2	9.5	309
3.	Haryana	1.9	2.4	2.1	3.1	2.9	251
4.	Tamil Nadu	7.1	10.3	10.3	10.7	9.9	225
5.	West Bengal	8.0	6.6	12.6	9.8	11.0	223
6.	Punjab	2.5	5.7	3.4	4.1	3.3	217
7.	Karnataka	5.4	5.7	4.8	4.5	5.2	156
8.	Kerala	3.7	3.2	3.7	3.1	3.2	139

(Contd.)

2	3	4	5	6	7	8
9. Andhra Pradesh	7.8	12.3	9.2	5.2	5.0	104
10. Rajasthan	5.0	2.7	2.5	2.6	3.3	98
11. Orissa	3.9	1.4	1.5	1.8	2.1	89
12. Madhya Pradesh	7.6	3.8	4.1	4.0	4.1	88
13. Assam	2.9	1.8	1.7	1.3	1.4	80
14. Bihar	10.2	5.0	4.6	5.4	5.0	79
15. Uttar Pradesh	16.2	7.2	9.3	6.4	6.3	63

TABLE 6

Percentage contributions of primary, secondary and tertiary sectors in the incomes of the major states in India (1970-71 and 1981-82)

Sl. No.	States	1970-71			1981-82		
		Primary	Secondary	Tertiary	Primary	Secondary	Tertiary
1	2	3	4	5	6	7	8
1.	Andhra Pradesh	57.19	13.44	29.37	53.73	16.58	29.67
2.	Assam	63.78	13.97	22.25	60.27	17.72	22.01
3.	Bihar	62.76	17.73	19.51	54.72	16.43	28.85
4.	Gujarat	48.90	20.87	30.23	35.59	26.68	37.73
5.	Haryana	64.79	15.07	20.14	50.25	20.52	29.23
6.	Karnataka	59.60	18.54	21.86	46.44	24.78	28.78
7.	Kerala	49.48	16.33	34.19	39.90	23.84	36.26
8.	Madhya Pradesh	63.18	14.77	22.05	54.98	20.96	24.06

(Contd.)

1	2	3	4	5	6	7	8
9.	Maharashtra	29.92	34.19	36.89	28.38	32.72	38.90
10.	Orissa	67.31	10.41	22.28	63.50	13.91	22.59
11.	Punjab	58.36	15.92	25.72	44.28	21.37	34.35
12.	Rajasthan	64.33	13.32	22.35	53.77	17.30	28.93
13.	Tamil Nadu	39.38	26.80	33.82	29.11	34.99	35.90
14.	Uttar Pradesh	60.12	14.39	25.49	45.17	20.72	34.11
15.	West Bengal	45.11	22.93	31.96	39.82	27.75	32.43

TABLE 7

Economic characteristics of human resources in major states of India

Sl. No.	States	Percentage of literate person (1981)	Percentage of urban population (1981)	Percentage of labour force employed in agriculture (1981)	Rate of unemployment (1977-78)	Percentage of population below poverty line (1977-78)	CMIE index of economic development
1	2	3	4	5	6	7	8
1.	Andhra Pradesh	30	23.3	70	10.67	42.2	107
2.	Assam	35*	10.3	@	1.81	51.1	58
3.	Bihar	26	12.5	79	8.01	57.5	51
4.	Gujarat	44	31.1	61	6.24	39 0	129
5.	Haryana	36	21.9	61	6.41	24.8	166
6.	Karnataka	38	28.9	65	9.36	48.3	126
7.	Kerala	70	18.8	41	25 69	47.0	126

(Contd.)

1	2	3	4	5	6	7	8
8.	Madhya Pradesh	28	20.3	76	3.09	57.7	62
9.	Maharashtra	47	35.0	62	7.99	47.7	163
10.	Orissa	34	11.8	75	8.13	66.4	67
11.	Punjab	41	27.7	58	4.82	15.1	220
12.	Rajasthan	24	20.9	69	2.99	33.8	72
13.	Tamil Nadu	47	33.0	61	15.59	52.1	131
14.	Uttar Pradesh	27	18.0	74	4.12	50.1	72
15.	West Bengal	41	26.5	55	10 15	52.5	103

*Pertains to 1971 census

@Not available

TABLE 8

Infrastructure and financial resources in major states of India

Sl. No.	*States Statistic*	*CMIE Indices of Infrastructure 1966-67*	*1983-84*	*Per capita plan outlay (Rs) 1951-1985*	*Centre's assistance to plan outlay (per cent) 1982-83*	*Per capita plan outlay (Rs) in seventh plan 1985-90*
1	*2*	*3*	*4*	*5*	*7*	*8*
1.	Punjab	201	208	2804	16.52	1757
2.	Haryana	129	151	3024	17.77	1973
3.	Tamil Nadu	171	144	1303	19.41	1097
4.	Kerala	135	140	1279	34.21	753
5.	West Bengal	152	124	1185	33.72	681
6.	Gujarat	111	126	2094	15.45	1558
7.	Maharashtra	117	115	1955	14.44	1498
8.	Uttar Pradesh	107	108	1148	37.41	840

(Contd.)

1	2	3	4	5	7	8
9.	Karnataka	90	99	1377	22.85	837
10.	Andhra Pradesh	93	100	1231	31.78	877
11.	Bihar	98	98	919	40.77	653
12.	Assam	73	93	1180	94.93	905
13.	Orissa	69	85	1218	48.89	931
14.	Rajasthan	59	77	1259	45.72	759
15.	Madhya Pradesh	53	68	1352	28.51	1199
Ratio of highest to lowest		3.79	3 06	3.29	—	3.02
C.V. (%)		37.88	30.51	40.43	—	38.33
S.D. of logs		.3840	0.2875	0.3439	—	0.3539

8

REGIONAL IMBALANCES AND SOCIO-ECONOMIC WELL-BEING IN TWO EASTERN STATES OF INDIA

SWAPNA BANERJEE—GUHA*
NANDINI DASGUPTA**
BHARATI BANERJEE***

The course of Indian economic development has been replete with failures to achieve the plan target in different plan periods. Since late sixties, with the introduction of input-based agriculture and at later stage, with the introduction of high technology and capital investment in industries, the G.N.P. figures have started rising fast. Since late seventies studies on interdependence between economic development and transformation of socio-political institutions have been undertaken by many social scientists where they have associated progress with mainly an increase in G.N.P.

The most crucial problem with the G.N.P. figures and productivity statistics is that they never conform with the

*Department of Geography, University of Bombay, Vidyanagari, Bombay
**Department of Geography, Kirti College, Bombay.
***Department of Geography, Parle College, Bombay.

regional space and therefore often fail to bring out the real pattern of growth. Very often economic growth is accompanied by rising disparities. As development is conceived as a process and state of being which encompasses the entire social and spatial phenomena, there arises a need to understand the relation between economic development and its expression in the quality of life. The spatial and temporal variations in this above aspect thereby can express how the economy works, how the surplus is appropriated, distributed or redistributed, how resources are allocated and how opportunities are competed for or services rendered to. Further, the phenomenon of economic development loses its holistic nature if it is not linked with the overall standard of living or quality of life. Analysis of the linkage between economic infrastructure in the form of basic resources, agricultural and industrial development and the social infrastructure in the form of health, education and communication facilities etc. thus calls for attention.

In India the pattern of development is a palimpsest with vestiges of colonial rule and post-independent national and regional policies. At each level, large number of forces operate that vary in nature from one level to another. A process operating at all scales, therefore, has differential impact at different levels.

The present paper aims at analysing the resource base and pattern of development in two eastern states of India—West Bengal and Bihar and their expression in the pattern of well-being. Pattern of social and economic well-being has been derived with the help of eighteen indicators. The data is at district level and has been standardized and standard score additive model has been used (Smith, 1973).

Indicators of economic development:

1. Average size of operational holdings.
2. Per capita consumption of fertilizers.
3. Per capita value of output of major crops,
4. Per capita bank credit for agriculture.

5. Average daily employment in factory/lakh of people.
6. Number of workers in non-household industry.
7. Employment in household industry.
8. Per capita outstanding credit of scheduled commercial banks to all industry.

Indicators of social well-being:

1. Infant mortality rates.
2. Number of hospitals beds per lakh people.
3. Percentage of literacy.
4. Percentage of female literacy.
5. Cognizable crime rate.
6. Surfaced road length/$Km.^2$
7. Number of post offices.
8. Percentage of villages electrified.
9. Per capita bank deposits.
10. Number of registered motor vehicles/10,000 people.

Bihar: *Resource-base, economic development and Social well-being*:

Bihar possesses the most important mineral belt of India and Chotanagpur plateau is the worth mentionable name. In mid-seventies, Bihar occupied the leading position in the total value of national mineral production. The region leads in the production of Copper, Kyanite, Coal, Mica, Bauxite, China-clay, Chromite and iron-ore. These are found in abundance in Ranchi, Hazaribagh, Giridih, Dhanbad and Singhbhum districts. Singhbhum is famous for iron-ore and copper. Concentration of Coal is found along Palamu, Hazaribagh, Giridih, Dhanbad and the central belt of the Santhal Parganas. Ranchi and Palamau are famous for bauxite and limestone and Gaya for mica.

Districts of Muzaffarpur, Purnea, Patna, Gaya, Bhagalpur, Munger, Champaran and Darbhanga have little or no concentration of minerals.

Plains of Bihar are one of the most fertile ones in the country. In North Bihar Plains, percentage of net sown area is eighty-eight per cent whereas in South Bihar it is eightyseven per cent to ninety per cent (Thakur, 1980). Some parts of Southern Bihar is less fertile and the rugged terrain of Chotanagpur Plateau is one of the least productive areas. But the largest tracts of fallow lands are found in North Bihar and East-South Bihar. And a large part of Chotanagpur highlands is covered by forest. The thickly wooded hills are found in Baudh-Khondurals, Sundargarh, Palamau, Hazaribagh, Singhbhum, Ranchi and Santhal Pargana. A substantial portion of forest lands remain fallow which is evident from the very high percentage of land under cultivable waste in Chotanagpur (Thakur, 1980).

Generation of electricity, however, is a major problem and in recent years there has been a large gap between demand and supply. From 1951-1980 the eastern region has fallen down in power production and Bihar has fallen short of its target by 220 M.W. (Gupta, 1986). However from 1981-1984 there has been a meagre increase in Bihar. But Bihar is one of the poorest states in India where fifty one per cent of the rural and fiftynine per cent of the urban population live below the poverty level.

Historically, if we look into the conditions of under-development in Bihar, we find that the present pattern clearly exhibits the vestiges of the colonial rule. The British were never concerned with the development or maintenance of the age-old handicraft centres and other trade and urban centres of Bihar. Industrial revolution in Britain hit U.P. Bihar and Bengal hardestand districts of Patna, Gaya, Bhagalpur, Purnea, etc., suffered from enormous loss of industrial population. The unemployed sections then either fell back on agriculture only to create more pressure on land or outmigrated to Calcutta and other big cities to work in the Jute Mills or other industries. The entire area gradually sank down, thanks to the declining prosperity of the average consumers, and the whole economy was geared to support the rise of the port city of Calcutta to facilitate the export oriented mechanism (Banerjee-Guha, 1985).

In the backdrop of the above resource base and the historical continuity, we may now look into the spatial pattern of socio-economic well-being. The whole of Bihar, except for the districts of Patna and Dhanbad, is an expanse of abject poverty. Only in Patna (1.93) and Dhanbad (0.63) composite scores are positive. Districts stretching over the North Bihar Plain are all well below the average level. Starting from the west, Paschim Champaran (5.37–), Gopalgunj (5.04–), Siwan (4.75–), Saran (3.30–), Purbi Champaran (4.92–), Madhuban (4.01–), Darbhanga (2.61–), Samastipur (4.09–), Purnea (5.82–), and Katihar (5.56–), the level of well-being is very low. The large resource base has not generated local/regional development in Bihar. On the contrary, the state has not even been able to evenly redistribute the gains of agricultural development in the fertile plains of the North. Districts which are at marginally higher level than the northern districts are Rohtas (2.90–), Gaya (1.65–), Nalanda (2.00–), Nawada (3.45–), Aurangabad (3.61–), Bhagalpur (4.69–) and Munger (3.20–). In south Bihar, all over the Chotanagpur Plateau area, the districts of Palamau (5.57–), Hazaribagh (3.86–), Giridih (4.98–) and Santhal Parganas (4.05–) have negative Z-scores in all the components.

The districts of Dhanbad, Ranchi and Singhbhum deserve more attention. Dhanbad, other than Patna, is the only other district with a level of living above average (1.61). It has the highest per capita bank deposits in Bihar, quite adequate road network, vehicles and postal services. Hospital facilities are above the average standard but with a low female literacy rate and low crime index. It is a district with surplus thermal energy but only twenty six per cent of the villages have been electrified. Mining activity started early in Dhanbad and saw gradual development of the secondary sectors and infrastructural facilities. Its pace of urbanization is second to Patna and fifty per cent of the people live in urban areas.

Though industrially a developed district, Ranchi has an unsatisfactory level of living with negative scores on all components. Similarly Singhbhum though has the second highest per capita bank deposits in the state, after Dhanbad, has not been able to meet people's needs for basic services and amenities (Dasgupta, 1984).

A look into the structure of the economy will help to bring out the regional imbalance at a micro level.

In North Bihar pressure on land is evident in the small size of holdings and a low per capita value output of major crops. In the seventies, the smallest farmers *i.e.*, those in the size class 0-1 hectares accounted for sixty four per cent of the holdings but only 15.3 per cent of the land area. In addition there has been a steady increase in the number of agricultural labours (Nayyar, 1979). The concentration of rich farmers in Bihar in the west, however, has not been able to raise the socio-economic well-being as the latter is largely a function of prevailing wage rates, amount of unemployment and the purchasing power of the people at large.

Despite attempts at land reform, the distribution of landownership and of the amount of land operated continues to be very unequal in Bihar There is a large mass of agricultural labourers, increasing both numerically and as a proportion of the agricultural working population at a very fast rate. Data on real wage of agricultural labourers is highly unreliable, but there appears to have been no tendency for real wages to rise.

The State Government claiming an awareness of the problems of the rural economy, took some steps, *e.g.*, the Kosi and Gandak River Projects designed to control flood and increase the amount of land under irrigation. However, studies on the impact of the Kosi River Project have indicated that there is a growing differentiation among the peasantry that mainly arises due to the inequality in the distribution of land. Increases n output arising from the various government schemes accrue largely to the bigger peasant farmers and large landowners who have access to credit and material inputs. Perhaps, as a result of this, rural discontent in Bihar has noticeably increased in recent years (Prasad, 1975; Das, 1975).

In the sphere of association between the mineral resource base and industrial development, wherever industries have been located in a district on the logic of availability of raw material, economy of transport and proximity to ultimate market, without developing the agricultural and human base and social and economic infrastructure, the industries have behaved like alien growth (Mitra, 1961). The districts of Singbhum, Santhal Parganas, Ranchi and Dhanbad have not been able to trigger off multiplier effects of growth that is evident from the low well-being index. Singhbhum district that had the first steel plant of Bihar is still predominantly rural with the major concentration of urban population restricted to the one city of Jamshedpur.

In Hazaribagh district, though a large proportion of the population is engaged in non-agricultural activities mainly in mica mines, the indexes of urbanization is extremely low and only fifteen per cent of the population live in urban areas. Impact of the Bokaro Steel Plant to improve the local quality of life is yet to be felt.

An important aspect in the industrial development in Bihar is the failure to integrate tribals in it. With the transfer of land from tribals to non-tribals, a large section of the former did not gain from the process of economic development even after independence. Further, in areas like Chotanagpur, where industrial development has taken place, local tribals have hardly been the beneficiaries. They have only entered in secondary sector as unskilled low paid labourers and in newer industries they are further unwanted as the latter require skilled labour more (Banerjee-Guha, 1985).

Thus the poorest district of Bihar show ample evidence of lack of integration of resource base and regional development.

West Bengal: Resource base, economic development and Social well-being:

In West Bengal excepting in Raniganj in Western Burdwan district and the South-Western parts of Bankura and Birbhum districts, mineral is not found. Very little concentration of copper is found in Darjeeling district and china-clay in Bankura and Birbhum. Northern West Bengal has a very rich forest cover and Darjeeling district is the biggest exporter of tea in the country. Power generation is a major problem in the state and after the fifth five year plans West Bengal fell short of the target by 580 m.w. (Gupta, 1986) and between 1981-84 only .52 units have increase.

The level of well-being peaks at Calcutta (28.58) and falls sharply away to its neighbouring districts of Haora (3.78), Hugli (4.98), Nadia (2.27) and in north feebly remain in Bardhaman (0.83). Adjoining this conclave are the poorest districts of West Bengal: Bankura (1.93—), Medinipur (3.42—), Purulia (4.11—), 24 Parganas (1.30—) and Birbhum (0.33—). This poverty plain stretches northward to Malda (2.61 —), Murshidabad (3.21—), and West Dinajpur (3.27—). The only exception in North Bengal is Darjeeling (3.47) while Jalpaiguri (1.49—) and Koch Bihar (1.12—) have negative scores. The entire state with the exception of six districts, experiences not only negative scores, but very low levels of living (Das Gupta, 1985).

Growth in West Bengal has been fully concentrated in Calcutta—the colonial centre of the British and later the state capital. The process of concentration of people and activity in Calcutta began with the settling down of the British here. It slowed down the growth of other centres under the Dutch and the French, *e.g.*, Hugli and Chandannagar. At the cost of the early historical island port towns like the above and Adi Saptagram, Dhaka, Bakharaganj in addition, Calcutta rose as the seat of the colonial sea-power. It was previously used as the port through which handicraft goods and textiles were exported. Later, with industrial revolution in Britain and with the change in the colonial policy towards indigenous handicraft industries—when growth of Indian handicraft was under-mined—Craftsmanship and art destroyed, Calcutta's alienation from the surrounding region was fast completed. Gradually more cash crops were introduced in the Southern fertile tracts. With the further establishment of the plantation areas in the hills of Darjeeling and Duars Calcutta became a collecting and exporting centre of raw materials. To facilitate export and growth in Calcutta, road and rail network focussed here, further accentuating the difference between Calcutta and the neighbouring districts.

This process continued with further growth of industries. When British realized that it was more profitable to manufacture jute goods in Bengal, they declared certain areas as 'Municipalities' providing them with the necessary infrastructure. Thus the adjoining areas of Calcutta aligning River Hugli started growing thereby creating a small area of industrial growth.

In the post-independence era, industrial dispersal did not materialize. Only in Durgapur a secondary centre emerged. Situated close to the mining districts of Bihar, the steel plant in Durgapur got power from DVC and the benefits of the existing major highways and railways. This partly explains (the other reason is a pocket of agricultural development) why Bardhaman has a higher well being index, though located away from the Southern conurbation.

The urbanization pattern is also one of over-concentration in Southern East Bengal; in the metropolis of Calcutta. Durgapur-Asansol is a week second node followed by Darjeeling. However, this does not conform to any real rise in the quality of life of the residents even in Calcutta, as extreme overgrowth has led to acute congestion and deterioration of the economic base and the social inputs. Additive factors are steady migration from Bangladesh, Bihar, U.P., Orissa associated with sluggish industrial growth. Actually in West Bengal, with economic stagnation, the gap between Calcutta and the next lower order centres have been accentuated. Durgapur and Asansol in Burdwan district have not been able to relieve the pressure from Calcutta and though Siliguri in Darjeeling district is growing very fast it is not associated with development of the secondary sector inspite of North Bengal having a rich forest resource. In 1981, Class I cities in West Bengal accounted for fifty eight per cent of the total urban population, all of which excepting Siliguri, were located in Southen West Bengal (Banerjee-Guha, 1983).

The urban growth in Calcutta is not positively correlated with industrial development. Rather, with the constant flow of rural migrants and migrants from small towns of West Bengal and the neighbouring states, the tertiary sector of the metropolitan area has swelled over leading to an unholy association between urbanization and tertiarization.

A recent survey by the Association of Indian Engineering Industries has pointed out that the growth centres at Kalyani, Haldia and Kharagpur have failed to attract industries to a desired level because of the lack of infrastructural facilities, particularly social infrastructure like housing, schools, health facility, education, etc.

In the agricultural sector Hugli and Bardhaman districts are the fortunate ones. In their eastern parts with network of canals, fertile soil and concentration of the richest farming families of the state, they received the benefit of the 'Green Revolution' (Banerjee and Barman 1983). In Malda, Murshidabad, West Dinajpur, Purulia, Jalpaiguri and Koch Bihar, agricultural productivity is considerably low.

Conclusion

Unlike Bihar which is uniformly poor in all its districts, West Bengal has a very high degree of disparity. However, the existing space economy and the pattern of well-being in both these states do not match the needs of the people. From the primate city of Calcutta, growth and development have not been diffused rather the former acts as a focus of exploitation mechanism. (Raza and Hebia, 1976).

When both the states are taken together into consideration, the pattern of disparity that emerges, indicates a case of 'internal dependency' as expressed by Gilbert (1974) while explaining the exploitation of the poorer areas in Latin America by the privileged ones. In the present study also the existing pattern of economic growth and distribution of well-being evidence increase of gap between the core and the peripheral areas and shows Calcutta as the only dominating core amidst a vast plain of poverty.

The poverty pattern is highly asymmetrical. While the resource rich areas of Koch Bihar and Jalpaiguri in West Bengal are not industrially developed, the industrial development in Chotanagpur plateau in Bihar has not been able to revive the regional economy and has behaved like alien growth without any spread effect. This is because most of the output of these public sector industries comprises products of the first stage of processing which are exported to feed the industrial activities and their concomitant multiplier effect elsewhere. In the agricultural areas of the two states, introduction of H.Y.V. crops has increased the social disparity among the farmers and has created a large number of agricultural labourers. On the other end, the forest and tribal tracts of the Santhal Parganas in Bihar, and Birbhum, Purulia and Koch Bihar in West Bengal have always been bypassed in developmental projects.

Policy changes in recent years towards a more distributive justice and a shift to small area based approach and decentralized planning have aroused again fresh expectations. The results, however, are yet to be seen.

REFERENCES

Smith, David, M. (1973): 'The Geography of Social well-being in the United States, McGraw Hill, New York.

Thakur, Baleshwar (1980): 'Urban Settlements in Eastern India', Concept Publishers, New Delhi.

Gupta, Gautam (1986): 'Bidyut Sankat: Ek Rajye O Sara Deshe', *Desh*, Vol. 53 (13), February 1.

Banerjee-Guha, Swapna (1985): 'Colonial Spatial Organisation in India: Does it perpetuate', contributed to Prof. Minocha Felicitation Volume, University of Bhopal.

Dasgupta, Nandini (1984): A Geography of Socio-economic well-being in India, unpublished M. Phil Dissertation, Department of Geography, University of Bombay.

Nayyar, Rohini (1979): 'Poverty and Inequality in Bihar' in Poverty and Landlessness in Rural Asia, I.L.O. Publication, Geneva.

Prasad, P.H. (1978): 'Agrarian Unrest and Economic Change in Rural Bihar,' *Economic and Political Weekly*, 14th June, 1975.

Das, A.N. (1975): 'Bihar struggle of workers and Tribal peasants in Chotanagpur', *Economic and Political Weekly*, 1st March, 1975.

Mitra, Ashok (1961): Levels of Regional Development in India, Census of India, 1961, Part-I-A (i).

Banerjee-Guha, S. (1985): 'Colonialism New—colonialism and under-development—The Indian experience', Unpublished Monography, Department of Geography and Environmental Engineering, The Johns Hopkins University, Baltimore, U.S.A.

Gupta, Gautam (1986): Ibid, op. cit.

Banerjee—Guha, S. (1983): 'Spatial Disparity in Urban Industrial Growth in West Bengal—A Temporal Overview' Industrial situation in India, Vol. XII (2), pp. 47-52.

Banerjee, S. and Barman, S. (1983): 'Input availability and modern Agriculture in Burdwan Distrtct, West Bengal', in Transactions of the Institute of Indian Geographers, Vol. 5 (2), pp. 109-114.

Dasgupta, Nandini (1985): Ibid, op. cit.

Raza, M and Habib, A. (1976): 'Characteristics of Colonial Urbanization: A Case Study of Satellite Primacy of Calcutta, 1850-1921', in Alam—Pokshishevsky, ed., Urbanization in Developing Countries, pp. 187-218.

Gilbert, A (1974): Latin American Development—A Geographical Perspective, Penguin, Hammondsworth.

9

REGIONAL RESOURCE BASE AND PATTERN OF ECONOMIC DEVELOPMENT IN MADHYA PRADESH, INDIA

S. K. SHARMA*

Economic development is a very complex phenomenon, and depends on myriad spatial and non-spatial factors; natural resources being one of them. But the phenomenon of economic development in general and relationship between resources and economic development in particular could not arouse much interest among geographers (Keeble 1967). There are few geographical studies dealing with the relationship between physical environment, especially natural resources and economic development (Ginsburg 1957, Tosi and Voertman 1964, Perloff and Wingo 1964, Hodder 1971). There are other studies that have dealt with the national and supra-national resources and their exploitation in the context of changing technology and with the view to explain the processes of economic development. Therefore much emphasis has been on the mechanism of economic development and less on explaining it in perspective of local resouree-base. However, mention be made of core/periphery relationship postulated in the context of resource

*Reader in Geography, Doctor Harisingh Gour Vishwavidyalaya, Saugar.

transfer from developing countries to developed countries, the flooding of peripheral market with manufactured goods produced in the countries of the industrial centre and unfavourable terms of trade of primary goods (Friedman and Alonso, 1963 p. 211). Similar situation exists between developed and lagging regions within the territory of a nation itself. This has been important subject of discussion recently (Smith 1977, 1979). In the context of India, much has been said about the inequality in level of development; and so has been tried about Madhya Pradesh. But they have not explained explicitly the force generating the present spatial structure; and it gives the impression that level of development is directly related with the development potentials of the region. One of these potentials is the existence and exploitation of natural resources.

With this perspective, the object of the present paper is to portray the broad pattern of distribution of natural resources and to correlate it with the contemporary level of economic development in the State of Madhya Pradesh.

Existing Situation

It is a commonly accepted view that in the initial stage of economic development availability of local resources matters to a great deal; and economic activities related to the extraction of resources predominate. An advancement in socio-economic development involves a change in the existing use of resources to higher level or more efficient methods of production or more complete use of resources. But the process of such advancement is selective; and is determined by the efficiency of production. It follows the principle of least cost, and therefore, favours areas which have some initial advantages of production. This advantage may be the wants and abilities of people, availability of capital, market and initial linkages with other developed areas. With such advancement in the economic activities in these certain areas, supply of local resources appears to be inadequate to support them; and inadequacy of resources is met with the inter-regional transfer of resources. Thus the economy of the advanced areas unities the bounds of local resource base.

Contrary to it, there are certain regions which, for some reason or the other, could not increase the efficiency of resource use, and their resource bases appear much larger in relation to their level of economic development. Thus there is need of more resources in one region juxtaposition of their surplus in another. This creates a one-way channel of transfer of resources from surplus areas to the deficit areas. These two types of regions present dependent-dominant relationship. This is what exactly happening in Madhya Pradesh. As far as bounty of resources are concerned, the eastern part is the richest in the State (Kumar 1976), but in the economic development western part is far ahead, which has very thin resource base. Distribution of natural resources has been analysed with the perspecrive of the comprehension of their role in enhancing economic development in this State. Only major resources, *viz.*, land, water, forest and mineral resources, have been looked upon. Further, the situation has been made clearer with the example of the Baghelkand Plateau.

Value of Net Domestic Products

To assess the relative position of different resources, contribution of different sectors to the value of net domestic products has been present in the following table.

TABLE 1

M.P. Value of Net Domestic Products at Current Prices

(*Rs. in crores*)

Industry	*1970—71*		*1979—80*	
	Value	*Per cent*	*Value*	*Per cent*
Agriculture	1110	55.5	1752	41.1
Forests and Forestry	75	3.8	252	5.9
Mining	48	2.4	200	4.7
Manufacturing	189	9.4	515	12.1
Construction	98	4.9	311	7.3
Electricity, Gas and Water supply	17	0.9	87	2.1
Transport Comm. trade	251	12.5	562	13.2
Total	2002	100.0	4262	100.0

Thus more than half of the total value of net domestic products is contributed by the extraction activities. Agriculture stands at the top. Forests, mineral and power resources follow agriculture. The same sequence has been followed in this discussion.

Land Resources

Land is the basic resource and determines the economy of the State to agreat extent. It assumes special significance because it is non-transportable resource and yields benefits to the local people. But the state is endowed with limited good agricultural land. Most of the area presents typical characteristics of a plateau. The Malwa plateau, Madhya Bharat pathar, Bundelkhand upland, Vindhyachal scarpland, Vindhyachal range, Satpura range, Baghelkhand plateau, Baster plateau, Cnattisgarh basin and the Narmada valley of the north-central Peninsular India are the major physiographic units within the boundaries of the State (Map 2B). Most of these plateau are highly dissected and present high local relief which reduce their agricultural suitability. On reasons of unsuitable characteristics, land of the following region is usually not suitable for agricultural purposes:

However, there are some pockets of level land between hills and dissected areas. Most of these areas are under forests.

(i) Bastar plateau,
(ii) Baghelkhand plateau.
(iii) Satpura range,
(iv) Vindhyan range and
(v) Madhya Bharat pather.

Contrary to it, land classed as suitable for cultivation are confined in:

(i) the Chattisgarh basin,
(ii) Narmada valley,
(iii) Rewa plateau,
(iv) Malwa plateau and
(v) on part of the Bundelkhand upland.

Land of the Chattisgarh basin covered with red and yellow soils is rated as very good and good in the capability classification. While of the Rewa plateau and the Narmada valley, with deep and medium black soils are good land (Map 1A). Old alluvium and mixed red and black soils on level land of the Sindh-Pahuj plain of the Bundelkhand upland make it agriculturally productive area, gently sloping land of the Malwa plateau, covered with medium black soils, is moderately good.

The quality of land has manifested itself through the net sown area. It is because in the country like India where agriculture, by experimentation over centuries, has well adjusted itself to the natural conditions. All cultivable area is under cultivation which shows marked difference and corresponds with the nature of terrain. All the above regions with good agricultural land are widely cultivated. Proportion of net sown area above 70 per cent of the total area is in the Chattisgarh basin, excluding the marginal highlands, Malwa plateau, Narmada valley and the Sindh-Pahuj plain. The Rewa plateau, with land of good quality, has only 40 to 50 per cent of land under cultivation. Conversely dissected areas, with thin, poor and unworkable soils, have low and very low proportion of net sown area. It is extremely low in the Baghelkhand plateau, Bastar plateau Maikal plateau and major parts of the Madhya Bharat pathar and Bundelkhand uplands. And such areas are deprived of such basic resources which provides stable footing to the economy and people.

Use of land resource is determined not only by the capability of land but also by its distribution among cultivators as well. Like manufacturing units, size and ownership of operational holdings are among the determinants of the use of land, crop-structure and the use of inputs and efficiency of farms. Distribution—horizontal and vertical—of land holdings is very uneven in this state. There are more than 6.4 million operational holdings and their average size is only 3.42 hectares in 1980-81. Nearly one-third (32.8 per cent) of holdings have less than one hectare of land and possess only 4.2 per cent of area. More than half of the holdings are under 2 hectares in area (Table 2). On the other extreme, 6.8 per cent of landholders have large and very large sized (more than 10 ha) holdings and own more than one-third of the total area. Only these large holdings are capable of using modern capital intensive technology for agricultural development, while marginal and small farmers are bound to be traditional because of the smallness of holdings.

TABLE 2

Size of Operational Holdings in Madhya Pradesh, 1980-81

Size class	*Holding*		*Area*	
	Nos (000)	*Per cent*	*000 ha.*	*Per cent*
Marginal (under 1 ha)	2102.5	32.8	930.2	4.2
Small (1-2 ha)	1226.4	19.1	1791.6	8.2
Semi-medium (2-4 ha)	1371.5	21.4	3871.5	17.7
Medium (4-10 ha)	1275.4	19.9	7875.9	35.2
Large (above 10 ha)	435.0	6.8	7462.0	34.0

Source; Commissioner, Land Records—Agricultural Census of M.P., 1980-81.

This average situation varies spatially. There is wide spatial variation in average size of holdings. Average area per holding ranges from only 1.7 ha in Bilaspur to 6.7 ha in Vidisha districts. Most of the districts of eastern and southern parts of the state have exceptionally smaller average size. It may be generalized that marginal, small and semi-medium holdings characterise the eastern part; and semi-medium, medium and large holdings predominate the western half of the state. This distributional pattern has direct and significant relationship with the level of adoption of developmental measures and levels of agricultural productivity.

Water Resource

Useability of land is further limited with the availability of moisture. Rainfall is the primary source. There is wide variation in regional and seasonal distribution of rainfall. Usually, south-eastern half of the state receives higher rainfall than 120 cm. In the northwest, it gradually drops to 72 cm. in Jhabua and

68 cm in Morena. More than 90 per cent of the rain comes during the southwest monsoon season. *i.e.*, June to September. Vagaries of rainfall is so serious that eleven districts out of 45 have been identified as drought-prone districts (Balkrishna *et.al.* 1982, p. 3). Eight of them are in the southwestern part of the State, while Datia is in the north and Sidhi and Shahdol are in the east.

Nevertheless, the state has vast volume of surface water. Total volume of water drained by the rivers of this state is estimated, at 18,3294 million cubic metres. Rivers radiate from high lands of this state and are dammed as they reach in the bordering states. Potential of underground water is also vast, and is estimated at 5865304 hectometres and the present utilization is 599987 hectometres, which is only 10.2 per cent of the net recharge. Again, there is marked variation in distribution of these potentials, depending upon climatic and structural characteristics. Usually, level lands are also endowed with rich water resources. Ultimate potential of water resources of this State can irrigate 102 lakh hectares. Only 27.4 lakh hectares (1982-83) are irrigated at present, which is about 27 per cent of the ultimate potential. Most of the irrigate area is confined in the Chattisgarh the rice bowl of the State, Chambal region and Bundelkhand uplands. Conversely the eastern part of the State but Chattisgarh; and Vidisha plateau and Jhabua fail even to employ such basic input as irrigation (Sharma and Jain 1980).

Forest Resources

Forests are more abundant and valuable natural resources of this State. In all 140.2 thousand square kilometres are under different types of forests, which constitute 32 per cent of the total geographical area of the State. This proportion of area under forests is highest, but Orissa (42.2 per cent) among the neighbouring States. More than one fifth (21.0 per cent) of the total forested area and 29 per cent of the growing stock (410 million M^3 as against (1733-M^3) of the country is confined in this State.

Another remarkable feature about the distribution of forests is its close relationship with dissected topography. Generally dissected and rugged parts are widely covered with dense forests due to their unsuitability for cultivation and inaccessibility. There are five major areas of forest concentration (Map 2A). These are:

1. the Satpura-Maikal-Baghelkhand plateau, south of the Narmada-son valley and extending west to east across the State,
2. The Bastar plateau,
3. Sagar-Damoh plateau and Panna hilly tract,
4. Southwestern fringes of the Malwa plateau, and
5. The Morena-Shivpuri plateau.

Qualitatively forests of the Chambal region are highly degraded and are simply wastelands. Thus most of the forests are confined in the south and southwestern parts of the State. The forests of these parts belong to the Tropical Moist Deciduous type, while forests north of the Narmada-Son line belong to Tropical Dry Deciduous class. These forests have further classified on the basis of the composition into Sal (Shorea robusta), Teak (Tectona grandis) and mixed forests.

Forest Products: Traditionally forest products are classed into two groups—mojor and minor. Timber, fuelwood and charcoal are major forest products and others are minor produces. Value of all forest products has been estimated at Rs. 252 crores in 1979-80. Revence received from forests was only Rs. 140.77 crores in the same year, which was nearly fourteen times of revenue realised in 1960-61 (Rs. 10.12 crores). It was only 16.6 per cent of the total revenue of the Government. In 1977-78 total 1085.49 thousand cubic metres of timber wood, and 3289.12 thousand M^3 of fuelwood was extracted from the forests of this State. Total value of minor forest products was Rs. 2818 lakh in same year. Tendu leaves, bamboo, Khair tree, harra gums and lakh are worth-mentioning minor produces. Collection of tendu leaves, used for bidi making increased from 21.46 lakhs standard bags in 1964-66 to 30.79 lakh standard bags in 1979-80. It was nationalised in 1964. Consequently, revenue from tendu leaves rose from Rs. 86.08 lakh in 1963-64 to Rs. 3335 lakh in 1978-79. Thus as far as forest resources are concerned southern and eastern parts are capable of supporting several industries on all scale, particularly on medium and small scale. But there were only 1506 industrial units manufacturing wooden products employing only 10 thousand persons (0.05 per cent of all industrial workers). Among major units mention be made of paper mills located at Amalai (Shahdol), Hoshangabad and Nepanagar (Khandwa). Most of the forest produces are exported to surrounding States and as far as upto Punjab and Haryana.

Mineral and Power Resources

Madhya Pradesh has rich and extensive deposits of industrially important minerals and occupies significant place in the mining economy of the country. It is richly endowed with bauxite, coal copper, diamond, dolomite, iron ore, limestone and manganese ore. Besides them, andalusite, barytes, clays, corundum, floursspar, rock phosphate, ochre, sillimanite and steatite are also found. Distribution of these reserves are shown on Map 3B, and their reserves are presented in table 3 below.

Distribution of these minerals is very localized. Major tracts of their occurrences are the Baghelkhand plateau, Chattisgarh basin, Bastar plateau, eastern Satpura and Rewa plateau. Jhabua and lower Chambal valley are out side these tracts. Again, concentration of mineral and fuel resources is in the south eastern part of the State. For instance, coal occurs in districts of Sidhi, Surguja, Shahdol, Bilaspur, Raigarh in the east and in Chhindwara and Betul in the Satpura region (Map 3). Occurrences of iron ore are reported in many districts, however, workable deposits are in Bastar, Durg and Jabalpur districts. The state is India's foremost source for Manganese ore, important deposits of which lie in the districts of Balaghat and Chhindwara. Occurrences are reported in Jabalpur, Jhabua

TABLE—3

Reserves of Important Minerals in M.P.

(*Million Tonnes*)

Mineral	*Measures*	*Indicated*	*Inferred*	*Total*
Bauxite	61.198	65.119	61.147	187.464
China clay	—	0.50	23.01	23.51
Coal	4227	4067	7168	15482
Copper ore	—	76.19	23.58	99.77
Dolomite	270.01	168.25	1287.95	1726.21
Fire clay	1.31	14.62	105.68	121.61
Iron ore	1072.29	530.93	866.92	2470.14
Limestons	3979.55	1197.00	2289.88	7466.43
Manganese	11.436	8.213	5.157	24.806
Rock phosphate	2.00	9.55	2.31	13.86

Source: Indian Mineral Year book, 1980.

and Khargone districts. Rich and extensive deposits of limestone, associated with Cuddapah and Vindhyan formations, are found in a vast belt encompassing all districts of the Chhattisgarh basin, Jabalpur, Damoh, Satna, Rewa in the eastern half and in Jhabua, Morena and Mandsaur districts in western part of the State. Major deposits of dolomite are also located in and around the Chattisgarh basin and in Jhabua district. Bauxite, the ore of alumina is one of the major mineral resources and is widely distributed associated with laterite capping of the Deccan traps. Its mining is confined in Mandla, Bilaspur, Shahdol, Jabalpur and Satna districts at present. Recently one of the richest copper deposit of the country, occurring in the Archeans has been discovered in the Malajkhand area of Balaghat district. Most of the mineral deposits occur in the Archeans, Dharwar Purana and Gondwana formations. Bauxite is the only mineral found in the Deccan trap. Thus, stratigraphically, minerals are expected to occur in the southern parts which are composed on these rock systems.

Production: Madhya Pradesh ranked second in the value of mineral production in the country. Total value of mineral output in the State was Rs. 3650 million, which is 6 per cent of the total value of mineral produced in the country in 1980. It is remarkable that value of mineral output was only Rs. 82.3 million in 1951, contributing about 8 per cent of the country. Thus value of mineral production in the State increased by double the rate of the country during this period.

Coal, iron ore, limestone, manganese ore, bauxite, dolomite and phosphorite are principal minerals produced and they jointly accounted for 96 per cent of the total value of mineral produced in the state. Coal alone accounted for 76 per cent of the value. It is the sole producer of the diamond in the country and also largest producer of limestone (23 per cent), dolomite (8 per cent), bauxite (26 per cent) diaspore (65 per cent), and pyrophyllite (46 per cent). It was the second largest producer of iron ore (23 per cent), coal (23 per cent), phosphorite (19 per cent), Ochre (30 per cent), and quartzite (34 per cent). The value of output of minor minerals was Rs. 134 million.

Resource Regions

On the basis of the distributional pattern of natural resources, a critical combination of resources can be assigned to each district, and on the basis of similarity districts can be grouped into resource regions. These resource-bases must be taken into account while planning for development. Considering the connectivity and socio-economic background, these combinations can be rearranged into planning regions for optimum utilization of resources.

I LAND RESOURCE

Mandsaur, Ratlam, Ujjain, Indore, Dewas, Shajapur, Sehore,

TABLE—4

Trend of Production of Important Minerals in M.P.

Mineral	*1951*	*1960*	*1970*	*1980*	
				Quantity	% of India
Bauxite	13.8	47.5	340.7	470.7	26.4
China clay	30.0	5.2	15.2	11.0	
Coal	3593	6307	12556	25174	23.1
Diamond (Carats)		1159	20325	14432	100.0
Diaspore				3.9	65.0
Dolomite	13.1	171.3	414.1	767.3	38.0
Fire clay	29.4	59.1	72.5	96.1	
Iron ore		1448.7	7168.1	9745.3	23.2
Kaolin				18.6	
Lime stone	1018.1		4088.1	6582.8	22.6
Manganese	380.5	219.1	214.1	267.9	13.2

Ochre	2.4	11.0	12.0	28.2	30.0
Phosphorite				100.2	19.2
Pyrophyllite				16.0	46.0
Quartzite and Silica		24.8	48.7	37.1	34.0

Raigarh, Guna, Bhopal, Vidisha, Bhind, Gwalior, Datia, Tikamgarh and Rewa districts.

II LAND AND FOREST RESOURCES

Dhar, Khandwa, Khargone, Hoshangabad, Betual, Narsinghpur, Seoni*, Raisen, Sagar, Chhatarpur, Panna, Shivpuri, Rajnandgaon* districts.

III LAND AND MINERAL RESOURCES

Durg, Jabalpur, Satna districts.

IV MINERAL, FOREST AND LAND RESOURCES

Bastar*, Raipur, Bilaspur, Raigarh*, Surguja*, Sidhi*, Shahdol*, Mandla*, Balaghat, Damoh, Chhindwara, Jhabua* and Morena district.

*USUALLY POOR LAND

Economic Development

Performance of economic activities should be taken as an index of level of economic development. Probably gross national product may serve this purpose and per capita GNP can offer a rough indication of the degree of inequality among districts of this State. But at present level of statistical information it is just not possible to compute the district level GNP. Therefore, to meet the need of an aggregate district-level index through selective indicators, several studies have been attempted. For instances, Datta (198) selected twenty-five indices to measure the regional variation in level of development in this state, while Agarwal and Khan (1983) selected only nine out of them. Almost indentical indices were used by Sharma (1981) to portray the economic development of the Baghelkhand plateau of M.P. At the same time, Centre for Monitoring Indian Economy (1982·0, 1-) has selected following nine indices to compute the index of level of economic development of districts of entire country:

1. Per capita value of crops,
2. Per capita bank credit for agriculture,
3. Number of mining and factory workers,
4. Number of household manufacturing workers,
5. Per capita bank credit for manufacturing sector,
6. Per capita bank deposit,
7. Per capita bank credit to services,
8. Literacy and
9. Urbanisation.

There seems much weightage given to banking services in this selection of indices.

In the present study, twelve indicators have been used to measure the level of economic development. They have been selected from all sectors of economy, *viz.*, agriculture, mining manufacturing, trade and commerce. These indicators are:

1. Value of crops (Rs) per hectare of net sown area,
2. Proportion of net irrigated area,
3. Use of fertilizers per hectare of cropped, area,
4. Percentage area under high yielding variety of seeds,
5. Per capita bank credit for agriculture,
6. Number of mining workers per lakh population,
7. Number of factory workers per lakh population,
8. Number of household workers per lakh population,

9. Number of registered shops per lakh population,
10. Per capita bank deposit,
11. Per capita electric consumption, and
12. Proportion of urban population.

Scores of each variable were standardized to zero mean and unit standard deviation, and these were then summed for each district. On plotting these composite development indices on scatter diagramme, the following pattern of economic development emereges clearly (Map 4A).

Areas of High Development: There are two well marked areas of high economic development. First and foremost region exists in the western Malwa and covers three districts, *viz.*, Indore, Ujjain and Ratlam. Khandwa in the Narmada valley is also highly developed. This is urbanised and industrialised belt of the State. Indore—the industrial capital of the State—is located here. Z scores for all economic activities, excepting mining and household industries, are positive and their sum is as high as 21.76. Similar is the situation in Ujjain, but Ratlam is below state average is agricultural productivity and proportion of irrigated area. This is pertinent to recall here that this region is poor in all natural resources but land; and probably agricultural produces, particularly cotton, have been the base of industrial development. Gwalior and Morena constitute second area of high development. Economic development in Gwalior is based on agriculture, manufacturing, trade and commerce; while Morena is solely dependent on agriculture. In addition, three districts—Bhopal (21.59), Durg (7.79) and Jabalpur (5.43) are isolated districts of high economic development. Bhopal's economic status is dependent on manufacturing, trade and commerce and similar is the case with Jabalpur. As far as resources are concerned, Jabalpur is on better position. Durg is rich district in resources and the Bhilai Steel Plant has contributed to its economic upheaval. All districts of this class, except Morena, have atleast one first class city which can be deemed as regional growth poles. Naturally all resources have been pulled for the development of these poles which elevate the average of the district.

Areas of Medium Development: Moderately developed districts (with scores ranging from 0 to 4) occur in contiguity with highly developed districts. Mandsaur (2.60), Dews (2.40) Hoshangabad (3.57), Chhindwara (2.42) and Narsinghpur (0.88) districts link Indore-Ujjain belt to Jabalpur in the east. Sagar (0.41) and Tikamgarh (3.63) from its northern offshoot. Major component in economy of these districts is agriculture except in Sagar which mainly depends on houshold industries and tertiary activities. Bhind (0.11), and Datia (0 66) are contiguous to Gwalior belt and again they depend on agriculture. In the east, Raipur (3.18) and Bilaspur (0.97) are linked with Durg. It is worth-mentioning that these three districts have diversified resource-base which are being used for industrial development in these districts. Balaghat also has achieved moderate economic development. Thus twentyone out of fortyfive districts have composite score higher than zero, and only five of them are in the east. Malwa plateau has the largest number followed by Chhattisgarh basin and the Gwalier region.

Areas of Low and very Low Development: Contrary to it, largest block of economically backward districts is in the east. It extends from Chhatarpur and Damoh to Surguja and Raigarh in the east, and Bastar in south. This belt covers thirteen districts, and excepting a few northern districts all are rich as far as natural resources are concerned, but they depend on extraction economies. Only Damoh, Chhatarpur and Satna could develop household industries to remarkable extent. Mandla (—9.53), Sidhi (—4.17), Baster (—8.99) and Seoni (—7.65) are most backward districts in this eastern part. Most of the districts of this part are at the bottom level of development in Indian context (Sundaram 1983, p. 161). Second block of backward districts encircles Bhopal, the capital of the State, and cover seven districts. Guna(—7.97), Rajgarh (—6.65) are most backward among them. These districts are poor as far as resources are concerned. South western Malwa, comprising Jhabua (−9.27), Dhar(−3.48) and Khargone (−2.17) constitute third area of concentration of backward districts.

A few studies have concentrated on this issue of poverty in plenty (Sharma 1981, Mishra 1977). The problems of rural economic development in the Baghelkhand plateau (comprising Sidhi, Shahdol and Surguja districts in the eastern part) have been examined by Sharma, which can be cited as representative of these problematic districts. The plateau is known for its resource potentialities, particularly, mineral, forest, land and water resources. About 84 per cent of coal reserve of Madhya Pradesh is confined within this plateau. Similarly, huge reserves of bauxite, clays, limestone and sizable deposits of several other minerals are found here. It accounts for 34 per cent of State's mineral output, but most of the minerals produced here are exported, and therefore, they have hardly initiated economic and industrial development, as is anticipated, in the region. Economic activities generated by them are related to mining and export. Forests, which cover 46 per cent of the plateau area and contribute one-fifth of State's total revenue from forests, are important sources of timber, fuel-wood as well as of raw minerals for paper, bidi and many small scale industries located mostly out side the region. The Orient Paper Mills Amalai is only large industry based on them. Neither forestry nor forest-based industries have played any significant role in the economy. In absence of congenial industrial atmosphere, all exploited resources, except essential agricultural products, are exported. This outward linkage of export of raw materials, in absence of reciprocal inward linkages, has created the colonial setting by developing a few nuclei as exporting ports. This export has acted as an instrument of drain rather than capital accumulation.

Explanations of Inequality

Thus, more appropriately, the present situation of resource management, exploitation and utilisation can well be described under the setting of 'internal colonialism.' As colonies were used as sources of raw materials, in the same manner lagging regions act as sources of required raw materials for dominant regions. This does not mean that natural resources of eastern part are utilised in the western part of the State, it simply means that resources have not been utilised for the development of the region of their occurrences, instead they are drained outside the region. Thus resource-scarcity is not the cause of backwardness of these resource-rich districts.

It is appropriate to examine two other cause of inequality specified by Sundaram (1983 p. 5-6) in context of the developing countries. Socio-economic status of the people and communities goes long way in effecting man's developmental efforts. In the present politico-economic structure, those people who are conscious to their rights and those areas which are dominated by such people get benefits of developmental efforts. One example of developmental expenditure proves this fact. The analysis of development expenditure in both urban and rural sectors clearly shows the bias towards developed districts. The Fifth Draft Plan of the State shows that per capita expenditure has been much lower in backward districts than in developed districts excepting during II plan period. This is caused because of appeasing more conscious people and their regions. Probably this is the core and crux of the problem of inequality. The consciousness of the people can be measured by their voting behaviour. The percentage of voters actually turned up to total voters in 1984 Lok Sabba election has been plotted on Map (Map 4B), which shows very close resemblance with the pattern of economic development. This also supports the contention of conscious.

Another fact which emerges from this analysis is that most of the districts dominated by tribes fall in lower quantile in the development hierarchy, despite of formulation of several strategies for the development of such regions. Major segment of population in all nine districts, with lowest level of development in the east is tribal. Similar is the case in the southwest. Relationship of these socio-cultural consciousness can be seen with the infrastructural facilities, which also follow the suit.

To sum up, it may be accepted that there is region inequality in distribution of resources in this State. Exploitation of these resources has increased tremendously. But they contributed least in the economic growth of the areas of their occurrences. The western part of State, known as the Malwa plateau, has inertia of industrialisation and development. Agricultural base, which is supposed to initiated it, seems to be inadequate for supporting its present economic structure. It draws resources from outside of its territorial boundary and gives higher efficiency of production. Contrary to it, resource-rich eastern districts have been acting as source areas of resource for other regions. These resources have created channels and parts of export in these areas. Thus resource base of these districts seems to be much larger than the existing level of economic development. The prevailing under development in this part is caused by the inequality is socio-cultural structure through the developmental efforts.

REFERENCES

Agarwal, P.C. and Z.T. Khan (1983) Spatial Analysis of the level of Regional Development in M.P., pp. 315-24, in P. Pandey, ed., *Modern Geographical Trends*, New Delhi: Today and Tomorrow.

Balkrishna, S. *et.al.*, (1982) *Socio-economic conditions of Drought Prone Areas in Madhya Pradesh*, Hyderabad: NIRD.

Centre for Monitoring Indian Economy (1982) *District Level Data for Key Economic Indicators*, Bombay.

Clawson, M. ed (1964) *Natural Resources and International Development*, Baltimore.

Datta, T.N. (1980) Regional Variations in the Level of Development of Madhya Pradesh, *Geog. Rev. Ind.* 42 No. 3 p. 254 (1980).

Friedman, H. and W. Alonso, Eds. (1964) *Regional Development and Planning A Reader*. Massachusetts: MIT Press.

Ginsburg, N. (1957) Natural Resources and Economic Development, *Ann. Ass. Am. Geogr*. 47, 197-212.

Grigg, D. (1973) Geographical Studies of Economic Development, pp. 18-84 in, Michall Chisholm and Brian Bodgers, eds., *Studies in Human Geography*.

Hodder, B.W. (1971) Natural Resources and Tropical Development, pp. 69-75 in Mountjoy, A.B. Ed., *Developing the Under Developed Countries*; Macmillan Press Limited.

Keller, F.L. (1953) Resources Inventory—A Basic step in Economic Development, *Eco. Geog*. pp. 39-47.

Kumar, P. (1976) Regional Evaluation of Resources in Madhya Pradesh as a Basis for Planning, pp. 209-227 in V.C. Misra *et.al.*, eds., *Essays in Applied Geography*, Saugar University.

Mishra, C.B. (1977) *Changing Pattern of Resource Use in the Eastern Satpura Region*. Unpub. Ph.D. Thesis, Univ. of Saugar.

Perloff, Harvey and Lowdon Wingo Jr. (1964) Natural Resource Endowment and Regional Economic Growth, pp 215-23 in John Friedmann and W.A. Conso, eds., *Regional Development and Planning*, Massachusetts, MIT Press.

Sharma, S.K. (1981) Problems of Rural Economic Development in the Baghelkhand Plateau, M.P. *The Geographer XXVIII*, No. 2. pp. 57-68.

Sharma, S.K. and G.K. Jain (1980) Use of Water Resource for Irrigation and Agricultural Development—A case study of M.P., 463-83 in Noor Mohammad, ed , *Perspective in Agricultural Geography*, Vol. II, New Delhi: Concept.

Smith, D.M. (1977) *Human Geography: A Welfare Approach*, Edward Arnold.

Smith, D.M. (1979) *Where the Grass is Greener*, Penguin Books.

Spengler, JJ. ed., (1961) *Natural Resources and Economic Growth*, Washington DC.

Sundaram, K.V. (1983) *Geography of Underdevelopment*, New Delhi: Concept, Pub. Co.

Tosi, J.A. and R.F. Voertman (1964) Some Environmental Factors in the Economic Development of the Tropies, *Eco. Geog.* 40 No. 3, 189 p.

10

RESOURCE REGIONS OF TELANGANA

P. PADMANABHA RAO*

The composition of association and the spatial pattern of distribution, production and processing linkages constitute the core of the region and provide the base to capture the in-depth structure of the resource regions. Such resource regions may be optimal for planning and development of each resource, but not for comprehensive spatial planning of multi resources.

Resource regions acquire national and international importance depending upon the market for the resources. Ancilliarisation of industries and development of linkages between the resource complexes and local resource based industries through a well-designed locational and linked clusters in small towns and central villages. The resource regions contribute to the development of a more balanced and integrated development.

The objective of this article is to bring out region specificity based on significant variables rooted in the region landscape measured by its high concentration and also on the basis of natural resource and resources used for the development of the

*Geographer/Cartographer, Centre for Economics and Social Studies, Hyderabad.

region. Four distinct regions are delineated in the backward Telangana region of Andhra Pradesh. They are:

1. Urban-Industrial region;
2. Forest-Mineral region;
3. Irrigation Farming region and;
4. Dry Farming region.

The talukas of Telangana region are classified and grouped in each of the typological region into larger and contiguous region based on the selected characteristics relating to natural resource endowment, land use. Population-demography and occupational structure etc. In a dynamic framework, region can develop new structural and linkage pattern or can stagnate or decline.

Out of the above four regions, two regions are further sub divided on the basis of source of irrigation and soil types. Irrigation farming region is divided into two sub-regions, namely, Canal Irrigation and Tank and Well Irrigation. The Dry Farming region divided into three sub-regions of red soil, black soil, and mixed soil.

The data taken for this analysis is on the basis of natural resources and also percentage of forest area to total geographical area and gross irrigated area to total cropped area of each of the 73 talukas which are grouped from 15 taluks of Telangana. The upper quartile value of the forest area to delineate forest region and upper quartile value of irrigated area and lower quartile value of the irrigated area were taken to delineate irrigation farming and dry farming region for the cut-off values to bring out the spatial concentration and the associated typological regions.

Urban-industrial region

The urban-industrial region comprises Hyderabad urban, Warangal, and Nizamabad comprising twelve talukas in the region which accounts 4.3 per cent of area and 20.26 per cent of population. (18.7 per cent in 1971). Hyderabad metropolitan city is classified as an administrative town accounting for eighty per cent of the total urban population of this region. While Warangal and Nizamabad are classified as industry-cum-manufacturing towns accounting 16 per cent of the regions urban-population.

Forest-mineral region

The Forest and Mineral region comprises 20 talukas of four districts namely; Adilabad, Warangal, Karimnagar and Khammam. This region accounts twenty six per cent of area and 11.7 per cent of population (11.66 in 1977). This area is naturally the largest in the forest and mineral zone where they accounts for 58 per cent of the total geographical area as against 24.3 per cent of the region. In the three remaining regions forests are much lower than the region average. Coal is the most important mineral in the regian is found extensively in the Godavari basin covering parts of Adilabad, Karimnagar and Khammam districts. Other important minerals found in the region are Iron ore, some low grade magnetite-hematite, limestone etc. besides forest produces like teak, nallamaddi, bamboo, gum etc.

Irrigation farming region

Irrigation farming region comprises 38 talukas of Karimnagar, Nalgonda, Medak and Nizamabad districts. Under the command area of Nagarjuna Sagar project, and Sriramsagar project. This is the second largest region in Telangana in terms of area and population after dry farming region which accounts 27.9 per cent of area and 32.26 per cent of population in 1981 (32.6 per cent in 1971). Canal irrigation accounts 27 per cent, tanks 45 per cent and wells irrigation 26 per cent, *i.e.* most of the irrigation is done by tanks which can be seen from (Map 1).

Dry Farming Region

Dry Farming region comprises 45 talukas of mostly from Mahbubnagar, Nalgonda and Rangareddy districts *i.e.*, southern and central part of the Telangana. This is largest region in Telangana in terms of area and population and accounts 42 per cent of area and 35.76 per cent of population (36.96 in 1971) as also seen from (Table 1a). This region is mostly dominated by three types of soils, of which 42 per cent of red soils, 37 per cent black cotton soils and 21 per cent are mixed soils. The black cotton soils in the region found in part of Adilabad district and Mahbubnagar district along the western border. The red soils are found in central and southern part of the Telangana region.

Density of Population

The density of population is highest in urban-industrial region *i.e.*, 822 person per sq. km. in 1981 (596 in 1971). Nearly two-thirds of population of this region is in three cities only. This is due to in-migration of population in search of better employment opportunities in these administrative and industrial cities. Very low density of population is seen in forest and mineral region which accounts 62 persons per sq. km. in 1971. This has slightly increased to 79 persons per sq. km. in 1981. The density is very low as against the region's average of 138 and 176 persons per sq. km. in 1971 and 1981 respectively. (Table 1b.) The density is more than region average *i.e.*, 20.3 persons per sq. km. in irrigated farming (161 in 1971) and in dry farming region the density is lower than the region average *i.e.*, 122 and 150 persons. per sq. km. in 1971 and 1981. But it is higher than the forest and mineral region.

The density of population in forest and mineral region talukas is less than 518 persons per sq. kms. While talukas of irrigation farming region the density ranging between 1036-1554 persons per sq. kms. and in dry farming region it is 518-1036 persons per sq. km. The density of population and Resource region of Telangana maps (Map 1) are both comparable, *i.e.*, the low density of population occurs in forest and mineral region and dry farming region and the higher densities in irrigation farming and urban-industrial region which was observed from the above maps.

Growth of Population

The growth of population in urban industrial region was highest (37.92 per cent) followed by forest and mineral region (28.12 per cent) (see Table 2). This growth is more than Telangana average growth (27.5 per cent). The larger the growth rate in the urban-industrial and forest-mineral region may be due to faster growth in non-agricultural occupation and also due to migration to other two region the growth rate is lower than that of region average growth. The growth rate in irrigation farming region is 25.99 per cent (Table 2) indicating that there might not have been a substantial netout migration from this region.

Urban Population

The urban population in this region accounts for 25 per cent to total A.P. However the largest concentration of urban population is in urban-industrial region which accounts nearly 75 per cent of which Hyderabad Metropolitan accounts 12.5 per cent. In other region urbanisation is very low. However, in dry farming region it is as low as 11 per cent indicating that this region is dependent on agricultural economy (see Table 3).

The growth of urban population is higher than the general population. This growth rate was higher in urban-industrial region *i.e.*, 44.5 per cent, lowest in forest and mineral region *i.e.*, 36.4 per cent. The growth of urban population is increased in dry farming region in 1981 *i.e.* 40.9 per cent as against 15.0 in 1971 (Table 3).

The small towns with a population of 20,000 and below are concentrated in dry farming and forest and mineral region *i.e.*, out of 36 towns 24 are concentrated in these region itself. Out of 20 towns in Telangana 35 towns are in dry farming region only (as seen from Table 4) of which 3 are Class-II and 15 are Class-III and remaining towns are Class-IV and Class V towns (*i.e.*, small towns). Out of 3 Class-I towns in Telangana three are in urban-industrial region only. In forest mineral region there are 14 towns which are called as medium and small towns with 85 per cent of urban population in this region belongs to industrial and manufacturing category. This percentage was smaller in case of dry farming region whereas it is only 23 per cent because most of the towns are smaller having primary activities. In irrigation farming region 11 out of 25 in this region are Class-III and 9 are Class-IV towns (as seen from Table 4). Due to the developed irrigation facilities (construction of Sriramsagar project) the towns in irrigation farming region are developed and also change their size class (as seen Table 1) in 1981.

This analysis brings out that the urban settlements in this region are very weak. Nearly 60 per cent of urban centres (except Hyderabad, Nizamabad and Warangal) belong to either industrial and manufacturing or administrative activities and 40 per cent of towns predominantly in primary activities of trade and commerce etc. Most of the forest region is very rich in terms of mineral deposits and forest products. But, due to backwardness and negligence of government, we are unable to utilise these resources. Proper utilisation of these resources leads to development of the region and it will solve unemployment problem and stop the migration to other areas and at least unemployed persons to the regions in search of employment and commercial activity also develop due to this region's development and this also leads to development of small towns in this region. Most of the small towns in the region have rural character with quite a few have developeded with urban characteristics due to their administrative on the whole, most of the small towns are potential for future development with their available resources or governmenl policy.

TABLE 1(a)

Telangana Area, Population, Density—1971-81

S. No.	Name of the Region	No. of Talukas 1971	No. of Talukas 1981	Area in Sq. Kms.	Population 1971	Population 1981	Density per sq. km. 1971	Density per sq. km. 1981
1.	Urban-Industrial region per cent to total	5	12	4,972.3 (4.33)	29,63,882 (18.74)	40,87,858 (20.26)	596	822
2.	Forest-Mineral region per cent to total	14	20	29,728.3 (25.9)	18,44,638 (11.66)	23,63,443 (11.72)	62	79
3.	Irrigation Farming region per cent of total	22	38	32,041.2 (27.92)	51,64,143 (32.64)	65,06,188 (32.26)	161	203
4.	Dry Farming region per cent to total	32	45	48,026.1 (41.85)	58,45,032 (36.96)	72,12,315 (35.76)	122	150
	Total	73	115	1,14,767.9	1,58,17,895	2,01,69,804	138	176

Source: Census of India, 1981.

TABLE 2

Telangana Population Growth

(in percent)

S. No.	*Name of the region*	*1901-51*	*1951-61*	*1961-71*	*1971-81*
1.	Urban-Industrial	140.64	30.31	35.56	37.92
2.	Forest & Mineral	155.45	31.38	30.40	28.12
3.	Irrigation Farming	106.60	17.11	23.31	25.99
4.	Dry Farming	96.05	12.61	19.15	23.39
	Total Telangana	112.19	18.79	24.60	27.51

Source: Census of India, 1981

TABLE 3

Telangana Population Growth

(Urban)

S. No.	*Name of the region*	*Population in lakhs*		*% to total population*		*G.R.*	
		1971	*1981*	*1971*	*1981*	*1961-71*	*1971-81*
1.	Urban-Industrial	21.27	30.75	71.8	75.24	41.8	44.57
2.	Forest-Mineral	2.61	3.93	14.1	16.63	37.07	36.47
3.	Irrigation Farming	4.49	7.86	8.7	12.08	28.7	42.8
4.	Dry Farming	4.85	8.21	8.3	11.38	15.0	40.90
	Total Telangana	33.22	50.76	21.0	25.16	35.1	52.8

Source: Census of India, 1981.

TABLE 4

Telangana Distribution of Towns 1971-81

S. No.	Name of the region	Class I 1,00,000		Class II 50,000 to 1,00,000		Class III 20,000-50,000		Glass IV 10,000-20,000		Class V 5,000-10,000		Class VI 5,000.		Total Towns	
		1971	*81*	*71*	*81*	*71*	*81*	*71*	*81*	*71*	*81*	*71*	*81*	*71*	*81*
1.	Urban-Industrial	3	3	—	—	—	—	—	1	1	2	—	—	4	6
2.	Forest & Mineral	—	—	1	1	4	6	5	4	2	2	—	1	12	14
3.	Irrigation Farming	—	—	1	5	6	11	10	9	6	—	—	—	23	25
	a) canal	—	—	—	4	—	6	—	4	—	—	—	—	—	14
	b) Tank	—	—	—	1	—	5	—	5	—	—	—	—	—	11
4.	Dry Farming	—	—	1	3	8	15	13	10	6	6	—	1	28	35
	a) Red soil	—	—	—	2	—	5	—	6	—	4	—	—	—	17
	b) Block soil	—	—	—	1	—	8	—	3	—	2	—	1	—	15
	c) Mixed soil	—	—	—	—	—	2	—	1	—	—	—	—	—	13
	Total Telangana	3	3	3	9	18	32	28	24	15	10	—	3	67	80

11

AGRICULTURAL MARKET CENTRES AND REGIONAL IMBALANCES

C.K. ARUNA*

Marketing geography as a relatively recent branch of study poses umpteen challenges to the researcher in exploring and discovering the spatial patterns and processes. Role of marketing function in the development process has received attention and gained significance in our country only in recent years. A path set by economists and sociologists is now exceptionally a geographer's arena. Of the various studies, regional studies at states level are an exception.

Present paper makes an attempt in this direction where an analysis of market arrivals by taluks in the state is carried out. Thus the objectives are follows:

(a) To examine the spatial distribution pattern of market arrival in the State of Andhra Pradesh.

(b) To examine the spatial relationship between market arrivals and agricultural production.

*Research Scholar, Department of Geography, Osmania University.

Methodology

Marketing system in our country is channelized through two types of markets *viz.*, weekly and wholesale markets each having its own distinctive role and function. Present analysis is carried out for regulated markets alone keeping in view their significant role in a wider perspective with respect to overall development. Unlike weekly markets that signify subsistence level of economy with marginal marketable surplus, regional markets with large scale agricultural surplus are capable of successfully functionnig as economic units in sustaining growth and bringing about a transformation in all spheres. Hence, it is intended to analyse the regulated market arrivals in the State of Andhra Pradesh. As an analysis at the district level would provide too generalized a picture it is intended to seek a keener insight into the details at a disaggregate level hence an analysis of three hundred twelve taluks of Andhra Pradesh is attempted.

Analysis is based on secondary source of information alone and the type of analysis is also restricted by time and monetary constraints. Market arrivals (agricultural commodities excluding fruits and vegetables) data is obtained from Department of Marketing, while agricultural production figures were obtained from Statistical Abstracts published by the Bureau of Economics while disaggregate area figures for taluks were taken from Crop Abstracts which are unpublished manuscripts by the same Department.

A temporal analysis is not attempted as market regulation is a deliberate action, and the total coverage of markets in the state is yet to be covered, with twenty three taluks remaining to be covered by the market function as such. It is not only the number of market centres that were progressively being regulated during the decades (Table 1) but also the uniformity with respect to legislation and nature of commodities is a recent achievement (Appendix-I). Hence it follows that temporal analysis for individual market centres is possible whereas it is not possible for all, as they lack uniformity.

A cartographic appraisal of the market arrivals by taluks,

substantiated and strengthened by correlation analysis provides the basic framework for the study.

Market Arrivals—Spatial Pattern

Market arrivals are no exception with respect to spatial irregularities like any other geographical phenomena they too exhibit distinct spatial patterns that emerge significantly, when appreciated cartographically. When a highly generalised description is attempted one observes a decrease in market arrivals with the progression towards hilly and forested areas *e.g.*, along the eastern ghats on the borders of Cuddapah, Nellore and Guntur districts known as the famous Nallamalai hills and Velikonda range, extending further (with a break in between) towards the northern side of Vishakhapatnam district and the forested hilly areas of Adilabad, Khammam and Mahbubnagar districts.

A second pattern that distinctly emerges is when examined in the context of core periphery patterns, *e.g.*, the deltaic districts of Krishna, West Godavari and East Godavari exhibit a significant concentration of high market arrivals along the rich alluvial soils of the delta and a decrease towards the interior of the districts away from the coasts. This is an exceptionally high concentration where these districts have twenty out of twenty six taluks of the State contributing to above 1,000,000 quintals of market arrivals (Table 2). In addition to this with respect to aggregate arrivals, these three districts together account for fourty eight per cent of the total arrivals in the state (Table-3). Similarly some of the districts, if observed keenly, have taluks with high arrivals as the core and values decrease away from these centres towards the periphery of the district, either gradually or with immediate shadow region surrounding them. Taluks which reveal immediate shadow region surrounding them, are those that have large urban centres of the state, *e.g.*, Hyderabad the capital and acting as the boom town of the state has a shadow region in all directions whereas Vishakhapatnam, Kakinada, Warangal, Nizamabad, Nellore and Khammam taluks which have larger urban centres next to Hyderabad display their shadow regions only in one or two directions. Adilabad and Chilkaluripeta taluks having Class II towns of the name-sake emerge as high concentration centres and a gradual decrease in arrivals away from these taluks is recognised. On the other hand, Jammikunta and Jedcherla taluks although do not have large urban centres their pattern in the district also coincides with the above as their market centres are the first to be regulated in their respective districts, this is also true with the larger urban centres as well which are the oldest markets regulated in their respective districts with the exception of Chilkaluripeta in Guntur district which remains next to many other older centres but emerged with distinction due to its advantageous location along the state highway cutting across Guntur district. It therefore remains to conclude that these market centres along with their high urban status and long duration exposure to market function emerge as high concentration of market arrivals. The only deviation is observed with respect to Nalgonda district where the taluks of high concentration do not coincide either with the location of larger urban centres or the older market centres of the district. This can be attributed only to the Nagarjunasagar Canal Irrigation tract which has led to high yields of agricultural production.

Yet another significant pattern that emerges is the belt pattern, where the concentration of market arrivals followed the transportation routes or canal irrigation. With respect to the former variable it holds good in Rayalaseema region, Vizianagaram, Medak districts. It's prominence in Rayalaseema region is very striking and it follows the Nandyal-Proddatur-Cuddapah and Chittoor route, while the pattern of Kurnool district follows the Tungabhadhra Canal and the Transportation route.

If these existing pattern are further substantiated by agricultural production data it may provide a keener insight into the problem as agricultural market arrivals are directly related to the agricultural productivity of the surrounding region. Hence in the foregoing analysis it is intended to examine the association between agricultural production and agricultural market arrivals.

Agricultural Market Arrivals Vs Agricultural Production

A well known fact that agricultural surplus of a region finds its outlet through the agricultural market centres and hence it follows that agricultural market arrivals reflect or indicate the agricultural productivity of the surrounding region.

In an attempt to establish the relationship statistically between the two variables firstly it was worked out at the district level as the agricultural production figures were available in a published and compiled form, and the results of the same reveals a high degree of association between market arrivals and agricultural production (co-efficient value +0.8) thus emphasizing the fact that marketable surplus of agricultural commodities is directly related to the agricultural productivity of the surrounding region.

While the above provides a generalized picture, it was intended to study the detailed spatial association at a disaggregate level *i e.*, taulk level the further understanding of the causative factors. Absence of production figures in a compiled form at the taluk level was the main set back for the analysis, but all the same a trail and error method was adopted in selecting a proxy for production data.

Firstly, experiment was carried out with the variable gross area sown as it covers the entire area under cultivation in a given area. Cartographical appraisal and statistical computation of the association between market arrivals and gross area sown show an insignificant relationship (co-efficient value+0.08), hence the map showing the distribution of gross area sown by taluks has not been included in the analysis.

With the above results proving unsatisfactory, it was intended to seek for a better proxy for agricultural production and in a second attempt a new method was achieved cartographically where the spatial distribution of the area under the first dominant crop (these crops also rank with high respect to agricultural production and market arrivals in the state (Table 4 and 4a) arriving into the markets by districts was plotted by obtaining per cent share of each taluk to the respective district. Commodity significance is highlighted by (Table 5), while spatial distribution of the same is highlighted in (Map 2). Correlation co-efficient value for this variable with marketable surplus stands as +0.5 which is quite significant and the spatial distribution further substantiates this relationship, where striking resemblances with (Map 1), occurs in many districts and it further highlights the role of large urban centres and old market centres in integrating the agricultural surplus of the surrounding regions and extending their influence beyond the taluk limits, as such emerging as nodal centres for their surrounding regions. For example the taluks of Hyderabad, Warangal, Vishakhapatnam, Jammikunta, Badepalli, Chilkaluripeta, Cuddapah, Proddatur and Nandyal to mention few, are the taluks with high market arrivals but low agricultural production and their surrounding taluks exhibit high agricultural production but low market arrivals. This itself suggests on intertaluk movement especially towards these large centres. There are yet other taluks like Nizamabad, Adilabad, Chittoor, Nellore. Nidamanur, Miryalguda. Huzurnagar and Kodad which are the taluks of high agricultural production and high market arrivals as such rule out the fact of their influence extending beyond taluk limits. Thus the preceding patterns could be attributed as the causative factor for the partial +0.5 coefficient value instead of a perfect (+1.0) correlation. While this remains a suggestion, a definite statement can be drawn only by substantiating and substituting by field knowledge as the jurisdiction area of a Market Centre, according to the Marketing Act does not specify but on an average extends upto a radius to ten km. This analysis also highlights the probability of treating market arrivals as a variable in identifying the core area of urban fields.

An inter regional movement of commodities is further suggested when (Table 5 and 6) are compared where the difference in the dominant crop with respect to production and arrivals varies for some districts. This also suggests some market centres specializing in selected commodities for the region, which of course should be substantiated and correlated with typology of markets.

In an attempt to find the quantitative difference between market arrivals and agricultural production of selected commodities, (Table 7), a pattern of inter-district movement of commodities emerges where knowledge limits to few district like Hyderabad with its large population size require the surplus for consumption while West Godavari and Vishakhapatnam districts are the major export districts of the state from where the commodities find their national market.

Thus the present paper is an exploratory venture which provides the preliminary framework for further interrelated analysis which the paper highlights simultaneously. Micro level studies substantiated by empirical analysis may possibly help to test the present findings.

REFERENCES

1. Government of Andhra Pradesh, Annual Report—1984-85 of Department of Marketing (unpublished).
2. Government of Andhra Pradesh, Statistical Abstracts—1984-85 (Published) and Crop Abstracts 1984-85 (Unpublished) Bureau of Economics and Statistics.
3. ICRISAT, *Agricultural Markets in the Semi-Arid Tropics* Proceedings of the International Workshop held at ICRISAT Centre, 1983.
4. Misra R.P., Sundram K.V., and Prakasa Rao, V.L.S, *Regional Development Planning in India*, Vikas Publishing, 1974.
5. NCAER, *Market Towns and Spatial Development in India*,— NCAER, New Delhi, 1965.
6. Smith Carol A (ed.), *Regional Analysis*, Vol. 1, Economic *System*, Academic Press, New York, 1976.
7. Subba Rao, K., *Rice Marketing System and Compulsory* Levies in Andhra Pradesh, Allied Publishers, 1978.
8. Vidyanath, V., *Spatial Variation and Change in Landuse and Cropping Pattern in Andhra Pradesh*, Project Report Sponsored by U.G.C., Department of Geography, Osmania University, Hyderabad, 1985.

TABLE 1

Distribution of Regulated Markets in Andhra Pradesh by Decades—1931-1985

Name of Districts	*1931-40*	*1941-50*	*1951-60*	*1961-70*	*1971-80*	*1981-85*	*Total*
1	*2*	*3*	*4*	*5*	*6*	*7*	*8*
1. Srikakulam			—	9	20	—	29
2. Vishakhapatnam			1	5	10	—	16
3. Vizianagaram			—	11	16	—	27
4. East Godavari			3	13	15	1	32
5. West Godavari			1	13	18	5	37
6. Krishna		1	7	10	12	1	31
7. Guntur		1	16	8	9	5	39
8. Prakasam			2	13	18	—	33
9. Nellore			—	4	22	1	27
Coastal Andhra		2	30	86	140	13	271

(*Contd.*)

1	2	3	4	5	6	7	8
1. Chittoor			4	11	16	5	36
2. Cuddapah			1	7	13	—	21
3. Anantapur			2	9	11	1	23
4. Kurnool			2	7	10	1	20
Rayalaseema			9	34	50	7	100
1. Adilabad	2	1	2	5	14	—	24
2. Ranga Reddy	—	3	1	—	7	—	11
3. Khammam	1	1	1	2	14	1	20
4. Karimnagar	2	5	—	6	12	4	29
5. Mahbubnagar	1	4	3	7	17	1	33
6. Medak	—	2	3	6	7	—	18
7. Nizamabad	1	1	—	11	7	—	20

8. Nalgonda	2	—	2	5	32	1	41
9. Warangal	1	2	1	8	10	1	23
10. Hyderabad	—	—	1	—	—	—	1
Telangana	10	19	14	50	120	8	221
Andhra Pradesh	10	21	53	170	310	28	592

Source: Compiled from the Annual Reports of Department of Marketing—A.P.

TABLE 2

Market Arrivals by Classes in A.P. 1984-85

Classes	*No. of Taluks*	*Arrivals of Quintals*	*As % of Total*
Very High—(>1,000,000 quintals)	26	43,531,000	51.0
High (5000,000-990,999)	16	11,230,000	13.0
Medium (100,000-499,999)	107	25 004,000	29.0
Low (10,000-99,999)	116	5,962,000	6.9
Very Low (<10,000)	22	107,000	0.1
State Total	287	85,834,000	100.0

Source: Compiled from the Annual reports of Department of Marketing—Andhra Pradesh.

TABLE 3

Market Arrivals by Districts in A.P. 1984-85

Districts	*Arrivals in '000 Quintals*	*As % of Total*
1 West Godavari	21,496	25.0
2. Krishna	12,317	14.0
3. East Godavari	7,970	9.0
4. Nalgonda	4,123	5.0
5. Guntur	4,108	5.0
6. Nizamabad	3,585	4.0
7. Kurnool	2,728	3.0
8. Hyderabad	2,690	3.0
9. Mahbubnagar	2,482	3.0
10. Karimnagar	2,466	3.0
11. Vishakhapatnam	2,421	3.0
12. Nellore	2,406	3.0
13. Cuddapah	2,226	3.0
14. Warangal	2,138	2.0
15. Prakasam	2,135	2.0
16. Khammam	1,929	2.0
17. Chittoor	1,599	2.0
18. Srikakulam	1,491	2.0
19. Vizianagaram	1,456	2.0
20. Anantapur	1,228	1.0
21. Medak	1,176	1.0
22. Adilabad	1,168	1.0
23. Rangareddy	496	0.6
Total	85,834	100 0

Source: Compiled from the Annual Reports of Department of Marketing—Andhra Pradesh.

TABLE 4

Per cent Share of Commodities to the total Market Arrivals 1984-85 in Andhra Pradesh

Commodities	*Quantity in Quintals*	*As % of total*
1	*2*	*3*
1. Rice	47442063	65.4
2. Groundnut	5227807	7.2
3. Cotton	3875258	5.3
4. Jaggery	2575223	3.5
5. Onions	2298687	3.2
6. Maize	1752081	2.4
7. Chillies	1227980	1.7
8. Tobacco	1155987	1.6
9. Green Gram	831927	1.1
10. Redgram	771048	1.1
11. Turmeric	764234	1.0
12. Jowar	632620	1.0
13. Jute	570620	1.0
14. Blackgram	581345	1.0
15. Tamarind	441465	0.6
16. Castor Seed	400466	0.5
17. Rovgi	314191	0.4
18. Till Seed	275105	0.4
19. Bajra	255306	0.3
20. Need seed	170530	0.2
21. Horsegram	135830	0.2

(*Contd.*)

1	*2*	*3*
22. Coriander	132450	0.2
23. Carad seed	130839	0.2
24. Wheat	117250	0.2
25. Other Pulses	83113	0.1
26. Bengal gram	59242	0.1
27. Cashewnut	58631	0.1
28. Garlic	53494	0.07
29. Sunflower seed	53494	0.07
30. Ajwan	47535	0.06
31. Tamarind seed	20998	0.03
32. Other oil seeds	18540	0.02
33. Other cereals	18291	0.02
34. Ginger	16978	0 02
35. Other condiments	13395	0.02
36. Cotton seed	10287	0.01
37. Ballar	9003	0.01
38. Ambada seed	8861	0.01
39. Linseed	8611	0.01
40. Niger seed	4731	0.006
41, Lobha	3753	0.005
42. Mustard seed	579	0.0008
43. Moath	309	0.0004
44. Jaw	265	0.0004
45. Mohva seed	25	0.00003
Total	72670447	100.0

Source: Compiled from Annual Reports of Marketing Departments—A.P.

TABLE 4(a)

Per cent Share of Commodities to the total Agricultural Production in Andhra Pradesh—1984-85

Commodities	*Agricultural Production of Principal Crops* *Quantity in '000 Tons*	*As % of Total*
1	*2*	*3*
1. Rice	6909	53.0
2. Groundnut	1258	10.0
3. Jowar	1216	9.0
4. Jaggery	1009	8.0
5. Maize	433	3.3
6. Chillies	254	2.0
7. Ragi	216	2.0
8. Bajra	206	1.6
9. Blackgram	189	1.5
10. Greengram	173	1.3
11. Tobacco	171	1.3
12. Cotton	167	1.3
13. Onions	144	1.1
14. Jute	88	1.0
15. Turmeric	79	1.0
16. Korra	74	0.6
17. Horsegram	62	0.5

(*Contd.*)

1	*2*	*3*
18. Redgram	56	0.4
19. Castor	56	0.4
20. Varagu	35	0.3
21. Coriander	34	0.3
22. Bengal gram	18	0.1
23. Samai	10	0.1
24. Wheat	8	0.1
25. Seasmum	8	0.1
26. Ginger	7	0.05
27. Other small millets	5	0.04
28. Other pulses	3	0.02
29. Garlic	3	0.02
30. Cowgram	2	0.01
Total	12893	100.0

Source: Compiled from Statistical Abstracts.

APPENDIX-I

I. Salient Features of Hyderabad Agricultural Market Act-1930

There was a Market Committee, established for each trade Centre and the areas of the market and the limits of the market yards to be notified. The notified area extended to a radius of eight to twenty kms around the market and no other market was allowed to function within this area.

The Act was operative to Agricultural produce numbering fiftyfour commodities besides fruits and vegetables and livestock.

Seventytwo markets in Telangana Region are regulated under this Act.

II. Salient Features of the Madras Commercial Crops Market Act-1933.

The jurisdiction of the Market Committee extended to the entire Revenue District for establishment of Market yard in the notified area. Only a few commercial crops in each district were covered for regulation.

Fortyfive markets in Andhra Region are regulated under this Act.

III. Salient Feature of Andhra Pradesh Agricultural Produce and Livestock Markets Act-1966.

As there was great variation in the modern-operandi of the markets regulated under two different market legislations, an imperative need was felt for the coverage of the entire marketable surpluses in Andhra Pradesh under a single markets legislation to give the benefit of regulation squarely to a large number of grower-sellers. Thus with a view to bringing about uniformity in functioning of markets in Telangana and Andhra region and to extend the scope of the Act to regulate the trade in livestock products, pisciculture, horticulture, besides agricultural produce, the Government of Andhra Pradesh, enacted the 'Andhra Pradesh (Agricultural Produce and Livestock) Markets Act, 1966' and the same was promulgated in the State with effect from 19th October, 1967.

Source: A booklet on Regulated Markets in Andhra Pradesh, issued by the Department of Marketing—Andhra Pradesh.

TABLE 5

Per cent Share of Important Commodities to total Market Arrivals in Andhra Pradesh by Districts- 984-85

Districts | Quantity in Quintals*

1	2	3	4	5	6	7	8	9
	Rice	% of Total	Jute	% of Total	Others	% of Total	Total	
1. Srikakulam	705717	57.0	195676	15.8	(14) 337681	27.2	1239074	
	Jaggery	% of Total	Rice	% of Total	Others	% of Total	Total	
2. Visakhapatnam	915438	38.1	901958	37.5	(22) 586278	24.4	2403674	
	Rice	% of Total	Jute	% of Total	Others	% of Total	Total	
3. Vizianagaram	448910	32.2	348127	25.0	(21) 594702	42.8	1391739	
	Rice	% of Total	Others	% of Total	Total			
4. East Godavari	6015549	92.9	(22) 460014	7.1	6475563			
	Rice	% of Total	Others	% of Total	Total			
5. West Godavari	17120411	95.4	(14) 814890	4.6	17935501			
	Rice	% of Total	Others	% of Total	Total			

6. Krishna	8142061	81.1	(17) 1901051	18.9	10043112		
	Rice	% of Total	Cotton	% of Total	Others	% of Total	Total
7. Guntur	1641248	46.9	1202198	34.4	(10) 652056	18.7	3495502
	Tobacco	% of Total	Ricc	% of Total	Others	% of Total	Total
8. Prakasam	667500	35.0	614504	32.2	(17) 625488	32.8	1907492
	Rice	% of Total	Others	% of Total	Total		
9. Nellore	1630402	85.2	(16) 282334	14.8	1912736		
	Jaggery	% of Total	Groundnut	% of Total	Others	% of Total	Total
10. Chittoor	653941	42.7	358681	23.4	(14) 519478	33.9	1532100
	Groundnut	% of Total	Rice	% of Total	Others	% of Total	Total
11. Cuddapah	668213	31.0	623114	28.9	(14) 864519	40.1	2155846
	Groundnut	% of Total	Others	% of Total	Total		
12. Anantapur	753639	61.6	(17) 469014	38.4	1222653		
	Groundnut	% of Total	Cotton	% of Total	Others	% of Total	Total
13. Kurnool	944241	36.7	688216	26.8	(16) 937970	36.5	2570427
	Cotton	% of Total	Others	% of Total	Total		

(*Contd.*)

1	2	3	4	5	6	7	8	9
14. Adilabad	993521	85.7	(29) 165278	14.3	1158799			
	Onions	% of Total	Rice	% of Total	Others	% of Total	Total	
15. Hydrabad	1021700	44.0	875762	37.7	(23) 424622	18.3	2322084	
	Onions	% of Total	Redgram	% of Total	Rice % of Total	Others	% of Total	Total
16. Ranga Reddy	89649	19.2	80771	17.0	72865 15.6	(35) 223788	48.2	467073
	Rice	% of Total	Others	% of Total	Total			
17. Khammam	781206	44.4	(19) 842484	55.6	1623690			
	Rice	% of Total	Others	% of Total	Total			
18. Karimnagar	1055956	52.4	(21) 957691	47.6	2013647			
	Rice	% of Total	Groundnut	% of Total	Others % of Tot.	Total		
19. Mahbubnagar	982601	47.6	665881	32.3	(29) 414615 20.1	2063097		
	Rice	% of Total	Others	% of Total	Total			
20. Medak	567848	60.2	(37) 375602	39.8	943450			
	Rice	% of Total	Turmeric	% of Total	Jaggery % of Total	Others	% of Total	Total

21. Nizamabad	1202291	38.7	372831	12.0	313314	10.1 (33) 1217149	39.2	3105585
	Rice	% of Total	Others	% of Total	Total			
22. Nalgonda	24433709	77.5	(34) 706232	22.5	3139941			
	Rice	% of Total	Others	% of Total	Total			
23 Warangal	898606	51.2	(27) 854780	48.8	1753386			

*Figures in Paranthesis indicate the number of other commodities.

Source: Compiled from the Annual Report of Development of Marketing—Andhra Pradesh.

TABLE 6

Per cent Share of Principal crops to total Agricultural Production in A.P. by Districts—1984-85
(Production in '000 Tonnes)*

Districts					
	Rice	% of Total	Groundnuts	% of Total	Jaggery
1. Srikakulam	248	60.0	41	10.0	31
	Rice	% of Total	Jute	% of Total	Groundnut
2. Vizianagaram	175	48.0	58	16.0	53
	Jaggery	% of Total	Rice	% of Total	Others
3. Vishakhapatnam	103	30.0	88	26.0	(25) 153
	Rice	% of Total	Jaggery	% of Total	Others
4. East Godavari	882	84.0	106	10.0	(25) 62
	Rice	% of Total	Others	% of Total	Total
5. West Godavari	1194	84.0	(25) 226	16.0	1420
	Rice	% of Total	Others	% of Total	Total

6. Krishna	838	73.0	(25) 303	26.5	1141
	Rice	% of Total	Others	% of Total	Total
7. Guntur	622	63.0	(24) 361	37.0	983
	Rice	% of Total	Jowar	% of Total	Tobacco
8. Prakasam	138	31.0	59	13.0	50
	Rice	% of Total	Others	% of Total	Total
9. Nellore	366	75.0	(24) 122	25.0	488
	Jowar	% of Total	Groundnut	% of Total	Rice
10. Kurnool	245	38.0	129	20.0	126
	Jowar	% of Total	Others	% of Total	Total
11. Adilabad	138	52.0	(25) 127	48.0	265
	Groundnut	% of Total	Others	% of Total	Total
12. Anantapur	280	53.0	(25) 251	47.0	531
	Rice	% of Total	Jowar	% of Total	Groundnut
13. Cuddapah	105	30.0	74	21.0	73
	Groundnut	% of Total	Rice	% of Total	Jaggery

(*Contd.*)

Table 6 (*Contd.*)

14. Chittoor	245	34.0	224	31.0	183
	Rice	% of Total	Jowar	% of Total	Others
15. Ranga Reddy	90	32.4	88	32.0	(27) 100
	Rice	% of Total	Jaggery	% of Total	Maize
16. Nizamabad	288	47.0	139	23.0	105
	Rice	% of Total	Jaggery	% of Total	Jowar
17. Medak	151	38.0	85	21.0	80
	Rice	% of Total	Jowar	% of Total	Groundnut
18. Mahbubnagar	123	31.0	102	26.0	77
	Rice	% of Total	Others	% of Total	Total
19. Nalgonda	466	72.0	(22) 179	28.0	645
	Rice	% of Total	Others	% of Total	Total
20. Warangal	172	46.0	(26) 206	54.0	378
	Jowar	% of Total	Rice	% of Total	Others
21. Khammam	138	28.0	105	29.0	(23) 121
	Rice	% of Total	Maize	% of Total	Others
22. Karimnagar	357	54.0	190	29.0	(21) 111

Source: Compiled from Statistical Abstract.

*Figures in paranthesis indicate the number of other commodities.

TABLE 6 (*Contd.*)

Per cent Share of Principal Crops to Total Agricultural Production in A.P. by Disstricts—1984-85 (Production in '000 Tonnes)*

1	*2*	*3*	*4*	*5*	*6*	*7*
Districts						
	% of Total	Jute	% of Total	Others	% of Total	Total
1. Srikakulam	7.5	27	6.5	(18) 65	16	412
	% of Total	Jaggery	% of Total	Others	% of Total	Total
2. Vizianagaram	14.0	34	9.0	(18) 46	12.5	366
	% of Total	Total				
3. Vishakhapatnam	44.0	344				
	% of Total	Total				
4. East Godavari	6.0	1050				
5. West Godavari						
6. Krishna						

Table 6 (*Contd.*)

1	2	3	4	5	6	7
7. Guntur						
	% of Total	Others	% of Total	Total		
8. Prakasam	11.0	(25) 204	45.1	451		
9. Nellore						
	% of Total	Others	% of Total	Total		
10. Kurnool	19.0	(25) 150	23.0	650		
11. Adilabad						
12. Anantapur						
	% of Total	Others	% of Total	Total		
13. Cuddapah	21.0	(24) 101	29.0	353		
	% of Total	Others	% of Total	Total		
14. Chittoor	26.0	(25) 67	9.0	719		
	% of Total	Total				

15. Ranga Reddy	36.0	273		
	% of Total	Others	% of Total	Total
16. Nizamabad	17.0	(27) 76	13.0	603
	% of Total	Others	% of Total	Total
17. Medak	20.0	(25) 90	23.0	396
	% of Total	Others	% of Total	Total
18. Mahbubnagar	20.0	(26) 90	23.0	292
19. Nalgonda				
20. Warangal				
	% of Total	Total		
21. Khammam	33.0	364		
	% of Total	Total		
22. Karimnagar	17.0	658		

TABLE 7

Per cent of Market Arrives to Agricultural Production of Selected Commodities of A.P.—by Districts—1984-85

(Quantity in '000 Quintals)

Districts	*Rice Production*	*Rice Arrivals*	*% of Arrivals of production*	*Cotton Production*	*Cotton Arrivals*	*% of Arrivals to production*	*Tobacco Production*	*Tobacco Arrivals*	*% of Arrivals to Production*
1. Srikakulam	2480	706	28.5	N	—	—	N	—	—
2. Vizianagaram	1750	449	25.6	—	—	—	20	3	15.0
3. Vishakhapatnam	880	902	10.2	—	—	—	40	0.5	1.2
4. East Godavari	8820	6016	68.2	2	9	450.0	130	23	17.7
5. West Godavari	11940	1712	14.3	2	—	—	330	392	111.8
6. Krishna	8380	8142	97.2	75	294	392.0	120	17	14.2
7. Guntur	6220	1641	26.4	843	1202	142.6	60	—	—
8. Prakasam	1380	615	44.6	298	228	76.6	500	668	133.6
9. Nellore	3660	1630	44.5	12	21	175.0	60	24	40.0

10. Kurnool	1260	399	31.6	173	688	397.7	190	—	—
11. Anantapur	840	99	10.7	46	138	300.0	N	—	—
12. Cuddapah	1050	623	59.3	2	158	7600.0	N	—	—
13. Chittoor	2240	278	12.4	—	—	—	N	—	—
14. Ranga Reddy	900	73	8.1	N	1	—	N	—	—
15. Hyderabad	10	876	8760.0	—	—	—	—	—	—
16. Nizamabad	3830	1202	42.5	3	72	2400.0	N	—	—
17. Medak	1510	568	37.6	N	—	—	10	—	—
18. Mahbubnagar	1230	983	79.9	17	0.01	0.1	30	1	3.3
19. Nalgonda	4660	2434	52.2	5	34	680.0	20	1	5.0
20. Warangal	1720	899	52.3	70	79	113.0	20	—	—
21. Khammam	1050	721	68.7	3	28	933.3	140	26	18.6
22. Karimnagar	3570	1059	29.6	3	0.1	3.0	40	—	—
23. Adilabad	710	21	2.9	119	994	835.3	N	—	—

N=Negligible

Source: Compiled by the Author from Annual Report of Department of Marketing, A.P. and Statistical Abstract.

Table 7 (Contd.)

Distrrct	*Chillies Production*	*Chillies Arrivals*	*% of Arrivals to Prodnction*	*Jaggery Production*	*Jaggery Arrivals*	*% of Arrivals to Production*	*Groundnut Production*	*Groundnut Arrivals*	*% of Arrivals to Production*
1.	70	43	61.4	310	53	17.1	410	116	28.3
2.	40	21	525	340	166	48.8	530	167	31.5
3.	110	103	93.6	1030	915	88.8	270	172	63.7
4.	40	25	62.5	1060	52	4.9	90	63	70.0
5.	110	56	51.0	1510	214	14.2	110	29	26.4
6.	260	18	7.0	850	104	12.2	280	125	44.6
7.	630	382	60.6	190	—	—	530	121	22.8
8.	210	7	3.3	30	1	3.3	270	59	21.8
9.	110	43	39.1	90	11	12.2	440	92	20.9
10.	40	1	2.5	80	7	9.0	1290	944	73.2
11.	20	8	40.0	N	7	—	2800	756	26.9
12.	20	84	420.0	200	41	20.5	730	668	91.5
13.	20	4	20.0	1830	654	35.7	2450	359	14.6

14.	50	0.01	0.02	170	1	1.4	50	38	76.0
15.	—	40	—	—	25	—	—	8	—
16.	50	11	22.0	1390	313	22.5	60	18	30.0
17.	20	5	25.0	850	12	1.4	30	14	46.7
18.	70	0.01	0.01	N	—	—	770	666	86.5
19.	50	0.2	0.4	40	—	—	550	258	46.9
20.	130	165	126.9	—	—	—	470	206	43.8
21.	370	193	52.2	50	0.3	0.6	230	156	67.9
22.	100	15	15.0	40	—	—	220	191	86.8
23.	20	1	5.0	30	—	—	N	2	—

N=Negl'gible

Source: Compiled by the Author from Annual Report of Department of Marketing. A.P. and Statistical Abstract.

SECTION III

HUMAN RESOURCES

India with its population of over seven hundred millions is richly endowed with human resources. However, if we have to consider human resources as a base for economic development, the qualitative aspects of the resource should also be evaluated Quantity alone may not be helpful for eeonomic and social development of the country; on the other hand, it may tend to become a drag on the country's economy. Therefore, availability and proper utilisation of man-power, literacy levels, physical and mental efficiency of population should be the criteria for the estimation of human resources.

In the first article of this section, S. Jayachandran makes a scholarly analysis of human resource development as the base for economic development of the country. According to him, economic development of a region is dependent on two major factors, namely material development and human development. The basic issue is the lack of literacy to pursue and innovate things on the one side and gainfully use and accept diffused knowledge on the other. He adds that there should be a qualitative improvement in man who can be more meaningfully utilized in the economic development of a region.

The second paper in this section is on human time budgets in agriculture. The authors in their inimitable highly readable style putforth their views in detail on this novel topic.

The time is considered as a *subjective time*, as against general social time. They observe that the allocational attributes of human time budgets indicate use and under-utilization is merely a result of cultivation practices and seasons of cropping.' They think that a time geographic approach can act as a means to answering policy questions about how society should be organised and how activity patterns can be structured. 'It is possible to derive perspectives: one is the articulation of agricultural operations, and the other is the devising of means of overcoming and under employment via planning for increased use of time.'

12

HUMAN RESOURCE DEVELOPMENT–THE BASIS FOR ECONOMIC DEVELOPMENT

S. JAYACHANDRAN*

Planning in India has been an exercise that has been adopted only recently. No doubt, India has been registering some development before the dawn of independence but that was without any plan. Subseqently, emphasis was laid for the development of different areas but again this was done in a haphazard manner without conforming to any laid out plan. For example, agriculture was permitted to expand at the expense of forest lands. No appropriate steps were taken to increase the yields. The Agricultural Research Institutes have been conducting research more in the form of an academic exercise, mostly confined to the people engaged in research activities. The information thus acquired had not diffused among the larger society of agriculturists.

India adopted sectoral planning. It was found that only such sectors which came into the fold of planning were given priority and others were either neglected or totally left out. The system

*Dr. S. Jayachandran is Professor and Head, Department of Geography, Madurai Kamaraj University, Alagarkoil Road, MADURAI—625 002.

was found to be inadequate. Hence integrated planning was advocated in recent years.

During the days of the British Rule, the people of the country were introduced to higher education. This higher education was carefully planned by them mainly to produce the required man-power to be gainfully employed by them in the day to day local administration. The courses of education were planned to give a general education only with a very limited degree of specialisation. Even this specialisation was aimed to produce teachers in various subjects for teaching in the schools and colleges. Professional education such as legal, engineering and medicine had limited encouragement. Vocational training institutes were virtually non existant. The British were interested to keep India as their major consumer for manufactured goods and so they did not show any interest to encourage vocational training centres or opening modern factories. It is only under pressure from such Indian entrepreneurs who were mostly pro-British in their outlook were permitted to start certain industries. Their product was only to supply to the poor strata of the society who cannot afford to pay for the imported goods. A few of their family members were permitted to have higher education in England. So it was lack of encouragement that has held the Indian mass in bay but their capabilities of learning cannot be questioned.

With the advent of independence, India had to struggle against several problems. Scientific and technological knowledge which had by them spread widely and had taken deep roots in certain countries, which are now well developed, were not available to India. Adding to this misery the population had been recording very rapid growth and the influx of refugees has been enormous. So without adequate financial assistance from friendly countries, as well as technical know-how, India could not establish large industries to record economic development.

There are several stages that had to be gone through before achieving economic development in its true sense. Foremost among them is the assessment of potentialities of land, soil, water, mineral, biotic and human resources. Being primarily an agricultural country with a large population to be fed, it became the primary requirement to assess the resources for agricultural development.

In the true spirit of the traditional system, it was assessed that water is the most important requirment for the agricultural development. Steps have been taken to harness the water sources and make them available to the farmer for the purpose of cultivation. But it was realised nearly thirty years later that the farmer had to be told about water management and conservation. Only now, steps are being taken to educate the farmer in water management. High yielding varieties were introduced first. A few farmers were impressed and started using them. Subsequently they gave up the high yielding varieties mainly because other infrastructural facilities needed such as chemical fertilizers, insecticides and pesticides were not made available. Hence the yield became lesser than the conventional varieties. This was mainly because of the lack of adequate supply which had to be mostly imported. The HYV can yield only if all the components are made available together. Soil surveys are conducted only recently and the soil qualities of all areas are not available. As a result the farmers are unable to make appropriate selection of crops or the right type of chemical fertilizer that is suitable to the plant as well as the soil.

The country has not set apart grazing grounds though it has the largest cattle population. Marginal lands were used for grazing which has been taken away for agriculture in their extension programme. The villagers were permitted to graze their cattle in the forests by paying a very nominal sum. In course of time the cattle, sheep and especially goats were able to deplete the rich forest wealth. Added to this the villagers not only cut the trees for their use as firewood but make a living out of it illegaly. The Government granted licence for some contractors for felling trees to supply them as firewood for the neighbouring towns.

Most of the time our aim had been to use the resources of the land, but the proper method of utilization of the resources through training was not contemplated. In the sixth plan extensive measures were taken to give training to the farmers. Till then agriculture, forestry and mining lacked a systematic approach through proper training. This resulted in enormous wastages of precious resources. Only now it is realised that people should be trained for a systematic use of the resources in order to gain maximum advantages. It is not enough that a country has a variety of natural resources. It is also not enough that the country has sufficient population. If the people do not know the use of the resources then it may remain unused. On the otherhand if the people do not know the proper use of those resources, then the resources may be either used wastefully or exhausted by using them improperly. Therefore, it is necessary to have those people engaged in the utilization of resources properly trained so that the resources will be properly used in a more meaningful way. Hence attention is diverted now towards imparting the training at various levels for the people their.

The geographical diversity of the country has left us with a multitude of natural conditions each differing from the other, demanding a careful observation and analysis for their successful utilization. The conditions prevailing in the south are different when compared to those in the west, north or east. It is only by judicious use, man can succeed in imparting development. So knowledge about the regions—geographical or otherwise should be known.

The economic development ot a region in a country is based solely on the people. It is necessary to create an awareness among the people—awareness for identifying and using the resources meaningfully and gainfully—awareness of conservation and appropriate use—awareness of rearing and multiplying as in the case of livestock, fishery, poultry etc.,—awareness of scientific methods for improving the agricultural yield and economising the use of fuel of all types at all levels. To achieve all these above mentioned goals appropriate development of human resources is necessary.

This basic requirements of a society are to understand the above said things, to have the potential for creative thinking and to have a healthy mind and a healthy body. The first two can be achieved by educating our masses and the latter by providing nutritious food in sufficient quantity and providing health care facilities.

The country is endowed with adequate information in every walk of life but we do not have the followers in adequate numbers. There was a time when people were unaware of the existence of certain information. But in the last decade or more thanks to the mass media many useful information are repeatedly told so that people can benefit by using them. Still the rate of diffusion is considered to be rather slow, resulting in the large section of the society not being aware of many useful information.

In order to specifically give instances and lay emphasis on the development of human resources, Dharmapuri district in Tamilnadu is chosen. Dharmapuri district is situated in the interior plateau of Tamilnadu at an average altitude of 450m to 900m with a rainfall of about 850 mm. The rugged topography, low rainfall, inadequate surface drainage as well as groundwater resources have made agriculture difficult. Irrigation is possible only in patches, mainly due to topographic conditions. Though the entire district lies on the southern part of the Deccan Plateau, it is not endowed with adequate mineral resources worth mentioning. One of the important resource of the region is livestock.

The population of the district is roughly 20 lakhs which is approximately 4 per cent of the population of Tamilnadu. This is spread over 9619 sq. km. Which is roughly 7 per cent of the area of the state. Thus the density of population is only 207 persons per sq. km. as against the state average of 371 persons. Ninetyone per cent of the population is rural and only 9 per cent is urban. Though they are classified as urban it is interesting to note the number of towns found in the district and their average size. There are in all seven towns, out of which one has a population of little over 50,000, two are with 25,000—50,000 and four towns with less than 20,000 population. Out of the total population, 59 per cent are non workers. This speaks about the non-availability of occupation either in agriculture or in non-agriculture pursuits. Nearly 83 per cent of the workers are engaged in agriculture, while industry engages only 1.8 per cent. Since the rainfall is low and irrigation potential is very limited only 12 per cent of the total area under cultivation is irrigated. Only 2.6 per cent of the irrigated area of the state is found in Dharmapuri district. Under these conditions only dry farming is prevalent. The agricultural surplus is very small leaving little scope to engage people in tertiary activities of transport, trade and communication. Even the scope for service centres is neglegent.

Lack of literacy is a major constraint in the development of the society. Though primary education is compulsory, the enrolment recorded in this district is only 82 per cent of the children in the age group of 5-9 years. The state average is 95. But in the middle school, in the age group of 10-12 years, the percentage falls to 27 as against the state average of 56. In the high school from 13-16 years it is 14 per cent against the state average of 36. There we find a sudden fall in the middle school level. After the 10th year of age the parents take away their children for grazing cattle and sheep and to help them in their agriculture. The small land owners are unable to employ labour on wages. Without additional expenditure these children provide the labour force. Thus the district records very low literacy levels.

The number of children taken to higher education is very low. There are two colleges with an enrolment of about 1000 students in each of them. There are two Industrial Training Institutes where they are trained as artisans for various industries. The strength of these two institutes may not exceed 500. There are no polytechnics or engineering colleges of higher-learning. There is a conspicuous absence of any form vocational educational facilities in the district. But new industrial estates have been established thanks to the encouragement given by the State Government. But most of the skilled and semi-skilled labourers have come from outside the district. So the general educational level as well as vocational educational level of the people are deplorable.

Health problem embraces the entire society. Health care is an integral part of a developmental system. Our development plans addresses itself to the release of creative initiative of the vast masses of rural areas to improve their economic conditions but does not bestow attention on the health care system. Organised health care system in a developing country is out of reach for the majority of population, especially for those who are living in rural areas. One of the major problems is the rate of growth of population. The awareness of small families have not been instilled in the minds of the people in the villages and such family planning programmes will take more time to bear fruits. Until such time adequate facilities should be provided and expectant mothers and children that are born should be taken care of. Lack of health care and nutritious food has been responsible for a high rate of mortality and morbidity among the children. Even the facilities recommended by the State Health Department is not fulfilled in this district. As per health department recommendations based on population, there should be 199 health care centres at the rate of one centre for every 10,000 population. But there are only 68 centres at present, which works out roughly to 35 per cent of the requirements. There is one doctor for every 30,000 people, *i.e.*, he has to look after six times more number and one bed for every 5200 people which is tentimes more With such poor facilities, it is next to impossibility to think of a society with a healthy mind and healthy body.

With low agricultural productivity and with little scope for intensifying the agricultural operations, with very small proportion of the population engaged in secondary and tertiary activities, the per capita income is very low. People with such low income practically struggle to get adequate food every day. Many do not get even one adequate meal a day. Under these circumstances one cannot expect them to get nutritious food. Nutritional and vitamin deficiencies are widely prevalent through the entire cross section of the society in the district, irrespective of caste or even literacy. Those who have adequate income may get adequate food which need not be nutritious food. It is estimated that only 20 per cent of the upper strata of the society can afford to buy such nutritious food. But lack of literacy and awareness may leave him out from selecting nutritious food. The remaining 80 per cent of the expenditure of the people is on non-discretionary food. The calorie needs are better fulfilled in this district when compared to her neighbours. This may be mainly due to the fact that crops are highly diversified. But more than half of the population get less than 80 per cent calorie needs. A change and improvement in nutritional status is essentially a problem of behavioural change. Appropriate nutrition education of elders in the family and proper identifica-cation of supplementary good for the infants is more important than its relation to income. In order to check morbidity and mortality for among children, the State Government has launched an ambitious plan and mortality providing nutritious noon-meals to all school going children in the primary school level.

The foregoing discussions prove beyond doubt that the economic development of a region is closely associated with human development.

The economic development of a region is totally dependent on material resource development. Effective and meaningful resource development is a human endeavour. The man power behind it should be equipped with education, health and nutritious food so that there is better understanding and awareness, to exercise his ability and skill. In short there should be a qualitative improvement in man who can be more meaningfully utilized in the economic development of a region. At present this qualitative improvement is lacking which can be attributed for the poor resource development which in turn has resulted in poor economic development.

13

TIME AS A RESOURCE: HUMAN TIME BUDGETS IN AGRICULTURE

T. VASANTHA KUMARAN*
S. ARUCHAMY*

> A day has 24, a week 168, a year about 8,800 hours. From day to day, week to week, year, to year, this amount of time falls to the share of the poor and the rich, the young and the old, men and women—in short to everybody on this globe of ours, irrespective of nationality, mother-tongue, colour, political or religious conviction and of his position in society . . . The question of how he spends these . . . hours, how he must and how he may spend it is not so simple and not so equitably solved . . . It is primarily his fellow men's social activity that man quantifies and coordinates by means of time.
>
> —Szalai, 1964: 105 quoted in Parkes and Thrift, 1980: 147-148.

The present paper is about human time budgets in agriculture. Time considered here is the subjective time. As a social

*Department of Geography, University of Madras, Madras—600 005.

factor, in and of itself, it becomes variable in its own right because its quantity is finite. Time is a scarce resource because we perceive alternative uses for it. It is allocated for a variety of purposes, and any one set of time allocations is a time budget. In agriculture, human time budget is most important, for at least in the third world, human time accounts for the largest input (direct cost) value. That is human labour is the strongest input. Human time budget therefore is a quantitative measure of relationship, input-output, for evaluating agriculture. The paper stems essentially from the author's own earlier work and considers two important facets of agriculture: human-labour input via annual labour schedule and time-space budgets.

Time as a Resource

Time like space is a primitive form of human experience (Harvey, 1969:410). No matter where they live, people have always been concerned with *timing*, however little or much they may care about the use of it. They are necessarily pre-occupied with the practical problems of allocating time, of co-ordinating activities (Lynch, 1972:66). Since time sense is a component of behaviour which consequently makes an impress on the world, being aware of the possible significance of time, sense in human geography is the geographers' responsibility (Parkes and Thrift, 1980:67). Time is a resource in as much as it is allocated (or spent) and this allocation is difficult, not simple and not equitably solved even in a society like ours, which by Linder's (1970) classification, more so in an application of it, is a *time-surplus* culture.

It is true that in terms of time *unutilized* (or man hours lost through un-and under-employment) ours is a time-surplus culture. On the other hand, paradoxically, we find it difficult (as agriculturists, industrial workers, and service personnel) to allocate time between several activities because we do not indeed have unlimited time is thus. Time scarce, and it is this scarcity, as you will see, the paper is all about.

All economic activities, are social processes. They involve the principle of regulation of space and time: the timing of space and the spacing of time. If we consider our society as time-surplus, it (the idea) presumes that the variety of activity is limited. But as we know it, it is not true, at least from a scale society perspective. We have too many people (because of population explosion) to accommodate, even with a variety of activities. Considered in the context of total population, the time budget of our society appears to include a lot of slack or unused time. It is not an *individual worker's* time that is thus considered; it is time in general, such as it is objectively thought of by everybody in a single civilization (see Zerubavel, 1976:87). This category of *general* social time expresses a time common to the population.

The subjective sense of time, in the context of activities, cannot be allowed to assume the meaning of general social time, because it would unduly distort the meaning of time as a scarce resource, allocated to activities. Time has a *subjective character*, Time—subjective time—can be calibrated. Activities can be tagged as to their time use. And people order their behaviour (activity related) in correspondence with a fixed, but available time for an activity. Moore (1963:8-9) has stated that,

> 'if activities have no temporal order, they have no order at all.'

Since *timing* is an intrinsic quality of all personal and collective behaviour, activities indicate the nature of this behaviour, because they (activities) involve time ordering (or shall we say regulation?). In carrying out activities, time is partitioned, measured and standardized, satisfies practical need and common sense and represents thus a reality that, even where a culture is time-surplus in general social time sense, it (culture) is not necessarily so in a subjective time sense. In short, our society does express that time is a scarce resource, the allocation of which is significantly important in the context of activities. In agriculture, it is more so. Two important characteristics of our agriculture makes all the difference to the meaning of subjective time:

1. While a farm family—and even a regional aggregate of it—has some part of its available labour (in man labour days) un-or underutilized, it is also constrained by bottlenecks in peak labour demand, often resorting to hired and exchange labour.
2. The utilization is further constrained by the *seasons* of agricultural activity, as also the *indivisibility* of human beings (especially constraint): that is, the fact a single person cannot do *two* things at a time.

Human Time Budgets in Agriculture

The material for analysis is drawn from two studies carried out in 1983 and 1985 by the authors (Kumaran, 1983; Kumaran and Aruchamy, 1986). However, the conceptual basis is that of Timing Space and Spacing Time, or for short, TSST.

In recent times, TSST has been one of the several strands of geographic research carried out at the Madras University, Department of Geography (also see Kumaran, 1983; Suseela, 1985; Kumaran and Suseela 1986). Several western studies exist on this theme focussing however on different systems of agriculture (Carlstein, 1982), TSST (Carlstein, Parkes, and Thrift, 1978, in three volumes) and built environments, especially cities (Parkes and Thrift, 1980). Time space budgets, these studies indicate, have great relevance for landuse planning and human behaviour analysis.

In the context of agriculture, in India the philosophy and the methodology behind TSST is vary relevant, and at least two context warrant such an application:

1. Human capital (labour days, hence time use) as an input in agriculture is the most important link in the technological inputs (for example: Bharadwaj, 1974; Chakraborty, 1982; Kumaran, 1983; Aruchamy, 1986).

2. Use of time by workers (Family labour, hired or exchange or attached labour) in different, classified agricultural activities (field preparation to post-harvest operations) and the space-time budgets that can be generated out of such use.

The studies of Kumaran (1983) and Aruchamy (1986) have clearly brought out the fact that Indian agriculture (both cases are from Tamil Nadu) is still very largely traditional and that the efforts that have gone on in the past two and half decades have not, in the two cases, made a very appreciable dent in the *hold* of tradition, though it is possible to categorize it as one certainly moving in the direction of greater modernization.

Aruchamy's study, of the Kambam valley in Madurai district (ı986), a semi-arid area, is in a transition from *tradition to modernization* and also is in the prcoess of *From-Peasant-to-Farmer*, and this is clear from the tendency of the factor scorces clustering around zero, with low plus or minus scores (398 observations, 57 variables). This study has applied factor analysis to agricultural and managerial inputs by the owner-cultivation farm operators. On the other hand, Kumaran's study of the tribal agriculture in the Kolli hills of Salem district (1983) using factor analysis has concluded that agriculture here is still tradition bound, though modern inputs (seeds, fertilizers, etc.) have long been in use, following Green Revolution of the 1960s, and integrated Rural Development Programmes of the 1970s and their implementation in the tribal area under Tribal Block Development Scheme since 1963. In both, human capital input, the farm and crop profiles indicate, is found to be high, proportionally, and is over 40 per cent of the direct costs.

The two facets (or contexts) above are considered seminally important in both the studies for overcoming, besides others, at least two problems: one, regulating initially, and monitoring finally of the rural exodus into towns and cities (the imbalance in annual labour schedules, of family farms and collective regional, is the principal reason for it, we shall see this a while later), and two, human labour utilization problems in various agricultural activities with respect to family farms (small, medium farms, especially).

Time Schedules in Agriculture

Agricultural development, in terms of time budgets, presumes a change from a time-surplus culture to a time-affluent culture. Subsistance economy represents a time-surplus culture where productivity is low and that a certain proportion of time yields little or nothing. There is little need for precision in time reckoning. On the other hand, diversified and specialised economies have an adequate time supply; in these time-affluent cultures a process of economic growth has started and extended stretches of unfilled time have largely disappeared. Certain aspects of modern Indian culture is an example of this category (small scale industrial economy in the country) whereas the larger part of our society is still time-surplus (being traditional in agriculture and subsistence therefore for a great part). We would move into time-famine culture, where no slacks in the supply of the time resources would exist (our urban economies, especially the metropolitan ones, are in this category), and all that remain would be further colonization of time (see Melbin, 1978; Parkes and Thrift, 1980:88).

Time is however important in a seasonal context; and in our cultures, it is a *rhythmic order*: for a festivities mark a new cycle (Nalleru or 'first plough' in Tamil Nadu marks such a cycle; *Pongal* or the 'harvest festival' marks the end of it) and the reenactment of myth provides for periodic re entry into the past (Kritigai or the 'bonfire festival', and Deepavali or the 'festival of light in Tamilnadu).

Agriculture, in a seasonal context, also demands more accurate time and space measurement, though their joint status is not in fact as complex. And it is certain, agricultural schedules demanded by crops and their cultivation derive from the temporal behaviuor of crops, people, and animals and the need to produce surplus food to store over unproductive seasons and this is an insurance against unpredictable circumstances. Several events in our agricultural society are fixed in time and over space but have property of recurrence: for example, we are so tuned to climatic elemencies-rainfall—that our activities are fixed in time and that we are also fixed over space in the sense that our crops—paddy, wheat, etc.—have their own areas of cultivation. The tasks associated with these events—such as those of field preparation, transplantation, irrigation, weeding, application of fertilizers, harvest and post-harvest operations (see Table 1)—form distinct cycles of activities. These cycles of activities and the recurrence of certain physical events, monsoon for example, become the basis of time measurement.

A Simple Human Time Budget

Table 1 is indicative of several interesting features in agricultural schedules. The most important are:

1. A crop of about 3-4 months, paddy requires about 148 man labour days or 1480 hours of work, and the distribution of human time use varies with different activities.
2. Transplanting and weeding require 35 labour days or 350 hours each. Irrigation requires 15 man days only as most paddy areas are canal/tank irrigated areas and the flow of water is only regulated. Fertilizers/pesticides application involves the least number of labour days as they require only a few hours because of the practice of broadcasting and spraying.
3. The distribution of human time (in panel one) changes into an altogether different one when labour days are redistributed by months (panel two) and this happens because activities listed in panel one do not occur in the order they are presented but always in a mix of two or more. For instance, field preparation may also include 'basal dressing' in which either fertilizers or green manures are applied to enrich the soil nutrient.

What is not immediately clear may be the contribution of male and female workers. Weeding is an exclusively female dominated activity, though occasionally male workers do the job. Harvest and post-harvest operations are usually done by both male and female workers. And this is also true of transplantation, though there is a definite division of labour or role association: while Female workers usually transplant seedlings (the planting), male workers merely facilitate planting (uprooting seedlings from nurseries, bundling into sheaves, transporting to prepared fields, supplying the sheaves to planting women). For several areas however there is role-switching among the workers, that is, males do female work, females do male work. Thus, there is indeed no sex differentiated role playing. It is also important to note that the female workers' contribution is anywhere between 40-50 per cent of the work and in some areas female contribution in agriculture is the largest (the tribal agriculture for example, Kumaran, 1983).

One labour day is never strictly eight hours. In agriculture, it is often of longer duration; even as much as twelve hours a day for both man and woman. Marx for example has conceived of time as a resource in his equations defining *surplus* value. In our agriculture, exploitation of labour consists of extracting more time from a labourer than is required to produce goods having the value of his or her wages (also see Heirich, 1964:387). This is true of 'attached labour' who works on oral contracts for rewards in kind and gifts. Thanjavur district is a good example where such a practice exists. And the work cycle is often without interruptions except the hours of sleep and includes seven days of the week. Only social occasions and sickness provide for respite. As for cycles of activities, two cycles are particularly important: the daily and the yearly. It is true also that the cycles are influenced by the calendars a society uses. Such calendars influence the society's perspective on time. In our agriculture, the traditional agricultural runs side by side with other calendars. Chaptamn (1978) has documented the use of agricultural almanacs in Bihar. The traditional calendor enshrines folk knowledge and is thus a source of agricultural knowledge. This contains divisions and periods which are ideal *time slices* for the organisation of agricultural activities.

TABLE 1

Distribution of human time use in Agriculture (Paddy)

Panel one:

Activities	*Human Labour Days (area: 1 hg.*		
	*Actual**	*Cumulative*	*In hours** (cumulative)*
Field Preparation	20	20	200
Transplanting	35	55	550
Irrigation (all through)	15	70	700
Weeding (three times)	35	105	1050
Fertilizer/Pesticides	3	108	1080
Application (thrice) Harvest	25	133	1330
Post-Harvest	15	148	1480

*Only one crop human time budget is given to indicate the activities involved and the time allocated by the farm family It should be noted that in double cropped areas, the activities are recurrent, and more or less indicate the same kind of budget.

**One labour day is equal to 10 hours of work.

Panel two:

Months	*Labour days*		*Labour days*	
	Actual	*Cumulative*	*Actual*	*Cumulative*
June	59	59	590	590
July	21	80	210	800
August	28	103	280	1080
September	40	148	400	1480

Source: The author's computation.

Multiple Human Time Budgets

The time budgets in agriculture are not as simple as the one explained through figure 1. They are complex and there are indeed multiple budgets: as many as there are crops. For the purpose ot explanation, however, we take the example of a three crop human time budget, though we are sure that a certain farm family may cultivate in a given agricultural year, five to eight crops. Time budgets take on additional complexities, if the crops are cultivated in fragments separated by distances, small or large, resulting in time-space budgets, which are still more complex.

It is important to recognize, in time resource analysis, that there is not only '*sparing time*' (time allocation between activities) but also '*timing SPACE*' (time allocation with respect to crops in space), and the perspectives gained from the two can greatly aid in planning and development of agriculture,

In order to explain figure 2a, we have to assume a few things, even though such assumptions are never true. We assure that the family with the three-croptime budget *does not* hire labour for operating its farm; on the other hand, hires itself out of farm work in other family farms to supplement income. Assuming that the family has four workers (man, wife and two children) and that the labour (potential) days available for use is 1080 a year (360+360+180+180), the family has an average of ninety days a month. If we assume further that this is a small medium farm family (70-80 per cent of the farm families fall under the two categories), the time budget for the whole year indicates that there are a few peaks of labour utilization. Yet the total for all three crops is only about three hundred seventy four days of 10 hours duration or about 35 per cent of all labour days. (1080 days). This means that a susbstantial part of the annual labour days within the family (706 days or 65 per cent) is unutilized. Given the fact that the family members cannot utilize sixty days of the total labour days available for reasons of illness and attendance at various social functions and festivities in a year and can only find jobs for about 60 days on wage labour (both assumed), then the family yet has a substantial part of labour days available for use (586 days at 54 per cent).

The facts about above mean that the time schedule is not balanced in terms of availability of labour days to be expended and the opportunities for full utilization: labour days utilized in productive activities is not equal to potential labour supply in the family. This is indeed the most serious problem of subsistence economies, a large pool of unemployed population. In certain villages in Tamilnadu, it has been time and again observed by the authors, a practice of what we may call '*work stretching*' exists which helps overcome the 'boredom' from inactivity. Also the un-and under-employment caused by the lack of opportunities for full employment push people off the land and rural exodus is the consequence of this imbalance in the labour schedule: at least, this is one of the major causes for rural-urban migration. An aggregate schedule for a region will be the same no matter what is the number of working population. The multiple time budget under discussion suggests a strategy. for full employment, which isthe balancing of labour days available with new opportunitiesfor employment. Several scholars have suggested that diversification of cropping systems, through the introduction of newer branches of agriculture (Kumaran, 1983: Aruchamy, 1986; Weitz, 1978, for example), and also rural industrialization programmes. All strategies, or rather their recommendations, are for filling-in gaps (the troughs in the graphics, so that the farm families are assured of a certain level of employment throughout the year, even if there are a considerable number of labour days unutilized. However, this number should not exceed ten per cent of the labour available for use. The present schedules, however, have levels of labour utilisation in slack months only to the tune of ten per cent or so. The utilization in any given month never exceeds seventy per cent of the capacity of the families, because in peak demand periods, the families for want of timely labour, because the family labour alone cannot meet all the needs, go in for wage and exchange labour.

Figure 2b illustrates a time space budget of a family with four workers and four fragments of land which requires their attention. Though this time space budget represents how the family's labour days (a week) are distributed between the spatially separated fragments, it does express the possibility, for expressing time-space budgets in terms of aggregates. Time-space studies conducted elsewhere, some of which are listed under references, do provide other modes of time-space budget mapping.

The Utility of Time Budgets in Planning Development Strategies

The time budgets interpret primarily activities in an accounting medium: the time allocated is a measure of utility. However, treated as a linking medium, time becomes a path which orders events as a sequence. Time budgets in agriculture can be a basis for the development of social accounting frame-works which could stimulate an interest in time allocation, or help find ways of utilizing effectively time available, so that we may develop indices of the richness or otherwise of life in rural communities.

The budgets can indeed become units of analysis in the study of patterns of activity in order to understand how productive people and rural environment interact, and also to relate spatial aspects of activities to time patterns (time-space budgets).

There is however a problem of classification of activities. But it is possible, as we have done in this study, to adopt a classification scheme from observations in the field.

We think, a time geographic approach can act as a means to answering policy questions about how a society should be organised and how activity patterns can be structured. Importantly, it is possible to derive perspectives: one is the articulation of agricultural operations, and the other is the devising of means of overcoming un-and under-employment via planning for increased use of time.

REFERENCES

Aruchamy, S. (1986): *Land Management for Rural Development: Case of Kambam Valley*. Ph.D. Thesis (unpublished), University of Madras.

Bharadwaj, K. (1974): *The Production conditions in Indian Agriculture*, Cambridge University Press.

Carlstein, T, (1982): *Time, Society and Ecology*, Cund University, Sweden.

Carlstein, T., Parkes, D, and Thrift N, (Eds), (1978): *Timing Space and Spacing Time*, Three Volumes, London: Edward Arnold.

Chakraborty, S.C. (1982): On Feeding the Cities: Some Aspects of the Indian *Scenario, Geo Journal*, Supplementary Issue, 4: 15-25.

Chapman, G.P., (1978): *Thc Folklore of the perceived Environment in Bihar*, London.

Harvey, D., (1969): *Explanation in Geography*, London: Edward Arnold.

Heirich. M. (1964): The use of Time in the study of Social Change, *Sociological Review*, 29: 386-397.

Kumaran, T.V., (1983): *An Anthropo-Ecological Study of Agricultural Development* in *Tribal Areas: The Kolli hills of Salem district*, An ICSSR Project Report, University of Madras.

Kumaran, T.V., (1984): The space-time Budgets, Travel Modes. and the Spatial Choice, *Proceedings*, National Symposium on the Ecology of Urban Areas, University of Mysore.

Kumaran, T.V., and Aruchamy S, (1986): *The Farm and Crop Profiles: A Budget Analysis*, University of Madras, (unpublished).

Kumaran, T.V., and Suseela, P, (1986): *Time-Space Budgets for Health Services in Madras City*, (forthcoming).

Linder, S.B., (1970): *The Harried Leisure Class*, New York; Columbia University Press.

Lynch, K. (1972): *What time is this place*? Cambridge, Mass. MIT Press.

Melbin, M. (1978): The colonization of Time, in Carlstein, T., Parkes, D. and Thrift, N. (Eds.): Vol. 2, *Human Activity and Time Geography*, London: Edward Arnold.

Moore, W.E., (1963): *Man, Time and Society*, New York: John Wiley.

Parkes, D. and Thrift N. (1980): *Time, Spaces and Places*, London, John Wiley.

Suseela, P. (1985): *Space-Time Budgets for Health Services in Madras City*, M. Phil. Thesis (unpublished), Univereity of Madras.

Szalai, A. (1974): Differential work and Leisure Time Budgets, *The New Hungarian Quarterly*, 5:105-119.

Weitz, R., (1978): Integrated Rural Development: *The Rehovet Approach*, Settlement Study Centre, Rehovet: Isreal.

Zerubavel, E., (1976): Time Tables and Scheduling: On the Sociological Organisation of Time, *Sociological Inquiry*, 46: 87-94.

SECTION IV

ENERGY RESOURCES

It has come to be accepted that provision of energy is an important factor in development process. There is a correlation between levels of energy consumption and economic output. It has been estimated that the industrialized countries use nine times as much per capita energy as developing countries. However, this estimate may be a bit misleading since most of the developing countries still depend heavily on primitive energy sources, the estimating of which is not an easy task. We often tend to overlook the fact that in a developing country like India, considerable inputs of energy still come from muscle power of men and animals, waste and dung etc. Half of India's energy consumption comes from this source, according to one estimate.

Due to the manifold increase in world oil prices consequent to the decision of OPEC countries, most of developing countries have been reeling under stress imposed by increased import bill. India especially has started exploring new energy sources like drilling off-shore wells and developing non-conventional energy resources.

Four articles pertaining to different facets of energy situation in India are included in this section. In their paper on 'Non-conventional Energy for Rural Development', Dr. V. Bhakthavatsalam and Mr. D. Chakravarthi Reddy describe the energy crisis and the imperative need to depend upon non-conventional energy resources such as Bio-gas, Bio-mass, solar and wind energies. They hold the view that non-conventional energies are so appropriate specially in the case of remote areas for irrigation, cooking and lighting purposes because of its potential for inputs such as dung, crop residues etc. The energy needs and the energy graphs are also explained. The article provides a future scenario to plan further in terms of conserving the conventional energy sources in order to have alternative utilization of conventional energy.

S.N. Tripathy, Kali Charan Pattanayak and Anjali Tripathy take a critical look at the non-conventional energy system and development of Orissa. While asserting that non-conventional energy resources are inevitable in the near future because of rising population and rapid technological advancement, they describe the available energy resources of the state of Orissa and also give estimates regarding the potential energy that can be generated by non-conventional energy rerources. They suggest that Hydro and thermal electricity and petrolem should be used for large scale industries and transport, solar, wind and geo-thermal energies for medium scale industries and agriculture, and solar and bio-gas for the house-hold purposes.

An assessment of energy potentials of raw-dung slurry for agricultural production is made by H.K. Singh in the penultimate article of this section. Maintaining that the lack of organic matter in soils leads to infertility and consequent disaster, the author establishes the superiority of fresh dung slurry throughout the cropping sequence. Besides its nutrients value, the fresh dung slurry is more effective in controlling all types of weeds, flora and particulary the Johnson grass which interfered with the normal growth of other forge crops.

P. Rama Rao in his paper on 'Energy Policies for Rural India' reviews the present policies for the development of new and renewable energy resources for rural India in order to assess the benefits of such policies and to suggest some alternatives within the institutional structure of the Indian economy. He is of the view that the Indian development policy for new and renewable sources of energy is designed in the light of technical matters which are non-disputable all over the world. This policy neglects the role of institutional matters like asset distribution, income distribution, employment etc.

14

NON-CONVENTIONAL ENERGY FOR RURAL DEVELOPMENT

V. BAKTHAVATSALAM*
D. CHAKRAVARTHY REDDY**

The oil crisis all over the world has brought to the fore the urgent need for developing non-conventional source of energy and their optimum utilisation with special reference to energy needs of our rural population 76.3 per cent of which spread over 6.3 lakh villages live in the rural environment. High rate of population growth and excessive pressure of population on agriculture have impelled our rural population to make heavy demands on the environment to meet their energy requirements. Deforestation and destabilisation of the environment in various other ways has been the net result affecting adversely climatic conditions and productive systems.

In view of the energy crisis and its impact on the economy, the Fuel Policy Committee set up by the Government of India has strongly recommended popularisation of biogas and other non-conventional energy sources as an alternative. In the plan documents also these programmes have figured as important items of planned activity. However, what comes in the way of

*Chief Executive and** Project Manager, APIL, HYDERABAD.

utilising energy from non-conventional sources is lack of appropriate technology and in such cases where technologies are available their fabrication and popularisation on mass scale.

In view of the wide gap between the requirement and availability of conventional energy, it is necessary to innovate and propagate non-conventional energy sources such as biogas, solar stoves, wind mill and energy from other bio-mass like kitchen waste etc. in rural areas so that if and when the conventional energy becomes plentiful to meet the rural demands, it can be better utilised in industrial sectors. The question, therefore, is not whether the non-conventional energy sources should be utilised on such a large scale but whether the country can afford to do without them. The answer lies in taking such steps as may be helpful in identifying non-conventional sources of energy, innovating appropriate technology for them and propagate their adoption on mass seale keeping in view the cost and various other factors of suitability,

Meeting Energy Needs

Several socio-economic factors hamper the progress and adoption of non-conventional energy technology. For example, convincing the local people about the importance of non-conventional energy sources for rural development, financing, creating the necessary infrastructure and integrating the scheme with other rural development programmes would have to be undertaken. Motivating and mobilising rural population for this purpose is one of the basic conditions for the adoption of non-conventional energy source.

During the seventh plan period the Government of India aims at rural development with emphasis on Food, Productivity and Employment. This needs improving their resources, enhancing their work period and income, reducing human drudgery and sufferings arising from poverty and generating durable assets and opportunities at decentralised levels for gainful employment. All these objectives hinge on energy sources. The existing energy situation in rural areas is part of the vicious circle of low energy input and low productivity and hence rising poverty. Hence, there is a need to assess the existing needs, availability and utilisation pattern of rural energy from conventional and non-conventional sources. Having identified, it is necessary to gear a suitable and appropriate non-conventional energy programmes in such areas. It is not only to gear up the programmes but also it is necessary to assess technical preference for different sources of non-conventional energy for adoption and use in the rural activity pattern such as irrigation, domestic lighting, cooking and agro-based tiny industries etc. Moreover, it is very much essential to understand the social aspects of users and adoption behaviour of the people based on techno-economic feasibility and socio cost benefit analysis.

Energy Planning

A number of government departments and institutions and non-governmental and voluntary agencies at different levels are directly and indirectly engaged in rural development. The planning for meeting energy needs of rural population should be made in such a way that it fits in the scope, resources, infrastructure and ongoing activities of the Rural Development Agency (DRDA) or Zilla Parished. Here, the quantitative and qualitative shifts in energy requirement resulting from increasing expectations, population increase and physical and natural resources changes in rural areas owing to reasons like rural development schemes, changes in agricultural, animal husbandry, village industries and crafts, soeial and domestic needs should be provided for adequately in the village planning. Again, only incremental efforts in energy inputs will not bring forth the desired improvements in the living conditions and socio-economic well-being of the people. It is the cumulative and integrated approach of all development schemes which can make an impact; energy would of course be an important component. In planning for application and utilisation of technology, there is need for education, extensive demonstration, training, action/adoption research, production and supply of inputs, credit and incentive and the needed maintenance services. These should also be integrated with the rural development plan of the village, block and the district. In some cases, energy planning may have to be done for a cluster of villages, a group of blocks/districts. The main concern of such integrated planning should be to ensure optimum economy and efficient delivery of location specific energy supply at the doorsteps of rural beneficiaries. In planning, the interest of rural poor must be considered as a special case. This may perhaps require a different approach and operating features to respond to praticular need of a group.

Energy planning and related technologies linked closely with the ongoing schemes of 'food, productivity and employment', health care, nutrition and literacy programme might have advantage. Since all these are inter-dependent, integrated planning would be more effective and useful.

Strategies for Meeting the Energy Needs

The Government of India had launched a massive programme of non-conventional energy sources programme. To create awareness and to bring the programme into take off stage and motivating people to go in for the non-conventional energy sources and to adopt them a number of incentives in the form of subsidy has been provided to the users of non-conventional energy sources. The programme and the pattern of incentives implemented by the Government of India through the State Government and its Nodal Agencies are as below:

National Project on Biogas, Community/Institutional Biogas Projects

The potentiality of producing energy from non-conventional sources is illustrated by the fact that cattle population in the country now exists 237 million. It has been estimated that if the entire quantity of dung available is processed through biogas plants, it would produce 66,000 m. Cum. per annum of gas to meet energy needs of our rural population for irrigation, lighting, agro-based industries and cooking, in addition to producing twenty million tonnes of waste material which is a rich source of fertiliser for agricuiture.

Subsidy Pattern: On an average one third of subsidy is provided to all categories of users and matched with loan facility from co-operative, commercial and rural banks. Nominal interest, repayment period five to seven years is provided to the users. The essential inputs such as Steel and Cement is provided with control rate. In the case of Community/Institutional Biogas Plants, cent per cent and 75 per cent subsidy is provided respectively.

National Project on Wind Energy

This project aims at drawing water from under ground wells, bores etc., for irrigation purposes. Also it envisages for farm applications such as gain winnowing, shelling, cutting and grinding. It is also used for power generation.

Subsidy Pattern: Hundred per cent subsidy for installing windmills under demonstration programmes. However, civil works for installing windmills and transportation charges are to be borne by the individuals.

National Project on Demonstration of Improved Chulhas

This programme provides high efficiency, wood burning stoves which provides clean and hygenic environment. This also helps in reducing the denudation of forests and it helps in the conservation of fire wood.

Subsidy Pattern: Fifty per cent to seventyfive per cent subsidy depending on the model and category of the beneficiary for portable chulhas and hundred per cent subsidy for fixed model for all categories.

National Project on Solar Energy

This project aims at distribution of Solar Cookers, Solar Stills, and establishing Solar Water heating systems, Solar pumps and Solar Photovoltaic systems for different forms of use.

Subsidy Pattern: Regarding Solar Cookers, the Central Government provides an amount of rupees one hundred fifty for all categories of users. In addition, State Government provides one third of subsidy and twenty per cent of Margin Money through DRDA for IRDP beneficiaries. In the case of Solar Stills hundred per cent subsidy is provided in consulation with Ministry of Works and Housing. In the case of Solar Hot water Systems hundred per cent subsidy is provided for Central Government Organisations, Public Trusts and Public Institutions like Universities and seventy five per cent subsidy will be given to the Co-operative Societies. In the case of Domestic Systems fifty per cent subsidy will be given to the users subject to a maximum of rupees three thousand.

Training Programmes on construction-cum-maintenance of Biogas Plants, Construction of Improved Chulhas and users programme for women

This programmes aim at Construction-cum-maintenance of Biogas Plants, National Project on Demonstration of Improved Chulhas and One day Women Education Programme under national project on biogas development to provide technical skill, awarness and the utilisation of the Non-conventional energy sources.

Rural Renewable Energy Systems (RRES)

This programme is implemented by Department of Non-conventional Energy Sources, Government of India, one village in one block. This Programme envisages integrated rural energy systems.

Integrated Rural Energy Programme (IREP)

The main feature of IREP is the preparation of an area based, block level rural energy plan through which the optimum mix of different sources of energy, conventional and non-conventional, commercial and non-commercial are provided for meeting the different energy needs for subsistence (cooking, heating, lighting etc.) and productive purposes (agricultural, Irrigation, Mechanisation) and non-farm activities (rural, Industries, Commercial activities etc.), of the different income groups living in that area (block).

Impact of the Programme

All the Renewable Energy Programmes are sponsored by Department of non-conventional Energy Sources, Government of India through department of Energy, Environment, Science and Technology, Government of Andhra Pradesh are mostly meant for the people in rural areas for meeting their energy needs. The programmes like National Project on Biogas development is low technology based and also the input materials are available with users of Biogas. It conserves fire wood, diesel, which in turn saves foreign exchange for the nation and provides clean and smokeless gas in the kitchen, thus providing healthy environment to the rural women. Also it provides rich manure to the farmer.

The energy conserved due to various non-conventional programmes and the energy savings are represented in the following table.

The Wind energy programme helps the small and marginal farmers to draw water from under ground wells and bores for irrigational purposes and the power generation through the wind energy will help the farmer in farm application such as grain winnowing, shelling, cutting and grinding. As an indirect benefit out of it the conventional power *i.e.*, electricity will have an alternative use in large scale industrial applications.

Another important programme, National Project on Demonstration of Improved Chulhas will help the weaker sections in the villages by providing clean and hygenic environment which indirectly plays in controlling the polluion. Also it restricts the denudation of forest which results in development of ecological balance in the universe. It also provides to the Rural Women healthy atmosphere by protecting from irritation to their eyes while they blow the traditional stoves.

Sl. No.	*Sources of saving*	*Type of Saving*				
		Gas production	*Fire Wood*	*Diesel*	*Slurry*	*Electricity conservation*
1	*2*	*3*	*4*	*5*	*6*	*7*
1.	Family Size Biogas Plants	70.20 m. cum	2.44 lakh tonnes	36.50 m. ltrs	8.01 lakh tonnes	—
2.	Community/ Institutional Biogas Plants	2.58m. cum	898 tonnes	1.34 lakh tonnes	2580 tonnes	—
3.	Wind Energy	—	—	0.72 lakh tonnes	—	2.21 lakh K.W.
4.	a) Photovoltaic lighting system @ 8.4 KW per day	—	—	—	—	3066 KW
	b) Photovoltaic pumping system @ 8.4 KW per day	—	—	—	—	20400 KW
	TOTAL	72.78	2.44898	36.706 m.lit.	8.03580	2.44466

National Project on Solar Energy provides the heating and lighting systems in the remote areas such as tribal areas where there is no possibility of taking the conventional energies into those areas. This indicates the non-conventional energy *viz.,*

Solar Energy, Biogas, Biomass and Wind Energy are the boon to the tribal villages as well as backward villages.

In addition to the programmes it involves in imparting training in the areas of non-conventional energy programmes for both skilled and un-skilled workers which in turn creats skilled and unskilled employment to the rural youth.

The above programmes generated both skilled and unskilled employees is presented in the following table.

Under the above cited direct and indirect benefits the programme implementation through it is generating an employment opportunities in rural areas, bridging the energy gap in rural areas and conserving the energy for an alternative and advanced economic development of the nation.

Conclusions

From the foregoing analysis the following conclusions can be derived:

1. It is apparent that there is a lot of energy crisis and also wide gap between the requirement and availability of the conventional energy in Rural areas.

2. There is an imperative need to depend upon non-conventional energy sources specially in rural areas for rural demands such as irrigation, cooking, lighting etc.

3. Non-conventional energies are so appropriate specially in the case of remote rural areas for irrigation purpose and in other rural areas for cooking and lighting because of its potential for inputs such as generation of Biogas for cooking and lighting etc.

4. There is no proper link up non-conventional energy programmes with other rural development programmes such as IRDP in order to achieve forward and backward linkages of inputs and outputs of different rural development programmes that are being implemented.

Employment Generation

Sl. No.	Programmes	During the Period of 1982-85		During the period of 1985-86		Total	
		Construction of employment	Continuous employment	Construction of employment	Continuous employment	Construction of employment	Continuous employment
I.	1. National programme for Biogas plant	17.1957 (lakh man hrs.	471.1192 person year	13.50	369.86	30.69	840.98
	2. CBP/IBP	0.05	1.37	1.35	36.99	1.40	38.36
II.	1. Solar PV Pumpsets	544	1.0625	256	0.4375	800	1.5
	2. P.V. Street Lights	896	1.1662	784	1.02	1680	2.1862
III.	3. Wind Energy						
	1. Wind Mills	625	37.5	312.5	18.75	937.5	5625

5. The strategies that are being adopted for bridging the energy gap by the government has achieved in conserving energies, saving foreign exchange and contributing to the socio-economic condition of the rural poor to a greater extent.

Recommendations

1. Carefully and clearly drawn programme implementation of non-conventional energy sources will further take, the weaker sections and the rural population into a better standard of living.

2. It is essential to link up the energy programmes with other developmental programmes in the rural areas in order to provide maximum benefit to the rural poor and to meet their minimum energy requirements such as cooking, lighting etc.

3. There is a great need to promote R and D activities in order to make the energy devices as cost effective as possible so that they can be with in the reach of the rural poor.

15

NON-CONVENTIONAL ENERGY SYSTEMS AND DEVELOPMENT IN ORISSA

DR. S.N. TRIPATHY*
KALI CHARAN PATTANAYAK**
DR. (MRS) ANJALI TRIPATHY***

Energy in of fundamental importance in economic development of any region which in turn helps to increase the standard of living of people. The increasing rate of power consumption has a close relation with the exponential growth of population in the state. To discover new sources of energy, to obtain essentially inexhaustable supply of energy for the future, to make energy available wherever needed and to convert energy from one from to another and use it without creating the pollution which will destroy our biosphere constitute one of the greatest challenges facing this state today. In order to apply energy without making undue demands on the consumer, it must be converted into a form that may be rapidly transported, distributed and used in a variety of devices. The electric power system is one of the

*Reader, P.G. Department of Geography, Utkal University, Vani Vihar, Bhubaneswar—4.

**Research Scholar, P.G. Department of Geography, Utkal University, Vani Vihar, Bhubaneswar—4.

***P.G. Teacher, Regional College of Education, Bhubaneswar—7.

tools for converting and transporting energy which is playing an important role in meeting this challenge because of the fact that this form of energy can be used over a broad spectrum of applications. The trend has been toward grids, for obvious reasons specifically towards electricity.

Present power Consumption and Strategy For New-Energy Resources

The rate of power consumption has been increased due to the rapid growth of population and widespread industrialization in the state. During the decade 1971-81 Orissa's population has increased from 2.2 crores to 2.6 crores *i.e.*, 19.72 per cent increase during the decade. On this account, our state will require 4.42 million tonnes of oil by the end of this century while the coal requirement will go upto 91 million tonnes and electric power from up 1755 MW. But available data shows that the proven coal reserves of 3,4596 million tonnes will last only for 50 years.

Of the total 18,832-05 MW of hydro power resource, only 4032 MW is being harnessed now. The thermal power generation is being facing problems with restricted supply of coal and oil along with pollution problems, while sitting of water resources is being posing a threat to the life span of hydro-electric projects.

Recently the sea-beach sands of south Orissa coast contains large reserves of Thorium bearing monoazites will be utilise for the nuclear power generation. But this will last only for 10 years.

New Vistas in Energy

There will certainly not be enough power for the future but of the vast unemploited resources, which are otherwise known as democratic sources of energy being renewable in nature or it may be called non-conventional energy system. The non-conventional energy sources are derived from a number of forces: from the gravitational forces of the moon and sun which create the tide: from the decay of radio-active minerals and the heat of the earth which provide geothermal energy, and solar energy which generates ocean currents and the winds and in turn waves: from solar energy and the gravitational power of the earth which create the cycle of evaporation and precipitation of water and finally from the direct heat of sun itself. All these sources are in-exhaustible, atleast in the sense that little change in their energy output is expected over a span of million of years. Continuous or non-conventional energy supply can be divided into two categories: Solar and non-Solar. Solar constitute direct conversion, thermal conversion, wind power and hydro-power, while non-solar constitutes tidal, geothermal and ocean thermal (thermo-marine) energy.

Overview of Non-Conventional Energy sources and their potentiality in Orissa

Tidal Energy: So far, no Tidal power station have been commissioned in Orissa but, the possibilities of Tidal power development have already been identified in one location. That is on *River Panchapara* in Balasore district. The total power that may be generated in Orissa through tides is of the order of maximum power developed (instantaneous) during spring tide 1673 KW and during average tide 1049 KW. The total average power potential (over generation period only) during spring tide is 1345 KW and during average tide 786 KW. The total annual energy output during spring tide is 5.61 GWH (Fictitious) and during average tide 3.11 GHW. This large power can be utilised for electrification and industrialisation. *Asuradiha* of Balasore district is the only selected site in Orissa state for the extraction of tidal power from river *Panchapara*. The fluctuating output of 1500 KW can be easily absorbed in the H.T. Grid net work.

Wind Energy: Orissa is mostly an agriculture state. The location and the maritime conditions of Orissa favour for the generation of wind power which will be more useful for agricultural purposes. Wind blows with uneven speed both spatially as well as temporally with a maximum annual mean wind speed of 17.8 (4.98) Km/hr/(m/s) at Puri and the minimum annual mean wind speed is 3.3 (0.91) Km/hr/(m/s) at Titilagarh. Gopalpur and Puri experience wind speed over 3 m/s during the months from February to October. Ghandabali and Cuttack have wind speeds over 2.5 m/s from March to August. Economic exploitation of wind energy at these stations is possible. The total estimated wind energy potential in Orissa is of the order of 14.88×10^9 KWH is more than the power consumption in the State.

TABLE—I

Estimates of Wind Energy Potential

S. No.	*District*		*Annually extractable energy 109 KWh*
1.	Balasore	...	0.179
2.	Phulbani	...	1.010
3.	Balangir	...	0.658
4.	Cuttack	...	0.658
5.	Dhenkanal	...	0.514
6.	Ganjam	...	0.688
7.	Kalahandi	...	0.615
8.	Keonjhar	...	0.295
9.	Koraput	...	3.200
10.	Mayurbhanj	...	0.475
11.	Puri	...	5.82
12.	Sambalpur	...	0.409
13.	Sundargarh	...	0.827
	Total	...	14.880

Source—Orissa Renewable Energy Centre. (Fig. 1)

The total power that may be generated in Orissa through windmills is of the order of 8.49×10^9 KWh and with suitable escarpments 28.69×10^9 KWh which is more than that of the electricity consumed in the state (2.424×10^9 KWh). The Government of Orissa has already taken steps to construct a farm having ten big windmills at Puri sea-shore which will produce electricity. The electricity which will produce from the windfarm, will be connected with the regional grid. This wind power will help rural electrification, agriculture and irrigation in the state.

Solar Energy: The united nation conference on new and non-conventional source of energy of Nirobi in August 1981, which defined there renewable sources of energy include fourteen technologies, from among which, much stress is on Solar.

It has been calculated that the sun sends into the space every second radiant energy equivalent to about one million times of the earth's coal, petroleum and natural gas supplies before these were tapped by man. The total output of all man-made energy producing systems in Orissa in 1980 was less than 0.0001 per cent of this. Orissa receives on an average about 5.7 KW per m^2 surface area, which on average of 240 days of bright sunshine in a year.

If the irradiance of only 1 per cent on the Orissa's surface could be converted into useful energy with more than 10 per ecnt efficiency, solar energy could provide the energy needs of all the people of this state. Broadly, solar potential can efficiently be used as low and high temperature solar heat applications besides direct use as solar photovoltaics.

Bio-gas: *Energy*: In the context of the present energy crisis in Orissa development of bio-gas as a non-conventional source of energy has assumed great importance. While population growth has been putting pressure on land under forests, the increasing use of power implements and farm machines has created bigger demand areas for diesel and electricity. Villages are, therefore, fuel hungry both for household and farm needs. Bio-gas is a cheap fuel which can be used by each and every village of Orissa. In Orissa, it is the most relevant source of renewable energy that can make a significant dent in the much talked "fuel crisis," the less talked "fertilizer crisis" and the problems of rural health and sanitation. It is consodered most useful source of electrical energy for the rural habitats for their domestic and agricultural purposes. At present India as well as Orissa are facing the scarcity of petroleum, hydro-electricity and fuel wood. Hence for the replacement of all other power resources, now-a-days bio-gas may be the only substitute to make any individual of the state self-sufficient in the field of electricity supply. The first bio-gas plant was started in the year 1971 in Betnoti police station of Mayurbhanj district. This is a multi-purpose project. Because it encompass three important economic programmes, such as "white revolution," "Green revolution" and "rural electrification" programme.

Geo-thermal Energy: So, far no-geo-thermal power station have been commissioned in Orissa but the possibilities of geo-thermal power development have already been identified in one location. That is at Taptapani of Ganjam district. About 200 MW of power will be generated from the plant annually.

The stress on non-conventional energy sources is not expected to minimise the need to accelerate the supply of energy from coal, hydel and petroleum sources. The entire consumption of diesel for water pumping and rural industry and also 50 per cent of the Kerosine consumption could be replaced by non-conventional energy system.

Thus about 40 per cent of total oil consumption in all sectors could be replaced by renewable sources of energy. Moreover the non-conventional energy sources could replace 20 per cent of coal consumption and 7 per cent of electricity consumption of the state. Table-2 shows the consumption of cost, area requirement and efficiencies of non-conventional energy system.

And finally Verne's Prophacy; he had said that one day water can be employed as fuel that hydrogen and oxygen contained in it would furnish in-exhaustible source of light and as well as the running of industries.

TABLE—2

A comparison between renewable based power systems (10 KW decentralised power system)

Systems	*System Efficiency*				*Investments (Rupees in Lakhs)*				
	Major component	*Other component engine*	*Overall efficiency*	*Area requirement (Sq. metre)*	*Major component*	*Auxillaries other components*	*Land*	*Total*	*Qualitative complexity rating*
1	*2*	*3*	*4*	*5*	*6*	*7*	*8*	*9*	*10*
1. Solar Thermal System	30	8.5	2.55	2000	6.5	1.6	0.2	8.30	HC
2. Concentrating collectors cum-stems-engine									
3. Solar pond cum vapour engine system	25	2.0	0.5	3000	5.15	0.8	0.3	6.25	HC
4. Solar Photovoltaic system	12.5	—	10.0	3000	13.20	3.30	0.03	16.53	S
5. Wind energy conversion system									

(i) Low wind relocities 1 KW (10 units)	70.70	90	28.00	7000	1.6	0·8	0.7	3.10	
(ii) High wind velocities									
—3.5 KW (3 units)	75.70	90	28.00	1800	0.68	0.50	0.18	1.36	
—10 KW (1 unit)	75.70	90	30.0	1000	0.40	0.23	0.10	0.73	
6. Bio-Gas Plant-Cum-Bio-Gas-Engine-Gobar.	28.0	—	28.0	500	0.63	0.20	0.05	0.88	
—Water Hyacinth	28.0	—	28.0	2100	0.91	0.20	0.21	1.32	
7. Energy Plantation-cum-Wood Fired Boxler-cum-Steam Engine	55.0	8.5	0.03	2000	1.15	0.60	2.50	4.34	C

*H.C.—Highly Complex, C—Complex, S—Simple

16

ASSESSMENT OF ENERGY POTENTIALS OF RAW-DUNG SLURRY FOR AGRICULTURAL PRODUCTION

H.K. SINGH*

What do we really mean by biomass in relation to the soil? It is something more important and far-reaching consequence than just not using artificial fertilizers, insecticides and weedicides. The trend being away from nature in our modern living, the same way we are framing our modern agricultural production-technology by using artificial fertilizers and chemicals to meet plant requirement without taking care of the needs of microflora of the soil. Within everyone of us, there is an urge to return to the state of nature. The Yogis believed that we should get our hands into the soil as often as possible to enable us to live in complete harmony.

There is no magic wand which can be waved over the earth, no short cuts to fertility with potions, Powder or other means. Fertile organic soil is difficult to be produced by scientists or chemists in any shape or form. Chemical fertilizers have all

*Sr. Scientist, Agro-Energy Centre, I.A.R.I., New Delhi-12.

the ingredients but lack vitality and life giving properties. In the long run this results in an equally lifeless soil and an increase in pests, weeds and diseases. The only prosperous way is by allowing natural processes to develop by means of using organis biomass, something man can never imitate. The nature acts as mysterious as life itself. This natural method is as old as the world and besides providing health to the crops, it keeps the balance of nature.

All the creatures, worms, insects, birds and other forms of life, down to the tiniest microbes, are allcwed to grow and play their vital role in the natural cycle. In turn they are either consumed by the other species or allowed to die off, and in doing so, add a minute part to the everlasting organic mass, which in turn becomes the part of soil body. It is after more than hundred years since the discovery of the artificial fertilizer, many scientists have realized that the constant use of fertilizers and other chemicals without looking into soil organic health means abuse of the soil and natural resources. We the scientist have during the last few decades, witnessed a worldwide transformation of farming methods. Progress has been made with automations and artificial fertilization of soil for crop production. The scientists have come to the aid of the farmers, small farm holders and others who are involved in agricultural production processes. All manner of pests may be quickly exterminated by either sprying a liquid insecticide or applying it in powder form. There are as many chemicals used in the form of insecticides and pesticides as many are the pests to combat. The artificial fertilizers have become a part of agricultural life for farmers in many states of our country.

The time has now come for us to take stock and see what these miraculous discoveries have really done to our farm lands. Lack of organic matter in soils leads to infertility and disaster. After decade of misuse, arable land become a desolate waste. Now the most important of all, farm lands must be made so fertile during the process of farming that chemical additives will be needed the least. The simple and long term answer to this problem lies in the use of organic biomass more and more in our farming systems. Certain old customs like ploughing, digging of land and other operations like hoeing etc. which sounds convincing has come as an ancient tradition from father to son since man first cultivated the land. It is a very debatable for what they gain by doing this.

The contention that digging/ploughing makes for drainage plusaeration of the soil, and is essential is not upheld, if you examine an organically rich unturned plots. The worms do that job which we do by ploughing. Sometimes ploughing and hoeing bring an ever increasing number of weed seeds to the surface suitable for their germination other wise such seeds would have remained dormant for years.

Modern science is probing more and more deeply into the minute mechanisms of life and into the vast mechanisms of universe. These efforts are meeting with some success and must be given their due respect. But since they are based on a materialistic out-look and neglect the inter-relatedness of the whole cosmose they must lead to a one sided and uncoordinated control over life of the planet which could well end in catastrophe. For real success a different approach and a deeper understanding are necessary. Insecticide pollution brings disaster. The B.B.C's outstanding film on the destruction of Lochleven presents a vivid but terrible picture of the long term effects of insecticides and polution with total destruction of every form of life that slowly but surely turned a beautiful lake into a polluted cess pool.

Recycling of organic wastes as a source of nutrient is assuming increasing importance due to ever enhancing fertilizer prices. The live stock population is, cattle—191, Buffaloes—69, sheep and goats,—138, Pigs,—10 and poultry,—193 millions as per recent census (1982). This large population presents challange to retain the traits of adaptability. But this large population possesses tremendous potential to supply plant nutrients through scientific recycling of organic wastes. However, great deal of research efforts are called for to study the effect of raw dung slurry on plant growth. It is because various organic compounds are formed during the process of decomposition which, in turn, may have differential influence on plant growth. It was observed (at NDRI farm) that application of fresh cowding slurry in the form of thick sheet on the field resulted in control of Johnson grass weed. The dung slurry was applied in a continuous sheet to cover the ground. After thirty days of application, the land was ploughed add harrowed twice and three crops of maize+cowpeas (80:20kg seed rate/ha) and a mixture of turnip and oats crops were taken. In other treatment the three imrigation of sewage water were given to a normal season crop of maize+cowpeas followed by the turnip and oats in a sequence. The third treatment was chemical fertilizer (Table—I) in fourth treatment F.Y.M. @10-12 t/ha was applied along with chemical fertilizer. Three crop sequences were taken in this case. In the last treatment only chemical fertilizers were used. The details of treatments are given in (Table—I).

The yield data in (Table—II) indicate that fresh dung slurry gave 6.71, 5.11 and 3.21 t/ha green fodder from three maize+cowpeas crops. The early and late season crop of maize+cowpeas were not taken it did not fit well into the traditionally followed cropping schedule. However, comparing the yield of maize+cowpea forage in normal season sown crops under different treatments indicate the superiority of fresh dung slurry which produced forage (5.11 t/ha) followed by sewage water (3.97 t/ha) F.Y.M. (3.22 t/ha), chemical fertilizer (2.90 t/ha) check (2.54 t/ha) summation of three forage crops of maize copea yieldsin the treatment of fresh dung slurry gave (15.00t/ha) of green fodder which was highest of all the treatments. The residual effect of fresh dung slurry was also reflected by the succeeding forage crop of turnip producing 5.80 t/ha of biomass as compaired to 3.90 t/ha, in remaining other treatments. The residual effect of fresh dung slurry was further exhibited by oats forage producing (5.8 t/ha) 1.30 t/ha more as compared to other treatments. This demonstrated the superiority of fresh dung slurry through out the cropping sequence. Besides its nutrients value, it was (fresh dung slurry) more effective in controlling all types of weeds flora and particularly the Johnson grass which interfered with the normal growth of other forage crops.

These results further necessitate studies in depth on use of fresh dung slurry not only in forage but also in other crops to harness its potential profitability for economic utilization on a wider scale.

TABLE 1

Details of fertilizer dose and seed rate under different treatments (N.D.R.I. Karnal)

Treatment	Maize + Cowpea Nutrient			Turnip Nutrient			Out Nutrient			Total Nutrient applied		
	N	P_2O_5 (kg./ha)	K_2O	N	P_2O_5 (kg./ha)	K_2O	N	P_2O_5 (kg./ha)	K_2O	N	P_2O_5 (kg./ha)	K_2O
Fresh dung slurry												
a) Early Sown	40	—	—	—	—	—	—	—	—	—	—	—
b) Normal Sown	60	25	25	65	20	30	—	—	—	285	110	110
c) Late sown	60	25	25	—	—	—	80	40	30	—	—	—
Sewage Water												
b) Normal Sown	60	30	30	65	20	30	80	40	30	205	90	90
Farm yard manure												
b) Normal Sown	60	25	25	60	20	30	80	40	30	200	85	85
Chemical fertilizer (NPK)												
b) Normal Sown	60	30	20	60	20	30	80	40	30	200	90	80
Local control												
b) Normal Sown	60	20	20	60	30	30	80	40	30	200	90	86

TABLE 2

Effect of organic and inorganic sources of plant nutrients on the biomass yield (t/ha) at NDRI (Karnal)

	1981			*1982*		
	Summer (early) March—May	*Monsoon (normal) June—August*	*Mansoon (Late) August—Oct.*	*Winter Oct.—Dec.*	*(Late) Dec.—March*	*Total forage*
	Maize+Cowpea	Maize+Cowpea	Maize+Cowpea	Turnip	Oats	
i) Fresh dung slurry	6.70	5.10	3.20	5.80	5.80	26.60
	(62)	(60)	(60)	(72)	(88)	(342)
ii) Sewage water	—	3.97	—	3.94	4.50	12.31
		(70-80)	—	(80-85)	(80-90)	(255)
iii) FYM+NPK	—	3.18	—	3.94	4.50	11.62
		(70-80)	—	(80-85)	(80-90)	(255)
iv) Chem. Fertilizers	—	2.90	—	3.95	4.50	11.34
		(70-80)	—	(80-85)	(80-90)	(255)

v) Local check	—	2.50 (70-80)	— —	3.94 (80-85)	4.50 (80-90)	10.98 (255)

Figures in parenthesis indicate the crop duration in days from sowing to harvesting.
Average production in the treatment (i) from 2.8 ha.
Average production the treatment (ii), (iii) and (iv) from 5ha.
Average production in the treatment (v) from 210 ha.

17

ENERGY POLICY FOR RURAL INDIA

P. RAMA RAO*

The article aims to present theoretical aspect of the development of new and renewable sources of energy and to review the present policies for the development of such sources of energy. It is also assess is the beneficiaries of such policies in order to suggest some alternatives, technical and financial, within the institutional framework of the Indian Economy.

The author does not intend to make a quantitative analysis, but attempts a qualitative picture of the rural India and the current energy policies is given. The energy needs of the rural India are not far from soluble. All of the analysis is carried out in relation to class structure, the rich and the poor.

Energy problem is not independent of thermodynamic laws, a peculiar branch of physics. Man can neither create matter energy not destroy it (first law). Man can do only is to transform the matter energy from one form into another for his utility. There is a fixed potential for energy generation, so as we are extracting the matter energy from the earth, the fixed potential reduces to zero (The second Law, alias Entropy

*Research Scholar, Department of Economics, Osmania University, Hyderabad—7.

Law). Man cannot recreate the matter energy which requires zero temparature and never possible on this earth except as in micro laboratory experiments (Third Law). The upshot is that if we extract more and more resources from the earth, the potential for future generations will be low and the ultimate result is the exintinction of human being. We should use less and less terrestial stock for energy generation to alive the human special as long as possible. There are two sources for energy generation. The terrestial stock which is not renewable and flow stock which is renewable. Coat, Oil, Natural gas etc., represents the former whereas the second category consists of Firewood, Solar radiation intercepted by the earth via photosynthesis, etc. In view of increasing Entropy (unavailable energy in a given thermodynamic system), it is inept to depend on terrestial stock for energy generation with so much present technological advance. So we should use renewable energy sources for energy generation.

Why the development of New and Renewable Energy Sources: Evolution of man during the past few centuries has been speeded up, which disturbed the inbuilt mechanism of the earth causing more pressure not only on terrestial stock but also renewable stock of energy sources. This development is not only increasing the pressure on terrestial stock of matter energy but also the main cause of the decrease of renewable stock of energy sources. Thus we are guided to develop alternative sources of energy and which are also renewable.

*For a scientific and Economic interpretation of the Entropy Law refer to,

a) Georgeson--Roegen, *'The Entropy Law and Economic Process'* Cambridge, Mass, Newyork, 1971.
'Energy and Economic Myths; Analytical and EconomicEssays' pergmon, Newyork, 1976.

**On biological evolution and exintinction, see Haldane JBS, *The canses of Evolution*, Newyork, 1932. CHII, Passim.

The Indian Scene

India is essentially semi-feudal economy in its nature. Much of its population resides in rural areas with penurial conditions. Thus the aspect of rural development need not explain. Generally, higher per capita income associated with higher per capita energy consumption (Reddy AKN and Krishna Prasad K, 1977). Market forces are not able to solve their energy needs, so the government intervention is necessary. Agricultural production is also positively associated with the energy input (Makhajani and Poole, 1975). How to met these increasing energy needs is basically a problem that is to be solved. The conventional energy sources are limited in view of increasing needs and the costs associated with it are also considerably high. It is felt that there should be alternative sources to satisfy the increasing energy needs. There are much social costs and increasing from time to time in using conventional sources of energy like Firewood, Dung cakes. The wanton and wide denudation of tree cover raises the ecological problem as well as other side effects. The same applies to dung cakes which have alternative use as fertiliser. There are many pumpsets which are to be nergisized either through electricity or other non-conventional energy sources, like biogas. Thus to avoid environmeatal deterioration and other social costs, we have to provide alternative sourees of energy. This can be done through either electrifying a village or alternative sources of energy and or both.

With the formation a separate Ministry of Energy, Advisory Board on Energy. The Department of Non-conventional Energy Sources and the initiative taken by KVIC, the development of New and Renewable Sources of Energy (called as NRES herein-after) got the momentum. Is it reasonable to reserve the forests and other areas in the name of ecological balance? Yes isit, if we provide an alternative source for the people's fuel needs. The population explosion and the so called modern technology which led to the increase cropped area certainly reduced the availability of common property resource for an Indian village.* Economically and technically it is possible to satisfy the energy needs of rural population, but the present Government is not so interested to do this, thus the result is a mass movement of the poor (Makhijani, 1977). Energy crisis of the affluent is not a people's problem and the real energy crisis experienced by the poverty stricken can be met by technological alternatives (Reddy AKN). The policy makers have put forward the technology without considering it simplications sociologically. Such developments certainly are obstacles to the social progress.

Apart from rural electrification programmes through REC, the NRES development policies can be devided into three groups. These are Energy Sources Expansion Programmes (ESEP), Energy Source Substitution Programmes (ESSP) and Energy Efficiency Improvement programmes (EEPP).* Rural Electrification constitute as the main indicator of rural development. Statistics were forward by the officials as number of electrified villages and pumpsets but not as number of households having electricity and the adoption of electricity even lighting. It is futile to count a village as electrified as official documents said (A village can be counted as electrified villages if one house is electrified). Much of the population either below the poverty line or around the poverty line, certainly the adoptation of Electricity even as fuel for lighting is beyond their capacity in view of its initial high cost. The promotion of Co. operative electricity boards might led to the adoption to be quicker. Any how the village electrification leads to the entire village electrification is a myth which is never possible within this class structured due to its high cost in nature. It is not to be expected that the adoption of electrification as fuel for lighting. Unless there is a substantial cost reduction. Increasing population and bifurcation of joint families are also

*On common property resource argument and how the monetisation creates the problem to the poor, see Jodha MS *Market Forces and Erosion of Common property Resources*' Proceedings of the international workshop on Agricultural Markets in the Semi-Arid tropics, ICRISAT, Patancheru, India, 1985.

*This is a broad classification for analytical purpose.

causes of the high growth of the new houses than the growth of electrified households. The alternative new sources of lighting are bio-gas and solar systems which also requires high initial finances. In addition to this these sources are costlier than electrifying a village (Venkatraman K, 1972). The quality of there sources of energy is also somewhat inferior to electricity for domestic as well as non-domestic needs. In some situations, however, power generations from gobar gas may be a resumable alternative. In isolated regions, the transmission costs would be higher than those estimated (Tyner WE and Adams J, 1977). Thus a substantial cost reduction should be achieved through efficient methods of power generation or increase of the incomes of the poor or both to solve the problem. But each hasits own limitations so that there should a co-operative effort to provide electricity facility to every household through using a common connection. Otherwise the electrified villages will be there with much percentage of households without using the electricity as fuel for lighting. In this situation it is a distant dream to use electricity as a fuel for cooking needs.

As mentioned earlier the developments in regard to NRSE can be divided into three categories as Energy Expansion Programmes (ESEPs) and Energy Source Efficiency Programmes (ESEPs) and Energy Source Substitutions Programmes (ESSPs).

Energy Source Expansion Programmes: Energy plantations programmes are related to this category. The overall price situation of fuelwood in the country is keep on going and become are incentive not only using wastelands for plantations but also to shift the cropping pattern in favour of firewood plantations in which little risk involved. For this category of developments the controversaries of the nature fuelwood is also questioned (For example, the Eucalyptus, which erodes the ground water). Energy plantation growing should have been selective and purposive in regard to its variety. Every village should common property resource of fuel wood plantation. The land in this purpose can get through either land reforms or with some other measure. If we encourage the plantation programme through private ownership it certainly transforms the valuable cropping land into firewood plantations.

Energy Source substitution programmes: Bio-gas, wind-power, and Solar Energy are related to this category. These are efficient as well as suitable to Indian conditions. Basically these are encouraged through private ownership by giving subsidies. On regard to bio-gas plant, is it very important to give the subsidies in the name of encouragement. Normally, the nature of its high cost, it is out of the poor section accessibility. Thus the relative benefits goes to the rural rich who are not facing the energy crisis. In addition to this, the benefit-cost ratio is suggests that it is not economical to give subsidies since the benefit cost ratio is too high. But the benefit cost ratio itself depends upon the assumption made in the analysis. The cost benefit ratio is positively associated with the size of the plant. There is no dispute in this connection. Thus the basic question is why we should promote individual bio-gas plants when these are not economical and the benefits does not reach to all section of the society. In addition there are number of households who are able to neither feed bio-gas plant with their little amount of livestock not install a own plant with their limited income. To avail of economies of scale we should promote community bio-gas plants which also have the advantages to diffuse the benefits to all sections. In regard to wind power the research is still on its mother lap, as we are yet to develop the technology that is suitable to our conditions to develop wind power source. At the present level of international costs of a wind mill it is beyond the capacity of even the rural rich. The community wind mill can be erected as a source of energy for lifting water, power generation etc. The present subsidy system is also do the same as in the case of bio-gas plants. A detail study of wind flows throughout the country is greatly needed to know the wind movements. The case of solar cookers, it is very difficult to find a market for it in a mass scale except as a special commodity. The solar cooker is unable to store energy and requires long time for cooking. This ludes even the rich to own a solar cooker.

A solar energy system should be designed so as to supply the drinking water and hot water to the entire village. The present subsidy element will provide the market for solar cookers over a short period and reaches the saturation point where further expansion cannot be achieved sooner than latter.

Thus the upshot is clear. The present activities of NRSE through private ownership by subsidies greatly help the rich and reinforced their way of luxurly living. But whereas their counterparts who have no benefits of this alternative technology, found to be going number of miles for drinking water, fuelwood etc. The Energy substiution development programmes should have been expanded as common property resources where everyone is able to avail of the benefits.

Energy source efficiency development: Improved chulhas are related to this category: The improved chulhas are designed to obtain much of the fuel efficiency. 'National project of Demonstration on Improved Chulhas' is going on. The chulhas are useful in using less firewood for cooking needs and are also not costlier. These chulhas can be constructed for a village through IRDP, NREP programmes etc. The chulhas can be used as intermediatries in the transition from conventional source of Energy to NRES. Thus every household should have been constructed an improved chulha or given a portable chulha with low price.

The overall development policy of NRSE is under the veil of '*subsidy fetishism*' under the veil of this fetishism the poor are totally neglected and the richer sections are able to avoil of the benefits of scant technological developments for rural development. To avoid this type of class based development, policy should be readically altered so as to ensure development of NRSE as common property Resources. Otherwise the circular flow of rich cycles cannot be altered.

As common property resources, the development of NRSE would require huge funds. It is to be suggested that to lift the gift tax on industrial houses and make measures to flow the black money to rural areas through the development NRSE. With the present state of policy makers it is reasonable to expect this type of reform, though they are much favoured the urban sector where there are many voices for their demands. Otherwise history repeats to destroy the class based economy via mass movement.

REFERENCES

Makhajani A and Poole, '*Energy and Agriculture in the Third World*' Ballinger, New York, 1975, Ch. II, *Passim.*

Makhajani A,—'*Energy Policy for Rural India*' *EPW*, Spl. Number 1977.

Reddy AKN and Krishna—Technological alternative and the Indian Energy.

Prasad K,—Crisis, EPW, Spl. Number, August, 1977.

Reddy AKN and Krishna Prasad K,—*op. cit.*

Tyner WE and Adams J—'Rural Electrification in India's bio-gas versus large scale power', Asian Survey, August, 1977.

Venkatraman K,—Power Development in India, the financial aspects, Wilery, New Delhi, 1972, pp. 92-96.

SECTION V

WATER RESOURCES

Water is an essential resource required for use by human beings for consumption, power generation, irrigation, navigation andi ndustries. Though, water is found to be abundant on the surface of the earth, most of it is composed of unusable sea water. Only the inland water is most valuable. In addition to its major significance as a source of water supply, water resource wields great influence in shaping the economic, social and cultural life of the human race.

India's water resources are vast and varied. However, if we keep in view the requirements of the countrys's growing population, special climatic conditions and increased demand for developmental needs, the water resources of India seem to be limited. There is, therefore, a strong case for optimu utilization of this limited resource for achieving a high degree of economic development and a better life for the teeming millions of our country.

The present section comprises of six papers dealing with different aspects of water resource development in different parts of the country. Jasbir Singh, in the first article of the section, examines water resources of India with a geographical perspective. In an in-depth analysis of the subject, he estimates the ground as well as surface water available for use from different sources. He comes out with valuable suggestions for the development of the resources.

Aspects of water scarcity in Dindigul, Tamilnadu, are probed by G. So ndaravalli. She observes that analysis of rainfall and mo sture regime should be the first step prior to the introduction of water management techniques.

S. Simhadri and R. Ram Mohan Rao examine water resource as an instrument of social change. White stressing that in a developing country like ours where agriculture is the dominant activity, water resource has great relevance in the dynamics of societal transformation. They observe that accrual of economic benefits to the farming community widens the horizon of necessities of people. The authors endeavour to dig into the plethora of social changes in Sriramsagar Command Area of Andhra Pradesh by analysing such variables as house types and conditions, utilities, transportation facilities, social disparities, socio-political consciousness etc.

In the next article, Water Resource assessment in the Himalayan foot-hills region in the light of losses from rainfall is made by M.N.

Nigam. He observes that losses associated with rainfall are usually of two types *viz.*, interception and direct evaporation from the depression storage. A detailed analysis of these two types is attempted.

In the article entitled "Land and Water Resources Development and Management of Tambraparani river basin, Tamilnadu," M. Sambasiva Rao observes that the criteria for classifying lands susceptible for sustained irrigated agriculture involves consideration of land productivity, land development, water resource development, land drainability and interaction of water quality on soils and crops. He stresses that land classification surveys should express the land-water-crop and economic interpretations. Suggestion are also made in the article for optimum use of water.

The problems and prospects of well irrigation in Telangana are ennunciated by A. Kamalakar Reddy, K. Surender Reddy and K. Vithal Reddy. 'The Scenario of well Irrigation in Telangana is analysed by taking taluk as unit from 1970-71 onwards.' The analysis reveals that there is a marked increase in the number of wells, resulting in increase of net and gross sown area under will irrigation. The problem of inadequate water supply from well for irrigation is analysed in relation to the future needs of food requirements.

18

WATER RESOURCES IN INDIA: A GEOGRAPHICAL PERSPECTIVE

JASBIR SINGH*

Basically, India is an agricultural country, and has more than twenty per cent of the world's irrigated land. The country receives major shares of its rainfall—over seventyfive per cent during the period of south-west monsoon. Moreover, the rainfall is highly variable from year-to-year, and in some parts it is meagre in amount for successful agriculture. As such, storage is imperative for assured supply of water for irrigation agriculture. India is among the foremost in the world in exploiting its water resources, surface water in particular. Remarkable targets have been achieved in conserving the water resources for irrigation, generation of hydro-electric power and drinking water supply during the thrity years of planned development of Independent India. A more than ten-fold increase has been registered over the pre-independence storage capacity under the newly completed reservoirs: while the gross storage capacity of the reservoirs existing in 1947 was only about fourteen thousand million cubic metres (m.cum), it has been

*Professor of Agricultural Geography, Kurukshetra University, Kurukshetra (Haryana—India).

stepped upto about one hundred and sixty thousand m.cum. by the end of 1978. An additional gross storage of about thrity thousand m.cum. is envisaged to be created when the projects under construction are completed in the next few years ahead. The gross storage created under projects completed or in hand is about one hundred and ninety thousand m.cum. This would be about twenty seven per cent of the usable quantity of the surface water resources of India, which has been estimated at seven hundred thousand m.cum. In terms of average annual flows of the country it would amount to only about eleven per cent, ranging from about sixty per cent in the Krishna basin to a mere 0.30 per cent in the Brahmaputra basin.

The significance of water resources in regional development of agriculture hardly requires emphasis. The increasing need of water for agriculture may be met by intensive and extensive use of the available resources. Intensive use refers to the local circumstances such as minor or tubewell irrigation, the latter involves regional aspects of irrigation such as canal irrigation. Therefore one of the major purpose of inquiry into the water resources is to define the regional patterns of their quantity and quality as well as utilisation.

In areas having meagre, concentrated and highly truant rainfall, agriculture without irrigation is a suicidal uneconomic venture. Under such conditions the availability of water is the only redeaming factor. An assured and regulated supply of agricultural water from ground and surface resources is the basic input and essential aspect upon which the future planning of irrigation agriculture depends in drought prone areas in India.

Drought Prone Areas

The complex system, that is of monsoon currents, altitudinal alignments, variablity of rainfall, erratic cyclones and potential evapotranspiration (PE) in excess of rainfall, leads to excessively low rainfall and soil mositure deficit regions and pockets which are well defined in India. The drought prone areas in tropical latitudes may be defined as those which receive rainfall under seventyfive centimetres per annum and where intensity of irrigation is under thirty per cent.

The major drought areas comprises the Thar desert and the semi-arid regions in India, about six hundred thousand sq. km. in extent (Figure 1). The rainfall in this tract is under 75 cm and, at places even less than 40cm. Some of the areas in this region where irrigation facilities do not exist, are amongst the world famine tracts of the country.

The second region comprises the areas east of the Western Ghats upto a width of three hundred kilometres, known as the Rain Shadow Region of the Western Ghats. The rainfall in this region is under 75cm and is highly variable. This area is thickly populated and the periodic droughts cause considerable suffering to human life and damage to crops. Since the Eastern Ghats are low, and highly broken up in the Krishna Basin, the semi-arid conditions extend almost to within eightly kilometres from the eastern coast in this region of Tamil Nadu and Andhra Pradesh. The area of this region is about three hundred seventy thousand sq. kiiometres (Figure 1).

Besides the two principal rectangles of drought areas as shown in Figure 1, there are pockets of drought in several parts of India. The scattered pockets total to about one hundred thousand sq. kilometres.

The total area thus affected by rainfall under seventyfive centimetres is about 1070 thousand sq. kilometres which form thrityfive percent of the total geographical area or a little over one-third of the country. Area between 75cm and 100cm of rainfall per annum may be considered as transitionl area where droughts may recur. The areas that may be free of droughts, save in a few exceptional years, are those where rainfall is over 100cm or 110cm. However, fifty per cent of the country gets rainfall under 100cm and in many parts of these areas the scarcity conditions have been overcome with the utilisation of surface and ground water. Obviously, the best hope for the future, in many parts of India, lies in the provision of irrigation a basic size-neutral input as an input for all other inputs for the Green Revolution.

Sources of Water

There are, in fact, four major sources of water available to man, namely, surface water, ground water, forms of precipitation, and the oceans. Of them, for humanity surface water in the form of rivers, streams and lakes is by far the most important source to be utilised for irrigation purposes. Fortunately, many parts of India are endowed with vast resources of irrigation water (available from two sources, *i.e.*, surface water and ground water) alongwith tropical, sub-tropical, and temperate climates having potentials to grow crops round-the-year and to carry on irrigation agriculture. Unfortunately, in many parts of India its distribution is variable, and at places quantity is limited and quality is not fit for human use.

According to Rao (1975) the total flow in all the river systems (mjor, medium or minor) in India is broadly assessed at 1,645 thousand m.cum. (1,334 million acre feet). The ground water is estimated to be about two hundred fifty-five thousand m.cum. of which about ninety per cent occurs in the Sutlej-Gangetic plain. Thus, the total water available in India from all sources is estimated at about 1,900 thousand m.cum. It is unfortunate that no adequate, precise, reliable measurement of flows, and geographic assessment of ground water resources are available to plan an economic exploitation of the valuable natural endowment. The geographic assessment of water resources is essential for planning and to harness the precious natural resources economically, judiciously and conjunctively. Therefore, these should carried out immediatly having sufficient/coverage.

(i) Surface Water

A beginning has been made to determine the river flows in some of the river basins making use of conventional methods. More discharge observation sities are being established. Besides, the observations be taken for a long period (atleast over a period of three to four decades) so as to make them more reliable and useful in planning the use of water resources for future generations. These records are essential to plan irrigation, the more need of which would arise in the years ahead due to increasing population pressure on land. Therefore, wisdom lies in planning for the future based on the past experiences.

The discharge observations and catchment areas of major basins (Figure 1) as given by Rao (1975) are shown in correlation scatter diagram (Figure 2). The diagonal line in Figure 2 represents the discharge in major basins having moderate rainfall, such as the Mahanadi, the Narmada, Brahmani, and Subarnarekha. Above this line, lie the basins having high rainfall, and examples of these are the Ganga and the Brahmaputra. The basins falling below this line predominantly lie in semi-arid areas, and the Indus, the Godavari, the Krishna, the Tapi, Cauvery, the Sabarmati and the Pennar basins are examples of this category.

The following scale as given by Rao (1975) shows the relationship between rainfall and the average discharge in m.cum. per 100sq. kilometres of catchment area:

—River basins with predominantly high rainfall: 65.0 m.cum. per 100 sq. kilometres.

—River basins with medium rainfall: 45.0 m.cum. per 100 sq. kilometres.

—River basins with low rainfall: 25.0 m.cum. per 100 sq. kilometres.

Making use of this scale, here an attempt has been made to classify the major river basins on the basis of rainfall quantity (Table 1 and Figure 2).

Of the total annual discharge of the different categories of river systems in India, the major river systems contribute about 85.99 per cent; while the medium, minor rivers, etc. contribute only 14.01 per cent (Table 1). The comparison of the flow in some of the major rivers of the world reveals that the Brahmaputra and the Ganga are within the first ten rivers of the world positioned at eight and tenth ranks respectively. The total flow

TABLE 1

Drainage area and Discharge of Major River Basins

Sl. No.	*Name of the River Basin*	*Drainage area in square Kilometres*	*Annual average discharge in million cubic metres*	*Million cubic metres per 100 sq. kilometres of drainage area*	*Rainfall*	*Annual average discharge as percentage of total dischare of major. medium and minor and desert rivers (1,645,106 million cubic meters*
1.	The Ganga	8,61,404	493,400	57.28	High	30.17
2.	Brahmaputra	5,80,000	510,450	88.00	High	31.22
3.	Sabarmati	21,674	3,200	14.76	Low	0.20
4.	Mahi	34,842	8,500	24.39	Low	0.52
5.	Narmada	98,796	40,705	41.20	Medium	2.49
6.	Tapi (Tapti)	65,146	17,982	27.60	Low	1.10
7.	Subarnarekha	19,296	7,940	41.15	Medium	0.48

8.	Brahmani	39,033	18,310	46.91	Medium	1.12
9.	Mahanadi	1,41,589	66,640	47.06	Medium	4.08
10.	Godavari	3,12,812	105,000	33.57	Low	6.42
11.	Krishna	2,58,948	67,675	26.13	Low	4.14
12.	Pennar	55,213	3,238	5.86	Low	0.20
13.	Cauvery	87,900	20,950	23.83	Low	1.28
14.	The Indus	3,21,289	41.955	13.06	Low	2.57
					Total	85.99

Source: Rao, K.L., India's Water Wealth, p. 46

of all the rivers in India is about six per cent of the discharge of all rivers in the world.

The quality of surface water in a river depends upon the weathering of rocks and soils of the terrain it traverses. The presence of carbonates of calcium indicates the abundance of limestone in the catchment area; and sulphates and chlorides indicate pollution of surface water. In general, it can be mentioned that rivers flowing through Deccan Trap (black cotton soil area) contain higher soluble salt content than the rivers flowing over the alluvial, laterite and red soils. However, the chloride and sodium content is relatively low in the rivers. The quality rating of surface water used for irrigation in India reveals that water may be rated having moderate salinity and no alkali hazard, and is considered excellent for use in irrigation agriculture.

The conservation of surface water by storing it in reservoirs, tanks, etc., is important specially in India where most of the flow in the rivers, to the extent of about eighty per cent occurs in the monsoon months (June to September). For the rest of the year, there will be only inadequate or no water supply from the rivers. Therefore, storage of water is very essential for irrigation agriculture in India. It is also necessary for the generation of hydroelectric power. The effective storage capacity built or under construction in various basins in India, excluding small tanks, is about one ninety thousand m.cum. It was only about fourteen thousand m.cum. at the time of independence. In the United States where the total flow in the river system is comparable with India, the total storage-built capacity is four hundred fortyfour thousand m.cum., which *vis-a-vis* India is comparatively much high. Of the live storage-built capacity in India fifteen per cent is for hydroelectric projects, and the rest is for multi-purpose projects or irrigation.

The total storage capacity when expressed as a percentage of the total flow in the basins, is about 8.91 per cent. It means that about ninetyone per cent of the surface water is still unused, if storage in tanks and small ponds is included the figure may drop to only ninety per cent. The aim must be to built storage capacity to the extent which, at least, may store fifty per cent of the basin flows: conservative value. By having this value as a base, it will be seen that we have yet to go a long way in the planning of new stroages practically in all the major basins, except perhaps Krishna, and Tapi (Table 2). The surface water resources are not put to full use in the basins like Ganga, Narmada, Subarnarekha and Brahmaputar. The position is not encouraging in the Mahanadi and the Godavari basins. The situation is slightly favourable in the basins of the Indus (in Indian territory), the Sabarmati, Cauvery and Mahi.

TABLE 2

Average Annual Flows of River Basins, and Storage Capacities created upto 1975

Sl. No.	*Name of the River Basin*	*Annual Average discharge in million cubic metres*	*Cumulative gross storage in million cubic metres*	*Gross storage capacity as percentge of annual average flow*
1	*2*	*3*	*4*	*5*
1.	Krishna	68,283	38,866	65.92
2.	Tapi	16,967	9,251	54.52
3.	Sabarmati	2,883	1,269	44.02
4.	Cauvery	20.695	7,420	35.85
5.	Mahi	11,829	3,420	28.91
6.	Indus (Indian Share)	73,305	18,050	24.62
7.	Damodar & Kosai	24,032	4,721	19.64
8.	Godavari	1,18,982	16,600	13.95
9.	Mahanadi	66,879	8,981	13.43
10.	Ganga	4,44,053	30,286	6.82

(Contd.)

1	2	3	4	5
11.	Subarnarekha	10,756	706	6.56
12.	Narmada	42,966	2,983	6.94
13.	Brahmani and Baitarni	36,227	630	1.74
14.	Brahmaputra	5,90,714	184	0.31
15.	West flowing rivers	1,97,956	12,174	6.15
16	East flowing rivers	41,531	2,086	5.02
	Total	1,768,058	1,57,627	8.91

Source: Memorandum on storages in River Basins of India, New Delhi, Water Resources Utilisation Directorate, Central Water Commission (Government of India), January 1979, p. 1.

(ii) Ground Water

In India the yield of ground water is dependent on the geological formations. There are three important formations which have bearing on the ground water potentialities. There are:

—consolidated hard rock formations,

—semi-consolidated rock formations, and

—unconsolidated rock formations.

—The consolidated hard rock formations comprise a very large portion of the country, nearly 1,200 thousand sq. kilometres in Peninsular India. These include either basalts or granites, slates, gneisses, etc. These rocks have little pore space. As a consequence, there are little possibilities of ground water irrigation, *i.e.*, tubewell or well irrigation (Table 3 and Figure 1). However, ground water occurs only in the weathered porous material or in physical opening like joints, fractures etc., in the rock masses.

TABLE 3

Utilisation of Water Resources for Irrigation in Major Basins

Sl. No.	*Name of the River Basin*	*Surface Water irrigation as percentage of net area sown*	*Ground water irrigation as percentage of net area sown*	*Net area irrigated as percentage of net area sown*
1.	The Ganga	25·64	9.21	34.85
2.	Brahmaputra	20.09	—	20.09
3.	Sabarmati	18.91	0.87	19.78
4.	Mahi	11.08	0.75	11.83
5.	Narmada	4.65	0.24	4.89
6.	Tapi	9.22	0.10	9.32
7.	Subarnarekha	16.20	—	16.20
8.	Brahamani	14.64	—	14.64
9.	Mahanadi	21.23	—	21.23
10.	Godavari	12.02	0.19	12.21
11.	Krishna	16.68	0.18	16.86
12.	Pennar	19.55	0.58	20.13
13.	Cauvery	30.63	0.14	30.77
14.	Indus	46.28	22.17	68.45
	Average	21.66	5.30	26.96

Source: Rao, K.L., India's Water Wealth. pp. 61-63.

—The semi-consolidated rock formations, covering about fifty thousand sq. kilometres, consist of sedimentary rocks, such as sandstones, limestones and conglomerates. These have wide spaces and cavities. Therefore, their porosity is good, and installation of tubewells and deep dug wells is possible in these formations. These can yield good amount of water. These formations occur in Rajasthan, Gujarat and Tamil Nadu

—The large areas of unconsolidated rocks and soils are found in North India. These formations consist mainly of sand, gravel, boulder, laterite, loam and clay. The heavy capacity tubewells can be installed in these areas comprising the Sutlej-Gangetic plain, Bhabar areas, the Brahmaputra basin, Luni river basin in Rajasthan, coastal plains, and in valleys like Kashmir, Doon and Manipur. These are the areas where tubewell irrigation is practised on a significant scale (Table 3) and the future possibilities of extension cannot be ruled out. While the yields of the tubewells differ from area-to-area and season-to-season, it is considerably more than that available in other geological formations.

The geographic assessment of ground water made by researchers in India indicates availability of about 333 thousand m.cum., of which about ninety per cent is associated with unconsolidated formations, six per cent with semi-consolidated and four per cent with consolidated geological formations. On the whole, it is interesting to note that about seventy per cent of the future development of underground water has to take place in the Great plain of North India.

A word of caution, in areas where replenishment is neither available at present nor possible in the time to come, exploitation of static class of ground water must proceed in a limited manner, and exploitation be done judiciously *vis-a-vis* usable class which is replenishable and economically exploitable. As rain water dissolves many of the salts, it is known as *Universal Solvent*, and it contributes to the ground water many salts, and as a consequence the water becomes brackish in many parts of India, specially in areas having arid and semi-arid conditions. However, high sodium concentration ground water can be made suitable for irrigation by mixing it with fresh surface water in a desired proportion and by adding gypsum and organic matter to the soils.

Acknowledgements

The author is indebted to Dr. R.L. Sharma and Dr. J.P. Gupta for the preparation of base map and tabulation of data respectively, and Shri D.N. Sharma for the final preparation of the map and diagram.

Works Cited

1. Central Water Commission, *Memorandum on storages in river basins in India*. New Delhi, Water Resources Utilisation Directorate, Central Water Commission, Government of India, January 1979, p, I.
2. Rao, K.L., *India's Water Wealth; its assessment, uses and projections*. New Delhi, Orient Longman Limited 1975, pp. XV, 46-48, 60-63.

19

WATER SCARCITY IN DINDIGUL

G. SOUNDARAVALLI*

Dindigul, a city of 1.8 (mid year 1985) lakhs population has become the district headquarters for the newly organized "Anna District" of Tamil Nadu. This new district is carved out of old Madurai district, covering an area of five thousand eight hundred thirty two sq. km. This district population according to 1981 census is 1.64 million. As early as 1955, it was recognized that "not only the prosperity and safety, the very existence of the town depends on a proper water supply" (The Hindu, 1955). Even today position regarding the protected water supply has not changed. Therefore it is an attempt to analyse the historical growth of the city and the persistent water need for this growing city. Since any examination of water scarcity demands the evaluation of rainfall, this study deals with this natural input parameter related to water balance and to the geological characteristics within the city.

Water Requirement

The demand for domestic water supply is usually estimated taking into account of the population numbers. The accelerated growth of population will create manifold increase in water

*Professor of Geography, M. V. M. Govt. College, Dindigul,

requirement and Dindigul is no exception. Its population depicted variable trend in growth since 1901. Introduction of rail route, conversion into railway junction and the regulated administrative system through the town municipality had resulted in the accelerated trend in the past, from 1961 government incentive of subsidiary for the establishment of small scale factories attracted influx of rural population therefore the recent position of Dindigul as the District headquarters will add to the population growth thereby the water demand.

The following table shows the water requirement of Dindigul city.

TABLE 1

Population and water requirement

Year	*Population (lakhs)*	*Water requirement lakh gallons per day*
1961	0.93	—
1981	1.64	25
1985	1.80	28
1991	2.05	31

The first step taken towards the supply of drinking water was in 1866 under Odukkam water supply scheme. By 1954 demand for water supply grew and Odukkam scheme was found inadequate. Thereafter the Athoor scheme was planned known as Kamaraj Sagar situated at twentyfour kms from Dindigul. This had helped to harness Kodavanar water for then estimated population of 1.5 lakhs by 1986. The aim was to provide fifteen gallons per capita per day. Because of the population of the city has crossed this limit by 1985 (1.8 lakhs) this seheme is now inadequate to meet the water requirement of the city. The recent acute water problem in Dindigul had made everyone to accept the fact that water scarcity is nothing uncommon.

Therefore it is necessary to investigate hydrological aspects and to find a solution for the perennial water problem. An attempt is made here to bring a clear picture of the moisture regime of the city.

Data Base

As the present study aims at the moisture fluctuation rainfall values for fifty years on monthly basis are collected and evaporation particulars for the recent decade namely from 1975-76 to 1984-85 are obtained from the Central Tobacco Research Station, Vedasandur, Fifteen km away from Dindigual. These values are applied for Dindigul based on the assumption that temperature and evaporation do not very much in the tropical country. The water level fluctuation has been observed personally along the main artery road of the city.

Methodology

Rainfall for south-west monsoon, north-east monsoon and for the year has been computed from fifty years monthly data. These form the basis for further analysis. Arithmetic means ($\bar{x}$) standard deviation (σn-1) and coefficient of variabilities are calculated for the above mentioned rainfall break-ups.

TABLE 2

Season	$\bar{X}$ *(mm)*	*σn-1*	*M (mm)*	*CV%*
Annual	834.0	214.9	801.7	39.8%
North-east monsoon	400.1	145.0	416.1	36.2
South-West monsoon	257.9	102.7	250.5	25.8

$\bar{X}$=Mean *σn-1*=Standard deviation *M*=Median *CV*=Coefficient of variability

five year moving means are used to indentify the long" term trends in the rainfall. These trends are plotted. (Fig. 1) Rainfall percentage frequency with the recurrence interval are computed and plotted (Fig. 2) to estimate the rainfall amount with ten year recurrence interval from the frequency analysis the median values for annual, north-east and south-west monsoon season are obtained. Using these median value (M) and the standard deviation (σn-1) normal, surplus and drought years are identified within ten years period (1975-76 to 1984-85). The values which are equal to M, M+σn-1 and M -$\sigma(n$-1) are taken to represent the normal, surplus and drought years respectively.

Moving averages for these ten years are considered for correlation between annual, north-east and south-west monsoon rains (Table 3).

TABLE 3

Annual	*North-east monsoon*	*South-west monsoon*
Annual	0.68	0.34
North-east monsoon	—	0.16
South-west monsoon	—	—

Pan evaporation values obtained from the research station are used after applying standard correction for evaporimeter to derive potential evapotranspiration. Adopting book keeping procedure of Thornthwaite—Matter (1957), water balance for normal (1978-79), surplus (1977-78) and drought (1982-83, 1984-85) years are worked out. Moisture indices *IM* are computed as (*Ih*—0.6 *Ia*) (Subramanyan 1982).

Analysis

The coefficient of variability for north-east monsoon is higher than that of south-west monsoon rains. Besides, high correlation ratio between the annual and the north-east indicates annual amount will vary whenever the north-east monsoon amount varies 68 per cent of the latter fluctuation influences the former. Eventhuogh the South-west monsoon rain fluctuates it does not affect the annual amount to the same extent. The low correlation ratio between the north-east and the south-west monsoons shows that they are independent of each other. Therefore the annual rainfall will very because the two monsoons have independent influence on it.

The moving average plots infer the fact that annual variations are due to that of the north-east monsoon rains as they mark the similar trends. The south-west monsoon trend is an independent one and rarely affects the annual trend.

"The reliability of the frequency estimates depends on the length of the observed record" a ten-year estimate with 99.5 per cent" (Ragunath 1985) probability is derived.

It is therefore clear that surplus year will appear once (Table 4) in ten years. But every year there is a possibility of the rain falling below the normal values. The percentage frequency plot (Fig. 2) indicates that the values lesser than the median are closer to the estimated line. Therefore the occurrence of below normal and values are more frequent in Dindigul. The year 1978-79 is taken as the representative year of normal moisture regime. Similarly 1977-78 for surplus and 1982-83 and 1984-85 for drought are indentified (Table 5) Hence their moisture regime will speak for their fluctuations.

TABLE 4

Recurrence Interval and Percentage Frequency

T (Yrs)	*F%*	*Annual rain mm.*	*North-east rain mm.*	*South-west rain mm.*
1.3	75	700.4	293.8	194.2
2.0	50	801.7	416.1	250.5
5.0	20	986.4	504.8	348.0
10.0	10	1113.0	613.3	374.5

TABLE 5

Year	*Annual Rain (mm)*	*% Frequency*	*Indicator*	*PE (mm)*	*Ia*	*Ib%*	*Im%*	*Moisture regime*
1977-78	1372.4	3.9	Surplus	1900	69.3	31.3	—10.4	Moist subhumid
1978-79	811.3	45.1	Nearly normal	1702	51	0	−30.6	Semiarid
1982-83	504.7	94.0	deficit	1881	69.2	0	−41.5	Arid
1984-85	486.2	96.0	deficit	1879	43.8	2.9	−23.4	Semiarid

During the normal year index of moisture (*Im*) shows a negative value exceeding 30 per cent. It is clear that Dindigul is always facing moisture inadequacy. It is definitely an indicator of semi-arid regime. *Im* value touches the positive position yet index of aridity (*Ia*) is very high. It infeys that eventhough there is surplus flowing as surface run-off, most of the months remain dry. The drought years mark a negative trend in *Im*. These oscillations are the characteristic of semi arid station.

Soil Moisture and group water recharge

The critical moisture regime appears to be a common phenomenon in Dindigul. It is due to evaporation, soil type and bed rock characteristics. Evaporation is the function of day light hours, relative humidity, wind, sunshine amount as well as the elevation of a place. Dindigul is 29[illegible] above mean sea level. Lying in a rain shadow region, the winds are dominantly from north-west and north-east which are dry. During the cooler months, in late evenings dry winds descent from the Sirumalais. This is reflected in evaporation. During December, January and February evaporation is as low as 3mm per day. At other times evaporation remains high (6mm per day) and during August-September it shoots up to 10mm per day. Loss of moisture as a common phenomenon is marked by high potential evaporation values (PE). Soil moisture recharge and ground water recharge therefore depend on this factor.

Soil moisture recharge depends also on soil properties. The Dindigul series (red sandy clayey loam to clayey) have been described as "moderately well drained, with moderate to low permeability . . . the problem being alkalinity and surface run-off." (Soil Survey and Land use organisation 1984). As per their report, the water holding capacity of the soil ranges from 31 per cent to 58 per cent increasing with depth (upto 150cm plus) Therefore in water balance analysis field capacity of 200mm is assumed. (Fig 3) soil moisture usage extends from September to December normally. It gets replenished during the north east monsoon season. There is no surface run-off. There is always 51 per cent of moisture deficit. When the moisture regime is showing surplus or subhumid as in 1977-78, the soil moisture reaches to its field capacity. Excess of moisture gets drained of as surface run-off immediate because of evaporation.

When there is a drought (1982-83) high evaporative demand has resulted in rapid soil moisture reduction. The water balance of 1984-85 shows a different adjustment. The recharge period appears to be longer and there exists little surplus as run-off.

Ground Water Storage

Whenever there is a recharge, ground water storage is also receiving moisture for replacement. Water table fluctuation is the function of recharge rate and the characteristics of underlying rocks. The hard rock areas having charnockite and knodolite groups are poor areas of recharge. The joints and fractures help in the recharge. The depth of weathered zone and the transmissibility of the soil are the other controlling factors. Moderate depth of 150cm or less, low to moderate transmissibility (Soundaravalli 1982) of red sandy clayey loam (75 to 150m^2/d) and low storage coefficient of hard rocks in the city account for deep water lable even during the normal year. As the underlying rocks are similar to that of Chittar basin in Tamilnadu (Soundaravalli 1982) the threshold value of rain required to replenish the water table namely 400mm is taken into consideration.

TABLE 7

Ground Water Recharge

Year	*Percentage of recharge*
1977-78	30
1978-79	21
1982-83	9
1984-85	8

Adopting P=0.43 (R—400) (where P is the amount of rain entering in the ground water storage) it is worked out separately for the normal, surplus and drought years.

Normally the wells are deeper ranging from 20mm to 30mm., The recent droughts has resulted in drying up of most of the wells 8.9 per cent recharge was much less when compared to 21 per cent during the normal year. On account of continuous loss through evaporation, ground water level receded to greater depths. The lowest ground level within the city is a lake Gopala samundram) and the wells inside the lake bed had 30cm of stureted level in 1985. The failure of north-east monsoon in 1984 and subsequent prolonged drought are the reasons for the acute water shortage in Dindigul.

In April 1985 it was stated as "there has been a considerable fall in the ground water level in Dindigul. . ." (The Hindu 1985a) Even when Dindigul received 32.5mm rain on August 22, 1985, Kamaraj Sagar (the source of water supply to the city) did not receive any rain. (The Hindu 1985) the dam (full level 6mm) was practically dry. The cloud seeding operation was not successful.

Conclusion

Tamil Nadu Government has taken necessary steps to meet the drought and water requirement of the city. 'Water specials' were run in May 1983. Water was supplied by lorries and later on water supply was regulated through pipes once in five days, in 1985. There is a new, proposal like 'peranat' water supply scheme' which will be completed in the next four years to meet the growing demand of the city (The Hindu 1985d).

The effective planning is a must before the undertaking of any new proposal. The lesson learnt from the past years show that the maintenance of public wells were not proper. Major part of the district including the city itself has to be declared as drought prone area. Clear insight is necessary to make use of the available rains. On the other hand, wastage through improper maintenance of pipes, public fountains as well as private pipes has to be avoided. Depending off the existing wells and maintenance of bore wells which are in recently are very important because Dindigul by its nature is prone towards aridity rather than the moisture surplus. From this study it is clear that every alternate year rainfall below normal will occur. Surplus condition is of rare frequency only once in ten years. Therefore the zone of potential water storage are to be identified. In any new proposal to supply protected water to the city, proper stress is to be made on water management.

REFERENCES

Ragunath, H.M. 1985 *Hydrology—Principles, Analysis and Design*, Wely Eastern Limited, New Delhi, pp. 47-51 and 245.

Soundaravalli, G 1982 Geomrphology and Hydrology of Chittar basir (Tirunelveli district) Tamil Nadu, *Unpublished Ph.D. thesis, Osmania University, Hyderabad.*

Subrahmanyan, V.P. 1982 *Water Balance and Applications*, Andhra University Press, Waltair, Visakhapatnam.

Government of Tamil Nadu, 1984 *Dindigul Master Plan Official report*, Town and Country Planning, unit, Madurai.

The Hindu, 1955 Dindigul water supply scheme *July 4, 1955, pp. 6.*

The Hindu, 1985a Water Scarcity in 12 Taluks, *April 21, 1985 pp. 1.*

——— 1985b Serious water famine in Dindigul, *August 16, 1985 pp. 12.*

———1985c Water shortage cases in Dindigul town, *August 23, 1985, pp. 1.*

———1985d Tourist and pilgrim potential of New Anna District, *September 14, 1985, pp. 12.*

20

WATER RESOURCE AS AN INSTRUMENT OF SOCIAL CHANGE

S. SIMHADRI*

R. RAM MOHAN RAO*

Social change may be defined as modification in ways of living, doing and thinking of people. It refers to the modifications which occur in the life patterns of people. According to Anderson and Parker (1969) social change is the structure of functioning of socical forms or processes. Social changes are "Variations from the accepted or pre-existing modes of life—whether due to alteration in geographical conditions, in cultural equipment, composition of population, or ideologies and whether brought about by diffusion or inventions within the group" (Gillian and Gillian, 1950).

A number of gigantic irrigation projects have come up in India with the intention of providing much needed irrigation facilities to the parched lands in the semi-arid parts of the country. The primary aim in constructing these projects is economic upliftment of the command areas by increasing the productivity levels in the agricultural sector. However, it has

*Mr. S. Simhadri, Lecturer and Dr. R. Ram Mohan Rao is Reader in the Department of Geography, Osmania University, Hyderabad.

been observed that the provision of irrigation facilities is also found to cause transformation of the society. It is hypothesised that provision of water generates vibrations in the societal structure. The present paper seeks to examine what sort of these vibrations are and in what form they are reflected. It aims to probe the type and degree of social transformation as reflected by selected reflective elements.

The area of the study is the right bank command area of Sriramsagar irrigation project (previously known as Pochampad) irrigated by Kakatiya canal. Sriramsagar dam was built across River Godavari which is one of the great rivers of India next only to Ganga in importance. The water was let out in a phased manner during the early seventies. Kakatiya canal is the right bank canal of the project and was taken up for construction in two stages. The first stage encompasses an area from Armoor taluq of Nizamabad district to Warangal city, covering parts of Metpalli, Jagtial, Peddapalli, Manthani, Karimnagar and Huzurabad talukas of Karimnagar district. Irrigation facilities were provided to Metpalli and Jagtial taluq as back as fifteen years. Recently water facility has been extended to other talukas with the exception of a few stretches of Manthani and Huzurabad talukas.

The study is based on the data obtained from questionnaire surveys and observational studies. Taking a stratified random method, a sample of five per cent (thirty seven villages) was picked up. Village questionnaire was employed to collect information concerning the in-built potentialities and changing characteristics of the study area. The indicators chosen to reflect the nature of social change are: caste-wise housing, transport, utilities, commercial establishments, migration and socio-political conditions.

Indian social structure has been in operation mainly on caste lines with a hereditary and endogamous nature (Srinivas 1966). Brahmin, Vysya (traders), Velama (farmers), Reddy (farmers), Munnurkapu (farmers), Yadava (Shepherds), Padmasali (Weavers), Gouda (Toddy tappers), Tenugu, Perika (Money landers), Mere (Tailor), Avasali (Gold smith), Kammari (Black

Smith), Vadla (Carpenter), Kummari (Potters), Bestha, (Fisherman), Chakali (Washerman), Mangali (Barbers), Vaddari (Stone cutters), Erukali (Basket weavers), Muslim, Christian, Mala, Madiga, etc. are the significant castes found in the study area. Brahmin, Vysya, Velama, Reddy, come under forward castes. Mala, Madiga are the scheduled castes, and Erukalis are Scheduled Tribes and all others excepting Muslims, and Christains are considered as backward castes. Christains who have been converted from Scheduled Caste are treated as belonging backward class.

The type of house in which certain type of family lives besides reflecting the economic status, is also an indicator of the social status of that family. Bhavanti type country-tile roofed house built with indigenous building materials was the most commonly seen house in the area of study before the onset of irrigation facilities. This type of house used to be the aboode of most of the socially developed classes *e.g.*, Brahmins, Vysyas, Velama, Reddys, etc. Most of the other castes specially the Scheduled Castes and Tribes used to live in simple, easy to build and cheap thatched roof houses.

As the benefits of irrigation facilities have started accruing, the pattern of house types has markedly changed. Although country-tile roofed houses are still in existence, they have lost their predominant position. Relatively more and more modern houses built of R.C.C. and Mangalore tiles have spring up in the country side. There is also a substantial decrease in the number of thatched roof houses. Not only lhat, the ownership of pucca Bhavanti-type houses and modern R.C.C. houses is no more the monopoly of forward castes. A substantial number of newly built Mangalore roofed houses are owned by Scheduled Caste and Backward Class people.

Mobility as a social factor is much dependent on the availability of transport facility, level of economic development and social awareness. Transport facility acts as an instrument to deliver the information in the process creating interaction among the villages and towns which, in turn, infuses new ideas into the country side. It is observed that the people were deprived of access with the rest of the world for generations as there was no physical infrastructure. Irrigation gave the fillip to the economy as in the case of other fields.

Most of the villages in the command area are now well connected by motorable roads which were laid by project planners as a matter of policy. Four out of five villages in Metpalli, six out of seven in Jagtial, eight out of eleven in Peddapalli, two out of three in Manthani, three out of five in Karimnagar and five out of six sample villages in Huzurabad are provided with motorable road facility. Although some bus services were in existence before, provision of water made villages feasible to have greater bus access. Bus service frequency has also increased manifold. In Metpally, for example, it went up by four fold and is followed by Jagtial with three times increase. Bus service is a recent phenomenon in cases of many villages of the rest unirrigated segment of the command area. Private buses operation is predominant and introduction of RTC is a recent one. The utilities considered in this study are bicycles, motor cycles and cars. It is found that there is a spate in increase in the number of bicycles. Card are almost non existent in the country side. Study also reveals (Table 1) that the Man-bicycle ratio has been tremendously influenced by water. Prior to 1971, when the water was not yet released the Man cycle ratio was very low when compared to the sudden spurt in the ratio after the provision of assured irritation facilities which automatically led to prosperity.

The provision of good transportation facilities in the country side of the command area has led to a greater degree of mobility of the people specially those belonging to hitherto deprived classes. This has resulted in greater interaction between places and people and also diffusion of ideas, habits, life styles, etc.

It can be observed that as a consequence of greater degree of mobility a new set of attitudes and social relations have emerged in the changed scenario.

A more vibrant change is felt in rapid expansion of commercial establishments (Table 3) and their typology. Commerce in rural areas used to be the monopoly of Vysya community since generations. A striking change can be observed in the type of units and ownership pattern. Prior to the provision of water, the commercial activity was limited to Kirana shops only. Provision of water dismantled the age old tradition of commerce being run by Vysyas only. It led to the emergence of a different spectrum, in which, the activity is no more the monopoly of Vysyas. Not only people from other castes are now engaged in trade and commerce, but many new types of commercial establishments like cloth shops etc. have started making their appearance.

There has been a shift in traditional occupations. A marked transfer is taking place by the entry of backward communities like Padmasali, Gouda, and Perika and forward community like Muslim venturing into new non-traditional occupations. All the units, which have come up recently are captured by these communities resulting competition in the trade. Ownership pattern of Kirana (grocery) shops was traditionally with Vysyas and to a limited extent by Padmasali, and Muslim. Hotel, Cloth, Cycle Taxi, Pan shops belong to Padmasali, Gouda and Muslim and their involvement is very recent. The new class of businessmen participate in business in addition to agriculture. The profits in commerce range from Rs. 200 to 800 per month in most of the cases and this is an additional income supplemental to the income from agriculture. It can therefore, be inferred that increased commercial activity is creating a new frame to social structure upon which emerging social relations are to operate.

In response to the ripples sent by assured irrigation, some cammunities like Vysya, Padmasali, Gouda and Muslim have migrated to the area after 1970. Migration on insignificant scale also took place during 1960s. Sixty three per cent of sample villages have a migration composition of five to fifteen families in each village. In the other twenty seven per cent of villages, there has not been any in migration. It is found that the distance travelled by migrants is short. Some of the in-migrants are from the submerged villages of the reservoir. However, a few villages situated in the mining belt are experiencing rapid in migration.

Apart from this there has been some out-migration due to unstable political situation and extremist activity. Land lords belonging to upper castes fled the area and settled in urban centres. These land lords who mostly belong to Reddy and Velama castes, are no more a force to reckon with as far as the village society and economy is concerned. Their lands are being taken over by the people belonging to backward classes and scheduled class.

Political scenario is like smouldering caldera. There has been a mass upsurge in the extremist activities. The annihilation of feudal lords by extremists in retaliation of suppression of backward class and scheduled class people. One of the causes for the struggle seem to be of commissioning of irrigation project (Balagopal 1983) which increased the 'commoditization.' Another factor appears to be the grabbing large areas of land belonging to the villagers by feudal lords. Confrontation erupted between landlords and labourers as land has become more productive. It can also be observed that the growth of economy and monopolisation of resources by a small segment of the society polarised the class interests. Besides, there is a disproportionate balance between wages and production. Taking advantage of these conditions extremist parties took hold of the situation and organised the revolt against the landlords. There have been some incidents of stopping land transactions made by the landlords.

Apart from this, water flow is also making strides in the dilution of rigid traditional inter-caste relationships. It is observed that the untouchables, backward castes and forward castes use the same body of the water for drinking, bathing and washing. Hitherto, before the construction of canals, water was available at point locations which intrinsically led to the segregation of the facility. Now, since the water is available in linear pattern, it is no more possible to have caste wise segregation. All caste people have to obtain water from the same source, thus leading to the breakdown of social barriers to some extent.

Income generated from the economic affluence of the area has been siphoned off into the urban centres, leading to alarming growth of urban centres. Emergence of strong urban centres heralded a new era of social life and acquiring urban life styles. Cinema theatres have mushroomed, buzzing trade has taken roots, and new political power centres have emerged. These factors, together, led to the emergence of a new class of people. The emerging structure may lead of erosion of some of the traditional relations and in establishing a new social order. However, the extent of social change, its intensity, spread and consequences are yet to be assessed and probed in detail.

BIBLIOGRAPHY

Amarnath K. Menon, India Today, May 15, 1985.

Anderson and Parker, Society, pp. 385, 1964.

Balagopal K. AP: Peasant struggle and Repression in Peddapalli, EPW Vol. XVII, No. 20, May 15, 1982.

Gillian and Gillian, Cultural Sociology, pp. 561, 1950.

Srinivas M.N., Caste in Modern India and other Essays, Asia Publishing Home, Bombay, 1962.

—Social Change in Modern India, Allied Publishers, New Delhi, 1966.

TABLE I

Man-Cycle Ratio

Taluka	*1961*	*1962*	*1981*
Metpalli	27	28	17
Jagtial	186	178	47
Peddapalli	115	42	21
Manthani	—	—	143
Karimnagar	355	55	9
Huzurabad	469	166	51
S C A	100	55	19

TABLE II

Caste-Wise Distribution of House Types

	Brahmin				*Vysya*				*Velama*				*Reday*				*Munnuru Kapu*			
	RCC	*MT*	*CT*	*TH**	*RCC*	*MT*	*CT*	*TH*	*RCC*	*MT*	*CT*	*TH*	*RCC*	*MT*	*CT*	*TH*	*RCC*	*MT*	*CT*	*TH*
Metpalli	—	3	4	—	1	2	9	—	6	7	3	—	57	11	72	—	17	5	65	3
Jagtial	—	—	1	—	5	3	19	—	—	2	16	—	—	16	40	—	—	14	59	22
Peddapally	1	2	10	—	7	4	57	4	4	12	34	—	11	75	174	42	—	9	48	55
Manthani	—	—	—	—	—	—	13	—	—	—	—	—	—	1	24	5	—	1	7	3
Karimnagar	—	1	36	—	5	6	33	—	4	3	45	3	15	52	161	2	—	2	248	—
Huzurabad	—	—	17	—	12	1	31	—	—	15	28	10	6	44	225	3	—	3	154	21
% Houses owned by each caste.		0.65					1.84				1.67				9.00				6.38	

*RCC—Reinforced Cement Concrete, MT—Mangalore Tiles, CT—Country Tiles, TH—Thatched Roof.

TABLE II (*Contd.*)

Caste-Wise Distribution of House Types

Yadava				*Padmasali*				*Gouda*				*Tenugu*				*O.B.C*				*SC & ST*			
RCC	*MT*	*CT*	*TH*	*RCC*	*MT*	*CT*	*TH*	*RCC*	*MT*	*CT*	*TH*	*RCC*	*MT*	*CT*	*TH*	*RCC*	*MT*	*CT*	*TH*	*RCC*	*MT*	*CT*	*TH*
2	2	72	1	7	5	57	—	4	1	26	5	—	—	28	7	14	18	136	152*	—	46	174	112
1	9	40	12	3	29	56	10	—	6	18	4	—	3	20	—	2	32	205	209	1	39	24	83
—	11	208	112	1	21	137	88	—	38	153	64	1	48	265	234	5	38	653	170	—	10	144	452
—	5	29	10	—	—	15	4	—	3	13	4	—	15	26	72	—	—	328	24	—	1	24	79
2	9	239	20	10	50	291	4	2	20	278	31	—	7	167	61	5	41	416	42	1	151	176	26
—	22	234	59	—	15	155	10	—	3	247	60	3	16	122	129	9	51	389	124	—	13	125	312
8.87				8.41				8.52				10.64				26.62				17.38			

TABLE III

Population—Commercial Units Ratio

	1961							
	Kirana	*Cloth*	*Hotel*	*Pan*	*Cycle Taxi*	*Others*	*Kirana*	*Cloth*
Metpalli	3881	Nil	Nil	Nil	Nil	Nil	4061	Nil
Jagtial	1781	—	—	—	—	—	2392	—
Peddapalli	1712	—	13702	—	—	—	1674	—
Manthani	—	—	—	—	—	—	1129	3388
Karimnagar	1242	—	6211	—	—	—	828	6211
Huzurabad	977	—	11929	—	—	—	658	—
Sriram Sagar Command Area	1547	—	14310	—	—	—	1190	23800

1971						*1981*			
Hotel	*Pan*	*Cycle Taxi*	*Others*	*Kirana*	*Cloth*	*Hotel*	*Pan*	*Cycle Taxi*	*Others*
—	—	—	—	1424	14243	2373	4747	NA	4747
—	—	—	—	600	16043	3208	16000	1782	8021
8372	—	8372	—	424	2123	805	—	2595	11677
—	—	—	—	593	4151	—	—	—	—
2484	—	6211	—	403	2095	998	1048	1612	1905
7240	—	—	—	355	3403	896	17019	1418	8510
7934	—	35701	—	496	3302	1197	13680	2816	5400

21

AN APPROACH IN WATER RESOURCE ASSESSMENT IN THE HIMALAYAN FOOT—HILLIS: CALCULATING LOSSES FROM RAINFALL

M.N. NIGAM*

The Himalayas are the great reservoirs of moisture for the plains of northern India. The rivers in the area are either snow-fed or rain-fed. The rain-fed rivers depend entirely on direct rainfall or that part of rainfall which is absorbed by the soils and the rocks during the rains and is deposited in the rivers through various means. In order to put the water of these rain-fed rivers to its best use in all the reaches, it is very essential to have a correct assessment of their total water potential at each stage during different periods of the year. There are usually two types of losses associated with the rainfall over an area and they are technically termed as interception and direct evaporation from the depression storage. Both of these processes need separate treatment. In interception the loss goes on taking place due to evaporation of water falling on the leafy surfaces till the entire foliage is saturated. Even

*Department of Geography, Dayanand College, Ajmer-305 001.

after this saturation some evaporation take place. The water retained by the leaves at the time of cessation of rainfall is completely lost to the atmosphere through evaporation. It is estimated that a tree of 400,000 leaves will contain about 6 cubic metres of water (Hull, 1964). The enormous amount of water thus lost in a basin with 20,000 trees would come to 3946 cubic metre of water in one single storm.

Wind affects interception in two ways. It reduces the amount of maximum storage and accelerates the rate of evaporation. These two processes act in opposite directions. In steady rains when lighter winds prevail, the rate of interception is rapid in the beginning and diminishes as the storage is full. Wind, however, generally tends to increase total interception in a storm of longer duration while it decreases the same in a storm of shorter duration. The evaporation rates are always higher during the early part of a storm if the period before the rain was dry. Even if the rates of evaporation during the rainfall are low the total values for large foliage surfaces are much. more.

The surface litter also tends to intercept some of the falling rain water and some of it percolates downward while the rest is lost to the atmosphere through evaporation.

Direct Evaporation: The areas which do not have any vegetal cover like house roofs, roads, courtyards, playgrounds, recently ploughed fields, the stony blanks and the slopes subject to excessive grazing loose a substantial amount of water from the depression storage. The water accumulated in the innumerable cavities of the bare surfaces is finally lost to atmosphere through evaporation. Some evaporation may take place at the time of rainfall also but this is insignificant.

The two types of losses described above are to be distinguished from the evapotranspiration losses which though relate to similar process of evaporation but are confined to the period to follow the rainfall and take place from the entire depth of the soil through the root systems of the plants and the soil porosily.

Measurements of interception have usually been made with trees or other woody plants because of the difficulties in arranging adequate interception devices on more ephemeral or smaller plants. Views presented in the literature are widely divergent in their conclusion regarding the seasonal variations of interception and the observed rates. It is not proper to express interception as a percentage of total rainfall since two storms of equal duration but of different total rainfalls may intercept the equal amount of rain water.

In the preliminary work done at Forest Research Institute at Dehradum by Qureshi and Dabral (1953) the interception losses as given in (Table 1)*

TABLE A

Interception losses at forest research institute, Dehradun

S. No.	*Name of the tree*	*Age in years*	*Interception loss % of the gross rain fall*
1.	Chir Pine	23	33
2.	Teak	33	37
3.	Sal	37	40
4.	Khair	27	40

Lull (1964) has given values of interception for various forest types and they are given in (Table 2)*

Interception loss from forest cover vary on the basis of species, forest types and the degree of human interference in the area. The usual rates of interception for oaks in an indisturbed Himalayan forest should be entirely different from those in a highly lopped oak forest. The oaks heavily in almost all the forests of Himalayas for providing fodder to the cattle during the period proceeding the rains.

TABLE 2

Interception for various forest types

S.No.	Forest type	Not interception with leaves	% of the total rainfall without leaves
1.	Northern Hardwood	15	7
2.	Aspen birch	10	4
3.	Spruce, Spruce fir	32	—
4.	White Pine	26	—
5.	Hemlock	28	—
6.	Red Pine	29	—

Haynes (1937) calculated interception for various crops as given in (Table 3). According to Haynes interception losses for dense grasses and herbs approaching full growth are nearly as great as for deciduous trees in fall leaf. As the season of full growth of these grasses is very short the total interception from them is considerably less.

TABLE B

Interception losses far various crops

S.No.	Description	Percentage of the total rainfall			
		Alfafa	*Corn*	*Soybeans*	*Oats*
1.	During growing season	38.5	15.5	14.6	6 9
2.	During low vegetation development	21.9	3.4	9.1	3.1

Horton in his classical paper of 1919 expressed the total interception as

$$Vi = Si + Cp.\ Ea.\ tr. \qquad \ldots\ldots (1)$$

Where,

Vi is the total storm interception,

Si is the storage capacity per unit of projected area,

Cp is the ratio of the vegetal cover to the projected area.

Ea is the evaporation rate per units of surface area, and

tr is the duration of rainfall.

Eguation yields a value of interception which is independent of the total rainfall in a storm. It assumes that during each storm the interception storage is completely filled. If the rainfall is low and the interception storage is not full the calculated values of total interception will be more than the actual amount of interception.

Kittredge (1948) has expressed the total interception in a storm as

$$1 = S + KET$$

Where,

1. is the total interception.

S. is the interception storage.

K. is the ratio of the evaporating leaf surface, to the projectional area.

E. is the evaporation depth per hour during the rain, and

T. is the duration of the storm in hours.*

In fact Kittredge has given almost the same formula as given by Horton.

For all rainfalls of the totai exceeding 0.10 inch (0.25 cm) the interception storage should be taken different and for rainfalls of total amount less then 0.10 inch (0.25 cm) we should have lower values of interception storage. These values are given in Table 3.

TABLE C

Values of interception storage for different surface covers and different total of rainfall

S. No.	*Surface Cover*	*Storage capacity for*		
		R.F. 0.0.05"	*R.F. 0.05-0.10"*	*R.F. Ovcr 0.10"*
1.	Coniferous trees House roofs and metalled roads	0.02	0.03	0.05
2.	Broad leaved trees and all other bare surfaces	0.01	0.02	0.04
3.	Overgrazed areas, bushes and shrubs and tall	0.005	C.008	0.01

The rate of average evaporation during rainfall in the entire central section of the lower Himalayas (Nainital—as if centre) in the month of June 1982 has been calculated as 0.0009 inch per hour using Thornthwaite Holzman formula. We need some scientific method to find out the values of evaporation rates for the rest of the months of the year. Leaving out the few slopes of the outer ranges, the hills that have the towns like Nainital, Landdowne and Mussoorie, the rest of the area lying in the region beyond these outer ranges is climatically uniform, and is drier than the other ranges. In the absence of further research work in this direction the following procedure is recommended for finding out the values of E in the formula given by Kittredge.

Initial losses of rainfall can be measured as correctly as possible provided some data in respect of the land use, forest types, trees species, rainfall totals, rainfall duration, wind speed, mean monthly temperature and the relative humidity percentage are known for the entire basin. With the help of these figures and the observed rates of evaporation for some months, the rates for the rest of the unknown months can be worked out. With the help of these evaporation rates the losses associated with rainfall can be measured and this helps to understand the water potential of a basin as correctly as possible.

Evaporation is a function of three dominent factors, *viz.*, the temperature of the air, the relative humidity and the wind speed over an area. The combined influence of these three factors is to be determined for calculating evaporation each month. Keeping in view the function of each of these three factors in increasing or decreasing the rate of evaporation the value of the combined influence of these factors on the rates of evaporation during each month of the year can be expressed as—

$$ef = \frac{Tm - Ws}{Hr.} \qquad \ldots (3)$$

Where,

ef is the evaporation factor or the value of combined influenced of the temperature, relating humidity and wind speed on the rate of evaporation during the month.

Tm is the mean monthly temperature for the month.

Ws is the wind speed in miles per hour during the month, and

Hr is the average relative humidity for the entire month.

Thus the value of all the twelve months of the year can be calculated.

Of C is the ratio between observed rate of evaporation during the month of June and the evaporation factor for the month of June is different the ratio can be expressed as—

$$C = \frac{0.0009}{ef\ 6} \quad \ldots (4)$$

Where,

ef 6 is the evaporation factor for June and 0.0009 is the observed rate of evaporation in inches per hour during the month of June.

TABLE D

Climatic data is respect of determination of evaporation factor for different months of the year in the central section of lower Himalayas behind the outer ranges

S. No.	*Months*	*Average relative humidity (m.p.h.)*	*Average wind speed*	*Mean monthly temperature (CO)*
1.	January	57.2	3.5	7.09
2.	February	52.5	5.0	8.71
3.	March	47.0	5.0	12.67
4.	April	40.5	3.5	17.08
5.	May	41.5	3.0	19.62
6.	June	62.5	2.5	20.88
7.	July	89.0	2.0	19.16
8.	August	90.0	2.0	18.83
9.	September	85.0	4.0	17.97
10.	October	67.0	3.0	15.26
11.	November	58.0	3.5	11.33
12.	December	54.0	3.0	8.93

TABLE E

Values of K in Kitteradge Formula

Months vegetal covers	*Jan. Feb.*	*March Apr.*	*May June*	*Jul. Aug*	*Sept. Oct.*	*Nov. Aec.*
1. Temperate Deciduous undisturbed forests.	.20	0.40	.60	.60	.60	.40
2. Temperate Deciduous lopped forests.	.10	.20	.40	.40	.40	.20
3. Oak Undisturbed forests.	.20	.40	.60	.60	.60	.40
4. Oak lopped forests.	.10	.20	.40	.40	.40	.20
5. Coniferous forests.	.60	.60	.60	.60	.60	.60
6. Bushes and Shrubs.	.10	.20	.30	.40	.40	.20
7. Tall grasses	.05	.05	.05	.13	.10	.05

It is suggested that in the absence of more meteorological observatories in the region the figures given in table 4 can be taken representative for all hydrological studies of the river basins in the central section of the lower Himalayas excluding the outer ranges of heavy rainfall. For the outer ranges climate data are usually available. The climatic data given in table—D are for the locality known as Chaubatiya near Ranikhet situated at a height of about 6090 feet above sea level and lying in the region of low annual rainfall. The mean monthly temperatures given in the table and the average relative humidity percentages are for the period 1978-1985.

Kitteradge formula can be used for finding the total loss from the bare surfaces if the value of *K*. in that case is taken as 1. The value of *K* otherwise will depend on the density of the foliage or the ratio of the area covered by the leafy surface to the total projected area. These values will be different for different months of the year for the deciduous trees, shrubs and grasses. For coniferous trees they will remain the same for all the months of the year. For overgrazed areas the value of *K* is suggested to be 1.

REFERENCES

Hull, H.W., 'Ecological and Sylvicultural [aspects' in Hand Book of Applied Hydrology, Ven Te Chew Editor, McGraw Hill Book Co., Inc. N.Y. 1964. p. 1418.

Haynes, J.L , 'Interception of rainfall by vegetable canopy'; U.S. Dept. of Agricultural Soil Conserv. Serv. (Am. Soc. Agronom. Annual Meeting) mimeo.

Kittredge, Joseph 'Forest influences' McGraw Hill Book Co., Inc. N.Y. 1948, p. 394.

Qureshi and Dabral 'Evaporation and infitration factors contributing towards flood control measures in forested watersheds' Nortyern Forest Rangers College Mag., 1963. 64 pp. 57. 75.

22

LAND AND WATER RESOURCES DEVELOPMENT AND MANAGEMENT IN THE TAMBRAPARANI RIVER BASIN, TAMIL NADU

M. SAMBASIVA RAO*

Land, which forms basic physical unit to carry out various agricultural activities embraces the soils, hydrology, underlying geology, plants and atmosphere above and below a specific area of earth's surface. It includes the results of past and present human activities. Land classification and development includes both qualitative and quantitative analysis. The qualitative analysis of land classification may be carried out by studying aerial photographs, Landsats, Fcc's etc., aided with field studies with more emphasis on physical characteristics. In India, land classification using air photos and Remote sensing data has been worked out by Iyer and Srinivasan (1977), Raghavaswamy and Vaidyanadhan (1980), Nageswara Rao and Vaidyanadhan (1981), Sambasiva Rao (1982-1985) and Sambasiva Rao and Nageswari (1983). Water is essential for

*Lecturer, Department of Geography, Madurai Kamaraj University, Alagarkoil Road, Madurai—625 002.

the subsistance of life on the earth. The water resources consists of two components surface and sub-surface water resources. The increasing utilisation of water in modern civilisation is of vital importance for agricultural purposes to meet the increasing utilisation, management and conservation gains paramount importance. Already drought prone area sponsored by Government of India (Ministry of Agriculture and Irrigation, Department of Rural Development) has adopted watershed as the basic unit for land and water resources management. Appraisal of resources and diagnosis of problems involved in management of the resources is particularly important in areas of scarce resource availability.

The main objectives of the present paper is to make a study of the land resources of the Tambraparani river basin based on physical characteristics and to evaluate surface water and sub-surface water resources of the basin based on data on rainfall collected from 19 rain guage stations over a period 50 years and groundwater data collected from 72 controlled wells. A study of the water balance elements of the basin is also attempted and various measures for development and management of land water resources of the basin are suggested.

The land resources of the basin are studied using aerial photographs (1.60,000), Landsats (1.1 million and 1.250,00) of bands 5 and 7 and Survey of India topographic sheets on scale 1.50,000. The various physical characteristics like relief, slope, land systems, land forms, soils, landuse, erosion appraisal and Hydrogeomorphic units are studied using the photointerpretation and Remote sensing techniques. The rainfall data over a period fifty years has been collected from 19 rain-guage stations and the data is used to evaluate the surface water resources of the basin. The ground water resources of the basin are studied based on ground water level data collected over a period of ten years from selected 72 controlled wells of the basin from the Ground Water Division, PWD, Government of Tamilnadu. Based on the data the ground water level variation, fluctuation, recharge, change in ground water level after ten years and groundwater potential have been worked out. Based on ground water potential and extraction at block level, the blocks where groundwater over extraction of under extraction zones have been delineated. The water balance elements of the basin namely potential evapotranspiration, actual evapotranspiration, water deficit, water surplus, moisture adequacy, aridity index etc. have been worked out using Thornthwaite and Mather (1955) book keeping procedure. Based on the evaluation of land resources, water resources and water balance elements a few suggestions are made for better development and management of land and water resources.

Evaluation of Land Resources of the Tambraparni Basin

Physically the basin is bordered by Southern Ghats (Mahenderagiri hills) on the western side rised to a height of about 600 to 2000 metres above mean sea level. A few isolated hills/inselsergs lie on the plain regions rised to a height of about 100 to 150 metres above MSL. The slope of the basin has been worked out on one inch to one mile topographic sheets adopting Wentworth's method. They have been broadly categorised into 0°—1° (nearly level), 1°—3° (gently sloping), 3°—5° (moderately sloping), 5°—10° (strongly sloping), 10°—20° (very strongly sloping), 20°—30° (steeply sloping), and above 30° (very steeply sloping). The plain regions fall below 1° slope with a few isolated ups whose slope varies from 1°—3°, 3°—5° and beyond. The maximum slope of more than 30° is located in Central part of Southern Ghats. Much variations in the slope are noticed in hilly terrain where ridge and valey topography are clearly displayed. The foot slopes range in slope from 3°—5° and 5°—10°. The slope on the debris slope of the hilly terrain and terrace plains range from 5°—10° and 10°—20°. The landsystems of the basin have been delineated based on the concept that similar land units, soils, vegetation etc. reflect in similar graytones on airphotos and Landsats. They are:

1. hilly terrain,
2. undulating terrain,
3. rolling plains,

4. levelled plains,
5. fluvial plains,
6. delta plains and,
7. coastal plains.

The various landforms identified from study of topographic sheets, air photos and Landsats have been grouped into denudational, fluvio-denudational, fluvial coastal and aeolian landforms based on the processed involved in their formation, alignment, lying parallel to hilly terrain, major river courses and coastline, graytone, variations in landuse, textural characteristics etc. The detailed discription has not been deal here. The broad soil divisions demarcated are hilly or skeletal soils located on the parts of hilly terrain, deep red sandy soils along the piedmont part of creep built plains, brownish red sandy soils on lower extensions of creep built plains, pediments and pediplains, greyish sandy loams on wash plains, blacksoils on black soil plains covered with biotite gneisses, alluvial soils along the major river courses and delta plains alkaline clayey soils in lagoons, marshy lands and lower reaches of coastal plains and coastal sands on beach ridges and coastal dunes. The land use as on data of Landsats February 1985 reveal that the major parts of pediplains are left as current fallow land and reflects in very light graytone. The black soil plains are used for cultivation practices. The fluvial and delta plains reflect dark graytone and are used for cultivation practices. The terrace plains, colluvial fans, piedmont plains are also used for cultivation practices under various major/minor irrigation schemes. The parts of creep built plains are left as current fallow land. The coastal plantations like casuraina, coconut, cashew nut etc. are brought up on the beach ridges and dunes. Parts of hilly terrain are distributed for cultivation of tea, coffee and rubber plantations and the other part of hilly terrain is covered with sparse to dense forests in Southwestern part of the basin. The resudual hills and pediments are left as barren lands. In the foot slopes in a few pockets parts of the land is left as cultivable waste. Based on the relief, slope, land utilisation, nature of distribution of landforms, lineaments, drainage and other structural forms of the basin has been classified into various zones which are subjected to erosion both under normal and accelerated conditions. The land above 30° which are utilised for cultivation practices are subjected to much accelerated erosion. In between 20°—30° slope the land is subjected to both normal and accelerated erosion. The land lying between 10°—20° is subjected to normal erosion in the undisturbed pockets. In the zones disturbed for cultivation practices without adopting soil conservation practices is being subjected to accelerated erosion. Normal erosion includes the wearing of land under normal environmental conditions by weathering and mass wasting. The accelerated erosion is brought by changes made by man or climate. Neotectonic activity or reactivation of faults may also induce accelerated erosion. Various geomorphic processes and agents are involved in the removal of material in addition to vegetal cover, slope, lithology, structural activity, human interference, intensity of precipitation, thermal efficiency etc. The normal erosion such as hill side scarp retreat, dissection of valley fills, piedmont plains and pediplains by gravity, sheet was and soil erosion could be expected in the upper reaches of any major river system. The normal erosion is low to moderate on black soil plains and wash plains. Deep dissection by gulleying has resulted to severe erosion in land around Pattalapudur about eight km. east of Kadayam. In the coastal plains erosion due to wind erosion is severe. The terrai sands formed south of Nazereth are migrating inland due to severe gale in the months of May, June and July and encroaching the fertile lands. The average rate of encroachement for an year is about 100-200 metres. The problem to some extent has been retarded by Agricultral Engineering Department by planting shelter belts across the wind direction. The hydrogeomorphic units of the basin has been evaluated based on landuse, tonal variation, hydrogeological conditions, recharge, specific yield, infiltration capacity, depths of bed rock and weathered zone. The various units placed in the hierarchy of their ranks are 1. fluvial and delta plains (excellent), wash plains (v. good), creap built plains (good), piedomont plains (v. poor). The issue zone lying between fluvial and wash plains and other plains acts as the zone of break of slope in shallow groundwater movement and lies as a transition zone between one and the other. Based on the physical characteristics of the basin namely relief, slope, drainage, land systems, landforms, soils, landuse, erosion appraisal and hydrogeomorphic units the land capability of the basin has been evaluated. The various land classes grouped according to their hierarchy are class I (fluvial and delta plains), Class II (irrigated land other than fluvial plains under canal irrigation), Class III (wash plains and terraced plains), Class IV (creep built plains), Class V (pediments, pediplains and black soil plains), Class VI (coastal plains), Class VII (piedmont plains), Class VIII (hilly terrain with less than 30° slope) and Class IX (hilly terrain with more than 30° slope).

Surface and Subsurface Water Resources Evaluation

For evaluation of surface water resource a better understanding of rainfall characteristics is a pre-requisite which may enable the farmers to cultivate their crops during moisture adequate periods. Therefore an attempt is made to study the distribution of rainfall on seasonal and annual basis based on rainfall data collected from 19 rainguage stations in and around Tambraparni river basin over a period of fifty years. The studies reveal that during Winter the average rainfall varies from 50 to 173mm. The rainfall received on the plains receives rainfall exceeding 150mm. During Summer the average rainfall varied from 76 to 209mm. On the Eastern and Central plains the rainfall varies from 100 to 175mm. The rainfall exceeds 200mm on the western hilly terrain. In the southwest monsoon period the rainfall ranges from 35 to 322mm. On the eastern and central plains the rainfall varies from 50 to 150mm. The eastern coastal and delta plains receive rainfall less than 50mm. The rainfall on northwestern part of hilly terrain exceeds 200mm. During Northeast monsoon period the average rainfall ranges from 401 to 621mm. The rainfall on the plains varies from 400-500mm. On the western plains and hilly terrain the rainfall exceeds 500mm. The average annual rainfall in the basin varies from 691 to 1,103mm. One the plain regions the rainfall varies from 600 to 900mm. In the hilly terrain and western plains the rainfall exceeds 900mm. From the study of average rainfall distribution it is found that during northeast monsoon period the rainfall received is high in the basin and varies from 400 to 600mm. The total surface water resources of the basin is worked out based on average annual rainfall basin and geographical area of the basin.

Therefore surface water resource

=Average annual rainfall × geographical area

1. Western hilly terrain = 1712mm × 658.17 km^2

   = 1,128,370,230 M^3

2. Plain region = 848.33mm × 4,841.29 km^2

   = 4,107,011,545 M^3

Total surface water resources of the basin = 5,235,381,775 M^3

Groundwater Resources of the Basin

The distribution of groundwater potential worked out at lock level denotes that on the eastern blocks of the basin the potential is less than 25 million m.^{3} On the western part of the basin the potential varies from 25-50 millions m.^{3} In central and Sankarankoil blocks the groundwater potential exceeds 75 millions m.^{3} The groundwater potential has been workedout based on Rainfall Recharge Method and specific yield method. The annual distribution ground water recharge on plain region denotes that on major parts of plains the recharge varies from 10 to 15 per cent and 15-20 per cent. The recharge exceeds 20 per cent in the delta plains. The uniform nature of recharge in the basin is presumed due to uniform specific yield (3 per cent in hard rock terrain) and insignificant variation in lithological units.

The ground water extraction is high in northern blocks of the basin. The extraction ranges from 50-75 and above 75 millions m.[3] The extraction of ground water is low in zones where there are irrigational facilities by canal. An analysis of ground water potential and extraction depicts that there is over extraction of ground water resources in northwestern and southern blocks of the basin. Under extraction of ground water is noticed in Tirunelveli, Palayamkottai, Manur, Srivaikuntam and Tiruchendur blocks of the basin. The fall in ground water level ranges 2—4 metres due to over extraction groundwater resources over a period of ten years. The fall exceeds more than 4 metres in Nanguneri taluk. Rise in ground water level is less than 2 metres and is noticed only areas provided with canal irrigation.

Water Balance of the Basin

The water balance elements are studied from 11 stations in the basin. The annual potential evapotranspiration or water loss due evapotranspiration ranges from 1136 to 2095mm. The PE value exceed 1750mm on the central and eastern plains. On the hilly terrain the PE value is less than 1,250mm. The actual evapotranspiration or water available for transpiration ranges from 865 to 1125mm. The eastern plains posess AE value of less 900mm. In the central plains the AE varies from 900 to 1000mm. The value of AE exceeds, 1,000 mm on the western plains and hilly terrain. The water deficit is noticed on western, central and eastern plains of the basin and vary from 681 to 1156mm. The deficit is high on the northeastern and eastern plains and exceeds 1000mm. The water surplus is noticed only on western parts of hilly terrain and ranges from 597 to 924mm. The annual moisture adequacy on the plain regions varies 45 to 62 per cent and on the hilly terrain the range is from 93 to 96 per cent. The Aridity Index which depicts the amount of shortage of water in a region ranges from 38 to 55 per cent on the plain regions. The value of Ia exceeds 50 per cent on the central and eastern plains and denote that there is high shortage of water. On the hilly terrain the value of Ia is very low and range from 4 to 7 per cent. The Moisture Index indices is used to study the climatic classification of a region. he Tnegative values of this indices in the basin depict that the plain regions fall under the category of Dry Subhumid during normal years. On the western hilly terrain the Moist Subhumid and Humid climatic conditions prevail. From the study of water balance elements it denotes that the plain regions experience high water deficit for over a period of nine months in one year, and water surplus is noticed in the western hilly terrain. Therefore water balance of the basin is:

Total surface water potential: 5,235,381,775 m^3
(100.00 per cent)

Total groundwater potential: 1,112,773,562 m^3
(21.25 per cent)

Total runoff water to the downstream into reservoirs from hilly terrain : 500,654,488m^3 (9.56 per cent)

Total water loss in the form of evaporation and evapotranspiration

=(Total surface water potential—(Total ground water potential

+total runoff water to the downstream into reservoirs from hilly terrain)

5,235,381,775−(1,112,773,562+500,656,488)=
(5,235,381,775−1,613,430,050)=3,621,951, 725=
(69.18 per cent).

From the study of water balance of the basin it is found that out of 5,235,381,775 M^3 of surface water 3,621,951,725 (61.18 per cent) goes in the form of evaporation and evapotranspirations, 1,112,773,562 M^3 (21.25 per cent) recharges to the ground water and 500,656,488 M^3 (9.56 per cent) of water run-off to the downstream from hilly terrain and is stored in the reservoirs, tanks ponds, etc. In otherwords major part of water from the surface watergoes back in the form of evaporation and evapotranspiration into the upper atmosphere. Therefore the balance water resources store in reservoirs tanks or ponds and groundwater resources have to carefully managed for development and management of land resources with suitable crop culture.

Development and management of land and water Resources

Land development requires land survey and classification. The creteria for classifying the lands suceptable for raising sustained irrigated agriculture involved consideration of evaluation and mapping of land productivity, land development, water management requirements, land drainability and interaction of water quality of soils and crops for ranges of leaching fraction.

Land classification surveys or interpretations of soils surveys should express the land-water-crop and economic interpretation expected to prevail after resources and management modification. This involved identifying and evaluating changes anticipated to result from development or reclamation and management. The interactions should be expressed in terms of economic parameter reflecting future productivity and relating to financial returns to the farmer as well economic return to the society as a whole.

The land classification studied based on physical characteristics of the basin denote that the basin has been broadly divided into nine classes. Class I land constituting the fluvial and delta plains which are irrigated under canal and well irrigation has limited recommendations for land development. Land shaping, land smoothing has to be carried out to remove small irregularities in the land surface. Levelling will depend on the method of irrigation used and type of crops cultivated. Before undertaking grading or levelling of the lands, the depth of soil cover fertility of sub-soil, infiltration rate, slope of land and erosion characteristics should be thoroughly examined. The class II land (irrigated other then fluvial plains) with less then 1° slope under Tambraparni irrigation system in the downstreams on the plains posses silty, clayey sandy loams. Erosion is very low. Paddy is the predominant crop. Land shaping/levelling has also to be carried out depending upon the depth of soil cover for a modern farming operation. The Class III lands possessing wash plains and terraced plains range in slope from 2° to 5°. Paddy, vegetables and fruits other food crops are predominant crops. Erosion is normal and varies from low to moderate. Land shipping/levelling has to be carried out depending upon the slope of the land and mode of irrigation. The Class IV land is formed of creep built plains and very in slope from 1°-3.° The depth of soil varies from 1 to 3 metres and erosion is moderate to low. Land development has to be carried out by land shaping/levelling. The Class V land constitutes pediments, pediplains and pediplains and very in slope from 0° to 3° and are composed of shallow soil profiles, with very limited irrigated facitlties. Dry land farmins techniques have to be adopted in these land units because they are located in very high water deficit areas of the basin. The Class VI land consisting of coastal plains lies parallel to the present shorline with very high infiltration rate. The beach ridges with ridge swale topography has to be smoothened for cultivation of crops. However coastal plantations like casuriana, coconut, cashewnut and groundnut and brought up in these plains. The predmont plains fall in the category of Class VII land possess deep to very deep red sandy soild. Erosion is moderate to severe depending upon the crop culture. Land shaping, land graeing, land terracing etc., have to be adopted depending upon the slope. The Class VIII land constituting hilly terrain with ridge and valley topography has to carefully used for crop culture on the debris slope by adopting soil conservation practices by constructing earthern bunds, land terracing, land grading, graded bunds etc. In the zones where soil conservations practices are not adopted and disturbed for cultivation practices the accelerated erosion is severe. The Class IX land with more than 30° slope, constituting ridge and valley topography should not be disturbed for crop culture. However, in a few pockets on the hilly terrain these pockets are also disturbed for cultivation of plantation crops where careful soil conservation practices said above have to be adopted.

The water resources development and management also requires a detailed hydrological and geophysical survey and classification. Ground water resources management requirements both qualitative and quantitative assessment. In semiarid regions where surface and sub-surface water resources are not only limited, but also highly variable, assessment and management of water resources is of paramount importance. The basic theme is to findout an effective economic solution for optimum utilisation. An understanding of socio-economic conditions and land holdings in the basin is imperative for effective planning and development.

Unfortunately, the geographical location of basin is in the rainshadow area constituting mostly hard rock terrain with average annual rainfall of about 815mm, has given very limited scope for further escavation and development of water resources. Based on the studies of water balance of the basin it is found that about 61.18 per cent of the water is lost in the form of evaporation and evapotranspiration. 9.56 per cent of the water runsoff to the downstream from hilly terrain after water is lost in the form of evaporation and evapotranspiration and is stored in surface reservoirs, tanks, ponds etc. Therefore the basin could not be provided with canal irrigation facilities except in a few blocks covering an area of about 6.33 per cent (348.61 km^2), of the total area. The other sources of irrigation is mainly by well and tank. Tank is restricted to piedmont plains in the western blocks. In other blocks well irrigation is predominant. The total dependency of farmers on ground water resources for crop culture has led to over exploitation, which in turn, has rapidly lowered the ground water level. The annual fall in ground water level has made farmers to further deepen their wells year after year. The deeping of wells has not only given way for low yield but also created a new problem of over utilisation of power resources. In a State like Tamilnadu where production of hydro-electric power by natural processes is limited, the management of power resources has created crucial problems to supply power to farmers continuously. Therefore it is found sound to educate the farmers about the amount of groundwater available, groundwater that could be extracted and crops that suits to agroclimatic conditions depending upon available surface and sub-surface water resources for crop culture, to further minimise rapid depletion of ground water level. The recharge in the ground water could some extent be accelerated by conrtruction of artificial recharge ponds. However, it is restricted to small pockets in dimension. Therefore the assessment of groundwater that could be extracted will help to suggest ground water could be extracted and that is extracted. Unless the Government implements judicial measures about the use and misuse of groundwater resources with limitations by educating the farmers it is difficult to bring a revolutionary change among the farmers to retard over exploitation of groundwater resources.

REFERENCES

1. Iyer, A.S. and Srinivasan, T.R. (1977): Land resources inventories for integrated landuse planning with special reference to the catchment of Phoru river in Jammu and Kashmir State, Photonirvachak,. Vol. 5 (2)m p. 71-80.

2. Nageswara Rao, K. and Vaidyanadhan, R. (1981): Land capability studies from aerial photointerpretation. A case study from Krishna delta, Geographical Review of India, Vol. 43, No. 3.

3. Raghavaswamy, V. and Vaidyanadhan, R. (1980): Morphology and land systems part of Visakhapatnam district, Andhra Pradesh from air photo studies India, Photonirvachak, Vol. 8 (1), p. 9-21.

4. Sambasiva Rao, M. (1982): Flooc intensity and land evaluation in the Cauvery delta. Tamilnadu apply modern Remote Sensing Technique, Ibid. Vol. 10, No. 3, p. 23-30.

5. .... (1985): Land suitability of Madurai district using Remote Sensing data, Tamilnadu, The Geographer.

6. Sambasiva Rao, M. and Nageswari, K. (1983): Evaluation of land and water esources of Cumbum valley in Madurai district, Trans. Inst. Indian Geographers. Vol. 5, No. 1, p. 77-89.

7. Thornthwaite, C.W. and Mather, J.R. (1955): The Water Balance. Publication of Climatology: Lab of Climatology, Centerton, Vol. 8 No. 1, p. 104.

23

OUTLOOK FOR THE DEVELOPMENT OF WELL IRRIGATION IN TELANGANA

A. KAMALAKHAR REDDY*
K. SURENDER REDDY
K. VITHAL REDDY

The lack of archaeological evidence of the pre-historic period in Telangana makes it difficult to understand the sequences of development of irrigation practices of these ages. However, it can be assumed that the development of irrigation practices in the areas lying between the Godavari and the Krishna is associated with the settlements over the river banks and deltaic landscape which gradually moved into interior ares with the view to bring more areas under cultivation. Naturally, this situation might have easily made a demand for the development of irrigation practices and conservation of water to irrigate the areas newly brought under cultivation in upland tracts. The well irrigation development has emerged at a later period in the history *i.e.*, after the development of tanks and tank irrigation. Their widespread use and development is closely related to settled agriculture. (Mukherji, 1963).

*Dr. A. Kamalakar Reddy is Lecturer; Dr. Surender Reddy is Reader and Prof. K. Vithal Reddy is Professor in the Department of Geography, Osmania University.

Wells of various types depending on the nature of superficial rocks and underlying characteristics of the area are spread throughout Telangana. Quite a large number of percolation wells are found in the ayacut areas of the tanks and other irrigation sources, mostly in use for a part of the year. Stone lined rectangular, square or circular types are found largely in soft earth areas. In most of the districts of Telangana, wells are dug on the river banks, as they give good quantity of water. In the recent times bore wells have become common all over Telangana.

Distribution of Wells

In Telangana, greater emphasis was given to the development of well irrigation right from the beginning of planned Table No. 1 reveals this situation clearly. There is more than three times increase in the number of wells during the last decades during which period the number of wells rose by more than three-and-a-half times from 1,61,851 in 1959-60 to 5,63,723 by the end of 1980-81. However, the present rate of increase has come down of late. The decadal variation during 1971-80 was 77.72 per cent only as against 95.96 per cent in the decade prior to it. Successive drought conditions in large areas of Telangana for the last three years has led to greater use of wells for domestic and irrigation purpose which may lead to depletion of ground water potential at greater pace.

TABLE 1

Development of Wells in Telangana

Years	*Number of Wells*	*Decadal increased*
1959-60	1,61,851	—
1970-71	3,17,187	1,55,336
1980-81	5,63,723	2,46,536

Source: Bureau of Economics and Statistics, Government of Andhra Pradesh.

The distribution pattern as shown in from the figure 1 reveals, that there is large concentration of wells in Warangal and Karimnagar districts. The gross irrigated area as a per cent of gross sown area in Warangal district has increased from 4.2 per cent to 9.7 per cent during the last decade. In Karimnagar district, the same has increased from 7.3 per cent to a phenomental position of sixteen per cent during the same period, due to the expansion of rural electrification programmes.

The picture of expansion of well irrigation source in Telangana reveals considerable positive trend in this source except for the four taluks, three in Adilabad, (Asifabad Sirpur andLaxettipet) and one taluk (Narayankhed) in Medak district. The maximum development took place in Nizamabad, Karimnagar and Hyderabad urban districts. The driving force to such phenomenal development is the failure of rainfall for successive years (Subramanyam and Hemämalini) and liberal grants by the various agencies of the government. The cumulative effect of this driving force, combined with Governmental and private effort in developing the well irrigation in the last two decades resulted in increasing the net irrigated area by wells from 15.03 per cent in 1959-60 to 33.6 per cent by the end of 1980-81, out of the total net irrigated area of Telangana. However, by 1983-84 the net irrigated area by wells in Telangana dropped to 30.37 per cent, revealing the declining trend, as against the continuous increasing trend of last two decades.

Conclusion

The above trends of well irrigation if viewed from the larger perspective of national and regional angle, we come across face to face with the future needs of our food requirement in relation to the explosive situation of population front and also the process which will set in motion to meet the above challenges resulting in ecological imbalances.

The trends examined in relation to well irrigation in Telangana reveal that although that larger number of wells are being dug year after year, with availability of funds from various government and private agencies, the extent of area irrigated by these source is dropping, due to successive drought years and large scale depletion of ground water potential. It is estimated that 42,47,638 hectares meters of ground water potential is available in Andhra Pradesh, out of which 39.43 per cent lies in Telangana. Although the effort to tap this source is greater in comparision to the other regions in Andhra Pradesh (Table 2) being 48.7 per cent which is highest among the three regions. However, if we consider from the point of view of Telangana only 17.54 per cent out of the total available potential of Telangana has been utilised, and already there are signs of depletion of this source in several areas, particularly in drought prone southern areas of Telangana.

Another important aspect which has come recently to the light is significant depletion of forest, resources, revealed by LANDSAT imagery data processed by NRSA, as against the comportable feeling of security under the clout of statistics supplied by the forest departments. This degradation of forest resources will contribute immensely to the decline of ground water potential further in future, aggrevating the already existing and continuing/declining trend of well irrigation source in future.

To save our agriculture in general, and particularly in Telangana, there is no other way except to change the existing cropping pattern based on heavy does of irrigated water crops like paddy and sugar cane. Besides, there should be genera awareness to increase greening of the landscape, which will be a long term measure to reduce the soil erosion and silting of tanks. A short term measure is to save our wells from the exhaustion of ground water potential.

REFERENCES

"An outline of the Agricultural situation—1983-84," Bureau of Economics and Statistics, Government of Andhra Pradesh.

Mukherji, A B., "Cultural Geography of Wells in Telangana Reddy Villages," The Indian Geographer Vol. 8, 1 and 2, the Association of Indian Geographers, New Delhi, December, 1963, p. 79.

Reddy, K. Surender: "Irrigation Land-scape in Telangana", unpublished Ph.D. thesis, Agra University, Agra, 1970.

Reddy, A. Kamalakar: "Changing Agricultural Landscape in Telangana A Geographical study; unpublished Ph.D. thesis, Osmania University Hyderabad—1984.

Reddy, K. Surender and Reddy, A. Kamalakar, "Development of Irrigation sources in Telangana," Landscape systems and ecological studies, Vol. 6, Nos. I and II, pp. 69-72, 1983.

Subramanyam, V.P. and Hema Malini, B "Drought prone Areas of Andhra Pradesh." The Deccan Geographer, Vol. 17, pp. 442-449. 1978.

TABLE 2

Ground Water Potential in A.P. 1983-84

	Ground-water potential available	*Percentage to total A.P.*	*G.W.P. utilized*	*P.C. to total A.P.*	*Balance G.W.P.*	*P.C. to total A.P*
1. Coastal Andhra	19,41,185	30.69	1,85,220	30.69	17,55,965	48.18
2. Rayalaseema	6,31,865	14.87	1,24,301	20.6	5,07,564	13.94
3. Telangana	16,74,588	39.43	2,93,858	48.7	13,80,730	37.89
4. A.P. Total	42,47,638		6,03,379		36,44,259	

Source: APSIDC—Hyderabad.

SECTION VI

LAND AND AGRICULTURAL RESOURCES

Land resources, unlike other resources, are limited in extent since there is no scope for increasing them except on a very minor scale by means of reclamation at a great cost. Even these limited land resources cannot be put to full use because of climatic and topographic constraints. The major use for which the available land is utilised, is for agriculture. In a developing country like India, agriculture is important not only to feed its huge population but also to supply raw materials for many important agro-based industries. Of late, India has been successful in developing agricultural resources as reflected in self-sufficiency on the food-front. However, if India is to maintain its tempo of development, it is imperative to strive for greater out-puts and optimum utilisation of land resources by developing necessary technology in order to bring more and waste lands into productive ones.

The present section is concerned with the discussion of the problems related to land and agricultural resources. In the first article of this section B. Venugopal discusses assessment and planning of land utilisation with reference to forest and waste lands by making a case study of Vakadu taluk. He makes an attempt to present a comprehensive plan with an emphasis to increase and improve the deteriorating forest land and adopting the wasteland to multi-purpose silviculture pastoral system.

K. Krishna Reddy and C.R. Pathak in their article entitled 'An Approach to the Management of Land Resources in the Naturally Hazard Prone areas' observe that 'management of land resource has a significant role in the economic development of any region or country, whose thrust lies on its agricultural sector. Management finds its ways in two cases, when there is apparent scarcity of resources and when there are many hurdles in the process of their utilisation; the latter phenomena is very much observed in the case of naturally hazard prone areas. These are the areas of rich soil nutrient with good infrastructural facilities and densely populated.' The article attempts at a systematic analysis of the damage of the areas, present practices of land utilisation and employment generated. A suitable land resource management policy has also been suggested for the study region.

The problem of desertification in Rajasthan is lucidly discussed by H.S. Sharma in the next article. While stating that the existance of sand features in eastern Rajasthan has provoked much interest among geomorphologists, archeologists and palaeo-botanists, he says, some

Scientists have mis-interpreted their existence as a product of current aeolian processes. The author attempts to review the strategy adopted in VII plan for combating desertification in Rajasthan. He observes that over-exploitation of resources, over-grazing, large scale deforestation in the aravali range by men and animals have accentuated that re-activation of sand dunes and accelerated soil erosion in the area, causing serious ecological imbalance.

Evaluation of soil and land resources of a part of Mahabubnagar district of A.P., by utilising remote sensing data is made by K V. Sheshagiri Rao and R L. Karale. They stress that levels of abstraction and accuracy of data turn out to be the two very important aspects in this context, besides time effieiency, for proper utilisation of land resources. Based on the results obtained, certain stepts are suggested for preparation of soil and land use maps from MSS data by visual interpretation which should be further tested in various agro-climatie zones and geo-morphic surfaces to bring the remote sensing technique to operational stage.

Manoj Raj Sexena and V. Vidyanath discuss some aspects of geomorphology and its utility for land use planning in the next article of the present section. A reconnaissance level geomorphology and soil maps are generated by visual interpretation of land-sat imagery by employing ground data and subsequent field work. The outhors propose a rational land use plan based on geomorphology, soil and water potentials of the area.

C.K. Jain in his paper 'Modernisation of Agriculture and Changes in Agricultural Productivity in M.P.' observes that the first and prime need is to change the face of agriculture is regular and sufficient supply of water, besides several biological techniques. The author adopts a composite index of level of adoption of various agricultural innovations utilising the score method. The variables included in the modernisation index are high yielding variety of seeds, intensity of irrigation and density of tractors, irrigation pumps and tube well per unit of cropped area. It is found by the author that modernisation and agricultural productivity have significantly high co-relation.

In the last article of this section V.T. Gharpure and C.T. Pawar make an appraisal of agro-service centres in Panchaganga basin. They are of the view that the role of agro-service centres in the development of region is very important as they perform the function of arranging supplies of agricultural inputs and services to the farmers The paper highlights some of the salient features of the agro-service centres in Panchagana basin. The pattern of agro-service centre in analysed with the help of nearest neighbour analysis besides other techniques like dispersion analysis and pearson's co-efficient or correlation etc.

24

LAND UTILIZATION: ITS ASSESSMENT AND PLANNING WITH REFERENCE TO FOREST AND WASTE LAND (A CASE STUDY OF KOTA BLOCK)

B. VENUGOPAL*

The Ministry of Rural Reconstruction, Government of India requested the State Governments in 1980 for the formulation of block level plans and provided the necessary guide-lines for it. The forest and Rural Development Department, Government of Andhra Pradesh alloted the Kota Block to a voluntary rural development organisation known as SDRSI[1] for preparing the block level plan. The author of this paper is a consultant and a managing trustee of this organisation. The project "Micro-level plan for Kota Block" was taken up and completed by a multi-disciplinary group consisting of Geographers, Engineers, Economists and Administrators. The author is the geographer member of this group. *The material for this paper has been taken from this project Report.* The major thurst of

*Professor of Geography, Sri Venkateswara University, Tirupati.

1. SDRSI: Society for the Development of Rural Sericulture Industry. The organisation runs the development projects in Chittoor and Nellore Districts.

our investigation was our integrated approach for the development of resources and the development of target groups. It is also an action oriented programme with financial outlay etc., to be implemented by either the voluntary agency or any government agency (block).

In this paper the study is only confined to the land utilisation and assessment of forest area and the development of wasteland.

Study Area

The Kota Block is part of the Gudur taluk of Nellore District of Andhra Pradesh. It has a geographical area of 764 km,[2] 295 m.[2] The eastern boundary of the block is a coast facing the Bay of Bengal. The western portion is relatively an upland intersporged by hillocks here and there and is bounded by the Nellore taluk in the north, the Gudur block in the east and the Sullurpet taluk in the south. It has a small delta in the middle formed by a medium[1] river, Swarnamukhi. The economy of the block is mostly based on agriculture where paddy is the most important crop. The block consists of five firkas namely, 1. Kota, 2. Vakadu, 3. Yellasiri, 4. Ticcavaram, and 5. Ballarolu. It has eighty six inhabited villages. Half of the villages are located in the delta. The Vakadu firka, located in the deltaic region, has thirty one villages. Rest of the firkas have villages ranging between twelve and sixteen. The population of the block is about 1.1 lakhs (1981) and is hundred per cent rural.

Topography

Topographically, the block can be divided into three zones. 1. Deltaic plain consisting of the entire firka of Vakadu and half Kota, Yellasiri and Ballarolu, 2. Coastal lowland and

1. "River basins with catchment area between 20,000 sq. kms and 2,000 sq. kms are classified as medium river basins." The total area of Swarnamukhl basin is about 3,225 sq. kms and length is 130 kms. It traverses about 24 kms. in this block. K.L. Rao, *India's Water Wealth*, pp. 48 & 54.

waterlogged belt, and 3. The eroded rocky laterite zone in the west consisting of the entire Ticcavaram firka and the remaining half of Yeelasiri and Ballarolu.

The soils of the block can be classified into four categories. They are:

1. Sandy loam —Found in Kota, Vallamedu, Vakadu, Chitamur, Gunapadu and other Villages located in the Swarnamukhi delta.
2. Black loamy—Found mainly in Yellasiri, Chittomur, Chittedu and Vellipadu villages.
3. Red Soil —Found to the west of Chellakalva stream and the area between Chendodu and Kadivedu.
4. Saňdy land —The villages along the coast.

Drainage

This area lies in the lower Swarnamukhi basin. This sub-basin is further divided into micro-basins, namely 1. Mamidikalva basin, 2. Chellakalava basin, and 3. Pulikalava/Rottalavagu basin. Mamidikalva is a small stream which enters the block are at Rudravaram and joins Swarnamukhi at Guddu Challakalva, and Pulikalva/Rottalavagu are the distributaries of Swarnamukhi. Swarnamukhi is a perennial river. The Mamidikalva stream carries water during the better part of the year. The length of the Swarnamukhi river in this area is about twenty four kms. (15 miles).

The infiltration in the sandy zone is roughly estimated as twenty per cent and in the laterite rocky zone it is estimated as eight per cent.

Climate

This region has a hot climate with high humidity almost all the year round. The year may be divided into four seasons (i) Summer (March to May), (ii) S.W. Monsoñ season (June to

TABLE 1

General Land Classification of Kota Block (Area in hectares percentages in Brackets)

S. No.	*Land use category*	*Vakadu*	*Kota*	*Yellasiri*	*Ticcavaram*	*Bellarolu*	*Total*
1.	Ag. Lands including	4875	3045	6348	4100	4379	23739
		(49.5%)	(40.1%)	(30.5%)	(26.9%)	(21.4%)	(30.1%)
2.	Cultavable waste	1538	1200	4054	3620	4660	15120
		(16.7%)	(11.9%)	(20.0%)	(25.2%)	(20.9%)	(19.8%)
3.	Pasture	845	1411	891	907	198	4252
		(8.6%)	(14.2%)	(4.3%)	(6.0%)	(0.97%)	(5.6%)
4.	Cultavable barren land	793	6665	5385	3610	5415	16870
		(8.1%)	(18.5%)	(26.8%)	(19.2%)	(27.5%)	(21.12%)
5.	Forest	0.16	—	20.66	1110	1220	4303
		(0.16%)		(9.9%)	(7.3%)	(6.0%)	(5.6%)

6. Land under other non-Ag. Use.	1662 (16.9%)	1557 (15.5%)	1781 (8.5%)	2377 (15.6%)	4732 (23.2%)	12110 (16.0%)
Total Geog. area	9,8?2 (12.9%)	20,076 (13.2%)	20,840 (27.3%)	15,230 (19.9%)	20,424 (26.8%)	76,392

*In this system horticulture crops (fruit bearing trees), forest tree spieces suitable to the area are introduced and Pastoral land is managed for growing grass and rearing the livestock.

September), (iii) N.E. Monsoon season (October to December), and (iv) Cool season (January and February). This region is liable to damage due to cyclone storms of the Bay of Bengal. The mean annual rainfall for Gudur Station calculated on the basis of fifty years data from 1916 to 1965 and for another period of twelve year data from 1969-1980 along with the average number of rainy days for all the months and also for the year.

General Land-use

A brief description is give here of the general land-use to provide a background of the area and to give us some insight into the distructive processes at work of forest, pasture and other land. This also will help to suggest a plan for converting these lands for the development of Horli-sylvo—Pastoral system.*

The total geographical area of the block is of about 76,400 ha. (764 km^2s). The break-up of this area into six major land-uses is given above. They are:

1. Agricultural land including follows,
2. Cultivable non-barren waste land,
3. Cultivable barren land
4. Pasture land
5. Forests and
6. Land under non-agriculture use.

The table shows some interesting features. The land given to agriculture is not much as is generally expected in such coastal and deltaic area (30.9). The highest percentage of land noticed is the wasteland which makes above 40 per cent of the area. The forest and pasture land, each, make a little over five per cent. The distribution pattern of this landuse clearly indicates that this area has a lot of potentiality for increasing the land under agriculture as well as the land for the development of Horti-Pas toro-silviculture. We have already referred earlier to the water availability over the year and also water availability in various firkas.

Altogether the forest cover is about 4,300 ha. (43 km^2s) and is found in Ticcavaram, Ballardu and Yellasiri firkas with an area of roughly 11, 12 and 21 km^2 respectively. These are reserved forests known as Kadivedu R.F., Mamidi R.F., and Yellasiri R.F. These forests lack vegitation cover. Babul and wild bushes cover a major portion of the forest land. The area of all these reserve forests itself is dwindling. It was estimated recently that during the last seven years (starting from 1975) at the national level the reduction was of the order of three per cent.* Therefore the reduction of forest land over can be atleast four per cent decade in this area on an average. Therefore it is anybody's guess what would be the real forest cove in this area. Perhaps the conditions would be more or less the same in any other corresponding part of India.** Hence it is clear that the existing forest area itself requires treatment and intensive planning to bring it back to original vegitation. This aspect has been to catch attention of the union and state governments and various authorities are constituted, such as the National landuse and Wasteland Development Authority by the Government of India and shore belt Development authority by the Government of Andhra Pradesh.

Now let us look at the wasteland of this area. We have already noticed that the highest percentage of land (41 per cent) is under wasteland. Let us see the location aspects and other land characteristics of this block. The block lies under the coastal area. The length of the coast 50 kms. the river Swarnamukhi flows through the centre of the block traversing about

*Memorial lecture of by Dr. T.N. Khoshoo on Environment at Bangalore, delivered on 17 Feb. 1986.

**There is a big disparity between the area shown by revenue records and NRSA. The revenue records showed a percentage of 22.7 forsst area of the total Geographical area, while the NRSA showed 13 per cent (from satllite imagery). *From the statement from the Minister of State for Environment and Forest on 12th March, in Parliament.*

twenty four kms. with its channels. The southern part of this deltaic sandy coast is a waterlogged and marshy land. North of it is the sandy and sandy-scrub land. On an average the block extends roughly upto twenty kms from the coast. The three firkas, Ballarolu, Vakadu and coastal part of Yellasiri, extend about ten kms from the coast. Sandy and sandy-scrub area as well as hard soil area may be in the ratio of sixty per cent, forty per cent respectively.

The wasteland of this block can be grouped as (i) water-logged marshy land (ii) Coastal and deltaic sandy belt (iii) Sandy soil with scrub and wild bushes including palmira trees and (iv) non-sandy open scrub with or without rocky outcrops. About 32,00 ha. (320 kms^2) are available. Out of it about five to six thousand ha. lie under marshy land, about twenty thousand under sandy and sandy-scrub and another five to six thousands under non-sandy hard-soil with rocky out-crops. From the above analysis it may be said that much of the area of the block is easily developable into Horti-pastore-silviculture in the near future. The rest of the wasteland area *i.e.*, marshy land and open scrub area with rocky out-crops also can be brought under use with some treatment through the modern know-how and heavy inputs.

If we take the Kota block as a typical example of South coastal Andhra Pradesh, we may assume that this southern coastal belt lacks in forest cover and that perceptable wasteland in the form of open sandy area and sandy scrub area is noticeable.

It is a fact and needs no stress that over the present century much of the land was added under the plough and much more land which was under the vegitative cover (trees and grass) was destroyed by overuse for fuel, timber, wood and for grazing livestock. Over the recent decades due to increasing population pressure there has been no check to the distribution. Now the vegitative cover is being reduced at the rate of four to five per cent decade. Now this coastal belts which has a large cover of wasteland and which is developable by proper and intensive planning, gives a ray of hope for retrieving the climax vegitative cover and restoring ecological balance.

The problem of deteriotation and destruction of natural vegitation did attract in the past the attention of scientists, administrators and the planners. As far back as 1961. Food and Agricultural Ministry and other related ministries were making efforts to tackle this problem. Recently in 1982 a committee was set up by the union government to estimate the extent of wasteland. Now the landuse and wasteland developing authority is proposing to develop the wasteland @ of five million ha. every year, upto two thousand A.D. in order to meet the growing need of firewood, timber, pulpwood and grass. The question here is not one of fixing targets on paper but of assuring their achievement. Now there is a welcome change at the policy formulation level, making the wasteland developing programmes a peoples movement. Plans are to be prepared at micro-level and or gross root level and implemented by the district or block level agencies.

Keeping in view the above policy of the government and of the National Planning Authority let us take a look at the planning of forest, pasture and wasteland in the Kota block.

The planning is viewed here in four different contexts:

1. Restoring the original forest ecosystem by reforestation of degraded forest: *i.e.*, Environmental forestry.
2. Development of social forestry in open forest areas and wasteland.
3. Development of pastures, grassland and fodder crops in open forests, wastelands and cultivable wastelands of village communities.
4. Creating of economic and employment opportunities to rural poor (target group) through the forest development programmes.

Each of these aspects cannot be considered in isolation, as they are all integrated. Therefore, it has to be an integrated development; seen through Horli-Pastoro-Silviculture development systems of involving target groups, forest department and Panchayat Samithi.

Let us now see what can be done for the little forest cover that the Kota block has. On the records it is 4300 ha. of forest land, out of which about three thousand ha. of area is under reserve forest found in Yellasiri, Ticcavaram and Ballarolu firkas. The rest are unclassified forests.

The first and foremost thing is to be done controlling a pilferage and encroachment. This is easily said rather than done. This is to be followed by heavy inputs from the forest department (fuel and wood lifters and livestock grazers) by providing alternatives to the encroachers. Punitive and Preventive measures adopted till now have not been successful. Therefore the measures to be taken are:

(i) cleaning of the area and planting quick-growing, and high-yielding trees suited to the area and climate such as Casunina, Eucalyptus and sukabul in a phased manner in each reserve forest unit of this block. The sapplings have to be protected by completely preventing in the area till the plants reach sufficient height. Here the target group (landless labour) are to be employed.

In the rest of the area grazing is to be systematised and regulated by allowing only the cattle and the inferior cattle and other livestock and prevented from grazing. Though the studies on the carrying capacity of forest for grazing are lacking, it may be assumed here that one cow unit may be maintained per ha. in this area. Apart from checking the inferior cattle and other livestock the forest grazing area is to be closed for grazing, in order to allow the grass to grow for cutting at a later stage. All the measures suggested for improving the degrading forest is only possible when the task force of the forest department is increased and scientific management of forest operation is worked. Therefore, adequate investment and creating employment opportunity to the village poor living around the forest areas are needed. The preventive and punitive approach adopted by the forest department formerly was not aimed at National yield of forestry to meet the requirements of entire population.

Therefore the reforestation programmes and their implimentations have to be undertaken by the forest department or what we now call forest and Wasteland Development Authority.

Maintaining and Improving the Pastureland

The importance of pastureland development need not be stressed. Livestock rearing is to be scientifically managed. We have a good number of inferior cattle which are non-economic in maintenance and a heavy pressure on pastureland. To meet the growing demand for milk, dairy industry is encouraged and the number of milch cattle is being increased year after year. There are about twenty five thousand milch cattle (cow and buffaloes) in this block (1982). The total livestock census is recorded at eighty thousand cow units. The pastureland in this block is estimated at four thousand two hundred and fifty ha. We have two cow units per ha. This area has two times more livestock than it can maintain even on low nutrient level. During the loctation period the milch cattle fodder requirement is very heavy. On an average, the fodder requirement for a cattle will be twenty Kgs. per day. It comes to about three fourth ton of fodder per year per cattle. The yield of fodder per ha. is between twenty five to thirty five tons. Thus roughly forty cattle may be maintained in an hactare. In other words for proper maintainence we require about six to seven hundred ha to be brought under fodder cultivation. Since the number is likely to increase we may require one thousand ha. for fodder cultivation. Rest of the three thousand ha. of pastureland has to be managed as suggested for forest grassland area. This has to be organised by block/mandal/village level authorities by leasing the wasteland for a long period to the target group. It is needless to mention that the pastureland to be used for fodder cultivation has to near or at the outskirts of the village.

Pastureland is found in all the firkas. Only Ballarolu firka has very little area of pastureland (1981 ha.) Rest of the firkas have pastureland to the extent ranging from eight hundred ha. to fourteen hundred ha. This grassland can be profitably used for seven to eight months in a year *i.e.*, from July to February.

There is very little grass available for grazing from March to June.

Development of Wasteland

The extent of wasteland available in this block (along with the various categories of wasteland) has been discussed already under the general landuse study. Before we could take up programmes for the development of wasteland let us have a view of the distribution of wasteland in different firkas as given in the table below:

TABLE 2

Cultivable Wasteland Distribution in Hectares

(*from the Revenue Records**)

N. Firkas	*Wasteland easily developable*	*Westeland developable after treatment high inputs*	*Total Wasteland*	*Total Geographical field area*
1	*2*	*3*	*4*	*5*
Vakadu	1538(16.7%)	793(8.1%)	2331(24. [illegible]%)	9822
Kota	1200(11.9%)	1665(18.5%)	2865(30.4%)	10076
Yellasiri	4054(20.0%)	5385(26.8%)	9426(46.8%)	20840
Ticcavaram	3620(25.2%)	3610(19.8%)	7245(45 %)	15230
Ballarolu	4660(20.9%)	5415(27.5%)	10091(48.4%)	20840
Kota block	15120(19.8%)	16870(21.1%)	31990(40.9%)	76400

*The figures are rounded off and converted from acres to ha. The totalling etc., may not exactly tally. The figures are broadly used for analysis.

The data acquired by the Revenue Department is to be viewed together with the information about various categories of wasteland found in this area. Taking the two together the wasteland available in this block may be grouped into three major catagories. They are (i) Sandy and Sandy-scrub. (ii) Non-sandy hard soil with rocky out-crops and (iii) Marshy land. The estimate of the extent of these three types of wasteland is rounded off to '000s. Sandy and Sandy scrub wasteland is around twenty thousand ha. of which Ballarolu has eight thousand, Kota and Vakadu five thousand each and Yellasiri twenty thousand ha. While the hard soil with or without rocky outcrops has an area of four thousand ha. of which more than half is found in Ticcavaram. Rest of it is found in Yellasiri, Ballarolu. Almost all the marshy land (around five to six thousand ha.) is found in Yellasiri firka (coastal part).

About twenty thousand ha. of this area is easily developable into Horti-pasturo silviculture in near future. If five thousand ha. are reserved for pastureland development, the rest of the fifteen thousand ha. may be brought under the tree cover. If one thousand to fifteen hundred ha. are developed every year, by the turn of the century one hundred and fifty Km^2 area may be developed under social forestry.

Under social forestry, management to be aimed at National production programme to meet the demand, as well as make social forestry economically viable to the tree growing target groups. Experience has shown that it is profitable, less risky and yield can be harvested at the convenience of the farmer. Thus both small and marginal farmers as well as big farmers have already started taking up to social forestry.

By the turn of century with moderate inputs the percentage of area under forest may reach any where between twentyfive to thirty per cent of this area. Still this block will have hundred Km^2 to be developed at a later stage with intensive management and heavy inputs.

Here an attempt is made to discuss the plan of development of this wasteland involving the target groups of this block. (which make 70 per cent of the total population consisting of small and marginal farmers and landless labourer).

Different types of tree plantation programme envisaged under social forestry are:

1. farm or agro-forestry.
2. reforestation,
3. extensive forestry. We have already discussed reforestation programme under forest area development.

The farm forestry and the extension forestry programmes are discussed under the wasteland development schemes.

This area is suitable for the plantation of casurina, eucalyptus, sukabal, cashewnuts and coconut trees.* The farmers of this block have laready adopted the plantation of these trees. Even the small and marginal farmers have adopted social forestry. About two hundred ha. of land is under the cover of this casunna trees. The target group consists of 19448 families. Landless labour makes about fortyfive per cent. Each firka has roughly four thousand target families. The minimum is around three thousand and five hundred (Ticcavaram) and maximum is around four thousand seven hundred (Kota). It is proposed to involve about three thousand families from all the five firkas with more emphasis on the three coastal firkas of Ballarolu, Vakadu and Yellasiri where much of the sandy and sandy scrub and is available for social forestry.

About five hundred ha. of wasteland will be brought under the casurina plantation, and about one thousand families will be involved. The area will be covered by five lakh trees. In the same way, about eight hundred ha. will be brought under eucalyptus/sukabul plantation. One thousand families will be involved and the land will be covered by eight lakh trees. The sukabul is a new introduction in the area. It is being introduced in other parts of India too. Maharastra has taken the lead. This plant is drought resistant. Its yield will increase considerably when it is grown under irrigation. It is a multipurpose tree. Its leaves are used as cattle feed, its pole's as small timber for agriculture and domestic use in rural areas and it is also used as fuel. All the trees *i.e.*, casurina, sukabul and eucalyptus start yielding wood after five years, while sukabul tree leaves can be used after two years.

TABLE 3

Plantation Programme

S. No.	*Category*	*Hectares*	*Target Families*	*No. of plants per hectare*	*Total plants*
1.	Casunnia	500	1000	1000	5,00,000
2.	Ecalyptus and sukabul	800	500	500	8,00,000
3.	Casheunuts	100	500	500	50,000
4.	Coconuts	100	1000	1000	50,000
		1,500	3,000	—	14,000,00

*In the whole of the coastal belt of Andhra Pradesh where, sandy and sandy scrub land is available, we notice all types of trees except sukabul under plantation.

Another five hundred families of village are poor and proposed to be involved in the development of cashewnut plantation. It also starts yielding nuts around five years after planting. About one hundred ha. will be brought under it. Around fifty thousands trees can be planted. This has become a most profitable plantation industry which gives employment to women during harvesting and in the cashewnut small-scale industry.

Coconut plantation is not very common in this area. Under this plantation another one hundred ha. of wasteland will be developed. It will be undertaken mostly in the Swarnamukhi delta which is found mostly in Kota and Vakadu firkas. About five hundred coconut trees can be planted per ha. Thus fifty thousand trees can be raised. It can involve about one thousand families.

To make the programme effective, government would be providing the required infrastructure to the farmer by way of supply of seeding free of cost or at subsidised rates, loan and subsidies, and importing know-how, supply of pesticides and solving operational and other problems.

It is estimated that the farmer would get any where between six thousand to ten thousand rupees per ha. per annum for raising any of these plants.

This apart, development of extension forestry in this area is being considered. This area apart from having good road length it has about sixty to seventy Kms. of length of river banks, fifty Kms. of Buckingham canal banks and one hundred and fortyfour medium and small tanks. It is proposed to have a belt of trees consisting of four to five trees in a row all along the road, canal, river banks and tankbunds. We have been seeing that strips of land on either side of the roads and canals etc., are not put to any productive use in most places. In the prevailing conditions such strip planting schemes assume a very great importance. This has to be a public sector programme, involving the forest development and the Panchayat Samithis. It has to be treated as a commercial investment by the public sector.

The whole exercise will have to be an attempt at planning forest and wasteland development through integrated multipurpose horti-pastoral-silviculture planning by involving the target groups—forest department and the Panchayat Samithis.

REFERENCES

1. India Meteorological Department, Government of India: Climate of Andhra Pradesh, New Delhi, 1973.

2. Ministry of Agriculture and Irrigation, Government of India: Report on National Commission of Agriculture, 1976.

(i) Part IV Climate and Agriculture.

(ii) Part IX Forestry.

3. K.L. Rao: India Waterwealth, Orient Longman Ltd., 1975, New Delhi.

4. Ministry of Information and Broadcasting, Government of India: Kurukshetra: India's Journal of Rural Development.

   1. Vol. No. 5, Feb. 1985 and
   2. Vol. No. 10, July, 1985.

25

AN APPROACH TO THE MANAGEMENT OF LAND RESOURCES IN THE NATURALLY HAZRAD PRONE AREAS

K. KRISHNA REDDY*
C.R. PATHAK*

Of the three basic resources land, water and air, man has intervened with the land resource to the maximum extent due to ever increasing population pressure. Initially for sustenance, and later, to meet the demands of the people the land has been put to different uses depending upon its production capability. As a result, most of the land has been brought under cultivation. This started with Jhuming (Old field, 1960) and evolved to mechanised cultivation. The methods involved are extensification and intensification respectively. In the process of maximizing the production man has changed the form and quality of land. The ultimate effect is under-utilization, over-utilization and misutilization of the land.

Irrespective of future consequences on the society man has tried to exploit every piece of land, in his struggle for existence. As a result most of the available land of fertile flood plains which are vulnerable to natural hazards have been occupied.

*Department of Architecture and Regional Planning, Kharagpur.

This pattern of human occupance provided a new source of potential damage and added a new dimension to the crippling economic development of the region.

In India, according to regional delineation, the fertile agricultural tracks of Ganga and Brahmaputra valleys and the deltaic and coastal areas in Andhra Pradesh, Tamil Nadu and Orissa are most severely affected by floods. The average annual loss of food production is estimated at over one million tons. Average annual loss due to floods alone is eight hundred and seventy million rupees in value of which seventy three per cent is due to crop damages. In addition to this cyclones are having their fury on the public and private properties.

It has been observed that while the outlays for successive five year/annual plans have been enhanced and more area is being protected, the estimated value of damage has been increasing. This may be due to two reasons: Firstly, lack of proper landuse planning and rightful crop combinations which will cause the crop damage and secondly, the encroachment of human activities into such hazard prone areas, due to population pressure and richness of the soil.

The study is necessitated out of two reasons: The areas along the river courses, coastal tracts and confluence zones are agriculturally highly potential as well as thickly populated. But such potential areas are frequently affected by natural hazards disrupting occassionally the economy of the region. At this juncture it is necessary to a planner to develop certain strategies through which the economy could be developed and ecological balance can be maintained.

Aims of the Study

In order to derive suitable measures in such hazard prone areas, the planner was left with two choice—these are, either the land use management devices has to be changed according to the frequency of occurrence of hazards, or the human instrusion to such zones should be abandoned. Since these are the areas of high potentiality, the latter choice cannot be followed, on the other hand it calls for management of land resources. In order to attain faster economic development and optimum utilization of land in such hazard prone areas the study should aim at:

*reducing the impact of damages primarily to land and its associated activities by means of precaution or adjustment;

*efficient utilization of land by adopting suitable agronomical practices. In doing so the restrictions imposed by natural hazards should also be considered in such hazard prone areas.

The Study Region

The study region extends over 8727 sq. km. with a coastline of 88 km. The region is chiefly drained by the Krishna and other non-perennial rivers. The Kolleru lake, a shallow depression about 385 sq. km. in area lies in the northern part of the district.

Total population of the region is 30.48 lakh persons, in which 12.32 lakhs are working population, 64.53 per cent of the working force is engaged in agriculture. The irrigated area is 61.44 per cent to the gross cropped area. This region is endowed with rich nutrient alluvial soil, black cotton soil and red soils.

Methodology

The planning methodology which has to be adopted for such studies is as follows.

(a) Analysis of the damages to the land by hazards over a period of time.

(b) Observation of the relationship between the productivity changes, cropping pattern and occurrence of hazards.

(c) Calculation of the labour surplus/deficit in terms of man-days in relation with the existing cropping pattern, and

(d) Formulation of a suitable strategy for managing the land resource to attain maximum yield with least damages, marginal improvement in the employment opportunities and less disturbance to the ecosystem.

Analysis of damages to the land resource

The damages caused to the land area are of two types namely—damage to crops and damage to the land itself. Analysis of the data over a ten-year period (1975-84) reveals that, this region has experienced four times floods (Oct. 1975, 1978, Oct. 1982, Nov. 83) and three times cyclones (1976 Nov 1977, May, 1979).

Due to floods, 50 villages during 1975 and 416 villages during 1983 have been affected. The damage to crops in area is 2800 acres and 59,427 acres respectively. Major crops damaged are paddy, sugarcane, chillies, redgram and turmeric.

Due to cyclones property worth of Rs. 83.70 crore got damaged in 1976, crops worth of Rs. 147 crore in 1977 (8.547 lakh acres) and crops worth of Rs. 13.39 lakhs (18.440 acres) are damaged in 1979.

Apart from crop damage the land quality is altered due to sand and silt deposits. With this there is possibility of increase in the alkalinity of the soil which will have an indirect impact on crop productivity.

Land Use

The interaction between man and land will be reflected in the form of the activities carried over the land, which ultimately result in land use. In general, the basic objective of land use planning is how to utilize the basic resource in an efficient way to obtain optimum return. But in such hazard prone areas the objective is of two fold in nature. On the one hand optimization of production and on the other minimization of the damages caused by hazards.

The land use pattern reveals that the net area sown (58.19 per cent to total) is a dominant land use. The forest area occupied 7.69 per cent of the total area, which calls for improvement in coverage inview of the region's physico-climatic conditions and the problems of natural hazards.

From the past data, it has been observed that there is no change in the vegetal cover. But the net sown area increased with concomitant decrease in the current fallows.

Cropping pattern and productivity

In order to know the response of farmers to such natural events the cropping pattern and productivity was studied. The farmer enables us to know the existing cropping practices/rotations and the latter provide sound basis to know the farmers response. The response of the farmers to such hazards can be better understood by studying the cropping pattern. The response in the cropping pattern can be better understood by studying the productivity of different crops. Hence the farmer's response could also be known directly by studying the productivity of crops.

The changes in the yield of principal crops are calculated for a period 1975-80, by substracting the average yield rate for precedings 5 years from the corresponding year's actual yield rate. During this period, 1978-79 is considered to be a good crop year, where there was no cyclone but flood for very low intensity. The yield rates of all crops increased except groundnut. The impact of the cyclones and storm surges is reflected in succeeding crop year's yield. The percentage share of major crops remained unaltered though the productivity is decreasing and damages are increasing for a particular crop (See table Nos. 1 and 2).

From the table it can be seen that cyclones are having definite role in determining the productivity, initially by destroying the crop and later by changing the characteristics of the soil.

Employment Generation

The basic intention behind tackling any developmental problem is to achieve balanced economic development of the region, which will result in providing employment opportunity in order to increase the per capita income. In this region, agriculture is the basic sector which provides employment to 64.31 per cent of its working population.

The present study reveals that the labour availability is surplus than the requirement. The calculations based on the labour requirement per crop in terms of man-days showed that there is 1,85,457 surplus labour (See table 3). This calls for revitalizing the cropping pattern so that it can generate more employment.

A Strategy of Management

The above mentioned problems calls for management in two aspects. Firstly, the technological measures are unable to provide solutions for majority of such problems in such hazard prone areas. Because these measures are unaware of the ecological relations/balances. And secondly the existing agricultural practices could not be able to reduce the impact of the hazards and are unable to maintain proper land use proportions. Since major damage is to crops the emphasis should be made to reduce the crop damage. The strategy is given below:

Rescheduling of crops: The poor response of farmers to their cropping pattern illuminate the fact that they are unaware of modern short duration crop varieties and practices. This will provide a wide scope to reduce the impact by changing the cropping pattern, which will have good yield and will generate more employment. While rescheduling the crops it should consider:

(a) the existing crop combinations, the crops that are frequently damaged and their distribution over space,

(b) probable periods of occurrence of hazards and the rainfall distribution in different seasons,

(c) the traditional taste of the people and their food habits,

(d) soil conditions,

(e) availability of irrigation facilities,

(f) different varieties available in a particular crop,

(g) duration, sowing time, and harvesting time of crops, and

(h) of the types of hazards experienced.

Increase in the vegetal cover: In view of the region's low vegetal coverage, advantages of having shallow, sandy coast and frequent destruction by hazards calls for increase in the vegetal cover. Apart from maintaining good physico-climatic conditions and ecological balance it will serve two purposes:

(i) The increase of vegetation along the coast will protect the settlements from damage caused by violent cyclonic wind and storm surge effects.

(ii) It will bring the land into proper use which is otherwise uncultivable and provide employment opportunities.

But the growing of vegetal cover should consider the predominant path of the cyclones. There are two pattern in which it can be grown:

One pattern will take care of the wind velocity and it will regulate the path of cyclone on a 'settlement free zone.' The orientation of these plantations will be at right angle to the wind direction and will be developed in strips. This will be of 'even-aged form.' The advantage of this even-aged form is that there will be less damage than those of 'uneven-aged form' (Jensen, 1941). This is because of the difference in the arrangement of crown canopy.

In order to tackle the problems of storm surge and winds at lower level the trees of low 'from point' have been proposed. In a study, Curtis (1943) showed that the resistance windthrow depends upon the type of the crown and height of the form point.' In general, trees with a low 'form point' withstand the wind better than the trees with high points. Based on these observations and soil conditions cashewnut plantation has been suggested for this region.

Conclusion

From the study it is observed that the land resource of natural hazard areas can be better managed by natural method of adjustment, with least disturbance to ecological system. This is not being possible in Indian context, of two reasons:

(a) absence of organisations such as development authorities, planning boards to such problematic areas through which integrated planning is possible and

(b) lack of compilation of relevant data to derive definite conclusions.

For the present study, the non-availability of PH values of soil over different time periods limited the scope of establishing the relationship between productivity and natural hazards. If such problematic areas are delineated and treated as separate entities, with a body of diversified knowledge, people and experts in different disciplines—proper/ecological balance will keep pace with economic development of the region. This will enrich the culture of man and enhance the relationship between man and nature.

REFERENCES

Oldfield, F.—'Late quarternary changes in climate vegetation, and sea level in Lowland Lonsdata', Trans, Inst. of British Geographers, No. 28, 1960.

Ramachandran, R. and Thakur S.—'India and Ganga Flood plain in Natural Hazards—Local, National, Global' edited by Gilbert While, Oxford University press, 1974.

Jensen, V.S.—Hurricane damage on the Bartlett Experimental forest, Northeastern forest experimental station technical note, 4 , 1941.

Curtis, J.D.—Some observations on wind damage, Journal Forestry, 41 872-882, 1943.

Shamsingh, Krishnamurthy, and Katyal. S.L.—'Fruit Culture in India Indian Council of Agricultural Research, New Delhi, 1963.

Glendenning, R.M. and Logan, R.F.—'Land as a resource' in 'Natural resources' edited by Huberty, M.R. and Flock W.L., Mc Graw Hill Book Company, 1959.

Hawleyc, Raldh and Stickel, N. Paul.—'Forest Protection' John Wiley and Sons, New York, 1948.

Planning Commission: Sixth-Five Year Plan1980-85'. Vol. II, Govt. of India.

Planning Commission: Seventh-Five Year Plan1985-90' Vol. II, Govt. of India.

Krishna Reddy K. and Pathak C.R.—Alternative Strategies of landuse Management for Naturally hazard prone area", Paper presented in an International Conference—ASI on Regional Science and Planning for developing countries', I.I.T., Kharagpur, 30th Dec. 1985.

Krishna Reddy, K.—'Planning guidelines against natural hazards—case study of Krishna district (A.P.)' (unpublished) M.R P. Thesis, Dept. of Arch. and Regional Planning, I.I.T., Kharagpur.

TABLE 1

Percentage of area under different crops in Krishna district during 1975-76 to 1979-80.

Name of the crop	*Normal*	*1975-76*	*1976-77*	*1977-78*	*1978-79*	*1979-80*
1	*2*	*3*	*4*	*5*	*6*	*7*
Paddy	52.04	52.16	53.97	54.20	52.85	46.99
Jowar	8.46	6.19	5.64	8.18	7.16	15.03
Bajra	0.57	1.54	0.38	0.34	0.45	0.13
Maize	0.36	0.35	0.23	0.59	0.36	0.25
Ragi	0.07	0.11	0.11	0.06	0.07	0.01
Greengram	9.12	10.09	9.47	8.04	9.24	8.77
Blackgram	7.88	7.35	7.03	6.69	8.85	9.46
Horsegram	1.15	1.38	1.13	1.28	1.03	0.56
Redgram	0.52	0.59	0.55	0.52	0.51	0.43

(*Contd.*)

1	2	3	4	5	6	7
Chillies	1.38	1.21	1.57	1.35	0.94	1.81
Cotton	0.25	0.13	0.38	0.35	0.16	0.24
Groundnut	3.64	4.27	3.64	3.03	3.61	3.66
Tobacco	2.48	1.90	2.60	3.21	2.65	2.05
Sugarcane	2.07	2.21	2.40	2.39	1.99	1.34
Vegetables	0.45	0.42	0.41	0.44	0.47	0.50
Gross cropped area	—1723925	1719980	1677662	1754310	1732306	1735303
	(100%)	(100%)	(100%)	(100%)	(100%)	(100%)

Source: Assistant Director Planning and Statistics, Krishna/District.

TABLE 2

Changes in the yield (kg/acre) of principal crops of Krishna District

Sl. No.	*Crop*	*Average yield for preceding 5 years*	*1975-76*	*1976-77*	*1977-78*	*1978-79*	*1979-80*
1	*2*	*3*	*4*	*5*	*6*	*7*	*8*
1.	Paddy (K)	644	—52	—52	—146	121	66
2.	Paddy (R)	725	—103	45	—48	255	189
3.	Jower (K)	204	—75	—20	62	57	102
4.	Jower (R)	257	—69	84	—80	31	54
5.	Bajra	299	—4	—48	42	43	54
6.	Maize (K)	520	116	—170	89	—132	8
7.	Maize (R)	810	1	—26	—64	40	—149
8.	Ragi (K)	452	53	—61	—11	28	—40

(Cont.)

1	2	3	4	5	6	7	8
9.	Ragi (R)	588	—40	4	57	7	19
10.	Greengram	153	—4	25	—34	25	—79
11.	Blackgram	173	—6	—7	—49	66	14
12.	Horsegram	144	—3	—39	20	34	—21
13.	Redgram	78	1	—11	16	28	32
14.	Chillies	369	152	—196	—206	235	99
15.	Groundnut (K)	251	28	19	—17	—17	20
16.	Groundnut (R)	523	152	—39	—118	—73	—143
17.	Sugarcane	33.4 (M. tons)	0.2	1.4	—1.8	—3.0	—1.3

Source: Assistant Director, Planning and Statistics, Machilipatnam-2.
Note: (—) indicate decrease in the yield.
K=Kharif season; R=Rabi season.

TABLE 3

Cropping pattern and requirement of man-days for different crops in Krishna District – 1983.
(area in acres)

Crop	*Area under crop*	*Man-days equired per crop/acre*	*Total labour required*
1	*2*	*3*	*4*
Paddy (K)	810078	100	324031
Paddy (R)	245822	130	127827
Greengram	204583	50	40916
Blackgram	162161	50	32432
Groundnut	72594	90	26133
Jowar	50552	90	18198
Oil seeds	40931	65	10642
Fibres	23593	125	11796
Chillies	19651	90	7074
Redgram	16289	60	3909
Horsegram	13353	50	2670
Vegetables	9090	90	3272
Maize	4093	75	1227

Note: Total labour required = 610127
The available labour = 795584
Surplus labour = 185457
Col. 4 = Col. (2) × Col. (3)/260

26

THE PROBLEM OF DESERTIFICATION IN RAJASTHAN

H.S. SHARMA

Desertification has been defined as the 'diminution or destruction of the biological potential of the land, which leads ultimately to desert like condition and is an aspect of the wide spread deterioration of ecosystem under the combined pressures of adverse and fluctuating climate and excessive exploitation (UNCOD, 1977)'. In fact it is very difficult to define exactly the process involved in this phenomenon. At the U.N. Conference on Desertification (Nairobi, 1977) an attempt was made to review on a global scale the nature and causes of desertification. At UNCOD the data were reviewed and three possible causes of desertification have been defined (Baker, 1982) as:

1. *Climate change* resulting from changes in global atmospheric circulation.
2. *Mismanagement* resulting from an inexorable build up of pressure on resources and destructive misuse of resources reducing large areas to desert like conditions, *i.e.*, the same effect as first but cause differently.

*Associate Professor in Geography, University of Rajasthan, Jaipur.

3. *Biogeophysical feedback* relating (second) to (first) by which means, it is hypothesised that changes in land use are able to effect changes in climate. It is very difficult to prove the presence of climatic change from local data of Rajasthan. However, the impact of mismanagement of resources is often locally and regionally very clear and on an alarming scale. This is, however, something which unlike global climatic change, can be tackled at source as it is the work of man rather than nature.

Magnitude of the Problem

It has been estimated that about one third of the land surface of the globe is affected by desertification. This area contains about fifteen per cent of the total population of the world. The desertification and environmental degradation are the major problems in Rajasthan. The state embraces a huge area of approximately 3,42,261 square kilometres and population of 3,41,08,292 (1981). It is the second largest state in India. The Aravalli range divides the state in almost two equal halves. The north western part consists of Thar desert comprising various types of sand dunes as high as 20-25 metres and rocky plateaux. The state is frequently drought prone. Drought is a regular feature and its recurrence has rendered the problems very acute. The ecological imbalance of arid part of the state is marked by low annual rainfall and its great variability. High wind speed (10-20 km. per hour) aided by the lack of vegetation and intense solar radiation (450-550 calories per day per cm) cause high evapotranspiration (6mm—per day). The result is high aridity index-ranging from seventy six to seventyeight per cent.

The problem of desertification is not a new one, for already the Planning Commission of India described the magnitude of the problem that 'the great India desert of Rajasthan has been spreading outwards in a great convex arc through Ferozepur, Patiala and Agra towards Aligarh and Keshganj at a rate of about half a mile (0.8 km) per year for the last fifty years and is encroaching upon approximately fifty square miles (130 sq. km) of fertile land every year.'

The problem of desert expansion was thoroughly discussed in various seminars and symposium (1952, 1964, 1975). The studies of Central Arid Zone Research Institute (Singh, S. 1977) have also indicated that except much hue and cry the desert is not expanding towards north-east beyond Aravallis. Though in the past the north eastern part of Rajasthan has also witnessed arid phase in pre-Middle stone Age or early Holocene (more than 10,000 B.P) during which major dune formation took place (Goudie *et. al.* 1973). Alarming views are, however, still held about the continuous march of the desert in the form of sand movement to the north and north east along with the prevalent south west wind through various Aravalli gaps (Dhabria, 1984).

Nature of Dunes of North Eastern Rajasthan

In order to resolve the problem of desert encroachment, it is very essential to analyse the nature of sand dunes and sand sheets of north eastern Rajasthan which is climatically a part of semi arid region.

The north eastern Rajasthan is characterized by wide spread sand sheets and obstacle sand dunes on the windward side of the isolated hogbacks and hills of Aravalli mountain. A particularly large sand field occurs in the Sambhar area, West of Jaipur and extends almost to Jaipur. The dunes extend a considerable distance east and north of Jaipur. A large number of obstacle dunes are found at Banada, Jhir, Dausa, Lalsot, Karauli, Gangapur, Newai, Chroal and Tonk. This would appear to mark the eastern most extension of the aeolian features in Rajasthan (Fig. 1).

The existence of sand features in eastern Rajasthan has been misinterpreted as a product of the present aeolian process. Contrary to it, geomorphological, archaeological, pedological and botanical evidences suggest that the sand dunes of this part are fossile dunes and relict features of former arid phase of climate (later upper paleolithic, Allchin *et. al.* 1978). There are quite number of evidences that indicate the relict nature of sand sheets in eastern Rajasthan:

1. It has been found that most of the dunes are extensively moulded by fluvial action. In the foot hill dunes of Jaipur, Bhairana, Chroal, Newai, Samod, Boanli, Lalsot and Karauli gullying have developed, the phenomena indicating the aeolian phase was followed by fluvial erosion.
2. One consequence of the fact that the dunes are essentially fossil is that they have developed upon them extensive soil or weathering profile. The sand is highly oxydised and kankarized in the form of root tunes locally called 'Dikaka'. Such root rubes were exposed in abundance during 1981 flood at Jaipur in the course of Amanisa Nala near Shastri Nagar.
3. The oxydized red phase of sand still preserve archaeological material over their crest. In eastern Rajasthan many dune surfaces are covered by large number of microliths (Allchin *et. al.* 1978).

The sand dunes of the Sambhar area do not indicate any sand drift except local movement. The Jaipur city itself was planned on stable dunes about 255 years ago.

Reactivation of Stabilize Dunes

The phenomenon of wind formed sand ripples provide a clear indication of desertification processes on the stabilized dunes in north eastern Rajasthan. Loosening of sand through framing and large scale levelling sets the soil moving. As a result sand ripples appear, first on the crests of the so far stabilized dunes and then on the slopes and lower parts. The fact that these sand ripples appear in overused areas in the vicinity of Jaipur city and other settlements, which less used areas still preserve a part of the rich, original plant cover proves that ripple formation is anthropogenetically conditioned (rapid urbanization and expansion of city). After the formation of sand ripples the formation of fresh dunes on or along side the old one initiates. Then, the reactivation of the old dunes is complete. Recent dunes formation provides a sure evidence of desertification. But it is not easy to convince that this phenomenon is not simply a naturally controlled one, but, is a consequence of human impact, or that it is a process which is triggered off and enhanced by land misuse in the sand field. The most dramatic indicator of desertification is the encroachment of sand sheets upon buildings, roads, railways and cultivated areas. This process is quite natural in western Rajasthan, but its occurrence in semi-arid north eastern Rajasthan, however, indicates that ecological degradation has been imposed by the impact of men and animals. Thus, because of rapid urbanization in Jaipur and expansion of agricultural activities during last few decades, the old stabilized dunes have been reactivized and thus the loose sand moves locally and seasonally.

Climatic Change

Over hundred years data of rainfall and temperature do not give an indication of any departure from the normal. Besides, there are various studies expressing the view that, by and large, India has not undergone any significant climatic change since the beginning of this century (Parthasarathy and Dhar, 1973, N. Singh, 1984).

Population Pressure/Mismanagement of resources/consequences

In Rajasthan where only twenty per cent of the land is suitable for rainfed cropping, mounting population pressure has doubled the area under cultivation from 28.6 in 1951 to 45.00 per cent in 1971 and about fortyseven per cent in 1981, mainly at the expanse of grazing land, although animal husbandry is the main occupation in arid part of Rajasthan. With population density already twenty times of arid and semi-arid land elsewhere in the world, increasing pressure from human and animal, increased cropping, decreased grazing land, deforestation caused by rising demand for fuel and fodder and pressure on land from construction in urban agglomeration has rendered most parts of Rajasthan vulnerable for ecological deterioration. This deterioration of natural environment has created tension between shepherds of Rajasthan and farmer of Madhya Pradesh where more than a million sheep and goats sweep across the border to pasture. The sedentarization of nomadic population in Rajasthan during 1971-1981 has resulted into upsetting the ecosystem and the consequences are bad. Sedentarization is associated with over exploitation of the soil and moisture, over cultivation, limitation on grazing, increased salinity, greater deplition and gully erosion, devegetation, activation of sand dunes etc. all tending to a deterioration of the environment. Though the sedentarization in Rajasthan has a grand basis of the longest man made canal of the world. As a result of over use and mismanagement of water of Indira Gandhi Canal, salinity hazards in Suratgarh area have cropped up. Same is the case in the Chambal command and Jawai command areas.

The squeeze of pasture land has created huge stock of hungry, malnourished animals not only unable to provide economic yield, but adding to environmental destruction by creating soil erosion and destroying forest regeneration.

Deforestation

In Rajasthan the area of environment most depleted in the few decades has been forest land. Despite official data that 5.8 per cent area under forests that in reality less than half of this area now has adequate tree cover. The Aravallis of Udaipur, Dungarpur, Banswara, Ajmer and Jaipur are completely devegetated. The Bundi-hills which were well vegetated eighteen years ago, now have become rockey wasters. The thin soil cover has also been completely washed away. Therefore, the possibility of regeneration is deem. If the rate of depletion will continue the Aravallis will be barran by the twentyfirst century.

Ecological Crisis in the Aravalli Range

The Aravalli range of Rajasthan is facing serious ecological crisis. The diminishing mountain cover has adversely affected the climate leading to failure of rainfall resulting into severe famines and drought conditions. If the ruthless and indiscriminate cutting of trees, killing of wild life and mutilation of its topography is not stopped by now, a situation will be more serious than the Himalayan valleys like Alaknanda.

This mis-management of forest resources of Jaipur hills and their extension in the north east has made the surrounding hills barren. The removal of vegetation and large scale levelling of older fossilised dunes have aggravated gullying and choaking of natural water flows. With increased rainoff, reduced vegetal base and loosened sand there is a greater erosion than even before. This was seen earlier in 1978 monsoon and more spectacular so in 1981. In the event of 1981 large quantities of sand from dunal areas spread out on the entire fertile agricultural fields of southern Jaipur and adjoining areas of Tonk district (Sharma, 198).

Conclusions

From the above discussion, it can be concludedthat the environment of Rajasthan has been deteriorating as a consequence of human interference and mismanagement of land resources. The thesis of desert expansion towards east through various gaps of the Aravallis in the form of sand movement appears inadequate. However, over exploitation of resources, over grazing, large-scale deforestation in the Aravalli range by men and animals have accentuated the reactivation of sand dunes and accelerated sheet erosion in north eastern and south eastern Rajasthan, causing a serious ecological imbalance. The continued degeneration of the Aravalli forests would have serious repercussions and jeopardise the future of agriculture in Rajasthan.

Though Rajasthan has exerted some efforts partly by central assistance to control desertification in the form Desert

Development Programme and Drought Prone Area Programme, the results have not been remarkable. The main reason is the largeness of the affected zone. Added to this reason, there prevails among decision makers the idea that desert control is not an issue of high priority. Whatever development schemes which have been envisaged are more of a pilot projects than of development programmes. A successful plan to combat desertification in Rajasthan has to be all comprehensive. All recommended measures should aim at a reorganisation of land-use so as to retrieve the ecological balance between the land exploitation and the ability of plants and soil to regenerate. It is a matter of satisfaction that the decision makers in the centre have now realised the magnitude of desertification and the ecological crisis in the Aravalli range. As a result the allocation of funds for desert control by the central Government in the seventh Plan have been raised from fifty per cent to hundred per cent and eight hundred sixtyfour crores of rupees have been allocated for Aravalli Hill Area Development constituting one hundred twentynine development blocks.

REFERENCES

Allchin, B., Goudie, A. and Hegde, K.T.M. (1978): The Pre-history and Palaeogeography of the Great Indian Desert, Academic Press, London.

Baker, R. (1982): Desertification: Cause and control, A study of the U.N. Plan of Action and its possible Application, Scientific Review and Arid Zone Research, 1. pp. 285-313, Scientific Publishers, Jodhpur.

Dhabria, S.S. (1984): Intensification of Desertification Hazard Through Sambhar gap, A problem of Environmental Degradation in Indian Arid Zone. Paper Presented 18th International Symposium on Remotesensing of Environment, Paris (France) 1-5 Oct., 1984.

Goudie, A.S., Allchin, B. and Hegde, K.T.M. (1973): The Former Extensions of the Great Indian Sand Desert, *Geographical Journal*, Vol. 139 (v), pp. 243-57.

Singh, N. (1984): Fluctuations of Different Moisture Regimes in India, *Arch et. Geoph. Biocl.*, ser. B. 35, 239-256.

Singh, S. (1977): Geomorphological Investigations of Rajasthan Desert. Monograph No. 7, Central Arid Zone Research Institute Jodhpur.

Parthasarathy, B., Dhar, O.N. (1978): Climatic Fluctuations over Indian Region—Rainfall: A Review, Research Report, RR-025, Indian Institute of Tropical Meteorology, Poona.

U.N.C.O.D. (1977): Plan of Action, Nairobi.

27

REMOTE SENSING DATA BASE FOR EVALUATION OF LAND RESOURCES A CASE STUDY

K.V. SESHAGIRI*
R.L. KARALE*

Preparation of Soil and landuse maps in a conventional system involves field traverses for examination of soil and land characteristics at required intervals with the help of soil base and finally compilation of data. Depending upon the object of the survey and intensity of observations, the base maps used for soil surveys vary in scale from 1:4000 to 1:50,000. For detailed soil surveys cadastral maps in the scale of 1:4000 to 1:8000 are normally used, whereas for reconnaissance level mapping topographical maps of Survey of India on 1:50,000/ 1:63,360 are normally used.

Since over three decades the serial photograph proved to be a very good tool for soil and land use mapping. Ever since the first Landsat was launched in 1972 and acquisition of MSS data started, a probe is on as a base for soil and land use studies.

*All India Soil and Land Use Survey, Ministry of Agriculture and R.D. Deptt. of Agriculture and Co-operation.

Visual interpretation of Landsat images was tried by several workers in soil mapping (Krishnamurthy *et al*, 1973; Mirajkar *et al*, 1975; Bhandari *et al*, 1976, Karale *et al*, 1980, Seshagiri Rao, 1983 etc.). The results obtained in preparation of small scale soil maps, land use maps and even classification of ravines (Singh, 1977) entails a success story but only on an experimental level.

The individual, combined and reciprocal efficacy of various landsat paper products has been tested for their utility in soil and land resources mapping and the results are presented in this paper. Based on the experience obtained in this study a feasible methodology is suggested for soil and land resources mapping with Landsat data as a base, which is to be tested further in various agro-climatical zones and different geological tracts.

Study Area

The study area encompassing 950 sq. km. is located partly in Mahaboobnagar district of Andhra Pradesh and partly in Gulbarga district of Karnataka. It is geographically located between 16°32′ and 16°55′ N Latitude and 77°15′ and 77°35′ E Longitude. The area is influenced by semi-arid type of climate with mean annual precipitation of 738 to 745 mm and mean annual temperature averaging to 27°C.

Granite-gneisses predominate the tract with a patch vehicular basalts occurring on the north.

Materials and Methods

(*a*) *Landsat*: Landsat E2 scene of 864-041 with the code 155-048 dated 4th June, 1977 was used in the study. MSS data on bands five and seven and FCC in the form of 1:250,000 paper products were utilised.

Monoscopic interpretation was carried out with the aid of magnascope. Tone, texture, pattern and colour/grey tone variations were considered as primary factors for differentiating various mapping units. Data from topographic maps (Survey of India) such as contours, townships, etc. were superimposed and the imagery suitably annotated. Selected aerial photographs representing the mapping units, have been studied to assist subfacet delineations.

(*b*) *Aerial photos*: Glossy, single weight, panchromatic black and white photographs of 728 B task on 1:20,000 scale were systematically interpreted. Operational sequence advocated by Goosen (1967) was followed in compiling the aerial photo interpretation soil map.

(*c*) *Field work*: Conventional field work was carried out at rapid reconnaissance level with topographic maps of Survey of India (1:50,000 scale) as bases in accordance with the stipulations laid down in Soil Survey Manual, 1970. The soils were mapped at sub-group level of taxonomic classification (USDA, 1975).

Line maps have been prepared from the API and RS data delineations. The mapping units in each case were translated to soil and landuse units by selected field check adopting sample strip method supplemented by the field data from rapid reconnaissance survey. All the products were brought to a common scale of 1:100,000 for easy comparison.

Results

API: Stereoscopic analysis of APs yielded excellent results. Altogether fourteen physiographic mapping units were recognised which are best correlated with soil vaJiations. Owing to the reduction of the output to 1:100,000 scale the lower categorical levels had to be sacrificed and ultimately only nine distinct mapping units could be demarcated with precision (Fig. 1). Soils could be mapped at sub-group level (USDA, 1975).

RR Survey: Eight mapping units were recognised representing association of sub-groups which is in consonance with the level of survey. The subfacets, within the facets, that were recognised in API could not be delineated. Erosional features and salt affected lands could be separately demarcated (Fig. 2). The boundaries between the units are not as sharp as in the case of API map.

Band 5: Save for dark clays of both pediplain and basalt landscape no significant results could be obtained. Drainage patterns are seen predominantly in this output. Area under dryland agriculture, wet cultivation and vegetated hilly lands could not be segregated consistantly (Fig. 3; Table 1).

Band 7: Results obtained from band seven data are more encouraging. Eight mapping units are recognised. Vertisols of pediplain and basalt region could be segregated easily (Units 7 and 1 of Fig. 4).. Within the basalt region the pediments could be recognised because of their lighter tones which are caused by erosion and gravelly nature.

Erosion features could be demarcated well. Within the eroded lands some patches showed up higher reflectance which is attributed to the presence of sa t incrustation. However, these patches could not be separated visually as the boundaries are not distinct.

The granite hill, pediplain, interfluves and mess could be identified. Valley lands under irrigation and water bodies are promiscuous in band 7 data only.

FCC: Since the imagery pertains to the month of June, foliage coverage was almost nil except for a few patches of vegetated hills. These were, however, recognised prominantly in FCC than in any other RS product. The advantage of IR could not be harnessed otherwise. Tanks and paddy lands are mixed up with narrow patches of dark clays and could not be always identified separately which was possible in band 7 data. However, the boundaries of the units representing dark clays are more sharper than in other products. Altogether 10 units have been mapped (Fig. 5).

Combined data of and 7 band FCC: An attempt was made to combine the band 7 and FCC data results. Surprisingly it was found that several superfluous units have disappeared (Fig. 6) and the new units derived stand for conspicuous variations in soil and land use differences. The dark clays of basalt and granite regions standout separately, eroded soils and lands under rainfed agriculture also could be demarcated uniformly. The complexity of soilscapes is reduced in this map (Table 1).

Correlation of Results

(*a*) *Soils*: Typic Chromusters and the complex of Typic Chromusterts and Typic Pellusterts are the sub-groups where almost 100 per cent correlation could be obtained in all outputs, except mass Band 5 data. Orthents of Lithic and Typic Subgroups occurring in valleys and foot slopes could be demarcated satisfactorily on Band 7 imagery. FCC gave relatively better correlation than band 5 data.

Typic Natrustalfs and Lithic Ustorthents encountered in valleys have been classified together in almost all cases except in API. Band 7 presented slight variations in tones but separation was not possible visually. An optical mechanical system that can segregate narrow spectral differences could perhaps achieve this.

Table 1 presents the correlations achieved in various data bases. It could be seen that the complexity of results of Band 7 and FCC data is reduced in their combined product. API, however, yielded better results as compared to other systems.

(*b*) *Surface characteristics*: Correlation of selected surfacial characteristics attempted with various data produts yielded interesting results thus indicating resourcefulness of various bases (Table 2). This aspect is very essential since MSS data is more influenced by surface characteristics. Correlation with a particular factor or a set of factors provide a clue in decoding the soil and landscapes as manifested in various tones in that particular area of study.

In the present study MSS band 7 data appeared to be more promising followed by FCC. Erosion and land-use are the two factors where very good correlation could be attained. Overall evaluation revealed that the data from MSS Band 5 are not encouraging. The API remaining supreme over other data bases, the combined band 7 and FCC stands next to it.

Conclusion

Landsalt MSS data paper products are found to be promising data bases for mapping of soil and land resources for broad level characterisation and planning (1:25000 scale). The data of imagery supplemented by aerial photographs of selected sites improved the soil delineations supporting the results of Mirajkar, *et. al.* (1975).

MSS band 7 data yielded a better soil map than the RR Survey as was found earlier by Singh (1980).

Enlargements of the imagery to 1:250,000 scale displayed better disposition of gray tones in MSS bands 5 and 7 and colour patterns in FCC for better information extension.

FCC is found to be the best in separating the afforested hills from barren and sparsely vegetated areas.

A combination of MSS band 7 and FCC outputs yielded better results in many respects (Fig. 6 and Tables 1 and 2).

The results suggest the following stepwise approach to operationalise the utility of RS data which may be tried further.

—General study of MSS bands 5 and 7 and FCC data.

—Drainage map from MSS band 5 data.

—Interpretation of MSS band 7 and FCC products under magnascope and enlarging the line map to 1:100,0.0 scale for cartographic case.

—Study of selected APs from each of the imagery units.

—Subdivision of facets based on the results of above step.

—Preparation of a combined map of band 7 and FCC

—Limited field check adopting sample strip method

—Translation of units to soil and land use classes

REFERENCES

Bhandari, R.L.: L.F. Curtis and U.C. Shukla, 1976—Visual Interpretation Landsat-I Imagery of Central and Southern district of Haryana State, India., Jour. Ind. Soc. Photo-Int. and R.S., Photonirvachak, Vol. IV, No. 1 and 2, 37-42.

Goosen, D. 1967—Aerial Photo Interpretation in Soil Survey Soils Bull. 6, FAO.

Karale, R.L., Sheshagiri Rao, K.V., and Singh, A.N.

Krishnamurthy, G and T.R. Srinivasan, 1973—Interpretation of Appolo Space Photo for small scale soil mapping in respect of an area in Bihar; Jour. Ind. Soc. Photo—Int. and R.S., Photonirvachak, Vol. I, No. 1 and 2, 75-87.

Mirajkar, M.A. and T.R. Srinivasan, 1975—Landsat Photo Interpretation for preparation of small scale soil maps through multistage approach.; Jour. Soc. Photo-Int. and R.S. Photonirvachak, No. 2, Vol. III, 87-92.

Seshagiri Rao, K.V.; 1983—Acquisition of Soil Data from Landsat Paper Products by Visual approach; Project Report—Unpublished.

Singh, B.M. 1977—Interpretation of Satellite Imagery for Delineation of ravines; Jour. Ind. Soc. Photo-Int. and R.S. Photonirvachak, Vol. V, No. 1, 31-34.

Singh, A.N. 1980—Comparison of Reconnaissance Soil Maps prepared by Conventional method and Landsat Imagery Interpretation; Jour. Ind. Soc. Photo-Int. and R.S., Photonirvachak, Vol. 8, No. 1, 1-8.

Soil Survey Staff 1970—Soil Survey Manual, IARI, New Delhi.

USDA 1975 –Soil Taxonomy—A basic system of Soil classification for making and interpreting soil surveys, Agril., Hand book No. 436; U S. Govt. Ptg. Press, Washington, D.C.

TABLE 1

Correlation of Soil and Land Use Data (1:100,000)

Land facet	*Soil and land use*	*Symbols of mapping units*					
		API	*RR survey*	*Band 5*	*Band 7*	*FCC*	*Combined Band 7 and FCC*
Basalt Mesa	Complex of Typic Chromusterts and Vertic Ustochrepts, rainfed	B1	T	6	7	8	1
Basalt Escarpments and footslopes	Lithic and Typic ustorthents partly cult., and partly busy	B2	T	4,6	2,7	1.1,8	3
Rocky hills	Lithic soils in patches, barren, sparse veg.	P1	Q, R	3,4	2,5	2,6	4
Hill flats and footslopes	T. Ustorthents and Ustochrepts, rainfed	P5 (Not on 1:100000 map)	C	4	5	3,4 6.1,7	4.a
Interfluves, granite region	Assoc. T. Ustochrepts and T. Haplustalfs, rainfed	P3	D, H	4,5	3,3a,5	3,4	3,5

Lower pediments	T. Chromusterts and T. Pellusterts, rainfed	P4	F	1	1	1	2
Valleys	T. Haplaquepts, X. Wet lands	VI	A	3,4	4	—	6 not on map
Valleys	Lithic Ustorthents, edd; T. Natrustalfs salt affected, Barren	V2	E, J	2,4	2,4,6	2,3,4	3

TABLE 2

Resourcefulness of Various Base

Parameter	*API*	*RR*	*RS*		
			Band 7	*FCC*	*Combined band 7 and FCC data*
No. of units	14	13	8	10	6
Level of mapping					
(Soil Taxonomy)					
At 1:2000 scale	Series and Assoc.	—	—	—	—
At 1:10000 scale	Assoc. of families	Assoc. of families	Subgroup and their assoc.	Subgroups and complexes	Assoc. of sub-groups
Efficacy in identification					
Valleys/Paddy	Excellent	Excellent	Very Good	Moderate	Very Good
Hills					
—Barren	Excellent	Excellent	Good	Good	Good
—Vegetated	Excellent	Excellent	Moderate	Very Good	Very Good

Eroded, salt affected, Barren	Excellent	Very Good	Very Good	Good	Very Good
Dryland Agril	Excellent	Very Good	Good	Good	Good
Boundary					
Sharpness	Excellent	Good	Very Good	Very Good	Very Good

28

GEOMORPHIC STUDIES IN DINDI RESERVIOR BASIN FOR LANDUSE PLANNING: ANDHRA PRADESH

MANOJ RAJ SAXENA*
V. VIDYANATH**

Agriculture landuse study has acquired special significance in the realm of the present day problem oriented studies of the growth and resource utilization. As such, studies in this sphere have been made with a view to present analytically the different aspects of landuse pattern so that the basis of the scientific land resource allocation to various agricultural crops and planning for maximum productivity may be attained. The planning and development of land requires an intimate knowledge of land, its physical characteristics, present biological productivity, capacity and limitations (Nageshwar Rao and Vaidyanadhan, 1981). As a part of this endeavour the remote sensing technology is demonstrated and discussed as a tool for geomorphic study and its application for landuse planning.

*Senior Research Fellow (CSIR), Department of Geography, Osmania University, Hyderabad.

**Professor of Geography, and Director, Centre for Area Studies, Osmania University, Hyderabad.

The main aim here in studying geomorphology is to provide information that is of great value to the planners and others concerned. Reconnaissance level geomorphology and soil maps were generated by employing available ground data and subsequent fieldwork.

A rational landuse plan at regional level has been proposed based on the geomorphology, soil and water potential of the area.

Methodology

Satellite imagery of bands 4, 5 and 7 in conjunction with false colour composite on the scale of 1:250,000 has been used. Survey of India toposheets on the scale of 1:250,000 and 1:50,000 have been utilised for annotation and verification of certain ground features for proper orientation. The morphological and hydrological differences that could be discerned directly and indirectly were taken into consideration to compile a physiographic-cum-image element map. This map with the help of ground truth in the form of soil data for the selected strips on conventional rapid reconnaissance soil survey map for the area (Anon, 1982) was translated into soil map. Landuse/surface water map showing water bodies, was also generated by visual interpretation. While identifying the areas under different landuse classes, the ecological principles of landuse have been the guiding criteria. Nature of terrain, availabity of moisture and vegetative characteristics of the area have been considered. The landuse classes are only broad and generalised ones and would help in identification of the lead sectors and formulation of suitable measures for all round development.

Location and Size: Dindi River is a major tributary of the river Krishna and occupies a portion of Mahboobnagar district in Andhra Pradesh. The river basin covers an area of 3708 sq. km. The river takes its origin on crystalline rocks of Archaean age at an altitude of 570 metres above sea level near Balanagar village in Mahboobnagar district. It runs over a total length of 170 km being euphemeral in nature. It runs the first 25 km, in a southerly direction and takes a south-easterly course near the village of Alwanpalle. After flowing for another 40 km in this direction, it turns towards the east and flows for 30 km before joining the river Krishna.

A dam was constructed over three decades back across the Dindi River near Gundlápalle village in Deverkonda taluq of Nalgonda district, with an irrigation capacity of 5060 hectares during kharif season and 2024 hectares during Rabi season. The location and spread of the reservoir basin is shown in (Figure 1).

Results from Landsat data

Geology: The geology of the area varies from Archaean to recent river deposits. The rocks of the Archaean age are made up of the peninsular granitic-gneissic complex and Dharwarian schists, whereas the rocks of Cuddapah and Kurnool formations are made up of basal conglomerates and quartzites which are resting over granites. The rocks of the Deccan traps are mostly vesicular and sometimes massive and the recent river deposits consist of alluvial sediments along the banks of the Dindi River (Figure 2).

Geomorphology: Geomorphologically the area is made up of a rolling plain which is dotted with inselbergs, tors, pediments, rock outcrops, valleyfill deposits and dolerite dykes, which are typical of the semi-arid climate. The section to the east of the main Dindi stream is undulating with gentle slopes and lesser intensities of erosion, whereas the rest of the area is more undulating with steeper slopes. The hilly landscape accounts for 2 per cent of the total basin area. The maximum elevation is between 700 and 750 metres with an average elevation of about 400 metres. Other important landscape features within the basin are large loose blocks of granite and rubble, which are separated along the joint planes. The boulders which are brought down from the hill slopes occur at the base as well as along the slopes of the hills. The area shows dissected topography with intervening ravines and streams. The area is characterised by a network of tanks which receive water from the upper to the lower tanks successively as the relief decreases. Although the local relief accounts for less than hundred metres many tributary valleys are youthful, steep and narrow with irregular longitudinal profiles. The geomorphology of the basin is playing an important role in influencing the type of landuse that is prevalent in the area.

Soils in the Area: In the present work, a soil map of the area under study has been prepared from visual interpretation of landsat imagery (Figure 3). The map was compiled by systematic analysis of image elements and physiographic units. Landforms were identified and delineated and translated into soil units on the basis of ancillary data in the form of available soil map. Additional observations were made use of, in compiling the soil map at an abstracted level of subgroups and association of subgroups (Table 1). The morphological descriptions recorded from each of the mapping units have been studied carefully and soils classified according to the USDA soil Taxonomy (1975) (Table 2).

The area is dominated by granitic landscape and there is a close relationship between soils and physiography. The soils follow a definite catena. A major part of the area is covered by course and medium texture soils.

The foot slopes of hills, hillocks and tors are steep supporting a thin veneer of soil. They are skeletal 'Lithic' or Typic 'Ustorthents'.

Soils in valleys are deep to very deep and hydromorphic conditions usually prevail in the lower horizon. The soils are medium to fine grained. They mostly classify as Haplaquepts and Aquic Ustorthents of fine loamy and clayey families, whereas upland soils are coarser and classify as typic Ustochrepts and typic Ustorthents.

Soils occupying the physiograph c position in between the hills and relatively flat rice lands represent most of the cultivated area. These are vital lands contributing to most of the agricultural production from the catchment of Dindi. Shallow to moderately deep, coarse to medium texture soils occur on the lower slopes and lower plateaus. Argillaceous subsoils are common in lower plateaus and on the interfluves. Soils in this landscape classify as typic ustochrepts on the upper slopes, typic and udic subgroups of Haplustalfs in the lower regions. Rhodustalfs and other subgroups of Haplustalfs are usually seen associated with pink granites and ferruginous quartzites which occur in random patches.

Black clay soils classifying as typic chromusterts occupy the lower plateau and plains within the interfluve system and mostly occur in the upper reaches of paddy lands. Salt-affected soils are encountered in the valley regions and are seen overlying the tank spread areas. They occur as narrow elongated patches and support deep to very deep soils which classify as typic Haplaquepts and Aquic Natrustalfs.

Land use of the study Area

The present landuse pattern of the area is an outcome of the interaction of physical, social and economic factors. As much as 93 per cent of the area in the basin is under cultivation (Figure 4). The rest of the area is either hilly or under bush vegetation and forests or rocky wastes. Almost all the rainfed areas and culturable wastes show a high potential of erodibility. They account for 2.87 lakha ha. covering over 79 per cent of total basin area. Literally, no complete and comprehensive soil conservation measures are being implemented in these lands.

Three types of landuse could be readily discerned and demarcated from the landuse imagery. The narrow elongated dark-toned patches with moderate to coarse texture could be identified as land under irrigated agriculture. Lighter-toned areas with moderately fine texture, spotted with darker mottles (hills and tors) were recognised as land under dryland agriculture. Water bodies could be readily identified from their very dark tones and by their typical pattern within the courses of streams and rivulets. Forest areas are identified by their mixed tones. Bigger habitations could be identified by their spotted nature. The map prepared from the imagery (Figure 4) and the areas computed by different landuse are given in Table 3 and the types of landuse associated with particular land forms and soils are given in Table 4.

Present Landuse

Intensive agriculture is practised in the valley regions below the tanks, while small patches are put under cash crops such as groundnut, and the rest of the area is cultivated for cereals, pulses and oil seeds. Only in the kharif season the yield in the valley region where high yielding variety (HYV) of paddy is grown is good. Fertilizers are applied only here. In other areas the cultivation is patchy and the yield is rather poor.

Discussion

Abstracting soil information from the landsat imagery is a quick method but it has certain limitations. Since physiogrphy is not directly reflected in the landsat data, the help of corroborating evidence of geology and geomorphology as reflected in the drainage system can be taken in demarcating the soilscape. Murthy *et.al.*, (1982) demonstrated the close relationship between variations in the geomorphic patterns and the soil patterns in their studies under three different climatic conditions.

A great deal of work on soil identification and mapping has been carried out in all parts of the world. Biswas (1982) carried out reconnaissance soil surveys of eastern south Dakota using remote sensing technology for land development. Shankarnarayan *et al* (1979) carried out visual interpretation in conjunction with the ground truths leading to identification, delineation and mapping of various geomorphic units. Pacheco (1978) adopted visual analysis methods with field checks of landsat colour composite (band 4, 5, and 7) on 1:1,000,000 scale. He considered shape, size, tone, colour, texture, shadow patterns, location and association as image characteristics in the interpretation process and delineated physiographic units. Pacheco (1980) also adopted an approach for recognition and delineation of soil boundaries in association with:

(i) climate and vegetation;

(ii) edaphic parent material;

(iii) topographic change; and

(iv) landscape units by visual interpretation of landsat imagery at various scales.

White (1977) has discussed the use of techniques of aerial photography and remote sensing for soil surveys. Roy and Bhattacharya (1967) and Moutappa (1968) have examined the use of air photographs and their systematic interpretation in soil surveys and in the assessment of soil erosion.

In the present investigations, the areas infested with tors and inselbergs could be identified and segregated with sufficient ease, since the shadow pattern has been exhibited on the imagery with the mottled tone. Valleys have been predominantly depicted by darker and linear patterns and these are generally paddy lands with aquic soils. The chromusterts mostly associated with pediplains were identified by their coarse texture and darker tones.

The soil map prepared by the remote sensing technique (Figure 3) has been compared with the existing soil map by Rapid Reconnaissance (RR) Survey of the area (Anon, 1982) and fair agreement is seen between the two. The areas computed by both the methods are presented in Table 5.

Groundwater conditions of the Basin

Groundwater occurs in the study area under water table conditions, in weathered, semi-weathered, fractured portions of granite and saturated thicknes of alluvium. The development of groundwater in the hard rock area is by means of open-dug wells and the quantity of groundwater depends on the degree of weathering, thickness of weathered zone and the fractures and joints present in the rocks. The wells in the hard rock area are mostly rectangular in shape and most of the wells are unlined. The wells range in total depth from 3 to 22 metres below ground level. Of the total wells examined in the hard rock area 65 per cent fall in the depth range of 4 to 8 metres below ground level and 16 per cent in the depth range 1 to 4 metres below ground level and 19 per cent of wells lie in the depth range more than 8 metres. The weathered zone extends downward to a maximum depth of 22 meters and the depths to levels vary from 0.5 to 17 metres below ground level. It is observed that 70 per cent of the wells have the water levels less than 4 metres below ground level and 27 per cent of the wells indicate the range in water levels from 8 to 12 metres below ground level. Most of the wells have not pierced the complete thickness of the weathered zone. Some of the wells have 20 inches to 40 inches diameter bores drilled at the bottom of the wells for obtaining better yields. Yield of water in these wells of hardrock area is between 40,000 and 60,000 litres per day.

The groundwater is developed in the alluvial area by open-ring wells and filter point wells. The development of groundwater by filter point wells is only a recent technique adopted by farmers. The open-ring wells range in diameter from 1.5 to 9 metres. Total depth of these wells varies between 3 and 10 metres below ground level. Of the total wells examined in the alluvial area 70 per cent are in the depth range of 4 to 8 metres and 25 per cent in the range of 1 to 4 metres. Only 5 per cent of wells extend downward to a depth of beyond 8 metres. Maximum total depth observed is 10 metres below ground level at Sirsavada and Gudiganpalle villages. It is observed that most of the wells have not penetrated through the complete thickness of alluvium. Depth to water levels in these wells ranges between 1 to 6.5 metres below ground level. Study of water levels in the wells of alluvial area indicate that 88 per cent of the wells have the water levels less than 4 metres below ground levels and 12 per cent of the wells have water levels of 4 to 8 metres below ground level.

The wells in Vepur, Anantharam, Nainapalle, Nellikudur and Medipur vary in depth from 3 to 7.4 metres below ground level, and depth to water level ranges between 2 and 3.8 metres below ground level. The saturated thickness of alluvium is found to be in the range of 1 to 4.3 metres. It is seen from the lithology of the well constructed at Medipur village (Figure 5) that the thickness of clay soil is about 4.5 metres which is followed by medium-grained sand. The well was drilled down to a depth 8.5 metres.

The wells located in Polumar, Gattalapalle, Nedigadda and Raghupathipet villages vary in total depths from 3 to 6.7 metres below ground level and depths to water level range between 1.3 metres and 4 metres, respectively and the saturated thickness of the alluvium is found to range from 1.1 to 3.1 metres. The concentration and distribution of the wells are observed to be more towards east of the Dindi River flow.

As a corollary to the above discussion, it is recommended that the area to the east and northeast of the Dindi River, with productive soils (Haplustalfs and Rhodulstalfs) and suitable water potentials be entirely devoted to agriculture as basin conditions favour good agricultural production. Hydrogeological map of area (Figure 6) adopted from Central Groundwater Board supports these general observations. It is estimated that about 0.1 million hectares can be considered for improved land and water use. The following measures would increase the water potential and improve the subsurface water recharge.

(i) Creation of percolation tanks in the upper reaches of major stream courses (prospective sites indicated in Figure 6).

(ii) The valleyfill areas may be developed by open wells and filter point wells; the thickness of the valleyfill in most of the areas is limited, extending to a maximum depth of 10 metres.

(iii) Most of the open wells examined in the hardrock areas have not penetrated the complete thickness of weathered zone. Wells have to be deepened further or converted into dug-cum-bore wells for increasing the yield of water.

(iv) In order to study the base flow and stream flow checkpoints have to be established along the river.

Since the primary groundwater reservoir in the area is mainly constituted by weathered zone and to a limited extend by fissured, fractured and jointed unweathered zones, sinking of open wells or bore wells may be taken up on the lower slopes of interfluves and along the valley sides. Harnessing of water from the catchments in the percolation tanks is expected not only to improve the subsoil water recharge but also help to bring about:

(a) An improvement in the ecosystem;

(b) Regular recharge to the fissured, fractured and jointed zones; and

(c) Increasing the capacity of the existing wells and thus their command areas.

Proposed Landuse System for the Area

Not all drylands are suitable for arable farming. Further, serious imbalances in the ecosystem occurs by cultivating marginal lands. Besides food for the human beings, it is the firewood which is most wanting. Our forest wealth is fast depleting. So are our fodder resources. Timber is getting costlier with every passing day. We are, therefore, deep in the woods. Using marginal lands to meet requirements other than human food is the rational way of utilising land resources more efficiently in the study area.

Marginal lands could be profitably put to alternate landuse systems like tree farming or pastoral use. Trees and shrubs contribute substantially to the maintenance of a healthy balance in the ecosystem, besides meeting the human and livestock requirements for fuel, timber and top feed. The modern approach, therefore, calls for a system which can meet multiple requirements of the dryland farmers besides maintaining soil health. The various alternate landuse systems that could be implemented in the area are grass-legume, agro-forestry and Sylvo-pastoral management systems.

In the grass-legume forage farming system, marginal lands could be checked from further degradation by clothing them with a suitable vegetal cover. Perennial grasses serve this purpose the best. They check soil erosion and provide the much needed nutritious fodder to the cattle. A perennial legume component adds value to the pasturage and improves soil fertility and makes the forage more palatable. *Stylosanthes lamata* is a perennial legume which does not mind a shallow rocky and even undulating topography as its habitat. It is aggressive and knocks out weeds. It forms an excellent vegetal carpet on rolling plains as in the study area. It co-exists well with field crops jowar (sorghum), ragi (pearl millets), castor, bean etc. Growing it in mixture with crops saves on nitrogen bill. What is encouraging is the fact that it is a good choice to establish a grassed waterway. It makes the soil richer and more productive. Eventually, it can help convert marginal lands into productive arable lands.

In the Sylvo-pastoral system, a tree species (silviculture component) and a pasture species (pastoral component) are grown together in a systematic way so that they become complementary to each other. On shallow red soils in the area having rolling topography, this system could be implemented.

The agro-forestry management system means a landuse system which involves the use of trees and shrubs in combination with food and fodder crops (relying heavily on positive interaction) and livestock. The main objective is to increase/optimise the productivity of land, either in terms of increased total biomass or variety of biomass, or both, of economic importance. Lands with shallow soils and sloping lands could be put under such a system.

The success of the system lies in selecting appropriate tree and shrub species according to requirements and following proper management practices. In fact, there should be a variety of these systems, to enable the farmer to select the best for his requirements. A classical example is growing arable crops with *Leucaena leoucoceohala* at set intervals of 3 to 6 metres. The *Leucaena* has to be maintained at 0.6 to 1.0 metre height and pruned frequently, the loppings beings used as fodder or green manure or mulch for the arable crops.

Going a little beyond the well known landuse systems, marginal lands could serve as ideal sites for water harvesting and storage to be concurrently capitalised for increasing the productivity of reasonably good agricultural lands which may be available on the lower elements of slopes. The dug-out ponds meant for water harvesting could go a long way in providing additional income to dryland farmers by way of aqua fish culture sustaining live stock in years of crisis. Some green fodder or growing nurseries may also find a place if the dug-cuts are adequately large.

In addition to the above systems discussed, forests play a major role in reducing the runoff, checking soil erosion and restoring ecological balance in the area and would also provide employment to a number of landless labourers which would be largely of continuing nature.

The areas which could be developed for forests include rugged terrain and land with slope generally exceeding ten percent. This category includes all hilly areas where runoff is usually very rapid and where soil erosion is a serious problem. In view of the necessity to check runoff and to reduce the hazards of soil erosion, all such areas should be covered by thick vegetation.

This class of land includes much of the area under the existing state forests as well as areas which are presently under the control of individuals or the village panchayats. Usually, such areas are devoid of population. In some cases, a few hamlets may come under the forest area. In such cases, the villagers should be allowed to retain the land, but they should be advised to grow crops only and not keep too many animals. This will, of course entail tremendous extension work, persuasion and may be, legal force also.

Further care has to be taken to keep the forest area as compact blocks mainly with a view to reduce the expenditure on fencing. One of the serious impediments in the evelopment of forestry in this part of the area is the depredation by stray, cattle. As this area receives only scanty rainfall, the trees once destroyed by cattle rarely grow again. The safeguard against cattle by fencing is usually a costly affair. Hence while identifying the areas for forest development, contiguity and compactness should be taken into account to keep the fencing expenditure at the minimum. Further, the existing forests in the area are devoid of trees. They are forests only in the sense that the ownership of the land rests with the Forest Department. This situation is undesirable. It does not help to bring about the desired restoration of ecological balance. It does not check the heavy runoff and washing away of the fertile soil mantle, and lastly, landuse in this category should be enforced with rigidity. These areas are quite vulnerable becaues of the steep slopes and rugged terrain and any laxity will frustrate the very purpose of ecological landuse planning.

Conclusion

Present studies in the area reveal that the area to the east and north-east of the Dindi River, with productive soils (Haplustalfs and Rhodustalfs) and suitable water potential, favour good agricultural production. The deep to very deep alfisols provide good sites for introducing improved cropping pattern. Two-crops system can easily be introduced, both in kharif and rabi seasons. Improved varieties of jowar, maize and groundnut can replace the present traditional seed varieties. If a high level of fertilization can be adopted with assured supply of water, better seed and fertilizers, the cost benefit ratio (C:B) shall increase to 1:2:5 and easily compensate the initial costs of percolation tanks and borewells, within a period of five to ten years. Further, any industrial development and other future infrastructure can conveniently be planned in the north-west and south-west of the Dindi reservoir. In this way, if agricultural landuse is intensified and made production-oriented, the productivity for some crops may be raised to high level.

TABLE 1

Legend for soil map derived from imagery

Physiography	*Tone/texture/pattern*	*Soils/groups*
Hills, inselbergs and tores	Dark, coarse, mottled	Rocky
Interfluves	Light, smooth, scuettered dark patches	Assoc. Ustorthents and Ustochrepts
Interfluves	Light gray, moderately coarse	Assoc. Ustochrepts and Haplustalfs
Interfluves	Gray, moderately fine elongated nearer to valleys	Complex Haplustalfs and Rhodustalfs
Interfluves	Dark gray, coarse patchy and slightly mottled	Chromusters
Valleys	Very dark, fine smooth, elongated	Haplaquepts and Aquic Ustorthents

TABLE 2

Classification of soils according to USDA Soil Taxonomy, 1975

S. No.	*Order*	*Suborder*	*Great group*	*Subgroup*
1.	Entisols	Orthernts	Ustorthents	Typic Ustorthent Udic Ustorthents Lithic Ustorthents
2.	Inceptisols	Ochrepts	Ustochrepts	Typic Ustochrepts Lithic Ustochrepts
3.	Alfisols	Ustalfs	Haplustalf	Typic Haplustalfs Udic Haplustalfs
			Natrustalfs	Aquic Natrustalfs
			Rhodustalfs	Typic Rhodustalfs
4.	Vertisols	Ustert	Chromusterts	Typic Chromusterts

TABLE 3

Information on landuse derived from imagery

Details	*Tone and texture*	*Area computed (000 ha)*
Irrigated agriculture	Narrow, elongated darker tones, moderate coarse texture	69
Dryland agriculture	Lighter tones, moderate to fine texture mottled scattered patches	177
Barren land	Very light tones with moderate to fine texture	2.8
Forest	Mixed tones, coarse texture	4
Tanks	Very dark tones, smooth texture irregular pattern in the middle of streams	Not computed

TABLE 4

Terrain evaluation in Dindi reservoir basin

S. No.	*Landform terrain*	*Slope %*	*Soil characters*		*Landuse*	*Environmental hazards (erosion intensity)*	*Tentative soil class (subgroup)*
			Depth	*Texture*			
1	*2*	*3*	*4*	*5*	*6*	*7*	*8*
1.	Valley bottom	1	Deep to very deep	Medium to fine	Rice	Slight to none	Assoc. of Typic Haplaquepts and Aquic Ustorthents
2.	Uplands, interfluves	2 to 4	Shallow to moderately deep	Coarse to medium	Rainfed crops (Castor, Jowar etc.)	Moderate to severe	Typic Ustochrep s
3.	Rolling plain	2 to 4	,,	,,	Tur and caster	,,	Assoc. of Typic and Lithic Ustochrepts
4.	Convex lands, interfluves	2 to 3	Moderately deep to deep	Medium	Rainfed crops (Jowar, ragi, groudnut)	Moderate to severe	Assoc. of Typic Ustochrepts and Haplustalfs

(Contd.)

2	3	4	5	6	7	8
5. Lower pediments	1 to 3	Deep to very deep	Fine to very fine	,,	Moderate to severe	Typic chromusterts
6. Interfluves	1 to 3	Moderately deep to deep	Medium fine	,,	Moderate	Assoc. of Typic Haplustalfs and typic Rhodustalfs
7. Lowlands (salt affected)	1 to 2	Deep	Medium	Barren	Moderate to severe	Assoc. of Typic Haplaquepts and Aquic Natrustals
8. Foot slopes of hills, inselbergs	3 to 5	Shallow	Coarse skeletal	Shrub vegetation	Severe	Assoc. of Lithic and Typic Ustorthents
9. Foot slopes of quartzite hills	2 to 4	Moderately deep	Medium	Rainfed crops (Jowar, groundnut tur etc.)	Moderate	Typic/Udic Haplustalfs

TABLE 5

Table showing areas computed by Rapid Reconnaissance (RR) survey and Remote Sensing (RS) technique

Soil/groups	*Area computed by*	
	RR survey	*RS technique*
Ustorthents, Ustochrepts	169	189
Haplustalfs, Rhodustalfs	91	80
Haplaquents	68	70
Halaquepts, Natrustalfs	10	4
Chromusters	16	11
Total	354	354

REFERENCES

Anon, 1982—Report on demarcation of priority subwater sheds in A C (part) subcatchment (above Dindi Reservoir) of Nagarjunasagar catchment, Andhra Pradesh. All India Soil and Landuse Survey, Govt. of India, Dept. of Agriculture, IARI Buildings, New Delhi.

Biswas, R.R, 1982—Report on UNDP associated project for advance training in remote sensing technology for Land development in USA and Italy, Ministry of Agriculture, Govt. of India. pp. 45-49.

Moutappa, F. 1968—A beginning of aerial photograph interpretation in soil surveys in India, in Aerial Surveys and Integrated studies—proceedings of Toulouse Conference, UNESCO.

Murthy, R.S., Pofali, P.M. and Saxena, R.K. 1982—Remote Sensing techniques in establishing geomorphic soil relationships. Jour. Ind. Soc. Photo. Int. R.S., 10(2): 1-12.

Nageshwara Rao, K. and Vaidyanadhan R., 1981—Land Use capability studies from Aerial photo interpretation—A case study from Krishna Delta, INDIA. Geog. Review of India, Vol. 43, No. 3: 226-238.

Pacheco, R.A.. 1978—Application of Landsat imagery to soil and landuse mapping in the central region of the Yemen Arab Republic. FAO, Series AGLT 6/78: 1-18.

Pacheco, R.A., 1980—Landsat applied to soil surveys. FAO, RSC series 4/80: 30-35.

Roy, D.K. and Bhattacharya, P.B., 1967—Use of air photographs in assessing erosion in upper Damodar Valley, Jour. of Soil and Water conservation in India, 15:3-4.

Shankaranarayan, K.A. and Singer, S. 1979 –Application of landsat data for natural resource inventory and monitoring of desertification, U.S.A. SDSU—RSI—VISR—17, pp. 13 and 24.

White, L.P. 1977—Aerial photography and remote sensing for Soil survey,—Clarendon, Oxford.

29

MODERNISATION OF AGRICULTURE AND ITS IMPACT ON AGRICULTURAL PRODUCTIVITY IN MADHYA PRADESH

C. K. JAIN*

Efforts have been made to increase the efficiency of agriculture since the First Five Year Plan. One and the major line of changes introduced in Indian agriculture is its transformation from traditional to more scientific outlook. This transformation may be termed as modernisation. Modernisation implies a change in the method of farming and introducing yield-raising technology. In our perspective, first and prime most need to change the face of agriculture is regular and sufficient supply of water. Besides this, several geological techniques, such as high yielding variety of seeds, chemical fertilisers, pesticides etc. have been adopted to raise the yield per unit of area. Method of farming has been changing concurrently, and use of fossil fuel, tractor and several modern water lifting devices are used. But adoption of these methods and techniques is determined by a host of factors such as ecology, strategy, perception attitudes, values and socio-economic situation. (Edewes, 1969,

*Department of Geography, University of Sagar, Sagar.

61) Variation in these factors manifests in variation in level of modernisation, and modernisation, in its turn, effects the level of productivity.

Presuming vital significance of agricultural modernisation in rural development and accelerated growth of agricultural productivity the present paper has the objective of analysing spatial variation in levels of agricultural modernisation in the context of physio-socio-economic environment, and to see relationship between modernisation and agricultural productivity.

Methodology

Since modernisation of a society or an economic activity is reflected by several characteristics, it is a composite concept (Dayal 1983). Therefore, an index of agricultural modernisation must be a composite index based on different characteristics of agriculture, which are relatively new. The variables included in the analysis of modernisation are high yielding variety of seeds, irrigation, fertilizers, and density of tractors, irrigation pumps and tubewells per unit of cropped area. The aggregation of variables in the modernisation index was done by using the z-score method. Scores on each variable were standardized to zero mean and unit standard deviation, and these were then summed for each district. Taking the mean value of composite indices, fortyfive districts of this state are divided into seven level of modernisation. Indore stands at the top, while Bastar at the bottom. Further these scores have been correlated with the agricultural productivity measured in terms of value of cropsperunit of net sown area.

The Study Area

Situated in the heart of the country, Madhya Pradesh covers 443.4 thousand sq. km. (14.5 per cent of the country's) area. State has been divided into forty five districts which have been used as basic unit for the present analysis.

Modernisation manifests the complex relationship between physical and cultural millieus. Both of these environments present verified picture in this state. Most prominent physical features in the topography are the parallel ranges of Vindhya and Satpura with the valley of the Narmada river between them. Overlooking the Narmada valley in the north, the Vindhya range marks the edge of the Malwa plateau that slopes towards north. The plateau with gentle relief is bordered by the structural escarpments of the Madhya Bharat Pathar; and low hills of sveral forms developed on the ancient surface of the Bundelkhand; while land of escarpments and basins extends to the east. Again, south of the Narmada valley, hills and ranges of the Satpura present very high relief and even to the east of the Maikal range as the Deograh hills—a mass of tangled hills. The Chhattisgarh basin extending south of these hills, present characteristics of plain, which is bordered by the Bastar hills in south.

There are more than five hundred twenty one million people living in this state in 1981, which is more than 7.6 per cent of total population of the country; and thus state ranks sixth in the size of population. More than four-fifths of the people are living in the villages and more than three-fourths of the workers are engaged in agricultural occupations. The population in rural areas is heavily dependent on largely subsis tence farming, since only 16.8 per cent of the total cropped area is under non-food crops.

In Madhya Pradesh there are considerable regional disparities in the modernisation surface of agriculture. If the factors affecting disparities in modernisation surface ar identified, the process of modernisation of agriculture can be expedited in the lagging area. This can be reduce uneven development of rural areas, and thereby minimize regional disparities. Thus, an analysis of agricultural modernisation is functionally important insofar as it can help in planning and policy decisions.

Present Position

The position of this state in respect of the use of inputs is far behind the national average. For instance, only 12.4 per cent

(1982-83) of the total cropped area is irrigated (lowest among the states but Tripura), Morena stands at the top (39.5 per cent and Bastar at bottom (1.5 per cent) in respect of irrigated area (map 1).

Density of tractors per thousand hectares of cropped area, varies from 0.06 in Mandal to 5.03 in Raisen district. The mean of these district figures arrives at 0.90. Tractor is comparatively much costlier affair for poor peasants of this state. Density of irrigation pumps ranges from 1.66 in Bastar to 48.6 in Khargone district. On average, these are 14.53 irrigation pumps per thousand hectares of cropped area.

Tubewells are assuming important place in the present irrigational system. Density of tubewells per thousand of cropped area varies nil in Shahdol, Seoni and Mandsaur districts to 3.25 in Dhar district. The mean of these districts arrives at 0.40.

On average, 11.28 kg. of fertilizers are used per hectare of cropped area in this state which is less than one-third of the average for the country (36.6) in 1982-83. A comparision with Punjab (127.8), Tamil Nadu (58.6), Andhra Pradesh (53.0) and Uttar Pradesh (60.6 kg per hectare) show that the state is far behind in respect of consumption of fertilizers per unit of cropped area. It varies from 0.91 kg. in Mandla to 36.00 in Morena in 1982-83.

No doubt, provision of ensured timely water supply raises the productivity of land, but the real benefit comes only when improved seeds and fertilizers are used along with the irrigation. The correlation coefficient of value of crops per unit with the high yielding variety of seeds is very high ($r=+0.82$). It is also high with the extent of irrigated area ($r=0.77$). In the state only 35.65 per cent of total cereals cropped area are under HYV of seeds. It is highest (65.29 per cent) in Gwalior and lowest (8.53 per cent) in Baster (map 1).

Modernization Pattern

The pattern of agricultural modernisation that emerges by mapping the modernization index appears to fit some known realities but also reveals some less known areas, where the modernisation is quite high.

The striking feature of the pattern is the outstanding position of the north-central districts in the Malwa and Chambal valley. These districts are Morena, Indore, Bhopal and Narsinghpur (Map 2). Excepting Bhopal all these districts have well developed their water resources, and use the package inputs as fertilizers and high yielding variety of seeds, use of improved implements is also in vogue because of the dearth of agricultural labour. Because of the relative prosperity farmers in this region could save some capital which they invested in the new agricultural technology when it was introduced in the state. In these districts size of operational holdings are larger in comparision to other parts of the state. Agricultural productivitty is also high.

A second area, having a high level of agricultural modernisation, exists in the north-western part of the state, comprising the districts of Ratlam, Dhar, Mandsaur, Dewas and Gwalior. These districts are usually on higher side of the use of inputs. For instance, proportion of irrigated area is higher than state average, use of fertilizers is high and very high. High yielding varieties of seeds are also more popular. Only density of tractor is lower in these districts. These innovations result in higher productivity also.

Districts of medium higher class exist in the central and western parts of the state, comprising the districts of Tikamgarh, Khargone, Khandwa, Ujjain, Bhind, Raisen and Hoshangabad. Tikamgarh, Bhind and Hoshangabad have good irrigation facilities with fertile black cotton soil with average irrigation. Commercialization of crops has necessitated and facilitated modernisation. Twenty seven districts out of forty five have lower indeces of modernisation than the state. Districts with low and very low degree of modernisation are located in the Baghelkhand plateau, Rewa plateau and the eastern Satpura region. Eastern Malwa and Madhya Bharat plateau encompassing Datia, Shivpuri, Guna and Raigarh districts also are least modernized. The south-eastern part of the state is agriculturally poor, largely due to unfavourable physical environment. The districts of Chhattis garh, in the southern region, score high on fertilizer, HYVs and irrigation but not on modernization. The central-eastern part of the state is least irrigated. In these areas heavy dependence on agriculture has resulted in marginal and small sizes of holdings. Proportion of agriculture workers and their density on farming land is very high in comparison to the west. Thus, it seems that modernization, atleast mechanisation is, economically and socially not feasible in these areas.

Determinants of Modernization

Modernization is a socio cultural process and is determined by a host of factors. Means of transport and communication can play crucial role in interaction and spreading a modern technology. Adoption of these innovations also depends on socio-cultural capabilities of farmers. Literate farmers are supposed to accept profitable method and techniques readily. Sometimes, nature of crop can facilitate or hinder adoptability. For instance, commercialization of farming and its high productivity may help in accepting modern innovation. It can be compulsion also, as in densely settled areas use of modern yield raising inputs may be necessitated by the need of growing more food. Relationship of all these possibilities with the present level of modernization has been examined by calculating coefficient of correlation between them. In particular, seven variables have been selected, and their correlation with the composite index of modernization is presented in Table 1.

It is evident that modernization has no relation with accessibility in term of density of road length. At the same time, it has poor relation with density of rural population and literacy of ruralities. However, it has strong relationship with the size of holding, commercialisation of crops, agricultural productivity and also with the proportion of schedule tribes. Infact, commercial crops are mainly grown in the western part of the state, where average size of holding is comparatively, larger and agricultural productivity is also high. Consequently, these variables cover to a great extent. Significant positive correlation with the proportion of scheduled tribes is strong. Probably government subsides have acted as an initiative of their adoption.

TABLE 1

Correlation of some variables with the Index of Modernization in Madhya Pradesh

Variables	*Coefficient*
1. Per cent area under commercial crops	+0.51
2. Average size of holding	+0.36
3. Density of roads	+0.09
4. Rural literacy	+0.27
5. Density of Rural Population	+0.15
6. Per cent of Scheduled tribes	+0.48
7. Value of crops	+0.55

Spatial Patterns of Productivity

There are several methods for determining agricultural productivity but value of crops per units of net sown area has been selected for the present purpose. It is fact that agriculture in this state is dominated by food crops (83.2 per cent of TCA), but non-food crops are also significant in some districts, particularly in the western part. These crops occupy as much as 40.6 per cent of total cropped area in Khandwa district. After all, these crops also increase the supporting capacity of land by increasing the purchasing power (Sharma and Jain 1985). Therefore, agricultural efficiency in terms of calories output of food-crop is lower than the real one. To avoid the under-estimation, value of all agricultural produces per hectare of net sown area have been preferred. Total value of agricultural produces for each district was calculated at the rate of average state harvest prices. At the maximum, production of thirty-two crops, reported in the Agricultural Statistics of M.P. 1982-83, was used for the purpose. Value of agricultural produce per hectare of cropped area was obtained by dividing the total value by the total net area sown.

Value of all crops per hectare ranges from Rs. 2783 in Balaghat to only Rs. 909 in Sidhi and Rs. 956 in Jhabua. Twenty six districts out of forty five have lower value than the mean for the state (Rs. 1737). On the basis of these values districts can be grouped into six classes (Map 3). Districts with low and moderately low value are located in the Baghelkhand plateau, Rewa plateau and eastern Satpura region. Northern Malwa plateau, encompassing Guna and Rajgarh districts also has low value. It is difficult to describe this low value to a single reason. Dissected terrain and low fertility of the soil drag most of the districts to these classes. More than three-fourths of the differences in the value of crops is due to the variation in yield rates of crops. The correlation coefficient of cereal efficiency and value per hectare is positive and very high ($r=+0.77$). It is safer to say that districts of low yield have low value of agricultural produce (C.K. Jain 1985). In these areas level of modernization is low and very low. They also have significantly high proportion of tribal population.

Value of agricultural produces more than the state average is in nineteen districts, only five of them are in the eastern part of the state. These districts come in higher medium class in respect of both adoption of yield raising inputs as well as level of development. Most of the districts with high value per hectare are concentrated in the Madhya Bharat plateau have highly developed their water resources for irrigation which is followed by other yield raising techniques. The region is very close to the agriculturally developed north-western part of the country. This proximity has influenced this region to a great extent. High and higher medium productivity is dependent on comparatively higher use of yield raising inputs such as irrigation, HYVs of seeds and fertilizers in the Narmada valley and Malwa plateau. It is proper to mention that characteristics of agriculture in these districts are very much influenced by urbanization and industrialization which is reflected by comparatively higher proportion of commercial crops.

Correlation of productivity with input variables

From the preceding analysis, it is clear that agricultural productivity in terms of value of crops per hectare is dependent on yield rate. Expansion of irrigation, use of chemical fertilizers, high-yielding of seeds, and plant protection measures specially the use of pesticides are important methods introduced to increase productivity in recent years. The correlation and coefficient of some of these yield-raising inputs with the agricultural productivity are presented in table 2.

TABLE 2

Correlation of Agricultural Productivity with Input variables, 1982-83

Variables	*Coefficient*
1. Area under HYV	+0.48
2. Fertilizers per hect.	+0.66
3. Irrigated area	+0.78
4. Tractor per thousand hect.	+0.18
5. Pumps per thousand hect.	+0.18
6. Tube wells per thousand hect.	+0.18
7. Modernization Index	+0.55

The efficiency of agriculture is not related to number of tractor, irrigation pumps and tube wells per thousand hectares of total cropped area. Correlation coefficient of productivity with the use of high yielding variety of seeds is higher ($r=0.48$) and it is also very high (0.78) with the extent of irrigated area. The third important yield-increasing input is chemical fertilizer. It is remarkable that it has comparatively high direct correlation (0.66) with the value of per unit of net sown area. From the analysis it is found that among the yield-raising methods, the use of improved seeds, irrigation and fertilizers have direct and significantly high correlation with productivity.

Conclusion

The analysis reveals that state is moving towards modernisation of its agriculture. But there is wide regional variation in its level achieve. Western and north-western districts have high and very high level. Big size of holdings, commercialization of crops and urban influences have facilitated the modernization of farming in this area. Contrary to it, districts of the eastern half of the state are far behind the state level. It may be because of the preponderance of marginal and small holdings, scheduled tribes and high pressure of rural population. These variables also have their repercussions on agricultural productivity. Usually districts with high level of modernisation also have high productivity. But in some other districts productivity is higher due to inherent higher fertility of soil. Nevertheless, it is found that some of the variables of modernisation have significantly high positive correlation with the productivity. Mention be made of irrigation, fertilizer and high yielding variety of seeds, among them. It is suggestive that use of these inputs should be popularised in the lagging regions of the east.

Acknowledgements

The author is grateful to Prof. V.C. Misra, Head of the Department of Geography, University of Saugar for his encouragement, suggestions and facilities provided for this paper. He also expresses his thanks to Dr. S.K. Sharma, Reader in the Department of Geography, for going through the manuscript and giving valuable suggestions.

REFERENCES

Dayal, Edison (1983) Modernisation of Agriculture in Uttar Pradesh, pp. 471-474, in Pandey (ed.), *Modern Geographical Trends*, Today and Tomorrows Printers, New Delhi.

Eddowes, E. (1969) Crop Technology, London: Hutchinson, Educational, p. 61.

Jain, C.K. (1983): Pattern of Agricultural Development in Madhya Pradesh: A Geographical Analysis, Unpublished Ph.D. Thesis, Dr. H.S. Gour Vishwavidyalaya, Sagar.

Jain, C.K. and S.K. Sharma (1985): Changes in Agricultural Productivity in Madhya Pradesh: Spatial and Temporal Dimensions, pp. 34-55, *The Geographer*, Vol. 32, No. 2.

30

AGRO SERVICE CENTRES IN PANCHANGANGA BASIN-AN APPRAISAL

V. T. GHARPURE*
C. T. PAWAR**

The agro services centres located in the key communities are unique institutions in the agricultural landscape of a region. They perform an important function of arranging for the supplies of inputs and services to the farmers. Agriculture in the Panchaganga basin forms a significant sector of its economy. This main occupation of the people in the valley, is well organised. The rise of agro service centres is noteworthy which provides the basic facilities to the peasants. However, their spatial distribution is affected by several factors which is analysed in following pages.

The main body of the data used is collected from the primary and secondary sources. Villages and tahsil level statistics is collected from village officials and Mamledar offices of the study region. The information collected through interviews and discussions with entrepreneurs has also been added to test the validity of the results. The spacing and

*Professor and Head, Department of Geography, Vidyawardhini College, Dhule (Maharashtra)
**Department of Geography, Shivaji University, Kolhapur.

distribution of agro service centres is determined with the help of method of dispersion analysis. Pearson's co-efficient of correlative is used to test various observations which are formulated regarding the spatial organization of agro service centres. To analyse the pattern of agro service centres Hammond and Mcullagh's (1974) method of nearest neighbour analysis has been used.

Where R = 2 $\bar{D}$obs $\sqrt{(N/A)}$

'R' = is the nearest neighbour index

Dobs = is the measured mean distance between nearest neighbour points observed in a given area.

'N' = is the number of agro-service centres.

'A' = is the area of spatial unit.

The Region

The area under investigation is well wateıed and agriculturally developed part of Kolhapur district in South Maharashtra. The river Panchaganga itself a tributary of the Krishna, is formed by the four tributaries. the Kasari, the Kumbhi, the Tulsi and the Bhogawati. The traingular tract of the district comparising the seven tahsils, Shahuwadi, Radhanagari panhala, Gaganbavada, Karveer, Hatkangale and Shirol is regarded as the panchaganga basin region. The region covers about 45,752.2 sq. kms. area and supports 17,63,398 population.

Nature of Distribution

For the present study a place having minimum four or more functions (Appendix I) is called agro service centre. Out of the total 644 settlements in the area, 52 settlements thus are classified as agro service centres. However, their distribution affected by several factors is analysed below.

Agro Service Centres: Relationship

There are three noteworthy attributes which can be related to the number and distribution of agro service centres *viz.*, area, population and inhabited villages, Table 1 demonstrated the distribution of agro service centres at the Tahsil level. It is obvious from the table that Karveer (17) has the maximum, number of agro service centres while Gangabavada has the minimum. The large number of tahsils fall in the classes below the X. It is observed that the economically backward, tahsils, have less number of agro service centres.

(A) Area-Agro Service Centre Ratio

The number of agro service centres per 100 km^2 area stands to be 2.5 in Karveer Tahsil. In case of Shahuwadi and Radhanagari tahsil it is lower *i.e.*, 0.3. The spatial variations in area—agro service centre ratio at tahsil level are remarkable because Karveer tahsil (1.298) has the value higher than Shahuwadi (−0.948) and Radhanagari (−0.899) tahsils.

The dispersion analysis shows that three tahsils *i.e.*, Karveer, Hatkangale and Shirol fall in the class above $\bar{X}$ and remaining four tahsils below $\bar{X}$ as regards area—agro service centre ratio. The correlation between these two variables is slight.

(B) Population-Agro Service Centre Ratio

The number of agro service centres per 10,000 population comes to be only three in the Hatkangale tahsil level is again noteworthy. Hatkangale (0.857) ranks first while Radhanagari (0.198) with a very poor valueranks last. The dispersion analysis shows that two tahsils have their values above $\bar{X}$ and remaining five tahsils below $\bar{X}$.

Since the agro service centres develop to provide the needs of the agricultural population of the area, it is noteworthy that their number and distribution is related to the population of the area. The correlation between the two variables indicates very high positive relationship where r= 0.9822.

(C) Inhabited villages- ıgro Service Centre Ratio

The number of agro service centres per 100 inhabited villages stands to be 14.7 in Karveer tahsil. In case of Sahuwadi tahsil it is very low 2.1 (fig. 2C). The spatial variations at the tahsil level are quite significant. Karveer (14.782) ranks first while Shahuwadi (?.142) with a very poor value ranks last. The dispersion analysis shows that three tahsils *i.e.*, Karveer, Hatkangale and Shirol have value above $\overline{X}$ and remaining four tahsils are below $\overline{X}$.

It is observed that the density of settlements in the hilly areas is more where the number of agro service centres is less, while in the plain areas the density of rural settlement is less but the number of agro service centres is more. It is due to the size of the settlements which is big in eastern part and their number is less and vice-versa. This relationship is only 0.125.

(D) Agricultural Implement Score-Agro Serv.ce Centre Ratio

In case of this relationship Karveer tahsil ranks first (91,912) while Gaganbavada tahsil (16,592) with a very poor value ranks last. Fig. 2D reveals that the correlation between the two variables is positively high were r = 0.8030.

(E) Area Under Sugarcane—Agro Service Centre Ratio

In case of this relationship Karveer tahsil ranks first (11,997 Hectares) while Gaganbavada tahsil (923 Hectares) with a very poor value ranks last. Fig. 2E, reveals that the correlation between the two variables is positively high where r = 0.9560.

(F) No. of Sugarfactories-Agro Service Centre Ratio

In relation to sugarfactories, Karveer tahsil ranks first while Gaganbavada tahsil has not a single sugar factory. About three tahsils are without sugarfactories *viz.*, Shahuwadi, Radhanagari, Gaganbavada. There are three sugarfactories located in Karveer tahsil, while two in Panhala tahsil and one in Shirol and Hatkangale tahsil each. The correlation between the two variables is positively high where r = 0.8572.

Space of Agro Service Centres

Spacing refers to the measurement of linear distance. It helps in explaining the distribution of points over the space. The spatial pattern of agro service centres is characterised by their uneven distribution. There are clusters of agro service centres in some parts, while in others they are sparcely distributed. The techniques of nearest neighbour analysis shows the degree to which any observed distribution of points deviate from random distribution.

With the help of nearest neighbour analysis formula used by Hamond and Mcullaugh (1974) the values of distribution have been calculated for each tahsil. Since the study area presents a visible contrast in the density, pattern and spacing of agro service centres, the 'R' values give different results. It is observed that random distribution of agro service centres is found in Shirol and Gaganbavada tahsil.

Near to uniform and inform distribution is found in Karveer whereas clustered grouping is found in Panhala and Radhanagari tahsils. Only two tahsils namely Hatkangale and Shahuwadi indicate liner clustering distribution. It is observed that very few areas are favourable for the location of agro service centres, the 'R' values give different results, in western part due to rough topography.

Degree of Concentration

In general, a close distribution is considered to be a concentration and a wide distribution as dispersion. It is easy to distinguish them if they are found in extreme cases, however, it is rather difficult to differentiate in marginal cases (Reddy, 1970). The concentration of agro service centres is demarcated by a simple procedure, where a distribution in a region contains a number of discrete concentration. They can be grouped together if they are related to each other. They are considered to be related if the distance of separation between the continuous concentration across their settlements is less than the observed distance.

The region as a whole has clustered distribution of agro service centres where the degree of randomness is 0.55. However, the region has four concentration groups of agro service centres. Out of these first concentration zone includes Karveer Tahsil which has (17) highest number of agro service centres. This zone has near to uniform distribution of agro service centres where the degree of randomness is 1.40. The another concentration having linear clus tering (0.50) is found in Matkangale and Shahuwadi tahsil. The random distribution (80.3) is found in Shirol and Gaganbavada tahsil, whereas the Panhala and Radhanogari tahsils represent clustered grouping of agro service centres.

Conclusion

The foregoing analysis reveals that the spatial pattern of agro service centres is characterized by their uneven distribution throughout the region. There are clusters of agro service centres in some parts, while in others they are either random or near to uniform. It also indicate that small size agro service centres are more in number as compared to large size of agro service centre.

Broadly speaking, it appears that the density of settlements in the hilly areas is more where the number of agro service centres is less, whereas in the plain areas the density of rural settlements is less but the number of agro service centres is more. It is due to the size of the settlement whieh is big in eastern part and they are less in number and vice-versa in Western part. The Study reveals that the distribution of agro service centres in the region is largely influenced by the area under sugarcane, number of sugarfactories and technological development.

REFERENCES

1. Bureau of Economics and Statistics, Govt. of Maharashtra (1980-81): Socio-Economic Review and District Statistical Abstracts of Kolhapur district."

2. Clark, P. and Evans, F (1954): "Distance to nearest neighbour as a measure of spatial relationship in population" *Ecology, 35*—pp. 445-453.

3. Dixit R.S. (1983); Spatial Distribution of Market Centres in the Umland of Kanpur Metropolies—*Geographical Review of India,* Vol. 45, No. 1 pp. 39-54.

4. Govt. of Maharashtra (1980): Vocational survey of Kolhapur district." District vocational office Kolhapur. Education, Employment and Youth Services Department, Mantralaya, Bombay pp. 10, 12, 48.

5. Govt. of Punjab (1980): "Report on the evaluation study of agro service centre in Punjab" *World Agricultural Economics and Rural Sociology Abstracts Vol. 22 No. 3, p. 199.*

6. Hammond R. and Mcullagh P.S. (1974) *Quantitative Techniques in Geography*" Oxford pp. 238-239.

7. Reddy N.B.K. (1970): "Distributional Aspects of Urbanism in the Krishna and Godavari Deltas" *The Deccan Geographer, Vol. VIII. 1 and 2* pp. 1-18.

8. Shinde S.D. (1973): "The Panchaganga Basin" An appraisal of some aspects of Agricultural Geography" *Geogra. Review of India. Vol. XXV No. 3* pp. 263-276.

Appendix-I

A list of central functions and services selected for determining centrality

Sl. No.	*Central Function/Service*
1.	Agricultural Implements
	(i) Tractors
	(ii) Oil Engines
	(iii) Electric Motors
	(iv) Ploughs
	(v) Seed drills
	(vi) Blade harrow
	(vii) Bullock card
2.	Agricultural Credit Society
3.	Fertilizers distribution centre
4.	Pesticides distribution centre
5.	Seeds distribution centre
6.	Banks
7.	Hired Implements
8.	Repairs
9.	Extension services
10.	Veterinary Dispensaries
11.	Markets:
	(i) Weekly markets
	(ii) Sub-market yard
	(iii) Market yard
12.	Soil Analysis
13.	Petrol pumps.

SECTION VII

BIOTIC RESOURCES

31

RESOURCE DEVELOPMENT IN DANDAKARANYA AND ITS IMPACT ON THE TRIBAL ECO-SYSTEM

K.S. SIVASAMI*

"In the Dandakaranya, where magnificant trees are crowned with sweet fruits and where fruits and roots are in plenty, you (the development) are roaming who are you? We want to know your real nature" (Ramayana, Aranya Kandam).

Dandakaranya is a legendary territory mentioned in Ramayana. It gained popularity when the Central Government decided to settle in late 1950s the displaced person from East Bengal in this territory. Many heard about it but few can confidently locate it on the map. This territory is considered as a rail less region brodered by the railway line running from Nagpur via Raipur, Visskhapatnam, Vijayawada, Kazipet, Wardha and back to Nagpur (Subramaniam, U.K. 1969).

B.H. Farmer identifies it as a region comprising the districts of Bastar in Madhya Pradesh and Koraput and Kalahandic in Orissa and parts of Chanda district of Maharashtra (Farmer, B.H., 1974). However the development activities initiated by

*Centre for the Study of Regional Development, Jawaharlal Nehru University, New Delhi.

the Dandakaranya Development Authority were confined to the two districts, Bastar in Madhya Pradesh and Koraput in Orissa. These two districts are taken in this study as the Dandakaranya, covering an area of 66080 sq. km.

Dandakaranya is rich in natural resources, which are the least developed. There are plans to exploit in full these resources. The paper attempts to highlight the pit falls associated with resource development that can or should be avoided by considering the past experiences in this region as well as elsewhere.

The region way by passed by civilization over many centuries because of its isolation from the rest of India, by series of hills and ridges. The tribal people lived in their own way interacting in the least with the outside world. But in the last on hundred years the Central Government encouraged people to settle in Dandakaranya wherever large number of people were displaced elsewhere. The famine in 1876, anti-Indian riots in Rangoon in 1930 and immigration of refugees from East Bengal were such important events (Senapathi, U, 1969). The earlier immigrations had very little impact on the tribes. But the recent settlement of refugees under the agency of Dandakaranya Authority had a profound effect on the people of this region.

Land Resources

Dandakaranya is characterised by large upland plains interspersed by rolling hills and narrow valleys. The plain has moderately rich soil. The prominent soil types of this territory are red loamy soils in the valleys, red sandy soils on the slopes and hills. The average rainfall in the territory is about 1500mm. Which is sufficient for agricultural operations. Thus the area is highly suited for agriculture. The landuse in Dandakaranya is given in the Table No. 1.

It can be seen that nearly two thirds of the area is under forest. A large parts of the area do not have dense forest. They consists of scrubs and open forest. They can be either reclaimed for agriculture or afforested. The low density of population and large open forest in an undulating plain are suited for bringing more area under plough.

TABLE 1

Landuse Categories in Dandakaranya (Percentage to the Total Geographical Area)

Sl. No. Categories	*Percentage*
1. Forest	62
2. Not-available for cultivation	4
3. Permanent pastures and other grazing lands	3
4. Cultivable Waste	4
5. Land under miscellaneous tree crops	5
6. Fallow land	3
7. Net area sown	23
8. Intensity of cropping	109

Forest Resources

The vegetation is moist deciduous in the eastern part and dry deciduous in the western part. In the middle part, around the confluvence of Kotri with the Indravati are found the Savannas. Dense to open Tectora—Terminalia, Perocarpus—Marsecpium. Adina Cordifolia, Dalbergia, Latifolia, Hardwickia, Binatar, Termina Lati-Anogeisus—Cleistanthus are the main floral series in the dry—mixed deciduous type. The moist deciduous forest is characterised by dense to open Shorea—Termenalia Adina series and Baswellia Serrata.

Extensive forest is still found into western part of Bastar known as Abhuyjmarh. It is predominantly a tribal region, inhabited by Hill Marias or Abhujmarias. They practice shifting cultivation, known as 'Penda.'

Water Resources

Dandakaranya lies in the moist sub lubrid climatic region. The average annual rainfall is around 1500mm. The co-efficient of variation is Indravati and Sabari are the main rivers. The average flow of at 50 per cent dependability in Indravati at Pollavaram near to its conference with Godavari is M.Cu.m. This is approximately 600mm. Assuming there is no appreciable net ground water recharge the water balance of Indravati Basin is 1500mm. of Rainfall=600mm. of run off and 900mm. evapotraspiration.

Sabari is another river flowing through this territory. At the moment of writing the author does not have the discharge data. Considering the similar climate conditions, the water potential could be equal to that of Indravati.

Among the two rivers, Indravati is the least harnessed. There are two medium projects, in Indravati basin. They are Bhaskal and Paralhote. In the Sabari, Potteru and Satiguda are two major projects which are nearing completion. The area irrigated by these projects and by minor irrigation schemes are given in Table No. 2.

TABLE 2

Irrigation Potential Created and Area Irrigated by Major of Medium and Minor Projects in Dendakaranya

Name of the Project	*CCA*	*Irrigation potented in Hectares*	*Area Irrigated in Hectares 1981-82*
1. Satiguda	11336	13,600	9000
2. Baskal	4440	6,680	3280
3. Paralkote	9717	14,576	14576
4. Potteru	N.A.	61,034	18138
5. M.I.	45	64,199	16505

Source: India M.W.H. Annual Report, 1981-82.

There are two hydel projects under construction. They are upper Indravati and upper Kolalb. Upper Kolalb on completion may generate 95 m.w. of firm power with a generation of 8332 million units of power. Flow irrigation will be provided to an ayacut of 47985 hectares of C.C.A. (Orissa).

There are eight hydel projects proposed in the Indravati. They are: Chitrakot, Matnar, Kutru I, Kutru II, Bodhghat, Nagaur I, Nagaur II, and Kotri. The water spread area of these projects is estimated to be 106,060 hectares.

Mineral Resources

Dandakaranya is rich in mineral resources (Fig. 1). The region accounts for 217.7 the total resources in India of iron ore, 26 per cent of hametite and 34 per cent of higher grade with 62 per cent. The iron ore resource is estimated around 2200 million tonnes. Large resources of iron ore occur in Bailadila hills, and Roughat Hills. At Bailadella the estimated reserve is about 126 tonnes and they are mined by the National Development Corporation for Export to Japan and for use in the proposed Steel Plant at Visakhapatnam. Resources of Iron ore in Roughat and adjoining areas are of the order of 670 million tonnes.

Bauxite is another important mineral. The estimated reserve of bauxite is about 10 million tonnes. They are found to occur as pockets and lenses associated with laterite crapping in Bailadila, Roughat, Abujhmar, Keskal and Ambera areas and in the eastern ghats.

Limestone, the order of 880 million tonnes are found to occur in Kanger belt and in potnar-Baranj area of Bastar district.

Other minerals that occur in the area are corundum near Bhopalpatnam, Chromite near Kapsi, and alusite near Dantewara, and Roughat and tin in Katekalyan (T.C.P.D., 197.).

Resource Development and its Implication for the Tribal People

These rich resources forest, water and mineral will be developed in the large scale in the near future. While developing these resources can we avoid some of the pit falls associated with such developmental activities that has taken place in this region and elsewhere? Can some action be incorporated in the initial stages of development itself, so that an infuture accusing finger is not pointed out at those people who will be working hard in harnessing these resources? With these objectives, an attempt is made here to review the developmental activities associated with the Dandakaranya Development Authority and Bailadila Iron Ore mining and their impact in the local tribal population and the environment. In the end a course of action on suggested for incorporation in the initial stages of development.

A Brief Role of Dandakaranya Development Authority

Government of India constituted in July 1958 the Dandakaranya Development Authority for resettling the refugees from East Bengal in reclaimed lands, the area development and promotion of tribal welfare.

In the early years of the project about 350 kilometers of metalled road along with a large number of link roads were completed. As on December 1984 about 365000 families were rehabilitate. However a few families have since emigrated from this area. The number of families in actual position is 25153. Various facilities and financial help were provided to the settlers. Effective steps have been taken to eradicate malaria. Trees were felled over an area of 355 sq. and lands were made suitable for cultivation. Tne number of villages newly opened up was 103.

Modern methods of cultivation were demonstrated in few selected villages. The number of tube wells commissioned by 1981 was 1879, masonary wells 522, village tanks 324 and head water tanks 346. These works were meant to argument the water supply in this region (M.W.H. Annual Reports).

About 25 per cent of the reclaimed land was intended for distribution among the tribals.

Irrigation development was taken up in large scale. One major project and two medium projects and about 3580 minor irrigation schemes were taken up. The created potential as on

1980-81 was about 24,000 hectares and actual area irrigated was 18,350 hectares.

From the beginning the Dandakaranya Development Authority have run into trouble in implementing the projects. The foremost hindrance in the multiplicity of authority. The Central Government and several Departments of the State Government of Madhya Pradesh and Orissa are too numerous for carrying out in phased manner the developmental programmes (K.V. Sundram *et. al*, 1979). The tribals and the displaced persons were treated differently in resettlement process. The tribals were discriminated against the displaced persons. There was no coherent perspective plan of development for nearly 17 years. When the planning exercise was done the damage has already been done to the tribal people. The anthors of the perspective plan noted 'withdrawal of tribal population, either as a consequence of push of the people from outside or the tribals suspicious attitude towards modernization. (Town and country planning organisation, 1975—32.33). The tribals, unused to monetised economy, have gradually lost to the immigrants large portion of the land. The process of land alienation of tribes has been accelerated. The reduction in forest land have adversely affected the tribal way of life which is centred around forest.

The irrigation potential created is not fully utilised. There is not only under utilisation pointed and of the potential created intensity of cropping has not increased. Irrigation in the rabi season is very low.

The cropping pattern changed in favour of more food crops. This change is viewed as a back down of a tribal economy which has produced all major items of consumption within the region (Mishra, G.K. ed., 1979).

Impact of Basiladela on the Tribes and Hinterlands

Iron ores associated with the Basiladela hills of Bastar district have an estimated reserve of about 120 million tonnes and are under active exploitation by the National Mineral Development Corporation. It is a completely mechanised iron ore mine, exporting ore to Japan through the port of Visakhapatnam. The initial impact of the mining industry on the tribals resulted in the increasing number of landless labourers inflow of migrants, land alienation and monetization of tribal economy (C.R.S. Joshi, p. 373). The tribal migrants into this industrial complex are employed in organised and unorganised sectors. Literate migrant with technical know-how have found jobs in the organised sector of NMDC. Illiterate migrants with no aptitude for acquiring technical skills are employed in the unorganised sector often to do minial and unskilled jobs. The monetised economy is reflected in their consumption pattern use Money is spent on food, clothes, cosmetics, utensils and acquiring cycle, which ratio etc. Improved economic conditions have changed the social status of then original families in villages. The migrants also discharge their oblegation towards the parental family like improving agriculture regularly visiting them, meeting the occasional expenses on marriage, death etc., and in paying land resources.

Industrialisations has also created a negative impact in terms of: (a) water pollution, (b) increase in immoral traffic, (c) discrimination, (d) interference with the tribal life, (e) further displacement of tribals, (f) land alienation and (g) increase in urban created crimes.

Traditionals bond of tribal society are loosened. Agriculture in still primitive. These who adopted new techniques are constricated by tribal society.

Rainfall Trend

It is argued that reduction in forest canopy can have adverse effect on rainfall. This is tested by analysing 68 years annual rainfall data for Jagdalpur, which is the only observatory having a long period of reliable rainfall data. The normal rainfall in an year at Jagdalpur is 1570 mm. The average rainfall for the period 1910 to 1977 is 1536 mm.

It can be seen both from the Table 3 and the Figure 2 that in the last four decades, on an average, had less than normal rainfall.

TABLE 3

Decadal averages of annual rainfall at Jagdalpur

Decade	*Av. Rainfall mm.*	*Decade*	*Av. Rainfall mm.*
1911-20	1534	1951-60	1523
1921-30	1711	1961-70	1415
1931-40	1586	1971-77	1508
1941-50	1441	1911-50	1570
		1910-77	1536

The Five Year moving average is showing in Fig. 2.

The Status of S.T.

The status of the scheduled tribe in this region is given in Table 4. The scheduled tribe constitutes 61 per cent of the total population. Only 6.8 per cent of the tribal population are literates, 31.4 per cent of them are caltivatros, 10.2 per cent agricultural labourers. Other and marginal workers constitute 11.8 per cent of the tribal population. Tribal population engaged in household and other works, which can be considered as gainful employment is only 2.1 per cent.

Future course of Action

The tribals are facing great changes in their territory. The developmental activities cannot be revised or stopped.

Afforestation and Soil Conservation

The tribal people should be involved in afforestation programmes. With many hydel projects planned, lift irrigation can be introduced in forest areas and irrigated forests can be developed.

TABLE 4

Status of scheduled tribes in Dandakaranya, 1981

Sl. No.	*Characteristics*	
1.	Total Population in millions	4.3
2.	Persons—Scheduled Tribe	2.6
3.	Percentage of Scheduled Tribes to the total	62
4.	Literates	6.8
5.	Main workers	43.7
6.	Cultivators	31.4
7.	Agricultural Labourers	10.2
8.	Household Industry	0.3
9.	Other workers	1.8
10.	Marginal Workers	10.0
11.	Non Workers	46.3

Minor Irrigation

The rugged topography favours miner irrigation. Lift Irrigation check dam, and tanks can be encouraged. The local people should be trained in the maintenance and repairing of pump sets.

Resettlement

Plan for resettlement of people displaced in the wake of construction of hydel projects should be immediately taken up.

Flood Warning Exercise

The construction of hydel projects increases the risk of floods in the downstream area, particularly in Bhopalpatnam tahsil.

The reduction in flow in the stream bed encourage encroachment of the river beds. Periodical flushing will be hampered once the encroachment takes place. Proper measures should be taken up in regularity encroachment and educating the people on adjustment to flood flow.

Pollution Control

Mining authorities should take adequate steps in controlling the debris reacting rivers and polluting the water.

Land Alienation

Suitable measures to check the transfer of land from tribal to non-tribal.

Education

Vocational training should be introduced amongst the tribes so that tribal youth can develop skills, suited to the local conditions.

Conclusion

Developmental activities in the part has brought to automatic experience to the tribal people. In Dandakaranya suitable steps should be taken up in the initial stages of resource development so that the tribals have a smooth transition to the next level of development.

REFERENCES

1. Aijazuddin Ahmad, (1985): Regional Development Process and Redistribution of Tribal Population in Mid-India in Kosinski, L.A. and Elahi, K.M. (ed)—Population Redistribution and Development in South Asia. pp. 065-078.

2. Farmer, B.H. (1974): Agricultural Colonization in India since Independence, Oxford University Press, London.

3. India: Annual Reports Ministry of Works and Housing, 1957-81.

4. Misra, G.K., Kundu, A. (1979): *Rural Electrification in Bastar and Chandrapur, A Perspective Plan for Regional Develoment*, Indian Institute of Public Administration, New Delhi, p. 55, 56 and 63.

5. Sundaram, K.V., R.P. Misra and V.L.S. Prakasa Rao, (1972): Spatial Planning for a Tribal Region, a Case Study of Bastar District, Madhya Pradesh, Institute of Development Studies, University of Mysore.

6. Senapathi, U., Gazetteer of India: Orissa, Koraput (1969): Bhubaneshwar, District Gazetteers Department, Orissa, Government, p.

7. Subramanian, V.K., (1969): Dandakaranya—A Changing Landscape. The Indian Geographical Journal, Vol. XLIV, p. 44-59.

32

AN ASSESSMENT OF FOREST RESOURCES AND ITS PLANNING IN TUDA

DR. N. NAGABHUSHANAM*

It is a truism that there is no human life without forests. It is very difficult to imagine human life without trees as much our lives are entwined with them. While we are dependent on forests, they are independent of us. Forests had been existing for millions of years on the earth without man's interference but now the situation has changed.

More than half of the geographical area of the study area is under forests, but it is likely that they may undergo several changes due to changes in the climate of the area and also man's interaction with it, followed by different types of industries based on these forests providing only a little employment which is not substantial to the extent of the forests present and the quantity of the forest products available.

An Appraisal

India has about twenty three per cent of its geographical area under forests. This is not able to meet the increasing demands

*Lecturer in Geography, S.V. University, Tirupati.

of growing human and cattle population for fuel wood, small timber, fodder and raw materials for industries and other forest products. The devastation of forests poses a severe threat to the stability of the eco-system and civilization. The gap between demand and supply of forest products is so wide that all the efforts for plantations in forests, on road side and canal side, strips of land and village common lands cannot bridge it. Moreover this gap continues to widen. Therefore it has been suggested by an expert committee that the solution lies in adopting social forestry by all sections of the people of the country and thus bringing the forest area so thirty three per cent of the total geographical area.

The existing forest cover does not appear to be capable of meeting the multifarious demands of the growing population because of its gradual decline in area. According to NRSA report on the study of forest lands through land sat imageries, the nine per cent of the natural green cover has become barren. Owing to scanty rainfall and extensive cutting of forest trees twenty three per cent of the forest land of the total national geographical area has gone down from twenty three per cent to only fourteen per cent. The intensity of reduction is very high in Gujarat when compared to that in the other states of the Nation; that is, the normal per capita forests has been reduced from 0.1 hectare to only 0.06 hectares.

Study area and Landuse

Tirupati Urban Development Area is located in the Chandragiri taluk of the Chittoor district of Andhra Pradesh. It comprises eighty nine villages and occupies an area of six hundred and seventeen km^2 or sixty one thousand seven hundred and eighty three hectares, of which 51.6 per cent or 31,883 hectares of land is under rugged, hilly terrain forested area. The remaining plain with 18.6 per cent net sown area has a population of 2,54,460 with a density of four hundred and fiften persons/km^2 (1981). The high percentage of forest area has undergone changes and the green cover is now reduced to 20,600 hectares (according to the forest department estimates) leaving 11,183 hectares as bushy and barren.

Distribution and Extent of Forests

The forests are distributed between 470′ and 2800′ high from M. SL. having 1153 m.m. of mean annual rainfall from North-east and South-west monsoons. According to the location, these forests are classified as Chamala R.F. (7,347 hectares) which comprises fire wood and timber, Tirupati hill R.F. (7,308) which consists of Redsanders and Sandalwood bearing trees in an altitude of 300 m—600 m; Tirupati extension 'A' R.F. (1, 456) and 'B' R.F. (727) which have social forestry areas; Mamandur extension R.F. (4.064) and Mamandur R.F. (712) which have predominently Bamboo growth; Karakambadi R.F. (2, 990) and Napier R F. (7,299) which are dry grass, firewood and timber bearing forests (Table No. 1, Fig. No. 1).

Economics of the Forests

The green and thick forest growth is confined to 800′ and 2,100 altitude. The major forest products here are fire wood (4,264 tonnes per year), Tamarind (3,000 tonnes), Bamboo (480 tonnes) besides small quantieies of important products like red sanders, sandal wood, eucalyptus and tuki leaves (Table No. II). The entire study area depends on these forests for fire wood.

Tamarind is available in large quantities and is an important source of income of the area. Red sanders and sandal wood, though available only in small quantities, (Table No. III). earn a fairly good revenue of the several forest products of the area, the costiliest is sandal wood and it is exported to Japan, West Germany and to Australia, and only a small quantity of it is used locally for making dolls and powder. Red sanders are for making dolls, toys and wood carvings. Only a small quantity of it is transported to national markets.

The distribution of major forest products (Map No. 2) reveals that the yield of the Napier, Mamandur, Karakambadi, Krishnapuram and Tirupati extension Reserved Forests is much more than that of the o'her forests. The remaining forest yields mostly fire wood. Bamboo is obtained extensively from Napier and Mamandur forests, while sandal wood and eucalyptus are

TABLE I

Location and Classification of Forests in Tuda

Sl. No.	*Location*	*Classification*	*Area in Hect.*
1.	Chamala R.F.	Firewood and timber bearing forests.	7,347
2.	Tirupati Hill R.F.	Red Sanders and Sandal wood bearing forests (Alt. 300-600 m)	7,308
3.	Tirupati Extension 'A' R.F.	Social Forestry areas	1,456
4.	Tirupati Extension 'B' R.F.	Social Forestry areas	727
5.	Mamandur Extension R.F.	Bamboo Bearing forests	4,064
6.	Mamandur R.F.	Bamboo bearing forests	712
7.	Karakambadi R.F.	Drygrass, firewood and timber bearing forests	2,990
8.	NAPIER or Krishnapuram R.F.	Drygrass, firewood and timber bearing forests	7,299
	Total		31,883

Source: Forest Department, Tirupati.

TABLE II

Major Forest Products of Tuda
Averages for 5 years (77-78 to 81-82)

Sl. No.	*Name of the Product*	*Quantity available (in tonnes/ year)*
1.	Firewood	4264
2.	Bamboo	480
3.	Red Sanders	20
4.	Sandal Wood	15
5.	Eucalyptus	60
6.	Tuki leaves	18
7.	Tamarind	3000

Source: Forest Department, Tirupati.

TABLE III

Forest Based Small Scale Industry and Artisans

Sl. No.	*SSI/Artisans*	*No. of Units*	*Employment (Persons)*	*Location*	*Capital investment (in lacs)*
1	*2*	*3*	*4*	*5*	*6*
1.	Toys and Furniture making	10	259	Tirupati Chandragiri	14.96
2.	Carpenters	72	152	35 villages	1.28
3.	Basket makers	44	98	13 villages	0.42
4.	Wood Carvers	12	49	6 villages	0.86
5.	Mart makers	12	40	4 villages	0.16
6.	Miscellaneous	18	73	12 villages	1.91
	Total	168	571	——	19.59

(*Contd.*)

1	*2*	*3*	*4*	*5*	*6*
1.	Firewood Depots	82	380	Tirupati Tirumala Chandragiri Renigunta Tiruchanur	N.A.
2.	Fire wood shops (Sell small bundles)	209	209	Tirupati Tirumala Renigunta	N.A.
3.	Individual firewood sellers	—	611	Tirupati and Renigunta	N.A.
	Total	1771			

Source: Forest Departmen· Records, Tirupati.

confined to the Tirupati extension forests. Red sanders are distributed sparsely all over the green belt and a patch of teak plantation is limited to Mamandur forests only.

Besides these major forest products, some minor products such as honey, wax, gum, Karkkai, Sarapappu, Neredu, Soap nuts, seekai, mangoes, thandrakai, cashew, chillapandlu, Kanugakai, Sitaphalam, Velagakai, Bumgukai, Usirikai, Babul, Thangedu bark, Rela bark, Tahila, Modugu, Thada leaves and house building materials like dry grass, vengi, vepa, bagi and neredu wood stems are available in small quantities which are not useful for industrial and are used by people of the study area and surrounding areas.

Forest Based Industries and Employment Structure

The available major forest products to some extent encourage the people of the area to start some forest based small scale industries. The purchasing interests have been encouraging industrial and artisan products, Tirupati being a famous pilgrim centre attracting thirty thousand pilgrims a day on an average. The floating population and the population of the area provide opportunities for establishing industries which in turn give scope for employment in the region.

From the primary data collected, it is known that there are ten units of small scale industries, which make toys, wood carving and furniture located in Tirupati (nine units) and Chandragiri (one unit) Table No. IV). They provide employment to one hundred sixty persons. The forest products used in these industries are sandal wood, red sanders, teak, neem, neredu, vengi, etc. There are seventy two units of carpenters, forty four of basket makers, twelve units of mat-makers of the (Map No. 3), providing employment for four hundred and twelve persons The three hundred and eighty person employed by eighty two fire wood depots, those employed by two hundred and nine firewood selling (in small bundles) shops, six hundred eleven firewood cutters and sellers all together put up the total employment figure to one thousand seven hundred and seventy one persons.

Social Forestry Schemes under Operation

Realising the importance of the benefits of social forestry the forest department and the district administration under DPAP as well as Titumala, Tirupati, Devasthanams under the Bio-aesthetic scheme have planted 6,47,740 plants and provided employment for eleven hundred persons* (Table V).

The total employment figure due to forests raised 2871 persons which is 3.5 per cent of the total number of workers of the area.

Future Schemes

It is understood that a major part of the land under forests has not been providing substantial employment, because 1/3 of the total area *i.e.*, 11,183 hectares, has been converted to non-productive, for several reasons already explained. So to protext and develop the existing forests by preventing illegal and large

*Report on Bio-aesthetic scheme—TTD.

TABLE IV

Planning for the forests Social forestry under various schemes in Tuda

Name of the scheme	*No. of plants planted 1980-85*	*No. of plants to be planted 1985-90*	*No. of workers 80-85*	*No. of workers 85-90*	*Categories of trees*
1	2	3	4	5	6
Forest Department District Admn. Under D.P.A.P.	3,28,780 (185)*	5,62,800 (320)*	560	712	4
TTD under Bio-aesthetic scheme (Invanams of Tirupati and Tirumala)	2,00,000 (170)*	3,10,000 (195)*	410	590	6
TTD under beautification of road and rail lines and institutions. (Avenue planting)	1,18,960 (95)*	1,92,000 (110)*	130	212	6
A Biggest park in Tirumala	—	(300)*	—	285	116
Firewood forests	—	(2000)*	—	575	—
Total			1100	2374	

The Categories of trees—Neem, Kanuga, Cashew, Delonix regia, Tamarind, Eucalyptus, Casurina, Mango, soya.
*Figures in parenthesis indicate area in hectares.
Source: Forest Department and TTD forest office records).

scale cuttings of trees and to convert the non-productive land into green, the T.T.D. has proposed (1985-90) various social forestry schemes (Table No. V) with the technical help of the forest department.

TABLE V

Employment Structure

Sl. No.	*Category*	*No. of persons Present*	*Future*	
1.	Engaged in S.S.I.	259	1500	Permanent (3171)
2.	Working as Artisans	312		
3.	Workers in firewood depots	380		
4.	Individual firewood sellers	209		
5.	Firewood shops (workers)	611		
6.	Workers engaged in DPAP	560		
7.	Workers engaged in Bioaesthetic scheme	410	1514	
8.	Workers engaged in beautification of Tirupati and Tirumala and in laying parks in TUDA.	130	860	
	Total	2871	3874	

It is proposed to plant 10,64,800 seedings of cashew, tamarind, mango, neem, kanuga, delonix regia, causurina, eucalyptus, teak etc. in an area of six hundred and twenty five hectares. It is also proposed to grow fire wood in an area of 2,000 hectares aiming at supplying fuel to the people of the area so that the unauthorised cutting of other trees may be averted. These schemes are proposed with an objective of protecting the ecological balance of the area, to beautifying Tirumala and Tirupati and the surrounding areas by planting ornamental, flowring, shade-bearing fruit yielding trees and not only in the barren forest area but also in the twenty four institutional lands of Tirupati (Urban planting), along roads for a distance of 120 km (avenue trees), in tapovanams (spiritual forestry). The water facility for this purpose is created by constructing check dams for a selected number of non-perennial water-falls of the Seshachala hills. These schemes provide employment opportunities for about two thousand three hundred and seventy four persons.

Future Industries

The assessment of the quantity of forest products used in the industry or artisans tells that there is much scope for further development of the existing industries and artisans and also for establishing new industries and artisans. For at present out of the available forest products only 1/4th is utilised by the local industries and the remaining is exported and transported to other places. It is felt that instead of 1/4th, if 3/4ths of the total products are utilised by establishing another twenty units of small scale industries in Tirupati, Chandragiri, Tiruchanur, Renigunta and also engaging another two hundred and twenty artisan families of aeral villages, it would provide employment to fifteen hundred persons more.

The Planned social forestry and the planned industrial and artisan units together will create employment to 3874 persons. If this is successfully implemented the percentage of forest dependent workers will rise to eight per cent, of the total number, of workers. This type of plan must be repeatedly implemented with an interval of five years with the help of Tirumala-Tirupati Devasthanams, Government bodies, social workers, Commercial banks and other financial establishments.

REFERENCES

1. Agricultural Report of A.P., 1981.

2. A Report on Bio-aesthetic scheme, T.T.D. Tirupati, 1985.

3. A Guide to statistics, Chittoor district, Chittoor, 1984.

4. A Report on Tirumala Forests, Forest Department, A.P. 1984.

5. Forest Rescurces of Tirupati Range, A perspective study, an unpublished Dissertation, Department of Geography, S.V. University, 1983.

33

IMPACT OF DEVELOPMENT PROGRAMMES ON BIOTIC RESOURCE OF KALI RIVER BASIN

M. F. KARENNAVAR*

Man's impact on environment substantiates the wide spectrum of environmental changes brought by man, focusing on major processes of change, immediate and extended effects on the environment, and trends in time and space of processes and effects. (Detwyler Thomas R., 1971). Man is engaged in so many programmes of development through the exploitation of natural resources and scientific advancement for the betternment of society. In this process of development he gets the economic development for better way of life. Here he gives main emphasis on improvement of social needs and satisfaction without giving much importance on future consequences. To fulfil and meet the requirements on he has to destruct one or more natural resources which adversely affect the natural condition of environment in which we survive.

These development programmes may be either through the exploitation of water resources or forest resource or mineral

*Reader, Department of Post-Graduate Studies in Geography, Karnataka University, Dharwad.

resources or other resources. Even though these are meant for human welfare of the country but we have to use them very economically and some times we have to preserve for our survival.

But recently to meet out the requirements of the people, we are destroying various resources without taking much care of conservational methods. This situation arises due to large scale consumption of various resources for the betterment life. This is mainly on account of increasing population and technological development in the process of resource exploitation. According to me this has become world wide phenomena and resulting ecological imbalances.

In the present paper researcher has taken a case study of "Kali River Basin" in Uttar Kannada District of Karnataka State, where in the programme of water resource exploitation is undertaken for the development of hydro-electricity in the state. The aim of this paper is to assess and suggest suitable remedies in respect of destruction of biotic resources in the river basin under this hydel power project.

Kalinadi Project

Kalinadi hydro electric project envisages utilizing power potential by constructing a series of dams, tunnels and power houses. Construction of this project is spread over in one area of *25 Km radious* in the Kalinadi valley. This project consists of in all 10 dams (big and small), five on the main river Kali and the rest on its tributories like Tattikalla, Kaneri and Waki. This project is being built in three stages and estimated about 1298 million MW installed capacity.

In the first stage (a) Nagjhari power house installation (810 Million MW) by constructing a pick up dam near Bommanahalli across Kali river and Tatti hall dam to join these reservoirs. (b) Sup dam power house across Kalinadi. These have resulted destruction of 30,000 hectare of forest area under reservoir.

In the *Second stage* construction of Dandeli Dam, and Kadra dam across Kalinadi resulting about 10,000 hectares of area under reservoir. *Third stage* construction of lower Kaneri dam across Kaneri river and later upper Kaveri dam connecting tunnel to Supa reservoir and Waki dam and connecting tunnel to lower Kaneri reservoir. Under II and III stage about 25,000 hectares of forest area will be submerged under reservoir. Nearly about hundred kilometeres of road is being constructed to connect all points of power houses and spots by destructing hundred of hectares of forest area in the basin. The Kali river basin is a part of Western Ghats which covers important forest types and resources.

Biotic Resource of Kalinadi Basin

The richness of Uttar Kannada forests with a respect to flora and fauna has been amply referred to by various naturalists such as cooke (1901-1908) Talbot (1909), Blatter (1934) Champion 1936), Karamchandan (1949), Puri (1960), Santapau (1951), Richards (1952), Arora (1961-63) and others. These forests are a repositary of genepools of a large number of rare species of life and any destruction of the natural habitats (ecological riches) will result in irreversible changes.

Champion (1936) recognizes four types of forests in Uttar Kannada district—Evergreen, Semi-evergreen, moist deciduous any dry deciduous. These are governed by the factors of rain fall, soil and topography.

1. Evergreen forest assigned by Champion is called as Western Tropical evergreen forests in the belt of 200-500 cms rainfall between the attitude of 300 to 1500 mt.

2. Tropical semi-evergreen forests occur on the hill slopes between five hundred and eleven hundred seventy mattitude in the rainfall belt of 200—250 cms., where lateritic soil is found. These two type of forest exhibit great diversify of plant and animal life. There are number of major herbivorous animals like bison, deers, rabbits, Tigers, Panthers, langur, Squirrels, Lizards, Snakes and Birds. (3) Moist deciduous forest these are important sources of timber species. Dandeli is important region (4) Dry deciduous forests—these occur on the lee of the western Ghats in the North eastern part of the district with

seventy five to one hundred fifty cm. rainfall. On the whole more than one hundred and fifteen families of flowering plants are found in the region. As a result of construction of the above mentioned power projects thousands of forests area is being destroyed. Uttar Kannada district consists 10,22.678 hectares of area and out of it 8,27,956 (81.0 per cent) hectares of area is covered with forest resources. It is estimated that an important forest coverage of about 60,000 hectares will be destroyed in the above basin comprising Halyal, Supa, Karwar and Yallapur talukas. These talukas are loosing vast area of forest resource. Since forest resource is an important componant in maintaining the ecological balance of area, it will affect the environmental condition of the district. In addition to this animal resource is also being destructed in the district.

It is also observed that the workers of paper factory do not strictly follow the instruction given by the forest department. In the process of forest cutting of bamboo and soft wood they cut unmatured wood resource and causing lot of wastage of wood. It is also observed that unauthorised forest cutting is practiced by the people in the basin. Deforestian is taking place on large scale for timber exploitation and also for agricultural expansion.

Impact of Projects on Biotic Resources

As a result of the above said action by various agencies the following changes may take place in the eco-system of the district.

1. Rapid degrad tion of vegetation around the reservoirs is increasing on account of forest clearing as well as submergence of forest area.
2. Secondary communities with less useful plants like Maearanga, Trema, Hypericum, debregeasia, enqenia will appear.
3. Accelerated silting of the reservoirs on account of soil erosion and appearance of flash floods in mountain streams.

4. Soil erosion besides removing tremendous amounts of top soil results in huge loss of nutrients. It also creates gullies and ravines making the land unsuitable for cultivation.

5. The organic matter and sediments load carried by the run-off water contribute to entrophication and shorter the life of the reservoirs.

6. Deforestation causes the process of laterisation. Once the laterific soil laid bare to the air in the process of cultivation, it may even harden into stony laterite. Due to high temperature heavy rain fall most of the organic matter gets broken down and leached out of the top soil. The sillica and bases like calcium and magnesium are also leached away and as a result the proportion of oxides of iron, aluminium and other minerals in the top soil get increased and the soil becomes acidic in reaction.

7. Deforestation overgrazing and improper cropping of undulating lands are causing increasing run-off, reduced ground water recharges and sever erosion, resulting in land degradation including laterisation, flooding of low lands, sedimentation of tanks and reservoirs and wastage of precious water to the ocean.

8. Forest cover plays an important role in regulating the hydrologic cycle. Drving up of many of the streams and rivers during summer and severe floods during rainy season could be the negative impact of the forest cover. Alteration in the hydrological cycle could lead to a series of chain reaction. It could lead to changes in riverine ecosystem, affecting large number of plants and animals in the food chain.

9. Disappearance of wild life and plant species preferring river valley as the natural river valleys may get innundated. The wild life is becoming scarce and the execution of present hydel project may eliminate

whatever little is available due to serious disturbance of natural habitats, submergence, clearance for roads, townships, transmission lines, illegal clearance for roads, townships, transmission lines, illegal clearance and burning by villagers, planters and contractors etc. The population of Jackals, rodents and rabbits may increase disproportionately upsetting the ecological balance.

10. Diversion of land for agriculture, plantation, hydro-electric projects has destroyed the habitat and reduced the population of number of animals and contact with domestic cattle has resulted in the spread of disease to wild life.

11. Attempts to restock the area with Ecalyptus forests affecting wild life as it does not support and do not afford proper protection to the highly weathered hill slopes.

12. The overall possible decrease in humidity and soil moisture will seriously affect the plants.

13. The percentage of forest cover will go down in the district by nearly eight per cent. This is a serious matter since other districts are very much poorer in forest wealth in the state.

14. Due to decreasing trend in the rain fall the catchment area of the project may not get sufficient water in the reservoir. As a result it will upset the whole purpose of electricity supply and the money spent on this will be simply waste and the whole environmental condition will change.

15. Since the catchment area in the project is very limited the drought condition and inadequate rainfall may upset the storage of reservoirs. Already this is experienced in the Linganamakki reservoir in the Sharavati Project area in the State. Hence further construction should be stopped instead of causing ecological imbalance in the state.

Conclusion

The following suggestions are made below in view of the ecological imbalances and changes in the eco-system.

1. The Kali river power project may be completed only at the first stage instead of proceeding to the II and III stages, as the real benefit will be meagre in respect of hydel power. Real beneficiaries are contractors corrupt officials, poachers and smugglers.

2. The amount proposed for construction of number of dams and tunnels etc. is simply waste of money at the cost of people of Uttar Kannada in particular and Karnataka in general. Same amount may be used for agricultural development.

3. The factory people, who are using forest resource of the basin should be instructed to make use of forest resource economically and carefully in the process of cutting and transportation.

4. Unauthorised deforestation and smuggling etc. should be checked by the concerned authorities.

5. The Prime Minister had declared in the Parliament some times back that new projects affecting the environment would not be allowed and past mistakes would not be repeated. In the light of this assurance the State Government should abandon further stages of Kali as well as other Projects like Bedthi and Aghanashini rivers in the State.

6. Too many projects will definitely endanger the ecology of the region. To retain the biosphere in the state it is advisable to stop further projects as is being done with the silent valley of Kerala. Since Western Ghats are an important agent for maintaining the eco system of the state, such major projects should be stopped instead of creating the ecological hazards.

REFERENCES

Arora R.K. (1961, 62 and 63): The Forests of North Kanara District, J. Indian Bot. Soc., 40, 41 & 42.

Blatter E & Mecann C (1934): Revision of the flora of Bombay Presidency; Jour Bom Nat, Hist. Soc., 37,; 15-35, 255-277, 764-779.

Champion, H.G. (1936): A preliminary Survey of Forest Types of India & Burma, Indian For. Res. N.S.L., 1-386.

Cooke, T. (1901-1908): The Flora of the Presidency of Bombay, London.

Karamachaudari J.V. (1949) Game Sanctuary in North Kanara, Ind. For. 75; 505-511.

Mysore Power Corporation Ltd., (1980): kalinadi Hydor Electric Project (Booklet).

Puri G.S. (1960): Indian Forest Ecology, New Delhi.

Santapau H. (1951): Indian Bot. Soc. Excursion, Jour. Indian Bot. Soc. 30, 181-191.

Spillet J. Juan. (1968): A Report on wild life Survey in South & West India, Jour. Bot. Nat. Hist. Soc., 65 (2), 296-325.

Talbot W.A. (1909): Forest Flora of the Bombay Presidency and Sind, Poona.

Thomas R. Detwyter (1971): Man's Impact on Environment; McGraw Hill Comp., New York.

34

AN APPRAISAL OF POTENTIAL PRODUCTIVITY OF THE FORESTS IN THE CHHATTISGARH REGION

M.P. GUPTA*

The Chhattisgarh Region lies in the eastern part of the Madhya Pradesh State consisting of Raipur, Durg, Rajnandgaon, Bastar, Bilaspur, Surguja, and Raigarh Districts. The region is notable for its forests of all India importance. It has a forest cover 62,063.08 km^2 or 45.93 per cent of its total area. The corresponding percentage is less in Madhya Pradesh (38.91) and nearly half in India (23.05).

The forests of the region are predominantly of 'Tropical Moist Deciduous' type confined mainly to the middle and southern parts of the region, while the 'Tropical Dry Deciduous' type is confined to northern Surguja and small peripheral patches in Bastar, Durg, Rajnandgaon, and Raipur Districts. These two are the climatic climax types of the forests in this region. 'Sal' (Shorea robusta) and teak (Tectonal grandis) are the important economic tree species in the forest of the region.

The forest wealth of the region is enormous. Besides a large variety of tree products the forests of the region are rich

*Lecturer in Geography, Ravishankar University, Raipur (M P.).

in wild animals and animal-insect products, grasses, etc. To assess the wood resources *i.e.*, its growing stock, annual yield, and the potential productivity of the forests in the region is the main object of this paper.

Appraisal of wood resources

(A) *The Growing Stock*

The forest wealth is usually considered in terms of its wood volume. The wood volume at the time of assessment is technically known as the *growing stock.* For the assessment of the growing stock, *a stock mapping i.e.*, the statement of the forest-crop acreage according to its quality-classes is a prerequisite. The tree in the forests are enumerated according to their girth class and type and their area is also taken into account. The forests are then categorised according to their quality-classes based on the height of the tree (waheed Khan, 1971,)495. The I quality forests have above twenty seven metres high trees, the II quality have 21-27 metres, the III quality have 15-21 metres and the IV quality forests have trees below fifteen metres height. A further sub-division as 'a' and 'b' is also considered sometimes. The areas of forests of these different quality-classes of the region have been given in table 1.

TABLE 1

Area Under Forests by quality Classes (in hectares)

Species	*Quality Classes*				
	I	*II*	*III*	*IV*	*Total*
Teak	832	49,789	26,244	8,286	85,151
'Sal'	26,643	320,848	1,029,061	873,145	2,249,697
Mixed	4,623	323,788	1,358,167	1,348,128	3,034,706
Total	32,098	694,425	2,413,472	2,229,559	5,369,554

Table 1 gives the regional totals of forest areas of different tree species and their quality-classes. The I quality teak, 'sal', and mixed forests occupy about 1 or even less than 1 per cent of respective forest areas. The percentage of the II quality of teak forests is the highest being fifty eight per cent, while the 'sal' and mixed type forests extend over fourteen and 10.67 per cent area respectively. The III quality forests occupy 31, 46, and 45; and IV quality forests occupy 10, 39, and 44 per cent area of teak forests, 'sal' forests, and mixed forests respectively. The negligible per cent of land under I quality forests is due to the fact that the trees in this area, under the existing climatic and edaphic conditions, do not grow above a certain height. The near lack of I quality forest may also be assigned to the fact that the trees after reaching maturity and a particular height are usually felled. Thus, the trees mostly do not attain the height required for their inclusion in I quality.

The area under II quality of mixed forests is also not satisfactory. It is because the mixed forests include a large number of trees species many of which can not grow above twenty metres height, while teak and 'sal' are the tall growing trees.

By using the Standard Volume Table, prepared ont he basis of various experiments in the different regions, the growing stock may be calculated on the basis of 'the area under different quality classes and the density of trees in those areas.' In an easier method, suggested by Mathur (1949, 488-493), the growing stock* is calculated on the basis of:

(i) the area under the crop,

(ii) the period of crop rotation, and

(iii) the annual increment of a tree by volume.

The growing stock of the region is calculated to 430.9 million m^3 (Table 2) or 74.44 per cent of Madhya Pradesh State (579 million m^3) and 29.89 per cent of India (1442 million

$$\text{*Annual Yield} = \frac{\text{Actual Volume of Growing Stock}}{1/2 \text{ Rotation Period}}$$

m^3). The per km^2 growing stock in the region is about 6,950 m^3 which is 2.07 times that in Madhya Pradesh. It shows that the forests of this region are comparatively richer in wood resources. In the total growing stock of the region, 6 83 million m^3 is teak and 180.49 million m^3 is 'sal'. The per unit area growing stock per hectare varies between 52 87 m^3 in the North Raipur Division and 76.94 m^3 in the Jashpur Division. The high per hectare growing stock is found in those areas where forests have been least destroyed namely, most of the Bastar, Durg, Rajnandgaon, and South of Raipur Districts. On the other hand the low per hectare growing stock is found in those areas where the grazing incidence has been high or the trees have been felled indiscriminately, namely northern Chhattisgarh plain and south-western Surguja plateau.

(B) The Annual Yield of Timber

On the basis of the growing stock. the 'annual yield'* *i.e.*, the annual increment in the wood volume of the forests can be determined (Davis, 1964, 130-131). The annual yield of the forests in the Chhattisgarh region has been calculated to be 10.77 million m^3 as compared to 14.38 million m^3 in Madhya Pradesh. The shares of different species in the annual yield of the region is as follows:

Teak 1.59 per cent, 'sal' 41.89 per cent, and mixed species 56.52 per cent. The annual yield being directly related to the growing stock varies accordingly to the latter from one area to another area (Table 3). The annual yield varies between

*Growing Stock (GS) $= \frac{P}{2}\left[\sum_{t=1,}^{n} it\left\{2R+1-(2t-1)P\right\}\right]$

Where GS = Growing Stock
R = acreage and also the number of years in rotation,
P = age of the crop,
n = number of interval of age classes,
i = current annual inerement,
t = periodic interval, and
Σ = sum of.

132 m^3/km^2 in North Raipur Division and 192 m^3/km^2 in Jashpur Division.

(C) *The Potential Productivity Regions of Forests*

Related with the wood resources of the forests, there is a concept of potential productivity propounded by S.S. Paterson. The potential productivity means the maximum production from forest lands under ideal management. He considered the climatic factors to be the most important of all the ecological factors responsible for the forest growth. His CVP index* (showing climatic, vegetation, and production) depends solely on climatic factors. The potential productivity is calculated on the basis of this CVP index. The CVP indices and, based on them, the potential productivity values of the seven meteorological stations of the region *viz.* Ambikapur, Pendra, Champa, Raigarh, Raipur, Kanker, and Jagdalpur alongwith ten surrounding stations were calculated and then isopleths were drawn.

The forest under each category of potential productivity for each Forest Division in $m^3/ha/year$ was calculated and given in Table 4.

The potential productivity thus obtained varies between 3.06 $m^3/ha/year$ in south surguja and 6.50 in East Bastar. As the Fig. 2 shows, the potential productivity decreases in the region from south to north with an exception around Pendra.

$$*I=\frac{Tv}{Ta}\ P.\frac{E}{100},\ \frac{G}{12}$$

Where I = The CVP index

Tv = the mean temperature of the hottest month in °C,

Ta = difference between mean temperature of the hottest and the coldest months,

p = annual precipitation in mm,

E = evapotranspiration intensity, and

G = growth period in number of months (humid months aridity index 12 P/T+10 exceeding 20) (Champion and Seth, 1968, 39).

The high potential productivity in the south is due to a high rain factor *i.e.*, a high annual rainfall/temperature ratio. The high potential productivity around Pendra is found because of low temperature and its small annual range. The very high porential productivity *i e* , more than 6 m^3/ha/year is found in 20.19 per cent, high potential productivity (5-6) in 48.36 per cent, the medium potential productivity (4-5) in 20.79 per cent, and low potential productivity (below 4) in 10.66 per cent of the total forest area. The average potential productivity of the forests in the region is 5.23 m^3/ha/year, which is 77.29 per cent higher than the average for the whole country (2.95 m^3/ha/year). This indicates that the natural conditions for forest growth in this region are of a high order.

A comparision will now be made between potential Productivity and Annual Yield. While the former gives the expected annual production under ideal management and is based on climate, the latter is the expected annual production calculated from the actual growing stock and the length of forest crop rotation period.

The annual Yield of the forest in this region is 1.74 m^3/ha/year which is 33.27 per cent of the potential productivity (Table 5). The Annual Yield varies between 54.25 per cent of the potential productivity in South Surguja Division and 25.12 per cent in the South Bastar Division. The ratio between potential productivity and annual is low either in those areas where low temperature and high rainfall give higher potential productivity value such as in the Bastar area or in those areas where, because of indiscriminate felling of the trees in the past, the quality of the crop remains poor as in the Surguja area.

BIBLIOGRAPHY

Bose, K.J.C., 1973, "Thermodynamic Study of Plant Growth in Nature Part II, Method of Calculating Productive Capacity of Site", *Indian Forester*. 99 (9), 543-550.

Champion, H.G. and S.K., Seth, 1988, *A Revised Survey of the Forest Types of India*, Manager of Publications, Delhi.

Indian Forester (Editorial), 1932, "Forest Production and the Timber Trade", Indian Forester, LVIII (11), 597-599.

Mathur, R.B., 1949, "A Rational Way of Calculating the Growing Stock and Yield", *Indian Forester*, 75 (12), 488-493.

Sagreiya, K.P., 1971, *Forest and Forestry*, National Book Trust of India, New Delhi.

Waheed Khan, M.A., 1971, "Local Yield Tables for Sal", *Indian Forester*, 97 (8), 493-497.

TABLE 2

Chhattisgarh region: Growing stock of the forests (000 m³)

S. No.	Forest Division	Teak	'Sal'	Mixed	Total
1.	North Raipur	495.37	1,145.61	12,928.86	14,569.84
2.	South Raipur	65.00	8,640.20	7,859.94	16,565.14
3.	East Raipur	87.72	4,826.71	13,627.06	18,541.49
4.	North Durg	348.36	2,310.19	17,212.17	19,870.72
5.	South Durg	109.06	—	16,669.86	16,778.92
6.	North Bastar	200.62	23,366.31	9,695.98	33,262.91
7.	South Bastar	563.52	352.23	25,202.11	26,117.86
8.	East Bastar	49.99	20,082.97	11,028.35	31,161.31
9.	West Bastar	3,646.24	6.82	33,642.80	37,295.86
10.	Kanker	1,154.08	4,418.80	22,986.40	28,559,28
11.	Bilaspur	10.03	6,585.03	7,889.02	14,484.08
12.	North Bilaspur	14.04	22,969.11	17,392.44	40,375.59
13.	Raigarh	5.61	13,952.83	8,395.35	22,353.79
14.	Jashpur	—	15,268.43	10,678.74	25,947.17
15.	North Surguja	14.20	22,050.53	10,142.98	32,207.71
16.	South Surguja	—	19,785.13	3,650.18	23,435.31
17.	Korea	34.19	4,550.41	9,872.00	14,456.60
18.	Changbhakhar	35.31	10,182.87	4,693.53	14,911.71
	Total	6,833.34	180,494.18	243,567.77	430,895.29

TABLE 3

Chhattisgarh region: Annual yield of the forests (000 m^3)

S. No.	*Forest Division*	*Annual Yield From*			*Total Annual Yield*
		Teak Forests	*'Sal' Forests*	*Mixed Forests*	
1.	North Raipur	12.38	28.64	323.24	364.26
2.	South Raipur	1.63	216.01	196.50	414.14
3.	East Raipur	2.19	120.67	340.68	463.54
4.	North Durg	8.71	57.75	430.30	496.76
5.	South Durg	2.73	—	416.75	419.18
6.	North Bastar	5.02	584.16	242.40	831.58
7.	South Bastar	14.09	8.81	630.05	652.95
8.	East Bastar	1.25	502.07	275.71	779.03
9.	West Bastar	91.16	0.17	841.07	932.40
10.	Kanker	28.85	110.47	574.66	713.98
11.	Bilaspur	0.25	164.63	197.23	362.11
12.	North Bilaspur	0.35	574.23	434.81	1,009.39
13.	Raigarh	0.14	348.82	209.89	558.85
14.	Jashpur	—	381.71	266.97	648.68
15.	North Surguja	0.36	551.26	253.57	805.19
16.	South Surguja	—	494.63	91.25	585.88
17,	Korea	0.85	113.76	246.80	361.41
18.	Changbakhar	0.88	254.57	117.34	372.79
	Total of the region	170.84	4,512.36	6,089.22	1 .772.42

TABLE 4

Chhattisgarh region: Forest area under various categories of potential productivity of wood

S. No.	Forest Division	Area (Km^2) with potential productivity ($m^3/ha/year$)					Average regional potential productivity $m^3/ha/year$
		Below 4	4-5	5-6	Above 6	Total	
1	2	3	4	5	6	7	8
1.	North Raipur	—	1,173.24	1,582.70	—	2,755.94	5.07
2.	South Raipur	—	—	1,954.06	297.02	2,251.08	5.63
3.	East Raipur	—	—	1,848.70	693.41	2,542.11	5.77
4.	North Durg	—	—	2,767.00	—	2,767.00	5.50
5.	South Durg	—	—	2,359.38	—	2,359.38	5.50
6.	North Bastar	—	—	2,636.49	2,171.00	4,807.49	5.91
7.	South Bastar	—	—	1,194.59	2,984.98	4,179.57	6.21
8.	East Bastar	—	—	—	4,153.07	4,153.07	6.50
9.	West Bastar	—	—	3,100.02	2,232.82	5,332.84	5.92

(Contd.)

1	2	3	4	5	6	7	8
10.	Kanker	—	—	3,784.42	—	3,784.42	5.50
11.	Bilaspur	—	1,290.81	789.78	—	2,080.59	4.88
12.	North Bilaspur	—	2,810.25	3,039.47	—	5,849.72	5.02
13.	Raigarh	—	1,295.40	2,247.24	—	3,542.64	5.13
14.	Jashpur	—	2,705.11	667.20	—	3,372.31	4.70
15.	North Surguja	4,125.16	289.65	—	—	4,414.81	3.57
16.	South Surguja	2,317.48	1,222.19	—	—	3,539.67	3.06
17.	Korea	170.91	897.44	1,063.31	—	2,131.66	4.92
18.	Changbhakhar	—	1,221.53	977.25	—	2,198.78	4.94
	Total	6,613.55	12,905.62	30,011.61	12,532.30	62,063.08	5.23

TABLE 5

Chhattisgarh region: Potential productivity and annual yield of the forests

S. No.	Forest Division	Forest Area Km^2	Potential productivity $m^3/km^2/Yr$	Annual Yield m^3/Km^2	Annual Yield as % of potential Production
1.	North Raipur	2,755.94	507	132	26.04
2.	South Raipur	2,251.08	563	184	32.68
3.	East Raipur	2,542.11	577	182	31.54
4.	North Durg	2,767.00	550	180	32.73
5.	South Durg	2,359.38	550	178	32.36
6.	North Bastar	4,807.49	591	173	29.27
7.	South Bastar	4,179.57	621	156	25.12
8.	East Bastar	4,153.07	650	188	28.92
9.	West Bastar	5,332.84	592	175	29.56
10.	Kanker	3,784.42	550	189	34.36
11.	Bilaspur	2,080.59	488	174	35.66
12.	North Bilaspur	5,849.72	502	173	34.46
13.	Raigarh	3,542.64	513	158	30.80
14.	Jashpur	3,372,31	470	192	40.85
15.	North Surguja	4,414.81	357	182	50.98
16.	South Surguja	3,539.67	306	166	54.25
17.	Korea	2,131.66	492	170	34.55
18.	Changbhakhar	2,198.78	494	170	34.41
	Total	62,063.08	523	174	33.27

Average of the Region.

MAPS AND FIGURES

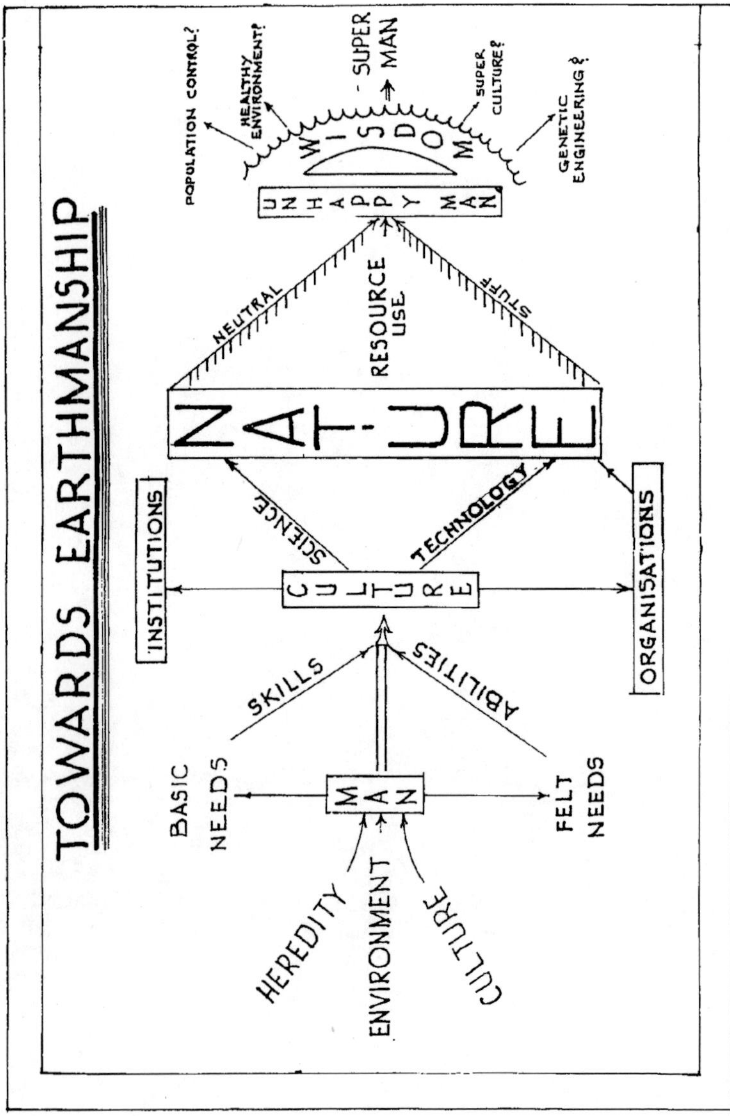
TOWARDS EARTHMANSHIP
HEREDITY
ENVIRONMENT
CULTURE
MAN
BASIC NEEDS
FELT NEEDS
SKILLS
ABILITIES
CULTURE
INSTITUTIONS
ORGANISATIONS
SCIENCE
TECHNOLOGY
NATURE
NEUTRAL
STUFF
RESOURCE USE
UNHAPPY MAN
WISDOM
SUPER MAN
POPULATION CONTROL?
HEALTHY ENVIRONMENT?
SUPER CULTURE?
GENETIC ENGINEERING?

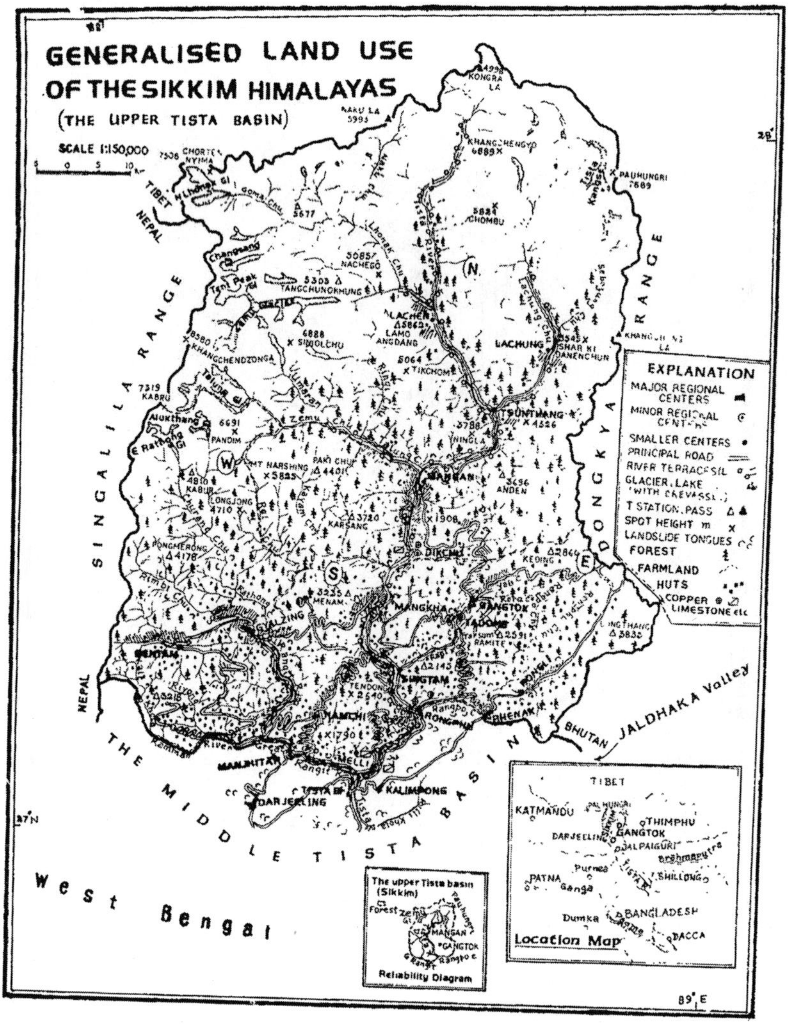
GENERALISED LAND USE
OF THE SIKKIM HIMALAYAS
(THE UPPER TISTA BASIN)
SCALE 1:150,000
EXPLANATION
MAJOR REGIONAL CENTERS
SMALLER CENTERS
PRINCIPAL ROAD
SPOT HEIGHT m
FOREST
FARMLAND
HUTS
SINGALILA RANGE
DONGKYA RANGE
THE MIDDLE TISTA BASIN
West Bengal
JALDHAKA Valley
TIBET
NEPAL
BHUTAN
LACHEN
LACHUNG
MANGAN
GANGTOK
DARJEELING
KALIMPONG
The upper Tista basin (Sikkim)
Reliability Diagram
Location Map
KATMANDU
THIMPHU
BANGLADESH
DACCA
89° E
27°N

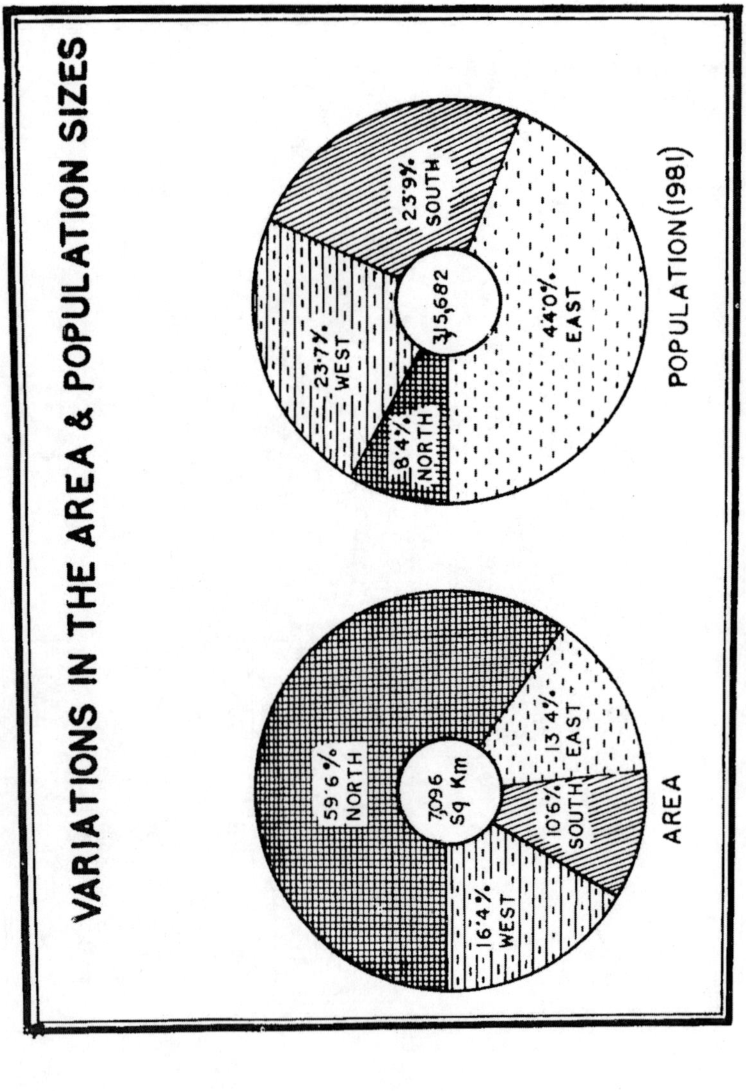
VARIATIONS IN THE AREA & POPULATION SIZES
59·6% NORTH
7096 Sq Km
16·4% WEST
10·6% SOUTH
13·4% EAST
AREA
8·4% NORTH
23·7% WEST
23·9% SOUTH
3,15,682
44·0% EAST
POPULATION (1981)

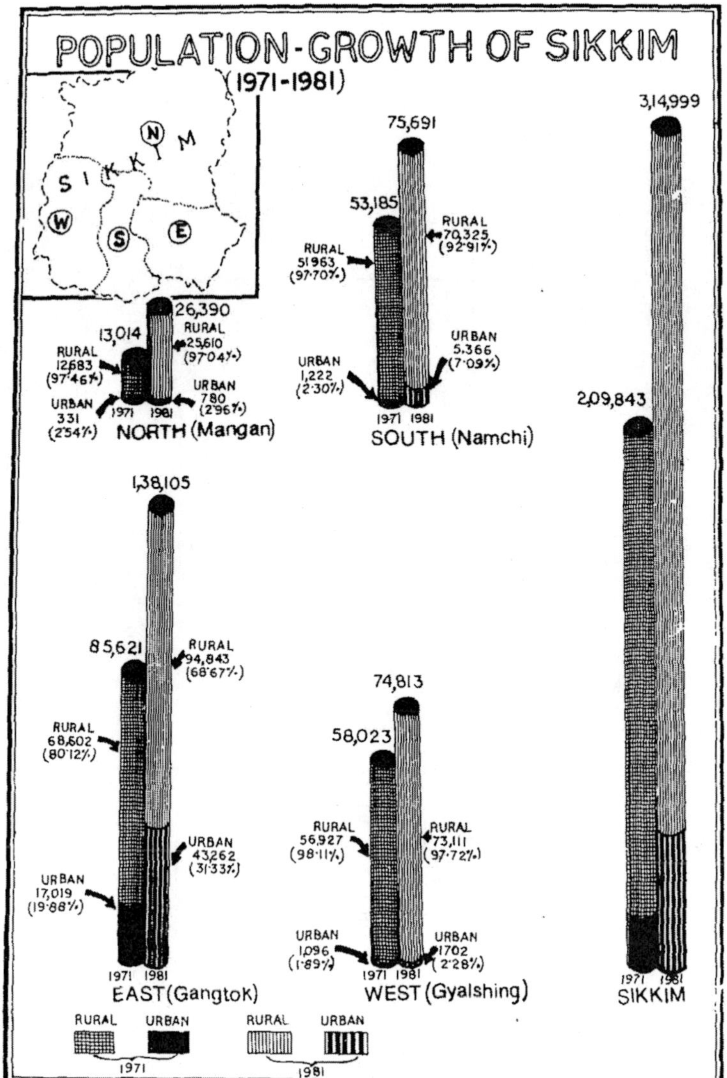
POPULATION-GROWTH OF SIKKIM
(1971-1981)
SIKKIM
N
W
S
E
NORTH (Mangan)
13,014
26,390
RURAL 12,683 (97·46%)
URBAN 331 (2·54%)
RURAL 25,610 (97·04%)
URBAN 780 (2·96%)
SOUTH (Namchi)
53,185
75,691
RURAL 51963 (97·70%)
URBAN 1,222 (2·30%)
RURAL 70,325 (92·91%)
URBAN 5,366 (7·09%)
EAST (Gangtok)
85,621
1,38,105
RURAL 68,602 (80·12%)
URBAN 17,019 (19·88%)
RURAL 94,843 (68·67%)
URBAN 43,262 (31·33%)
WEST (Gyalshing)
58,023
74,813
RURAL 56,927 (98·11%)
URBAN 1,096 (1·89%)
RURAL 73,111 (97·72%)
URBAN 1702 (2·28%)
SIKKIM
2,09,843
3,14,999
1971 1981
RURAL URBAN 1971
RURAL URBAN 1981

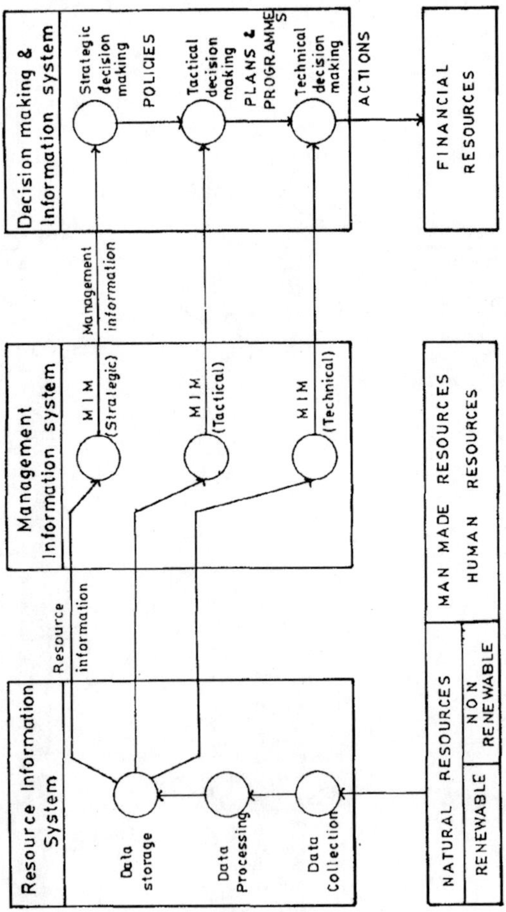

Fig. 1. Structure of the National Resource Information System

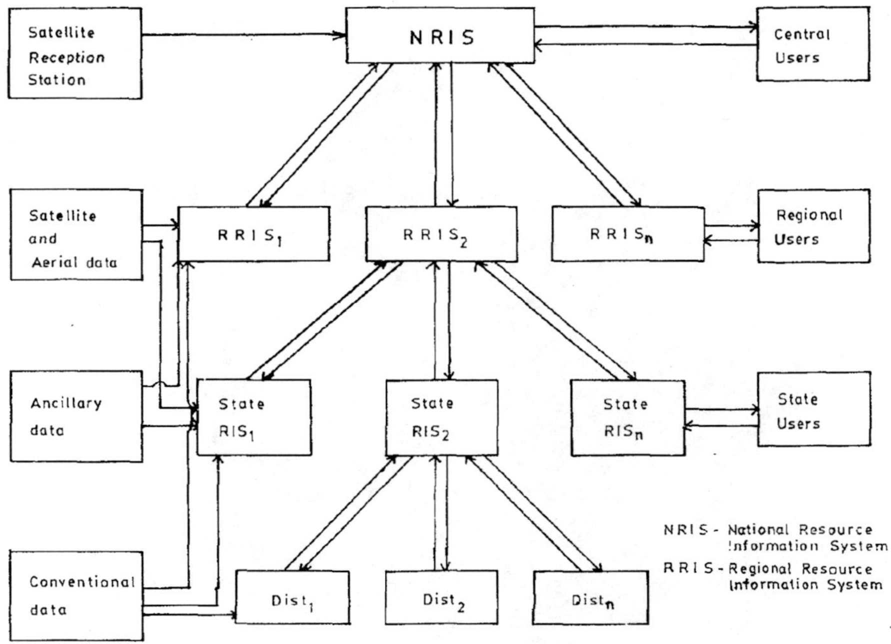

Fig. 2. Proposed Configuration of National Resource Information System.

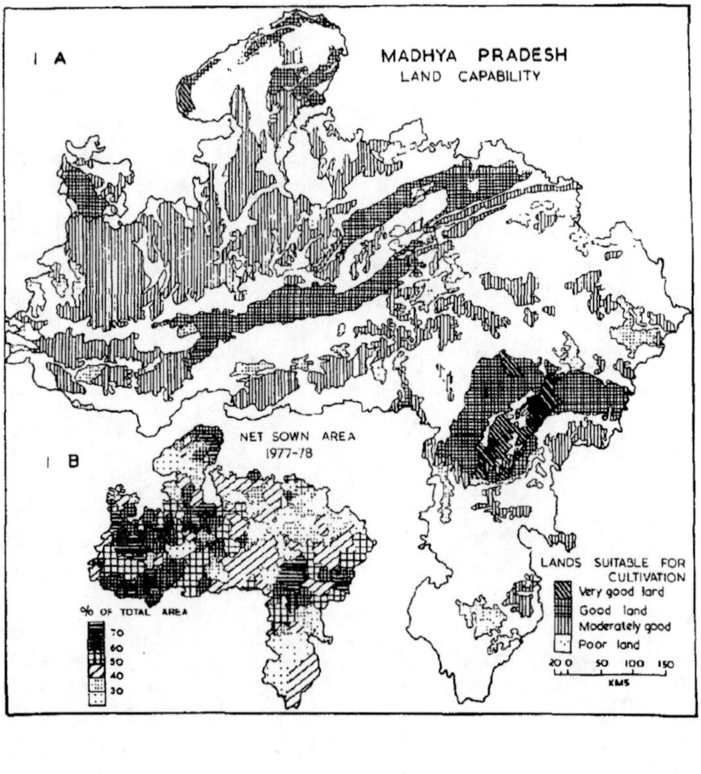

I A
MADHYA PRADESH
LAND CAPABILITY
NET SOWN AREA
1977-78
I B
% OF TOTAL AREA
70
60
50
40
30
LANDS SUITABLE FOR CULTIVATION
Very good land
Good land
Moderately good
Poor land
20 0 50 100 150
KMS

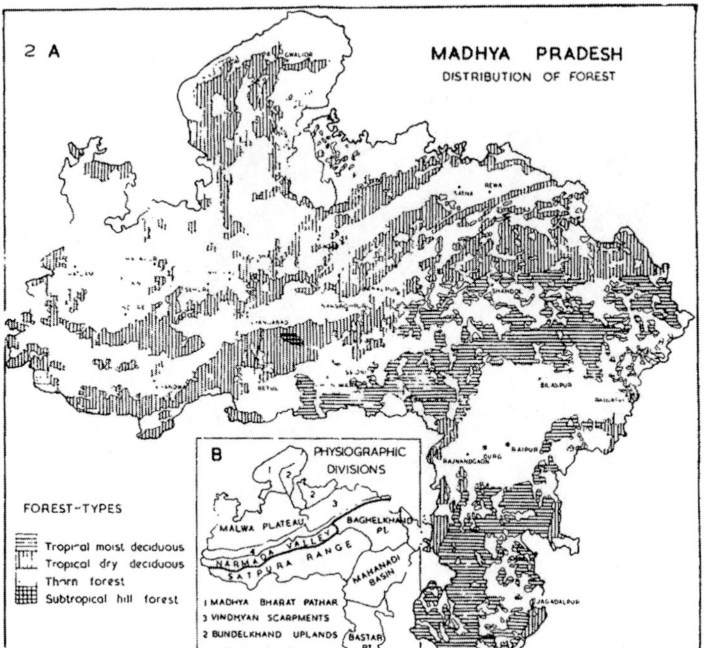
2 A
MADHYA PRADESH
DISTRIBUTION OF FOREST
FOREST-TYPES
Tropical moist deciduous
Tropical dry deciduous
Thorn forest
Subtropical hill forest
B
PHYSIOGRAPHIC DIVISIONS
MALWA PLATEAU
NARMADA VALLEY
SATPURA RANGE
BAGHELKHAND PT.
MAHANADI BASIN
BASTAR PT.
1 MADHYA BHARAT PATHAR
3 VINDHYAN SCARPMENTS
2 BUNDELKHAND UPLANDS
4 VINDHYA RANGE
20 0 50 100 150
KMS

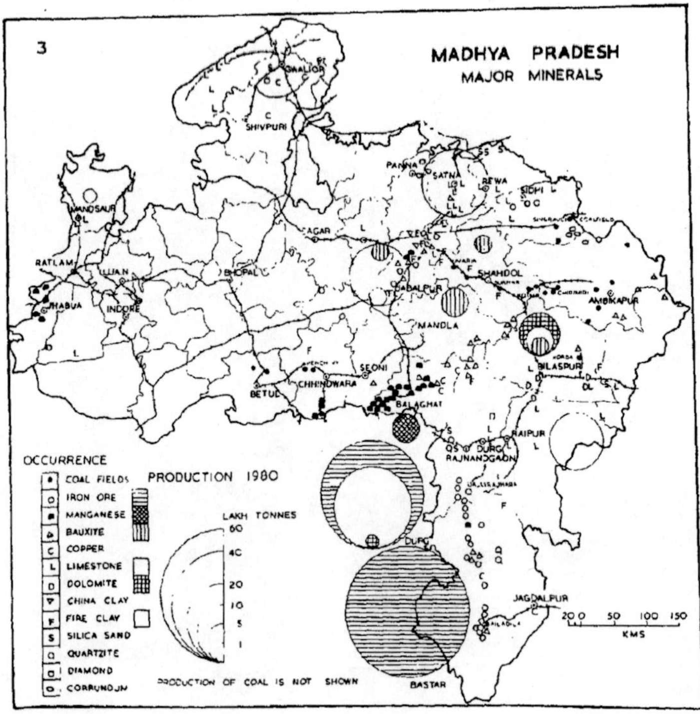
3
MADHYA PRADESH
MAJOR MINERALS
GWALIOR
SHIVPURI
PANNA
SATNA
REWA
SIDHI
MANDSAUR
RATLAM
UJJAIN
JHABUA
INDORE
SAGAR
BHOPAL
JABALPUR
SHAHDOL
AMBIKAPUR
MANDLA
BILASPUR
SEONI
BETUL
CHHINDWARA
BALAGHAT
RAIPUR
DURG
RAJNANDGAON
JAGDALPUR
BASTAR
OCCURRENCE
COAL FIELDS
IRON ORE
MANGANESE
BAUXITE
COPPER
LIMESTONE
DOLOMITE
CHINA CLAY
FIRE CLAY
SILICA SAND
QUARTZITE
DIAMOND
CORRUNDUM
PRODUCTION 1980
LAKH TONNES
60
40
20
10
5
1
PRODUCTION OF COAL IS NOT SHOWN
200 50 100 150
KMS

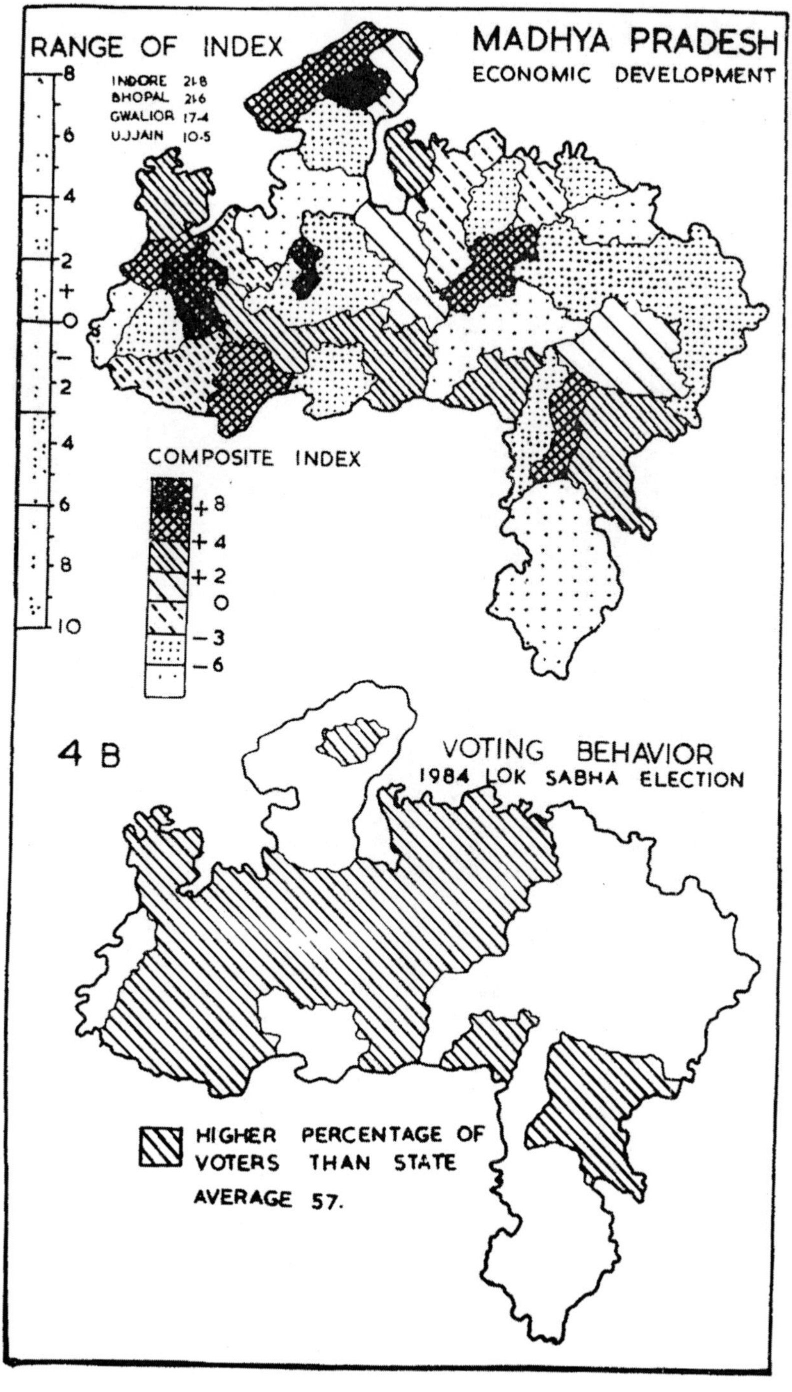
RANGE OF INDEX
8
6
4
2
+
0
–
2
4
6
8
10
INDORE 21·8
BHOPAL 21·6
GWALIOR 17·4
UJJAIN 10·5
MADHYA PRADESH
ECONOMIC DEVELOPMENT
COMPOSITE INDEX
+8
+4
+2
0
–3
–6
4 B
VOTING BEHAVIOR
1984 LOK SABHA ELECTION
HIGHER PERCENTAGE OF
VOTERS THAN STATE
AVERAGE 57.

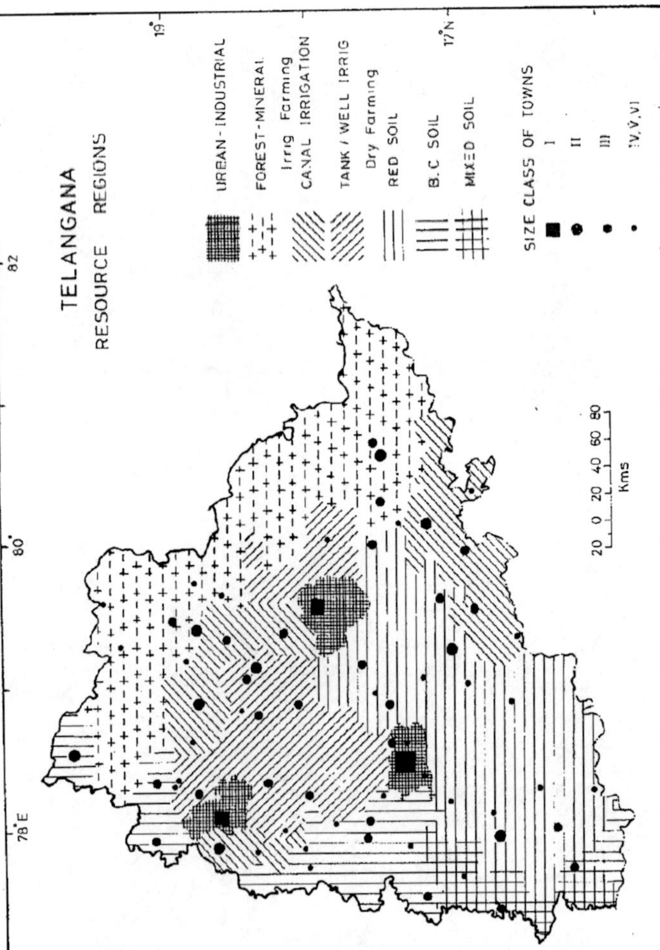
TELANGANA
RESOURCE REGIONS
URBAN-INDUSTRIAL
FOREST-MINERAL
Irrig Farming
CANAL IRRIGATION
TANK / WELL IRRIG
Dry Farming
RED SOIL
B.C SOIL
MIXED SOIL
SIZE CLASS OF TOWNS
I
II
III
IV,V,VI
20 0 20 40 60 80
Kms
78°E
80°
82
19°
17°N

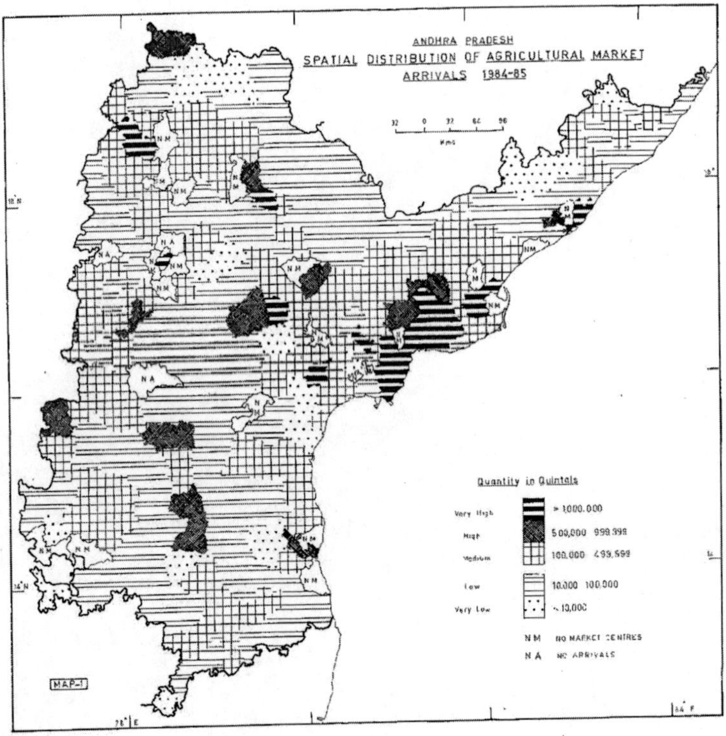
ANDHRA PRADESH
SPATIAL DISTRIBUTION OF AGRICULTURAL MARKET ARRIVALS 1984-85
Kms
Quantity in Quintals
Very High
High
Medium
Low
Very Low
> 1000.000
500,000 999.999
100.000 499.999
10.000 100.000
< 10,000
N M NO MARKET CENTRES
N A NO ARRIVALS
MAP-1

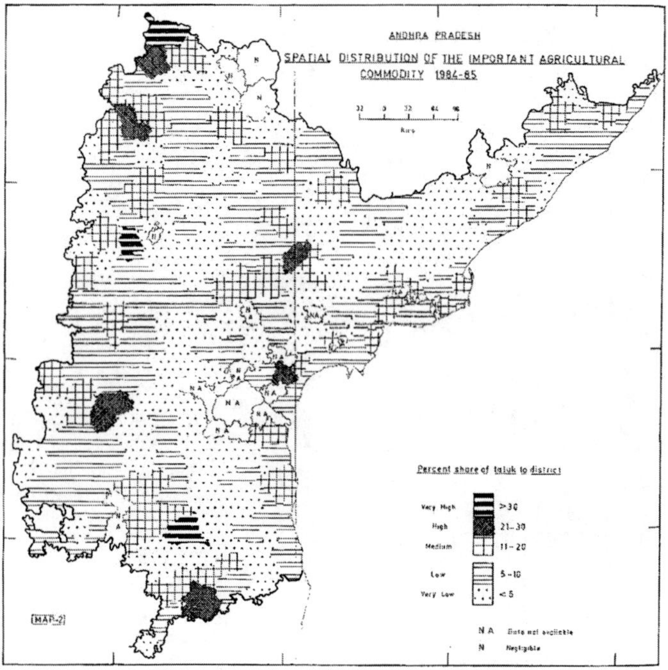
ANDHRA PRADESH
SPATIAL DISTRIBUTION OF THE IMPORTANT AGRICULTURAL COMMODITY 1984-85
Kms
Percent share of taluk to district
Very High >30
High 21-30
Medium 11-20
Low 5-10
Very Low <5
N A Data not available
N Negligible
MAP-2

Chapter 13

FIGURE 1 : HUMAN TIME BUDGETS IN AGRICULTURE (PADDY)

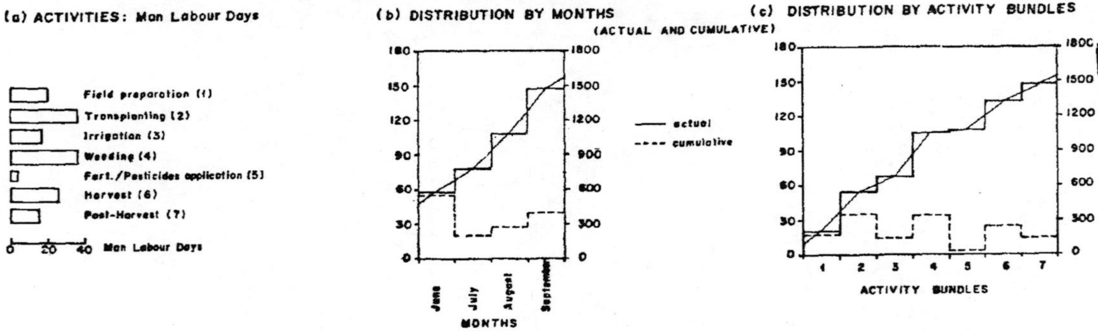

Paddy is a 90-day crop. Labour days and time in hours are for a 1 ha. farm. Labour includes family, wage, exchange and attached labour. The graphics here indicate the possibilities for data representation.

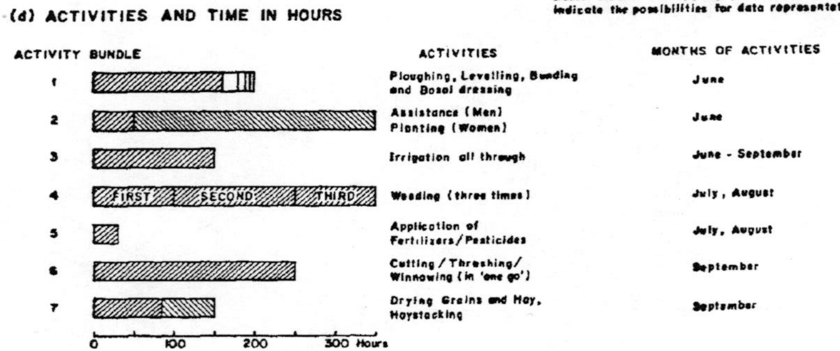

FIGURE 2. HUMAN TIME AND TIME-SPACE BUDGETS

(a) Multiple time budgets.

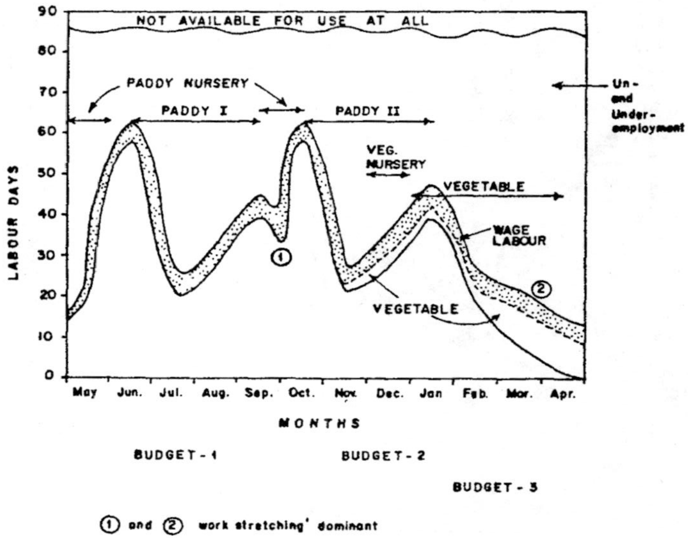

(b) Space-time budget.

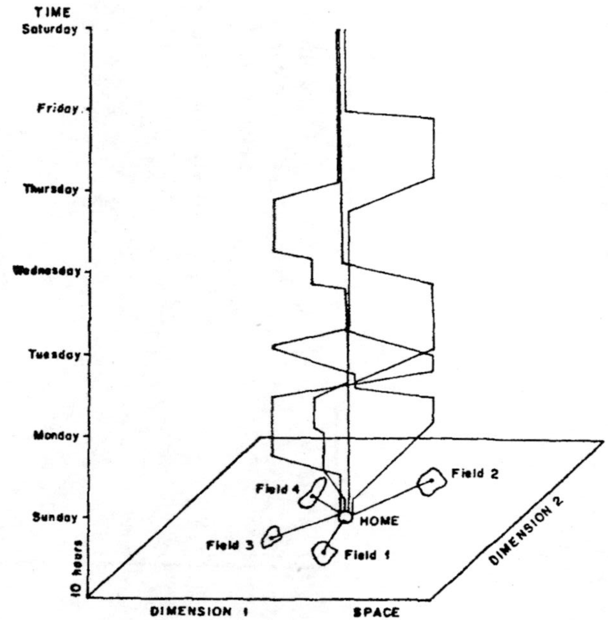

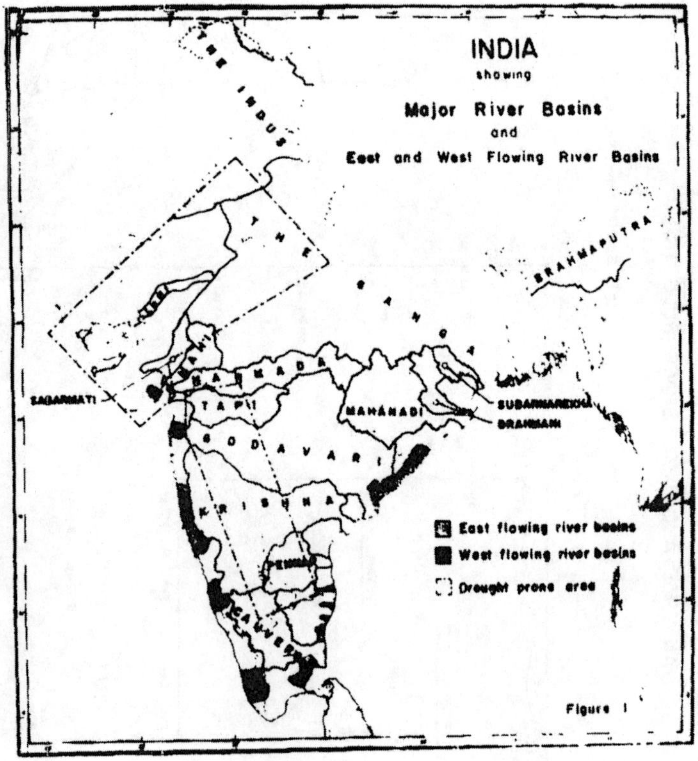
INDIA
showing
Major River Basins
and
East and West Flowing River Basins
THE INDUS
THE
GANGA
BRAHMAPUTRA
SABARMATI
NARMADA
TAPI
MAHANADI
SUBARNAREKHA
BRAHMANI
GODAVARI
KRISHNA
PENNAR
CAUVERY
East flowing river basins
West flowing river basins
Drought prone area
Figure 1

Correlation Scatter Diagram (Major River Basins)

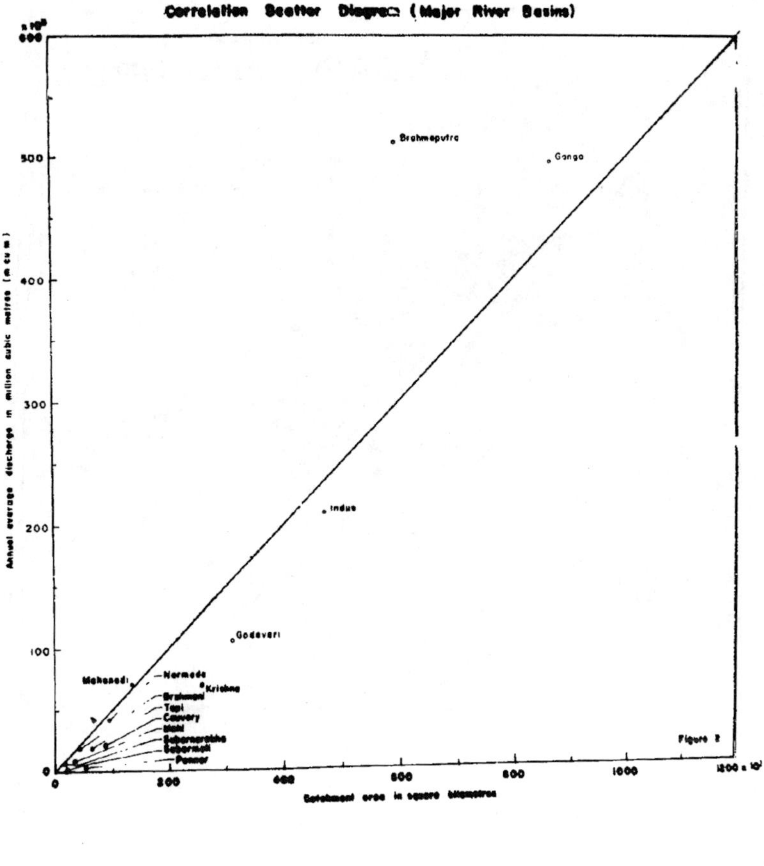

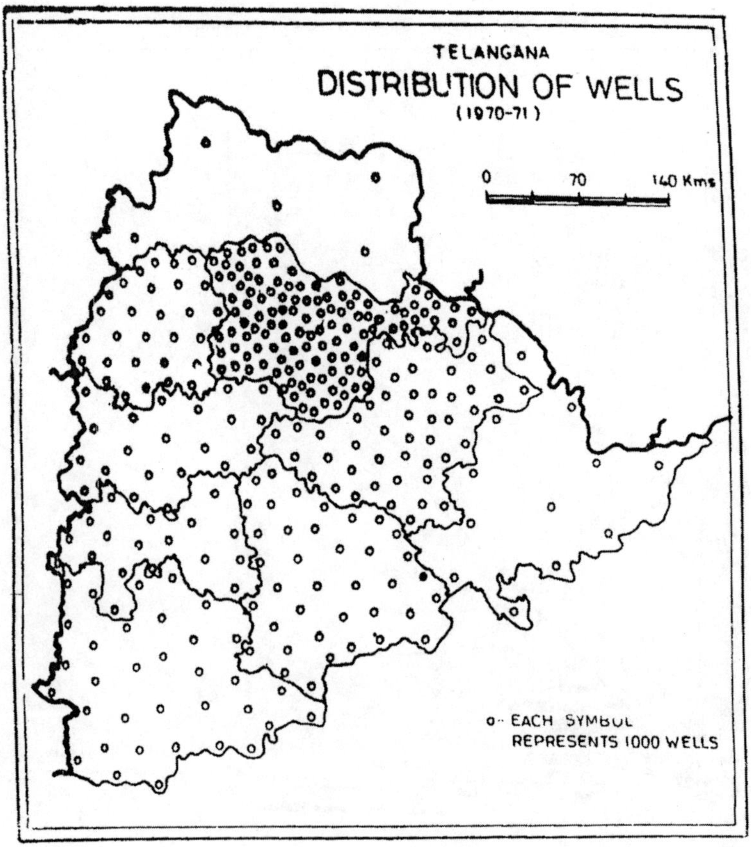
TELANGANA
DISTRIBUTION OF WELLS
(1970-71)
0 70 140 Kms
o- EACH SYMBOL
REPRESENTS 1000 WELLS

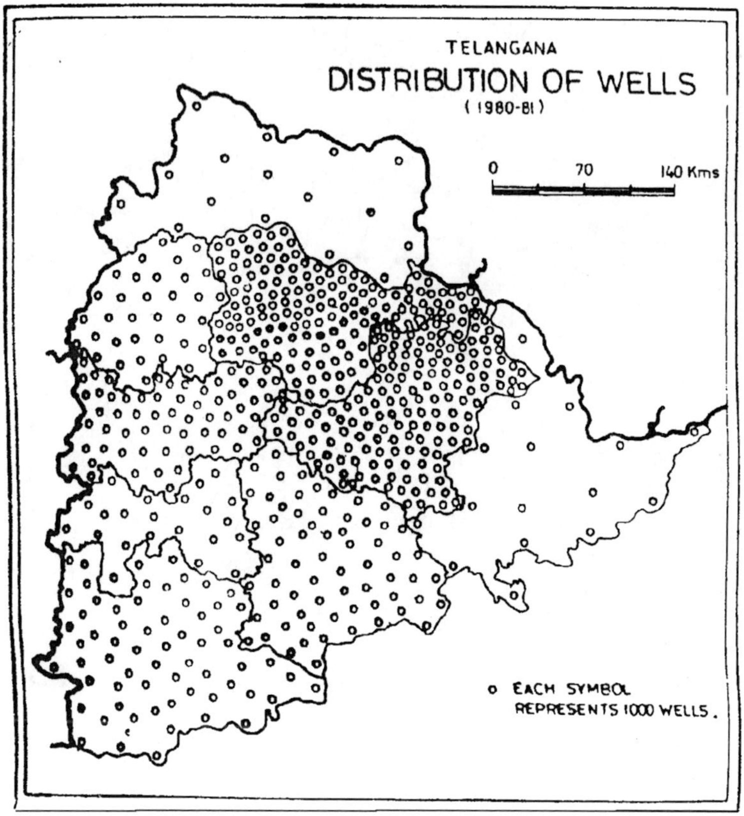
TELANGANA
DISTRIBUTION OF WELLS
(1980-81)
0 70 140 Kms
EACH SYMBOL
REPRESENTS 1000 WELLS.

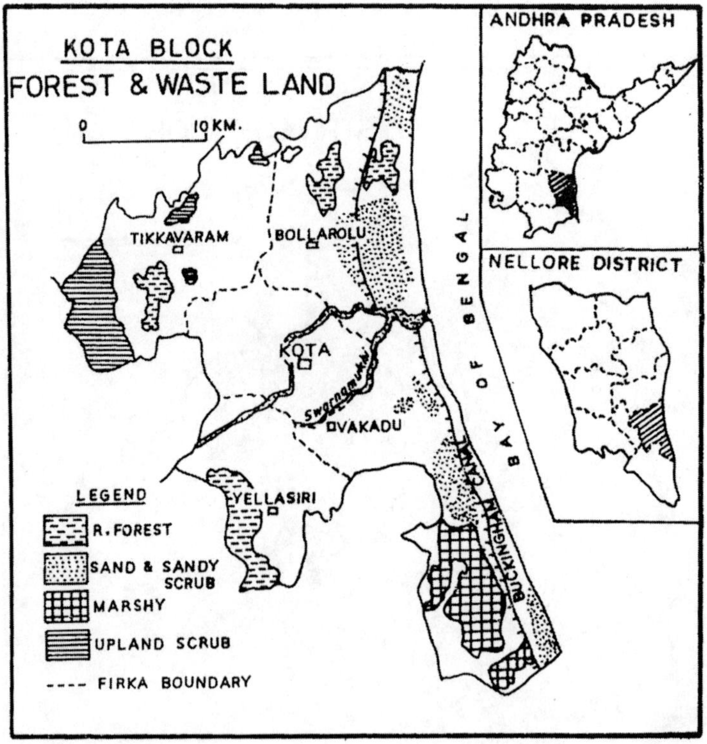
KOTA BLOCK
FOREST & WASTE LAND
0 10 KM.
TIKKAVARAM
BOLLAROLU
KOTA
Swarnamukhi
VAKADU
YELLASIRI
BAY OF BENGAL
BUCKINGHAM CANAL
LEGEND
R. FOREST
SAND & SANDY SCRUB
MARSHY
UPLAND SCRUB
---- FIRKA BOUNDARY
ANDHRA PRADESH
NELLORE DISTRICT

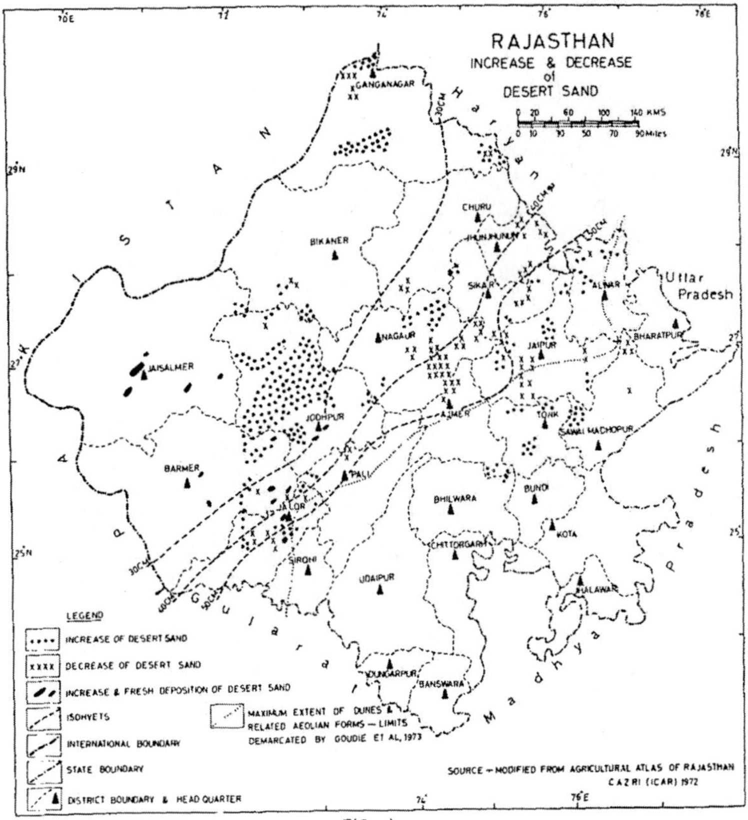
RAJASTHAN
INCREASE & DECREASE of DESERT SAND
GANGANAGAR
BIKANER
CHURU
JHUNJHUNU
SIKAR
ALWAR
BHARATPUR
Uttar Pradesh
JAISALMER
NAGAUR
JAIPUR
JODHPUR
AJMER
TONK
SAWAI MADHOPUR
BARMER
PALI
JALOR
BHILWARA
BUNDI
KOTA
CHITTORGARH
SIROHI
UDAIPUR
JHALAWAR
DUNGARPUR
BANSWARA
LEGEND
INCREASE OF DESERT SAND
DECREASE OF DESERT SAND
INCREASE & FRESH DEPOSITION OF DESERT SAND
ISOHYETS
INTERNATIONAL BOUNDARY
STATE BOUNDARY
DISTRICT BOUNDARY & HEAD QUARTER
MAXIMUM EXTENT OF DUNES & RELATED AEOLIAN FORMS — LIMITS DEMARCATED BY GOUDIE ET AL, 1973
SOURCE — MODIFIED FROM AGRICULTURAL ATLAS OF RAJASTHAN CAZRI (ICAR) 1972

FIG. 1

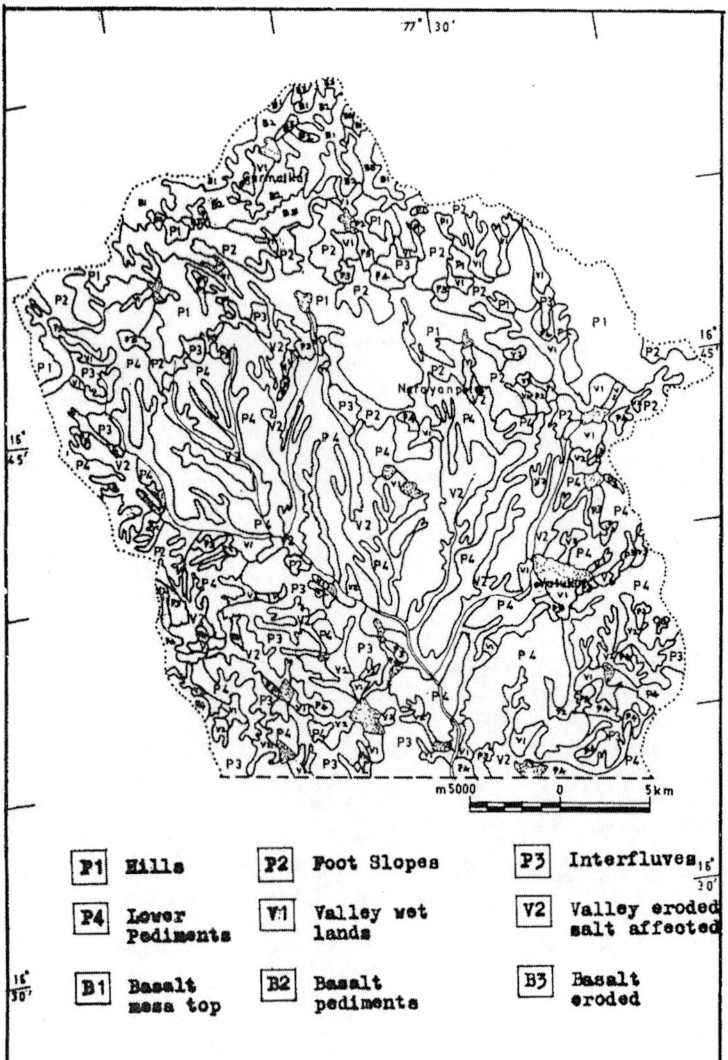

Fig. 1 .Physiographic soil map derived from A.P.I.

77° 15' 77° 30' M. No.32/86

cs/ksr

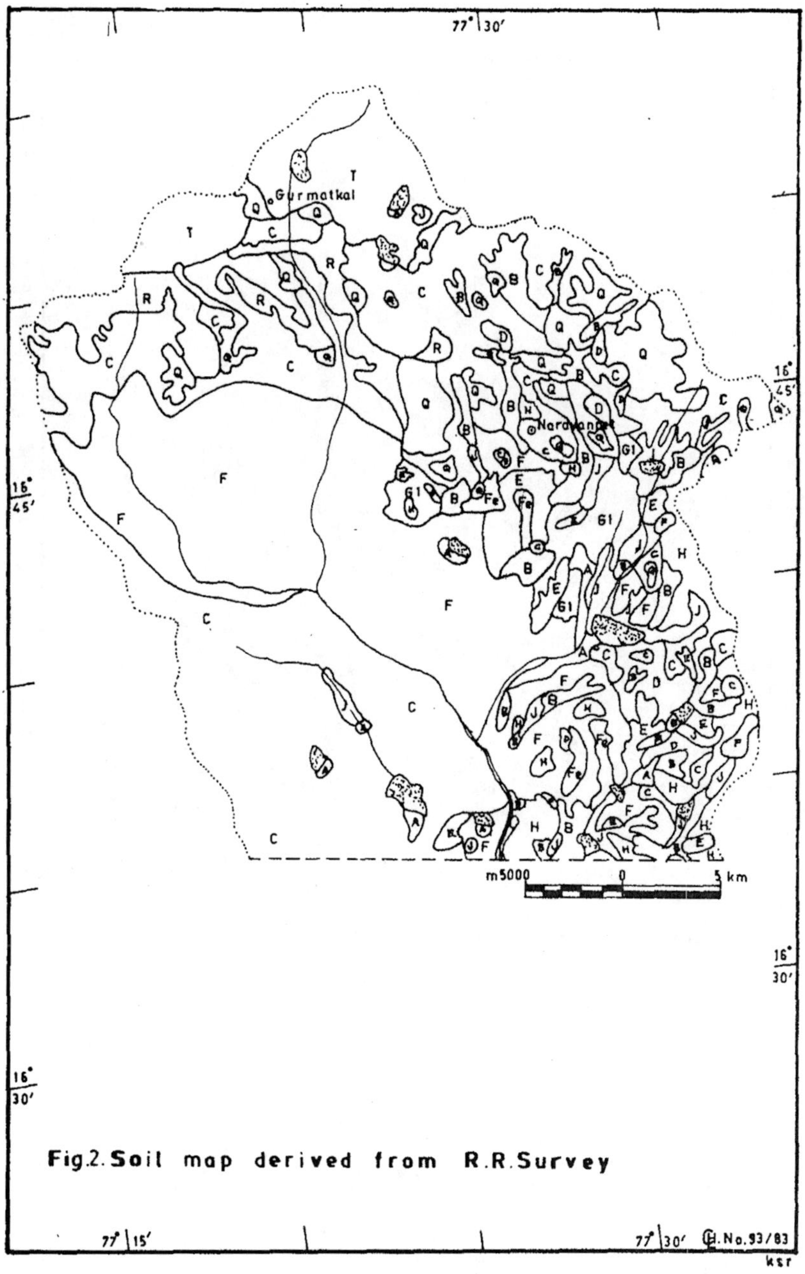

Fig.2. Soil map derived from R.R.Survey

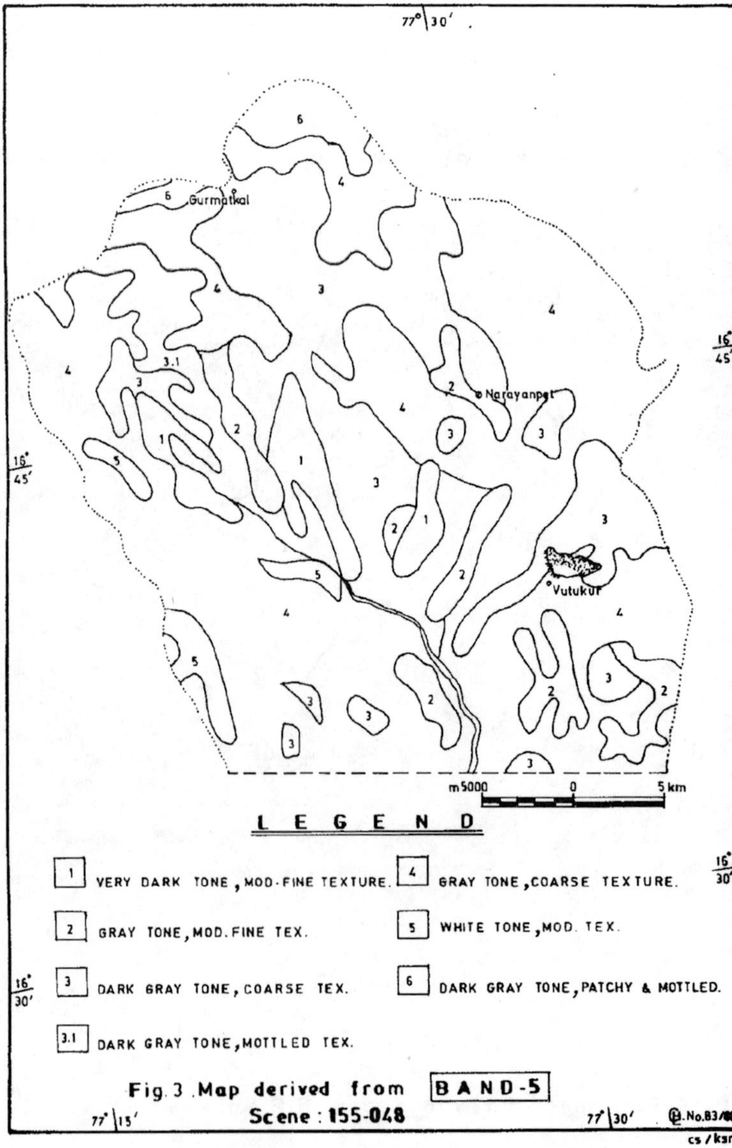

Fig. 3. Map derived from BAND-5
Scene : 155-048

77° 15′ 77° 30′ D. No. 83/88
cs / ksr

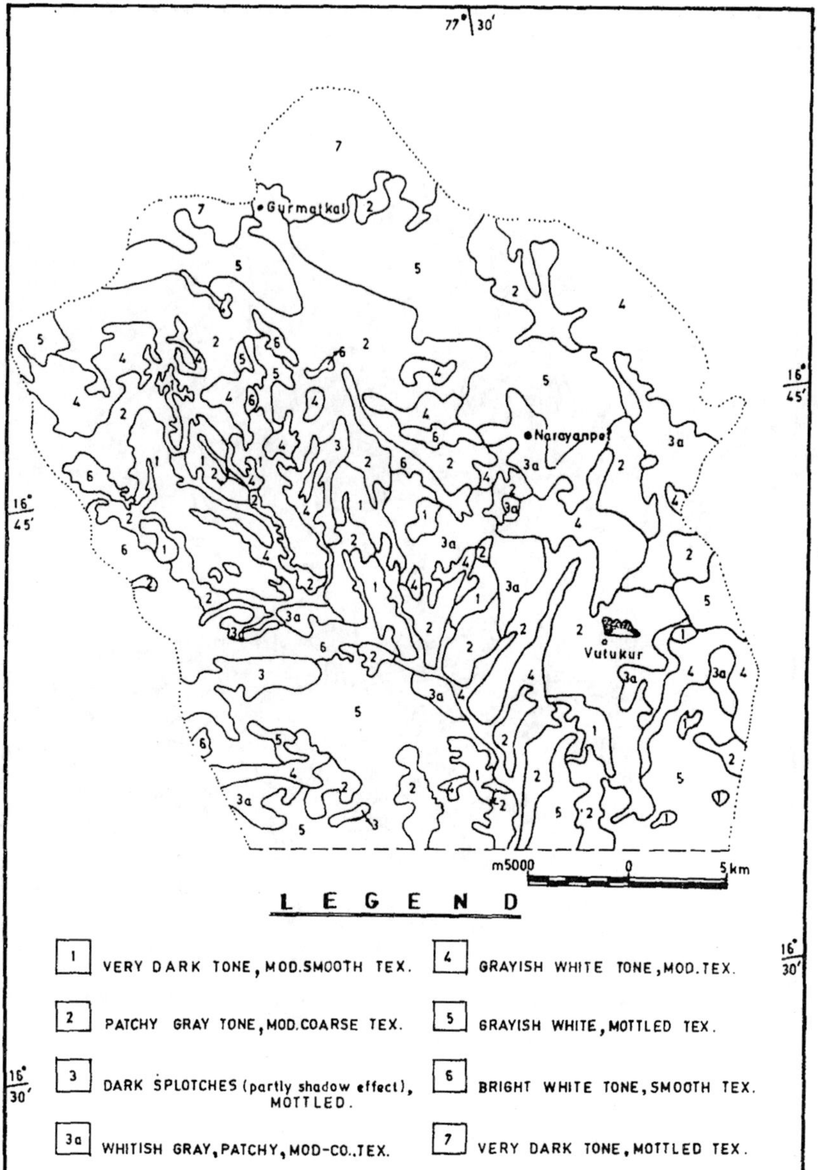

Fig. 4. Map derived from BAND-7 Scene: 155-048

77° 15′ 77° 30′ H.No.63
cs/ksr

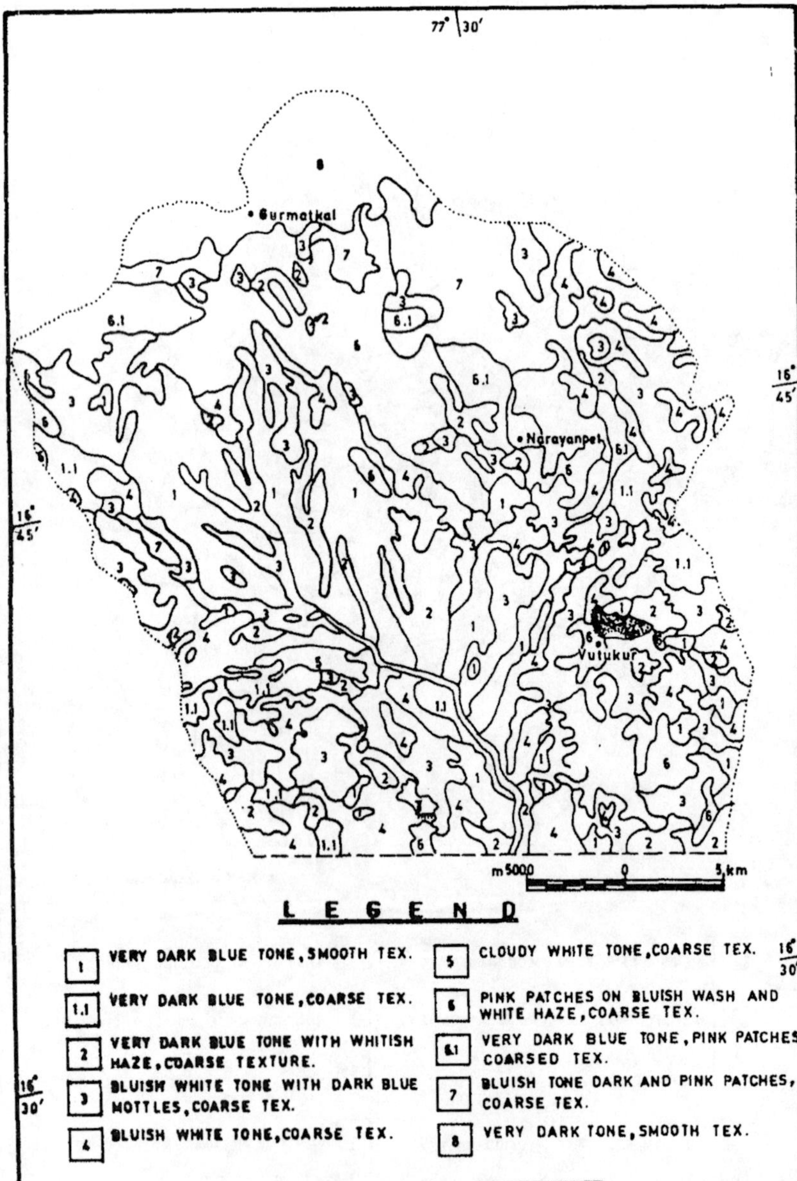

Fig. 5. Map derived from F.C.C
Scene: 155-048

77° 15′ 77° 30′ Dr.No.02/86
cs/ksr

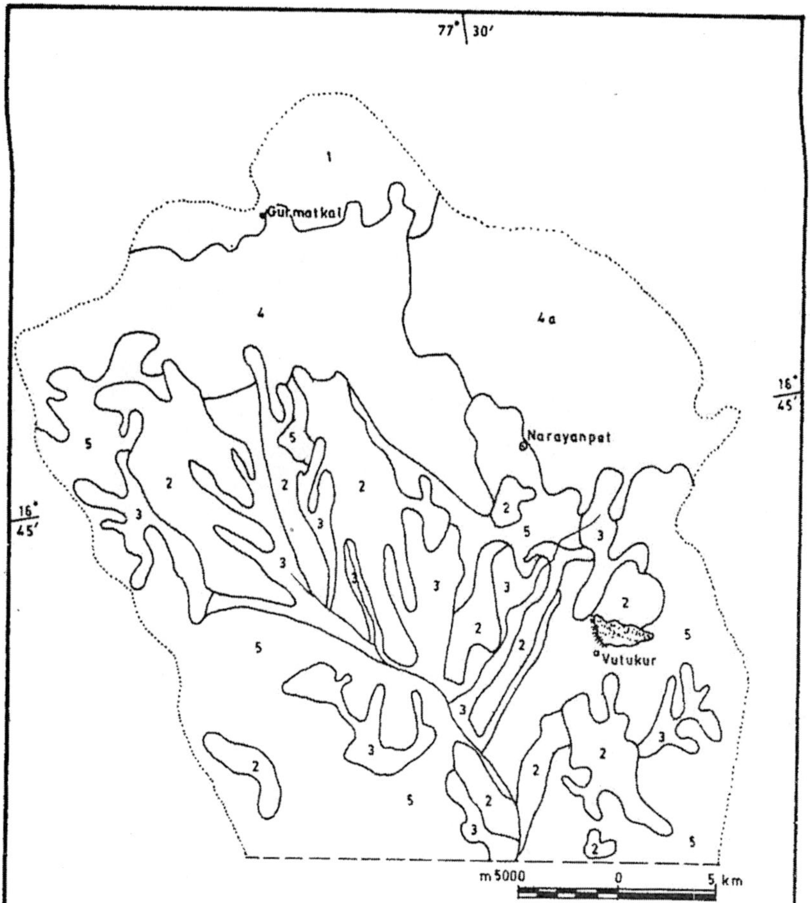

1. Assoc. T. Chromusterts and Pellusterts (Basalt Region)
2. T. Chromusterts - Granite Region
3. L./T. Ustorthents - Edd
4. Rocky (Hills and side slopes - Gr)

4a Assoc. T. Ustorthents and T. Ustochrepts (Hill flats and sideslopes - Gr. schist)

5. Assoc. T. Ustochrepts and T. Haplustalfs

Fig. 6 : Soil map derived from combined data of FCC and Band 7.

16° 30′ 16° 30′ 77° 15′ 77° 30′ G.No.91/86 cs/ksr

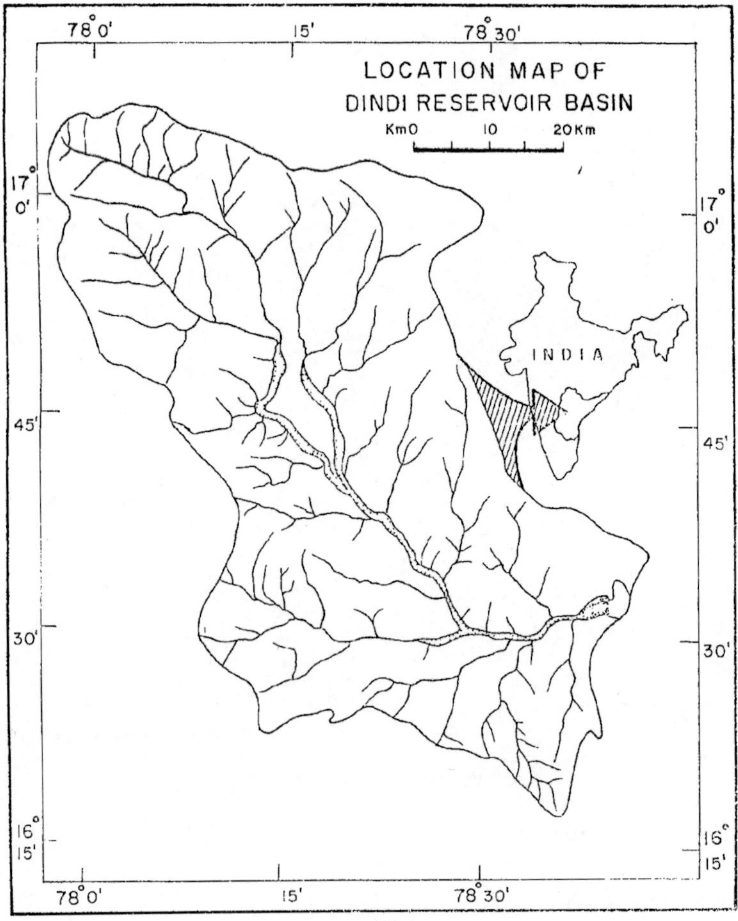
LOCATION MAP OF
DINDI RESERVOIR BASIN
Km 0
10
20 Km
INDIA
78° 0'
15'
78° 30'
17° 0'
45'
30'
16° 15'

FIG. 1

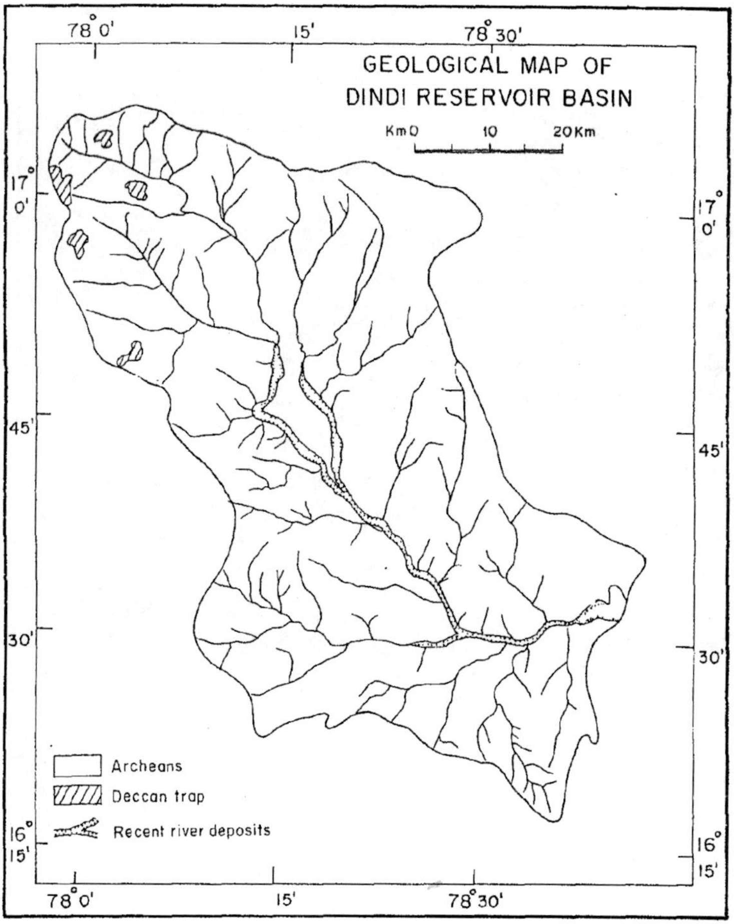
78°0'
15'
78°30'
GEOLOGICAL MAP OF
DINDI RESERVOIR BASIN
Km 0
10
20 Km
17° 0'
45'
30'
16° 15'
Archeans
Deccan trap
Recent river deposits

FIG. 2

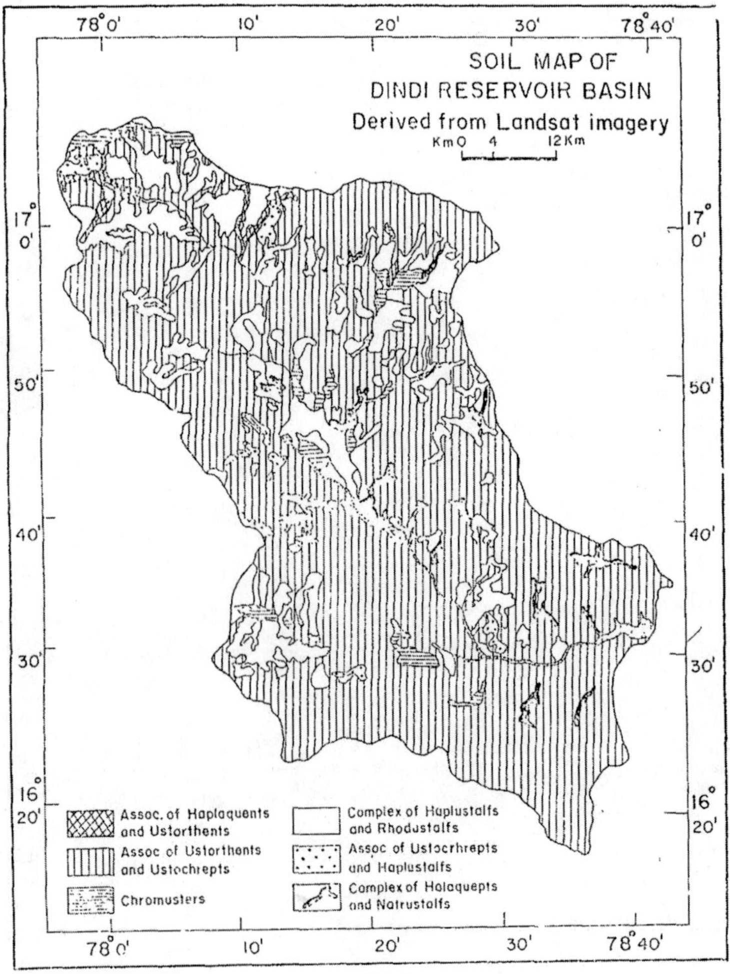

SOIL MAP OF
DINDI RESERVOIR BASIN
Derived from Landsat imagery
Km 0 4 12 Km
78°0'
10'
20'
30'
78°40'
17° 0'
50'
40'
30'
16° 20'
Assoc. of Haplaquents and Ustorthents
Assoc of Ustorthents and Ustochrepts
Chromusters
Complex of Haplustalfs and Rhodustalfs
Assoc of Ustocrhrepts and Haplustalfs
Complex of Halaquepts and Natrustalfs

FIG.3

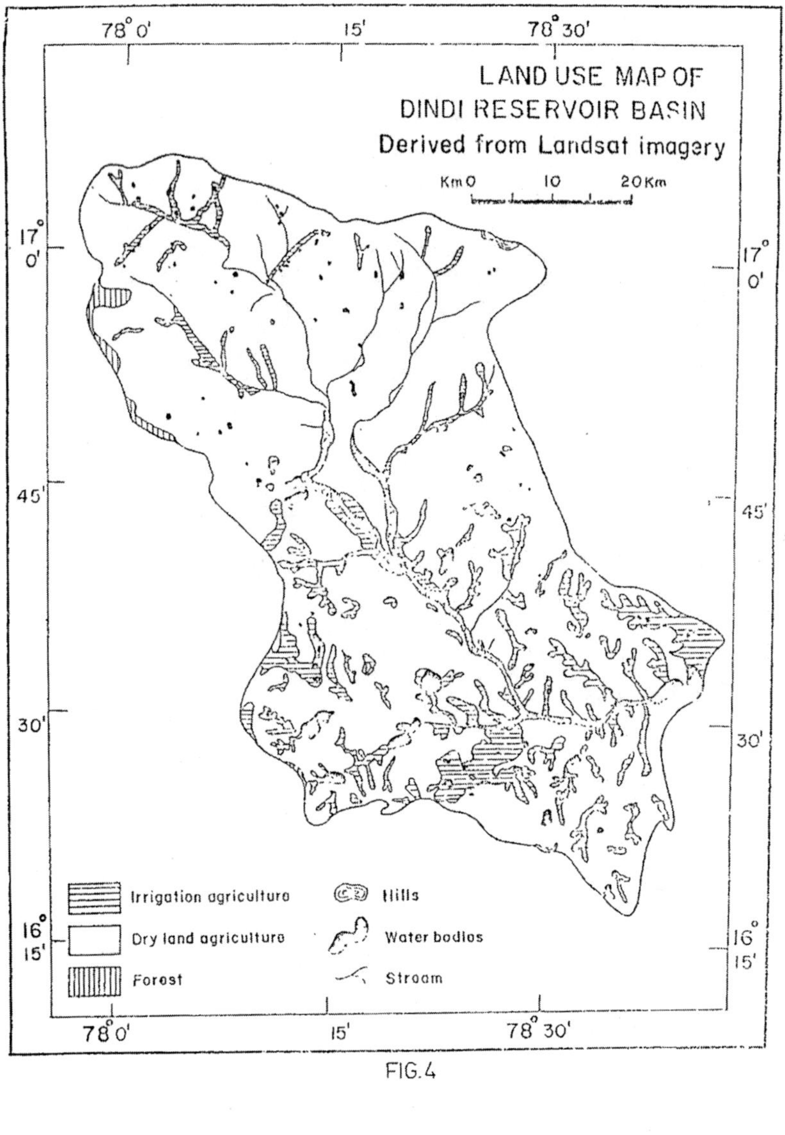
LAND USE MAP OF
DINDI RESERVOIR BASIN
Derived from Landsat imagery
Km 0
10
20 Km
78° 0'
15'
78° 30'
17° 0'
45'
30'
16° 15'
Irrigation agriculture
Dry land agriculture
Forest
Hills
Water bodies
Stream

FIG. 4

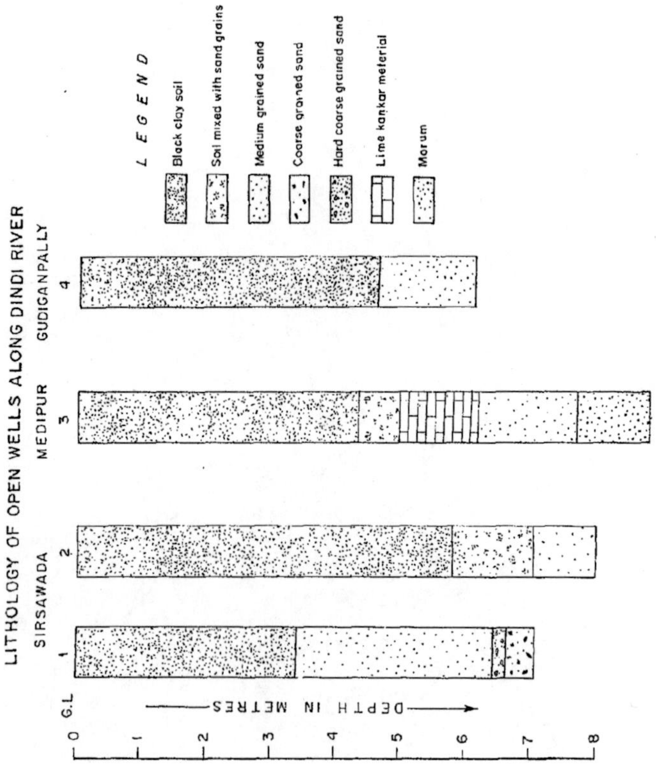
LITHOLOGY OF OPEN WELLS ALONG DINDI RIVER
LEGEND
Black clay soil
Soil mixed with sand grains
Medium grained sand
Coarse grained sand
Hard coarse grained sand
Lime kankar meterial
Morum
1 SIRSAWADA
2
3 MEDIPUR
4 GUDIGANPALLY
G.L
DEPTH IN METRES
0
1
2
3
4
5
6
7
8

FIG.5

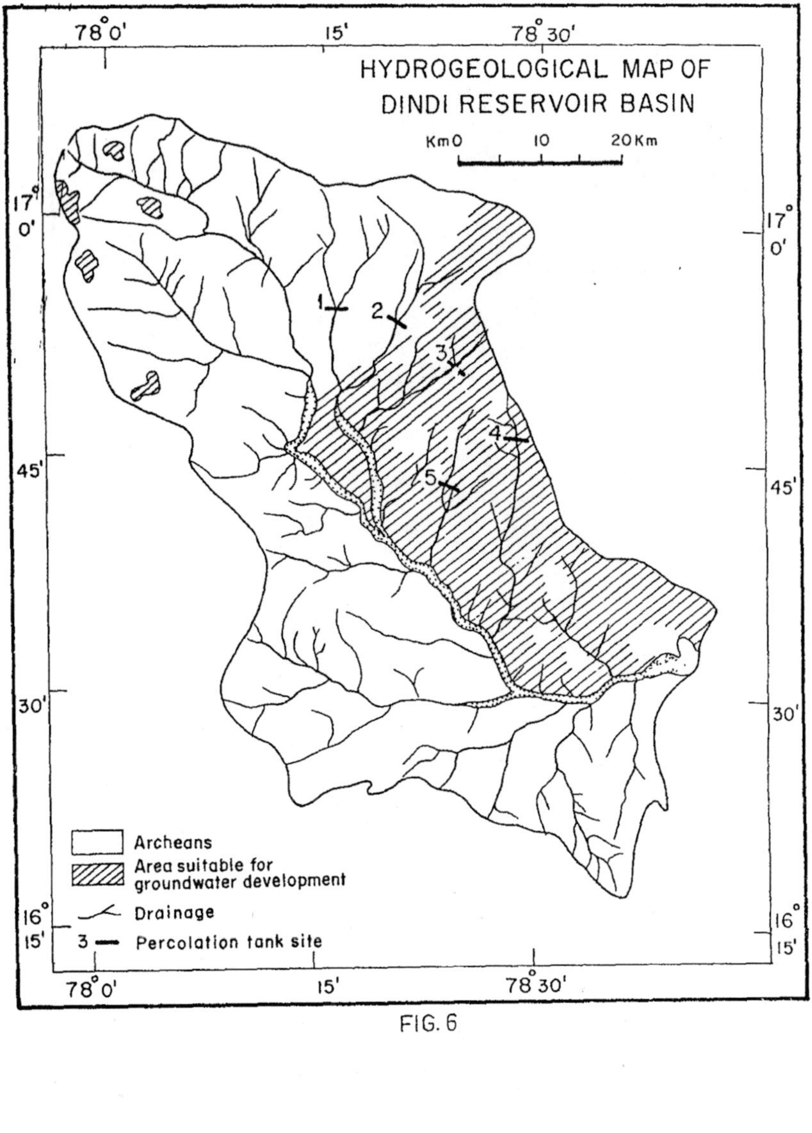
HYDROGEOLOGICAL MAP OF
DINDI RESERVOIR BASIN
Km 0 10 20 Km
78°0'
15'
78°30'
17° 0'
45'
30'
16° 15'
1
2
3
4
5
Archeans
Area suitable for groundwater development
Drainage
3 Percolation tank site

FIG. 6

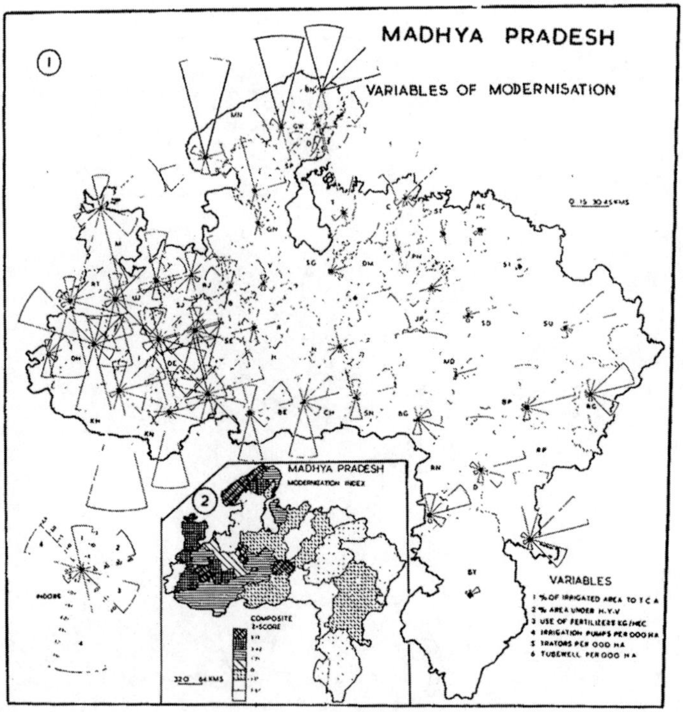
MADHYA PRADESH
VARIABLES OF MODERNISATION
MADHYA PRADESH
MODERNISATION INDEX
COMPOSITE Z-SCORE
VARIABLES
1 % OF IRRIGATED AREA TO T C A
2 % AREA UNDER H.Y.V
3 USE OF FERTILIZERS KG/HEC
4 IRRIGATION PUMPS PER OOO HA
5 TRATORS PER OOO HA
6 TUBEWELL PER OOO HA

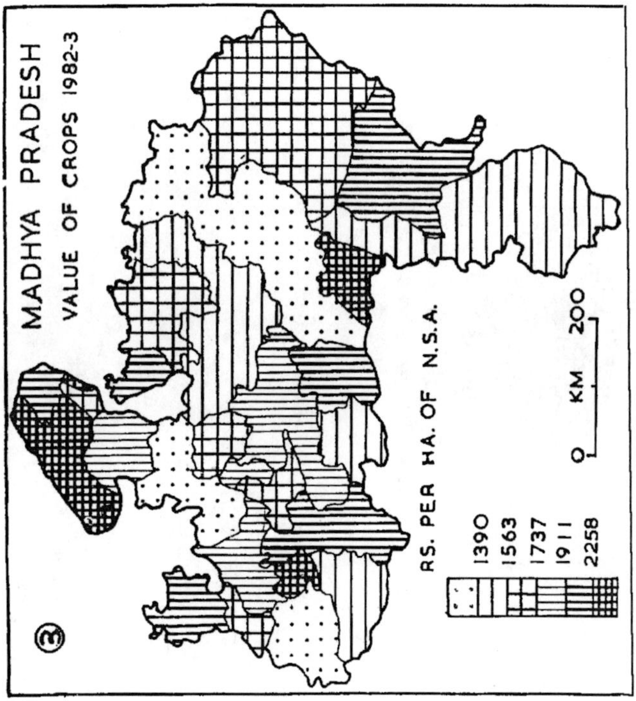
3
MADHYA PRADESH
VALUE OF CROPS 1982-3
RS. PER HA. OF N.S.A.
1390
1563
1737
1911
2258
0 KM 200

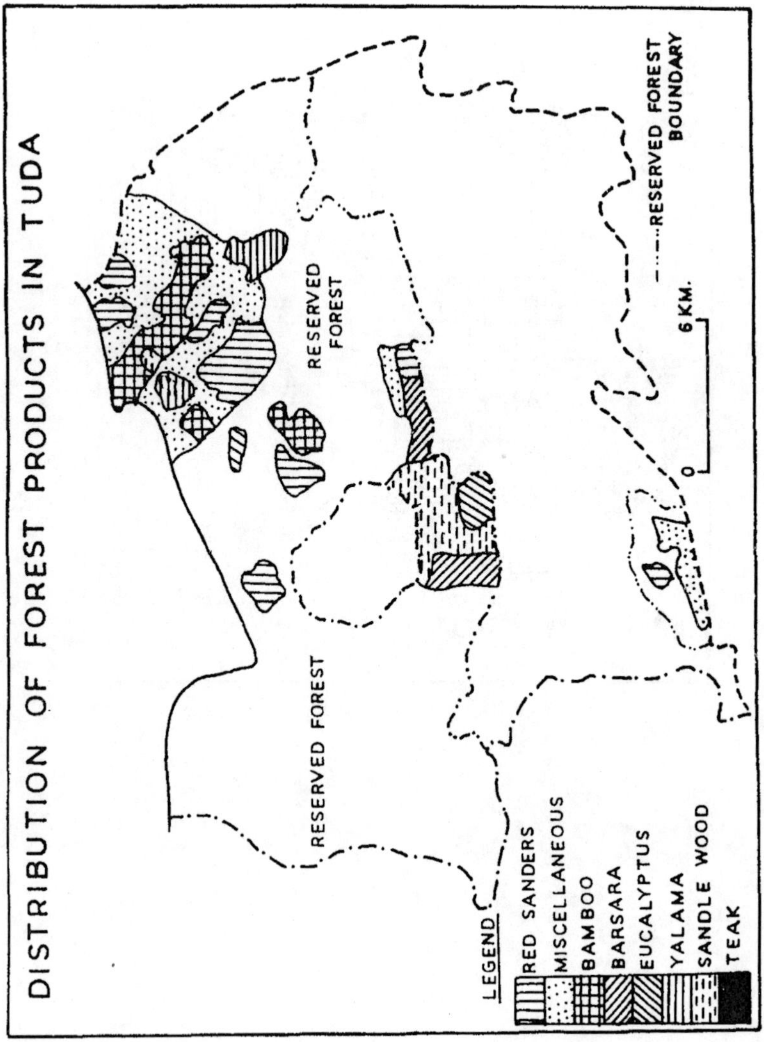
DISTRIBUTION OF FOREST PRODUCTS IN TUDA
LEGEND
RED SANDERS
MISCELLANEOUS
BAMBOO
BARSARA
EUCALYPTUS
YALAMA
SANDLE WOOD
TEAK
RESERVED FOREST
RESERVED FOREST
RESERVED FOREST BOUNDARY
0
6 KM.

FIG-1

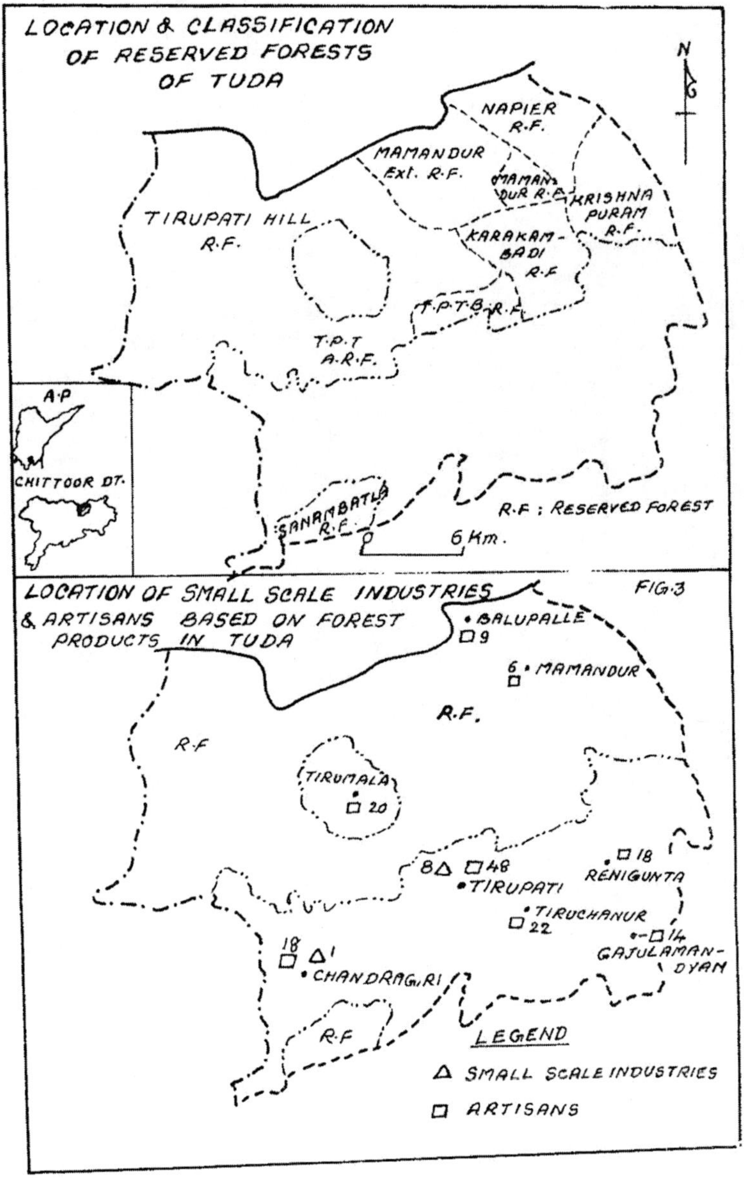
LOCATION & CLASSIFICATION OF RESERVED FORESTS OF TUDA
N
NAPIER R.F.
MAMANDUR Ext. R.F.
MAMANDUR R.F.
KRISHNA PURAM R.F.
TIRUPATI HILL R.F.
KARAKAMBADI R.F
T.P.T.B. R.F
T.P.T A.R.F.
A.P
CHITTOOR DT.
SANAMBATLA R.F.
0
6 Km.
R.F : RESERVED FOREST
LOCATION OF SMALL SCALE INDUSTRIES & ARTISANS BASED ON FOREST PRODUCTS IN TUDA
FIG.3
BALUPALLE
9
6
MAMANDUR
R.F.
R.F
TIRUMALA
20
8
48
TIRUPATI
18
RENIGUNTA
TIRUCHANUR
22
14
GAJULAMANDYAM
18
1
CHANDRAGIRI
R.F
LEGEND
SMALL SCALE INDUSTRIES
ARTISANS